WORLD EXPLORER

MEDIEVAL TIMES
TO
TODAY

PEARSON

Prentice
Hall

Needham, Massachusetts
Upper Saddle River, New Jersey

Program Consultants

Heidi Hayes Jacobs

Heidi Hayes Jacobs has served as an educational consultant to more than 1,000 schools across the nation and abroad. Dr. Jacobs served as an adjunct professor in the Department of Curriculum on Teaching at Teachers College, Columbia University. She has written a best-selling book and numerous articles on curriculum reform. She completed her undergraduate studies at the University of Utah in her hometown of Salt Lake City. She received an M.A. from the University of Massachusetts, Amherst, and completed her doctoral work at Columbia University's Teachers College in 1981.

The backbone of Dr. Jacobs' experience comes from her years as a teacher of high school, middle school, and elementary school students. As an educational consultant, she works with K–12 schools and districts on curriculum reform and strategic planning.

Brenda Randolph

Brenda Randolph is the former Director of the Outreach Resource Center at the African Studies Program at Howard University, Washington, D.C. She is the Founder and Director of Africa Access, a bibliographic service on Africa for schools. She received her B.A. in history with high honors from North Carolina Central University, Durham, and her M.A. in African studies with honors from Howard University. She completed further graduate studies at the University of Maryland, College Park, where she was awarded a Graduate Fellowship.

Brenda Randolph has published numerous articles in professional journals and bulletins. She currently serves as library media specialist in Montgomery County Public Schools, Maryland.

Michal L. LeVasseur

Michal LeVasseur is an educational consultant in the field of geography. She is an adjunct professor of geography at the University of Alabama, Birmingham, and serves with the Alabama Geographic Alliance. Her undergraduate and graduate work is in the fields of anthropology (B.A.), geography (M.A.), and science education (Ph.D.).

Dr. LeVasseur's specialization has moved increasingly into the area of geography education. In 1996, she served as Director of the National Geographic Society's Summer Geography Workshop. As an educational consultant, she has worked with the National Geographic Society as well as with schools to develop programs and curricula for geography.

Special Program Consultant
Yvonne S. Gentzler, Ph.D.
Iowa State University
College of Family and Consumer Sciences
Ames, Iowa

Content Consultants for *Medieval Times to Today*

**Barbara Brown, Laurence Michalak,
Ruth Mitchell-Pitts, Leslie Swartz,
Janet Vaillant, Robert Young**
Affiliations on page iii.

ISBN 0-13-062995-2

4 5 6 7 8 9 10   07 06 05 04 03

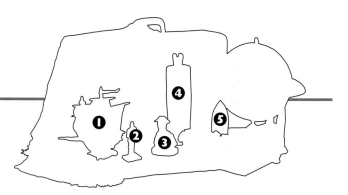

On the Cover

❶ Model of the Pinta

❷ Model of knight in armor

❸ Chinese sculpture based on an animal form

❹ African mask

❺ Griffin gargoyle plaque

Content Consultants for the World Explorer Program

Africa
Barbara Brown
African Studies Center
Boston University
Boston, Massachusetts

Ancient World
Maud Gleason
Department of Classics
Stanford University
Stanford, California

East Asia
Leslie Swartz
Vice President for Program
 Development and Harvard East
 Asian Outreach Program at The
 Children's Museum, Boston
Boston, Massachusetts

Latin America
Daniel Mugan
Center for Latin American Studies
University of Florida
Gainesville, Florida

Middle East
Elizabeth Barlow
Center for Middle Eastern and
 North African Studies
University of Michigan
Ann Arbor, Michigan

North Africa
Laurence Michalak
Center for Middle East Studies
University of California
Berkeley, California

Religion
Michael Sells
Department of Religion
Haverford College
Haverford, Pennsylvania

Russia, Eastern Europe, Central Asia
Janet Vaillant
Davis Center for Russian Studies
Harvard University
Cambridge, Massachusetts

South Asia
Robert Young
Department of History
West Chester University
West Chester, Pennsylvania

Western Europe
Ruth Mitchell-Pitts
Center for West European Studies
University of North Carolina
Chapel Hill, North Carolina

Teacher Advisory Board

Jerome Balin
Lincoln Junior High School
Naperville, Illinois

Elizabeth Barrett
Tates Creek Middle School
Lexington, Kentucky

Tricia Creasey
Brown Middle School
Thomasville, North Carolina

Patricia H. Guillory
Fulton County Schools
Atlanta, Georgia

Stephanie Hawkins
Oklahoma City Public Schools
Oklahoma City, Oklahoma

Fred Hitz
Wilson Middle School
Muncie, Indiana

Kristi Karis
West Ottawa Public Schools
Holland, Michigan

Peggy Lehman
Carmel Junior High/Carmel-Clay
 Schools
Carmel, Indiana

Peggy McCarthy
Beulah School
Beulah, Colorado

Cindy McCurdy
Hefner Middle School
Oklahoma City, Oklahoma

Deborah J. Miller
Detroit Public Schools
Detroit, Michigan

Lawrence Peglow
Pittsburgh Public Schools
Pittsburgh, Pennsylvania

Paula Rardin
Riverview Gardens Schools
St. Louis, Missouri

Kent E. Riley
Perry Meridian Middle School
Indianapolis, Indiana

Christy Sarver
Brown Middle School
Thomasville, North Carolina

Lyn Shiver
Northwestern Middle School
Alpharetta, Georgia

Mark Stahl
Longfellow Middle School
Norman, Oklahoma

TABLE OF CONTENTS

MEDIEVAL TIMES TO TODAY

1

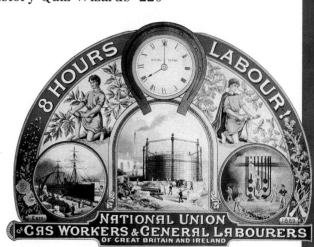

OF SPECIAL INTEREST

A hands-on approach to learning and applying social studies skills

Step-by-step activities for exploring important topics in medieval times to the present

Literature selections by authors who give us pictures of history

Profiles of people who made a difference in their country

Detailed drawings show how the use of technology makes a country unique

A view of a country through the eyes of a student artist

MAPS

CHARTS, GRAPHS, AND TABLES

READ ACTIVELY

How can I get the most out of my social studies book? How does my reading relate to my world? Answering questions like these means that you are an active reader, an involved reader. As an active reader, you are in charge of the reading situation!

The following strategies tell how to think and read as an active reader. You don't need to use all of these strategies all the time. Feel free to choose the ones that work best in each reading situation. You might use several at a time, or you might go back and forth among them. They can be used in any order.

BEFORE YOU READ

Give yourself a purpose

The sections in this book begin with a list called "Questions to Explore." These questions focus on key ideas presented in the section. They give you a purpose for reading. You can create your own purpose by asking questions like these: How does the topic relate to my life? How might I use what I learn at school or at home?

Preview

To preview a reading selection, first read its title. Then look at the pictures and read the captions. Also read any headings in the selection. Then ask yourself: What is the reading selection about? What do the pictures and headings tell about the selection?

Reach into your background

What do you already know about the topic of the selection? How can you use what you know to help you understand what you are going to read?

WHILE YOU READ

Ask questions

Suppose you are reading about the continent of South America. Some questions you might ask are: Where is South America? What countries are found there? Why are some of the countries large and others small? Asking questions like these can help you gather evidence and gain knowledge.

Predict

As you read, make a prediction about what will happen and why. Or predict how one fact might affect another fact. Suppose you are reading about South America's climate. You might make a prediction about how the climate affects where people live. You can change your mind as you gain new information.

Connect

Connect your reading to your own life. Are the people discussed in the selection like you or someone you know? What would you do in similar situations? Connect your reading to something you have already read. Suppose you have already read about the ancient Greeks. Now you are reading about the ancient Romans. How are they alike? How are they different?

Visualize

What would places, people, and events look like in a movie or a picture? As you read about India, you could visualize the country's heavy rains. What do they look like? How do they sound? As you read about geography, you could visualize a volcanic eruption.

Respond

Talk about what you have read. What did you think? Share your ideas with your classmates.

Assess yourself

What did you find out? Were your predictions on target? Did you find answers to your questions?

Follow up

Show what you know. Use what you have learned to do a project. When you do projects, you continue to learn.

MEDIEVAL TIMES TO TODAY

To understand today's world, we must learn about its past. Ancient civilizations laid strong foundations for modern cultures. The years between ancient and modern times have added greatly to the structure of those cultures. In this book, you will learn how the ideas, events, and people of these years have shaped our lives.

GUIDING QUESTIONS

The readings and activities in this book will help you discover answers to these Guiding Questions.

1 GEOGRAPHY How did physical geography affect the development of societies around the world?

2 HISTORY How did each society's belief system affect its history?

3 CULTURE What was the pattern of day-to-day life in these societies?

4 GOVERNMENT What types of government were formed in these societies?

5 ECONOMICS How did each society organize its economic activities?

PROJECT PREVIEW

You can also discover answers to the Guiding Questions by working on creative projects. You can find several project possibilities on pages 222–223 at the back of this book.

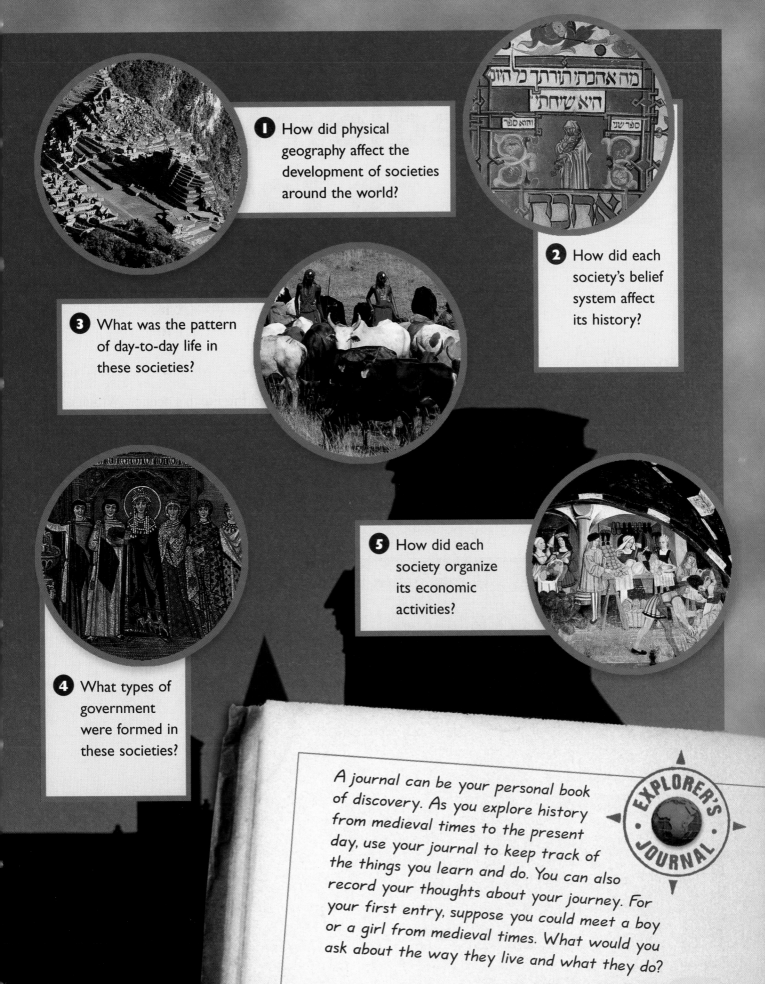

1 How did physical geography affect the development of societies around the world?

2 How did each society's belief system affect its history?

3 What was the pattern of day-to-day life in these societies?

4 What types of government were formed in these societies?

5 How did each society organize its economic activities?

A journal can be your personal book of discovery. As you explore history from medieval times to the present day, use your journal to keep track of the things you learn and do. You can also record your thoughts about your journey. For your first entry, suppose you could meet a boy or a girl from medieval times. What would you ask about the way they live and what they do?

EXPLORER'S · JOURNAL

Medieval Times to Today

Learning about history means being an explorer and a geographer. No explorer would start out without first checking some facts. Begin by exploring the maps on the following pages.

LOCATION

1. Look at the Earth's Continents How many continents are there? Use a ruler to compare the size of the continents. Find the smallest one. How much do the continents vary in size? Which two continents share the same landmass? Which continents are completely north or south of the Equator? Which ones lie on both sides of the Equator?

PLACE

2. Look at the Earth's Oceans Use the map below to find the Earth's oceans. Which ones appear on the map? Which ocean separates North America from Europe? Which one separates North America from Asia? Why do you think some people say that there is just one ocean, the "world ocean"?

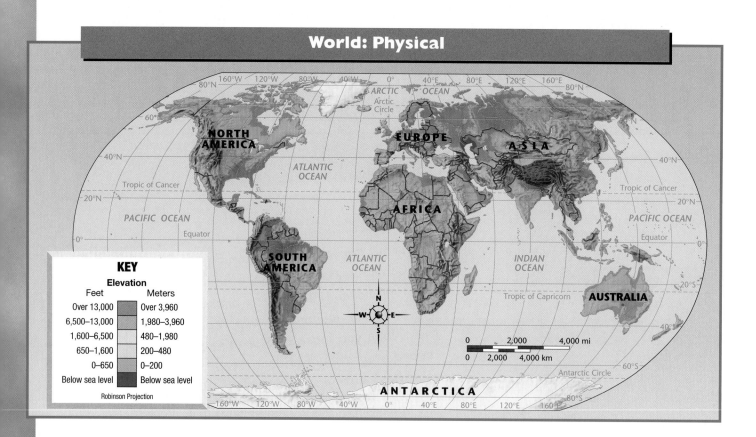

World: Physical

KEY

Elevation

Feet		Meters
Over 13,000		Over 3,960
6,500–13,000		1,980–3,960
1,600–6,500		480–1,980
650–1,600		200–480
0–650		0–200
Below sea level		Below sea level

Robinson Projection

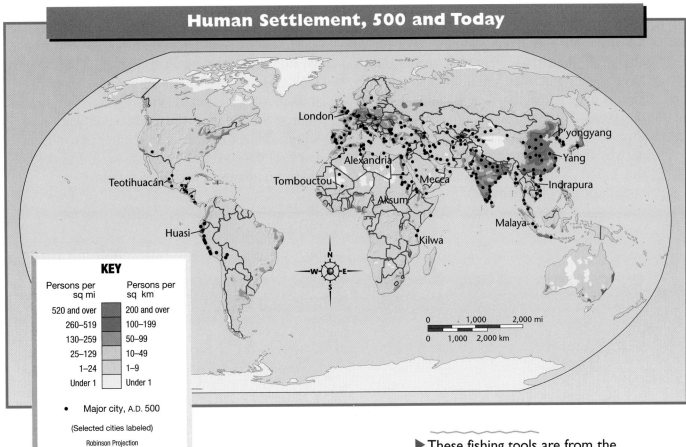

KEY

Persons per sq mi	Persons per sq km
520 and over	200 and over
260–519	100–199
130–259	50–99
25–129	10–49
1–24	1–9
Under 1	Under 1

● Major city, A.D. 500

(Selected cities labeled)

Robinson Projection

▶ These fishing tools are from the 300s or 400s. They were found in the country of Mali in Africa.

MOVEMENT

3. Investigate Human Settlement The map shows the major cities where people lived more than 1,500 years ago. The colors on the map show where people live today. What is the main difference between the two? Why do you think the change has occurred?

INTERACTION

4. Compare Human Settlement to the Location of Physical Features Look at the map on the opposite page. Identify at least three types of places where people have settled. For example, do people tend to settle along the edges of continents, at the coasts, or in the middle of continents? What natural features seem to attract human settlement? What natural features seem to discourage it?

5. Explore Changes in Political Boundaries

Many countries and political boundaries have changed since the 1500s, but some things have stayed much the same. Look at the map on this page and at the World: Political map in the Atlas. What changes do you notice in Europe? In North America? In Africa? In what part of the world have boundaries changed the most? Name two reasons that political boundaries might change.

6. Investigate Boundary Changes in Africa

Again compare the map on this page with the World: Political map in the Atlas. This time look closely at Africa. Africa in about 1500 was a land of kingdoms, empires, and trading states. Now look at the World: Political map, which shows Africa today. Name two differences between the two maps. About how many countries in Africa exist today?

The World About 1500

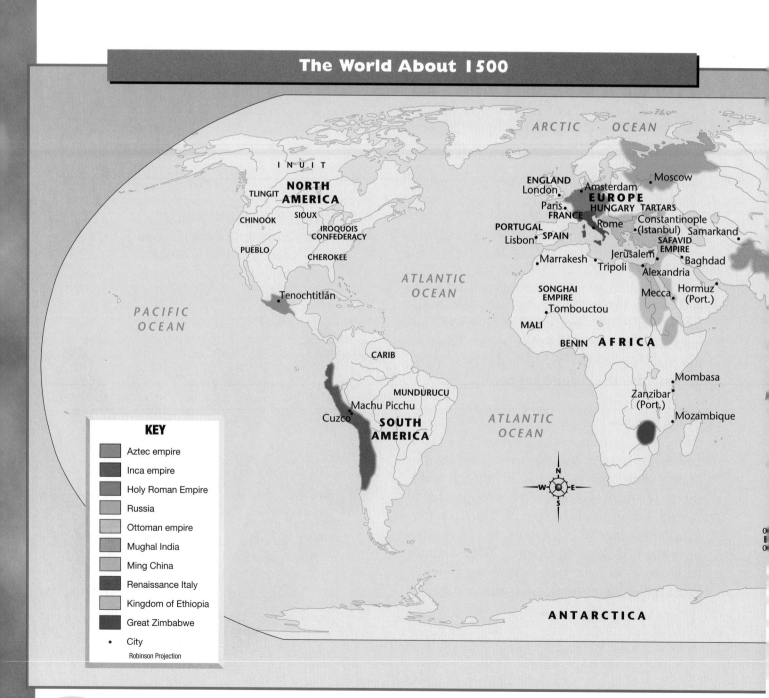

KEY

- Aztec empire
- Inca empire
- Holy Roman Empire
- Russia
- Ottoman empire
- Mughal India
- Ming China
- Renaissance Italy
- Kingdom of Ethiopia
- Great Zimbabwe
- • City

Robinson Projection

PLACE

7. Follow Geo Leo Geo Leo is looking back and forth between the map on these two pages and the World: Political map in the Atlas. He has a few things to say about them. Identify which map he means with each question.

"I will describe something on one or both maps, and you tell me which map I mean. Ready? Let's play!"

A. I'll start with an easy one. I see a world of continents and oceans, in which there are countries on nearly every continent. Am I looking at a map of the world in the 1500s, today, or both?

B. Look at this! The map shows the Holy Roman Empire in Europe. Which map do I mean? Am I looking at the map of the world in the 1500s or of today?

C. North America sure looks popular. There are dozens of nations who call this continent home. Each group has a different name, but they don't seem to have firm political borders. Which map am I looking at?

D. Look at North America now! Instead of dozens of different nations, the continent is covered by just three large countries. Is this the map of today or of the 1500s?

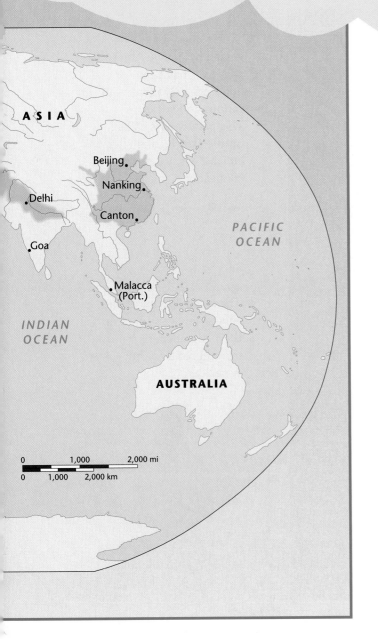

GEO LEO

BONUS

Which world map shows more countries? Why do you think this is so?

MOVEMENT

8. Investigate the Columbian Exchange

When Christopher Columbus and other explorers sailed from Europe to the Americas and back, they brought many things with them. People now call this movement of plants, animals, and diseases the Columbian Exchange. The map on the next page shows the Columbian Exchange. Study the map carefully. How does the map show you whether things came from Europe to the Americas or from the Americas to Europe?

Did more animals go from Europe to the Americas, or was it the reverse? What about plants? How many of the foods you usually eat first came from Europe? What diseases were transferred to the Americas?

◄ Wild rice is still harvested by Native Americans as it has been for hundreds of years—with canoes and sticks. This picture was taken on the Leech Lake Indian Reservation in Minnesota.

▼ These familiar fruits and vegetables were part of the Columbian Exchange from Europe to the Americas.

To Europe, Africa, and Asia

Pumpkin
Avocado
Peanut
Beans (lima, pole,
 navy, kidney)
Peppers (bell, chili)
Pineapple
Quinine
Wild rice
Corn
Potato
Tomato
Alpaca
Turkey
Llama
Guinea pig

ATLANTIC OCEAN

Coffee
Banana
Citrus fruit
Watermelon
Peach
Pear
Lettuce
Onion
Grains (wheat,
 barley, oats)
Sugar cane
Honeybee
Chicken
Sheep
Cattle
Horse
Chickenpox
Measles
Scarlet fever
Smallpox
Malaria

To the Americas

The Byzantine and Muslim Empires

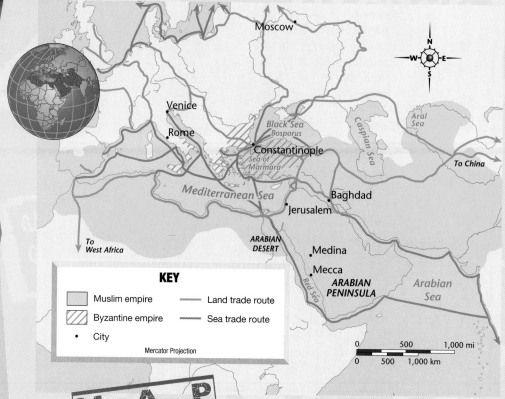

MAP ACTIVITIES

The Byzantine and Muslim empires covered a vast area stretching from Europe to India. The map shows lands and bodies of water that were important to one or both empires. To understand more about these empires, do the following activities.

Explore a city
Find Constantinople on the map. Study its location. Why do you think it is described as being at a crossroads between Europe and Asia?

By land and by sea
Look closely at the map. Notice that some routes are land trade routes and some are sea trade routes. How many places can you find where a land route and a sea route join to become one continuous route?

Byzantium

ROME'S EASTERN EMPIRE

BEFORE YOU READ

Reach Into Your Background

Think of the neighborhood in which you live. What advantages does your neighborhood have because of its location? Perhaps it is near a shopping mall, a park, or the beach. How important is location to a community?

Questions to Explore

1. How did the Byzantine empire survive for such a long time?
2. What major contributions did the Byzantine empire make to world culture?

Key Terms

strait   patriarch
icon   schism

Key People and Places

Justinian
Moscow
Constantinople
Rome
Venice

Prince Igor (EE gor) of Moscow, in what today is Russia, watched as a large force of his warships sailed across the Black Sea in A.D. 941. The prince was sure that Constantinople, capital of the Byzantine empire, would soon be his.

As his fleet drew closer to the city, the prince's excitement turned to horror. Byzantine ships hurled "Greek fire" at the invaders from Moscow. Anything the "fire" touched burst into flames. Soon, most of Prince Igor's fleet was ablaze.

"Greek fire" was made from a formula so secret that it was never written down. Even today, no one knows exactly how it was made, except that it contained petroleum. But this deadly weapon gave the Byzantines tremendous power throughout the Mediterranean area.

▼ This painting was made about 700 years after "Greek fire" was invented. It shows a scene like the one that shocked Prince Igor. "Greek fire" exploded into flame when it contacted water, making it a deadly weapon in sea battles.

Today, Constantinople is known as Istanbul. It is the largest city in Turkey. Centuries ago it was a large city, too. In A.D. 1000, it spread across the fringes of Europe and Asia at the Bosporus, and had a population of about one million people. **Critical Thinking** How did Constantinople's location help its development as a trade center?

Constantinople's Geography

From the 600s to the 1400s, the Byzantines used "Greek fire" to defend their capital against attacks by outside groups. All of these groups wanted to control Constantinople. The map at the beginning of this chapter can help you understand why.

Locate Constantinople on the map. Notice that it is located on the Bosporus. The Bosporus is a **strait,** or a narrow passage that links two bodies of water. It connects the Black Sea and the Sea of Marmara, which flows into the Mediterranean Sea. The Bosporus also links two continents, Europe and Asia.

Constantinople's location made it a natural crossroads of trade. The Byzantines grew rich from the trade routes that they controlled—from Moscow to the Mediterranean, and from China all the way to Western Europe. The Byzantines charged duties, or taxes, on all goods that went through the city. They made money off of every item traded.

Building the Byzantine Empire

Constantinople was not always a Byzantine city. First, it was part of Greece. Later, it was part of the Roman Empire. In these times, the city was called Byzantium.

In A.D. 330, Constantine, the first Christian emperor of the Roman Empire, moved his capital from Rome to Byzantium. The city was then renamed Constantinople, which means "City of Constantine." Today, the city belongs to the modern country of Turkey and is called Istanbul.

Yeats and Byzantium The great Irish poet William Butler Yeats wrote a poem called "Sailing to Byzantium." In it, Byzantium symbolizes a culture that stresses youth and art. Yeats describes an artificial bird made "of hammered gold and gold enameling." Legends said that birds like this "sang" from trees also made of gold. These legends also said that the goldsmiths who made the singing birds came from Greece.

The Roman Empire Splits into East and West

Perhaps you already know something about the great Roman Empire, from which the Byzantine empire emerged. At its height, the Roman Empire reached all the way from Britain to Egypt.

But even the greatest and most powerful empires do not last forever. In your own lifetime, the world has seen the breakup of an empire called the Soviet Union. Hundreds of years ago, the Roman Empire broke apart. It split into eastern and western divisions.

The western half of the Roman Empire was overrun by invaders in A.D. 476. The eastern half survived as the Byzantine empire until 1453. Why did the Byzantine empire last so long? The simple answer is trade. Because Constantinople was a trading crossroads, the empire remained strong.

The Byzantines also had a strong army, the best in the world. Byzantine fighters used not only "Greek fire," but many other weapons, including stone missiles, to drive back their enemies.

A Great Emperor

Clever rulers also helped to maintain the empire. Byzantine emperors had much more power than most rulers have today. They thought of themselves as representatives of God on the Earth.

Among the greatest of Byzantine emperors was Justinian, who ruled from 527 to 565. Justinian was not a typical emperor. He was born into a poor family, and he married an actress. He was easygoing and polite with everyone. He never lost his temper, even when provoked. Also, he

▼ In this mosaic made in the 500s, the Empress Theodora is shown wearing a crown. Theodora is famous for many things, including the work she did to gain rights for Byzantine women.

was ready to listen to the ideas of all his subjects, from the highest noble to the poorest peasant. At the same time, he was very stubborn. His advisers knew that once he had made a decision, there was no point in trying to change his mind.

Justinian ruled long and well. His success was due, in part, to hard work. He had great energy and self-discipline, and rarely gave up on a task until it was completed. Another reason for Justinian's success was his wife, Theodora. As empress, she took an active role in politics. Many of Justinian's most intelligent decisions were made on her advice.

Fall of the Byzantine Empire

After Justinian's death in 565, the Byzantine empire began to decline. In 1453, it completely collapsed. This fall was sparked by an argument about politics and religion.

A Religious Dispute   Most of the people and all of the rulers in the Byzantine empire were Christians. However, they did not agree on how to worship God. Some people prayed to saints or holy people represented on **icons,** or paintings of these saints or holy people. Others believed that people should pray only to God. The Byzantine empire grew weaker as its people took sides on religious questions.

The religious arguments spread from Constantinople to Rome. The **patriarch,** leader of the Church in Constantinople, and the pope, leader of the Church in Rome, took opposite sides. In 1054, they each took steps to throw the other out of the Church.

READ ACTIVELY

Ask Questions Think of questions you might ask about the role of religion in the breakup of the Byzantine empire.

Holy Paintings

Byzantine Christians treasured icons like this one of Mary and Jesus. They kept these holy paintings in their churches and their homes, where they worshipped and prayed before them. Artists made icons by applying color in hot wax or egg yolk to a board covered with plaster, glue, and cloth. **Critical Thinking** How did the issue of icons help to cause a split in the Christian Church?

In late March, 1453, a force of about 70,000 Ottoman Turks surrounded the city of Constantinople. The defending force, which numbered about 7,000, held out for two months. On May 29, 1453, however, the city fell to the Ottomans. This French painting of the attack shows a key to the Ottoman victory. The Ottomans dragged some of their ships overland and launched them into Constantinople's harbor—practically inside the city. **Critical Thinking** Why do you think so many different groups of people wanted to gain control of Constantinople?

These acts by the Church's most powerful leaders led to a **schism,** or split, in the Christian world. Like the Roman Empire, the Church was divided into eastern and western halves. In the Byzantine east, the Church was called Greek Orthodox. In the west, it was called Roman Catholic. The Roman Catholic and Orthodox Churches remain separate today.

The Fall of Constantinople Splitting from the Roman Catholic Church made the Byzantine empire a target for invasion. Encouraged by the Roman Catholic Church, an army from the west attacked Constantinople in 1204. This army captured, but could not hold, the city. Later, the Italian city of Venice took control of Constantinople. Eventually, in 1453, it was captured by the Ottoman Turks, non-Christian enemies of the Byzantines.

What the Byzantines Gave Us

Major achievements of the Byzantines affect our world today. Perhaps the most important is a system of laws.

The Code of Justinian When Justinian became emperor, laws were completely disorganized. Some laws repeated others. Some laws contradicted each other. The greatest minds in the Byzantine empire could not make sense of the law—much less enforce it.

Connect What happens when you play a game and the rules are not clear and easy to understand?

▲ Hagia Sophia, the largest church in the Byzantine empire, was the greatest monument of Justinian's reign. It took 10,000 workers five years to build the massive church with its 185-foot (56-m) high dome.

Justinian ordered his lawyers to clean up the mess. They worked long and hard to write a summary, called the Code of Justinian, that clearly spelled out the laws and explained their meanings. The Code became the backbone of the legal systems of many European nations.

Preserving Ancient Knowledge The Byzantines made another great contribution to our world. They recorded and saved the knowledge of ancient Greece and Rome. The period of Byzantine rule in the east was a period of disorder and destruction in Western Europe. If the Byzantines had not copied and cared for ancient books, Greek and Roman advances in science, mathematics, and health care would have been lost.

SECTION 1 REVIEW

1. **Define** (a) strait, (b) icon, (c) patriarch, (d) schism.

2. **Identify** (a) Justinian, (b) Moscow, (c) Constantinople, (d) Rome, (e) Venice.

3. On what was the power and strength of the Byzantine empire based?

4. How do Byzantine achievements affect the world today?

Critical Thinking

5. **Drawing Conclusions** Why do you think the disagreement over icons led to the split in the Christian Church?

Activity

6. **Writing to Learn** You are a foreign visitor to Constantinople. Write a letter to your country's leaders explaining why they might want to gain control of the city.

The Rise and Spread of Islam

Reach Into Your Background

If you spent a lot of time exploring wild and lonely places, what would you think about? In this section, you will read about a holy man who had an important experience while spending time alone.

Questions to Explore

1. How did the geography of the Arabian Peninsula affect Arab culture?
2. How did Muhammad's teachings spread?

Key Terms

nomad
prophet
hijra

Key People and Places

Muhammad
Khadijah
Mecca
Medina

The religion of Islam teaches that in about A.D. 610, a man named Muhammad went into a cave in the desert to pray. Suddenly he heard the voice of an angel cry, "Proclaim!" (To proclaim means to announce or declare something.)

Stunned, Muhammad asked, "What shall I proclaim?" The answer came quickly. He was to proclaim the one true God.

According to Muslim teaching, Muhammad was frightened at first. He was unsure that he was worthy of this mission. But he obeyed. And his acceptance of the command to "proclaim God" brought great changes to the world.

Geography of the Arabian Peninsula

Muhammad lived on the Arabian Peninsula, in the city of Mecca. Locate the peninsula on the map on the next page. Then find Mecca. It lies about 45 miles (72 km) inland from the Red Sea. As the map shows, Mecca sits on the eastern edge of a large desert. The desert takes up most of the Arabian Peninsula.

▼ In Muhammad's time—as today—a huge desert covered much of the Arabian Peninsula.

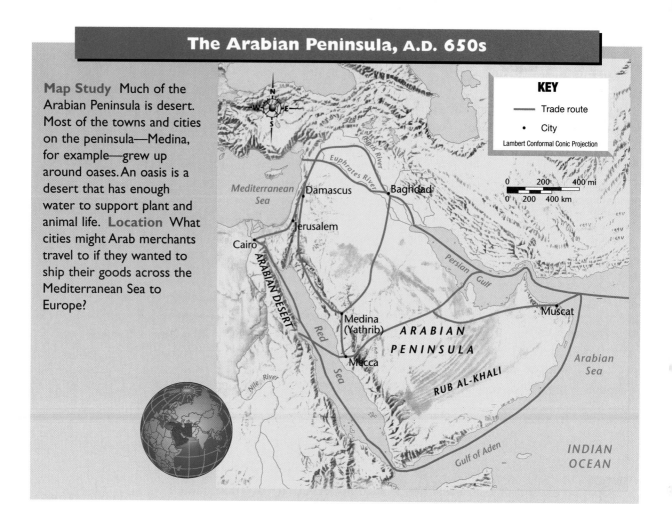

The Arabian Peninsula, A.D. 650s

Map Study Much of the Arabian Peninsula is desert. Most of the towns and cities on the peninsula—Medina, for example—grew up around oases. An oasis is a desert that has enough water to support plant and animal life. **Location** What cities might Arab merchants travel to if they wanted to ship their goods across the Mediterranean Sea to Europe?

KEY

—— Trade route

• City

Lambert Conformal Conic Projection

0   200   400 mi
0   200   400 km

Mediterranean Sea

Damascus   Baghdad

Jerusalem

Cairo

ARABIAN DESERT

Euphrates River   *Tigris River*

Persian Gulf

Muscat

Medina (Yathrib)

ARABIAN PENINSULA

Red Sea   Mecca

Nile River

RUB AL-KHALI

Arabian Sea

Gulf of Aden

INDIAN OCEAN

LINKS ACROSS THE WORLD

"Hub Cities" Trade hubs like Mecca became great cities all over the world. London, England, grew into a great city because it is a port. Ships from all over the world brought goods to London that were then sent throughout the British empire. St. Louis, Missouri, lies where the Mississippi and Missouri rivers join. These rivers were major shipping routes. St. Louis also was the jumping off place for settlers moving west.

An Avenue of Trade Mecca was a crossroads on a busy avenue of trade when Muhammad was growing up in the late 500s. Long camel trains filed through the city. They carried perfumes, ivory, spices, silk, and precious metals such as gold.

From Mecca, some caravans traveled northwest to markets in what today is Syria. From Syria, goods could be shipped across the Mediterranean Sea to Europe. Other caravans turned northeast after leaving Mecca. They made a dangerous journey across the desert to markets in the area now known as Iraq.

Bedouins and Merchants The desert was home to many groups of Bedouins (BED oo inz), an Arab people. The Bedouins were **nomads,** or people who moved from one area to another. To make a living, they herded sheep, camels, and goats. They followed planned routes, traveling from one water hole to the next. The desert yielded little food for the Bedouins' animals. Mostly they grazed on thorny bushes. Water was also scarce, for people as well as animals. Well water was often so bitter or salty that only the animals could drink it.

In addition to herding animals, the Bedouins acted as guides for trade caravans. Occasionally they would raid one of the caravans, stealing all the trade goods. To avoid being robbed, Meccan traders often made agreements with the Bedouins. Muhammad's great-grandfather, a wealthy merchant, helped to make these agreements.

Meccan merchants used religion to seal their alliances with the Bedouins. The merchants invited their Bedouin allies to worship in a holy place called the Kabah (KAH buh). The Kabah was a cube-shaped building in the center of Mecca. It held a rock known as the Black Stone, a meteorite that had fallen to the Earth from space. The Black Stone was sacred to the Meccans. The Kabah also contained many other objects that were sacred to Meccans and Bedouins alike.

Meccans closely guarded the Kabah and all the holy objects that it contained. The Kabah drew worshippers from all over Arabia. The Kabah is shown in the picture below.

Muhammad's Life

Though Muhammad's great-grandfather was a wealthy merchant, Muhammad did not grow up rich. By the time he was born, about 570, the family had fallen on hard times.

In addition to being poor, Muhammad was also an orphan. His parents died before he turned seven years old. An uncle took care of Muhammad until he grew up. Then Muhammad went to work in Mecca's brisk caravan trade. Muhammad's job took him to many other parts of the world. Several times he traveled to Syria, which was then part of the Byzantine empire.

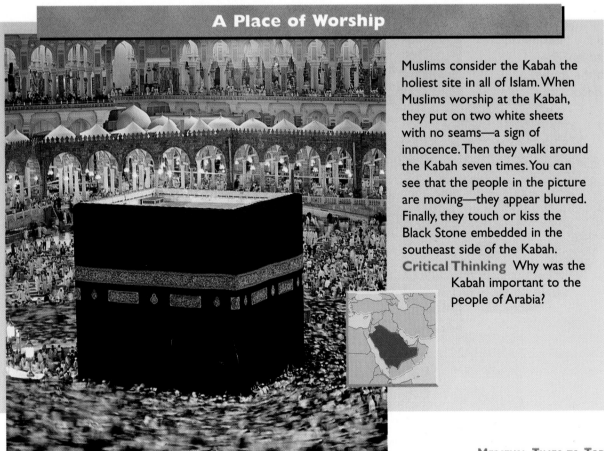

A Place of Worship

Muslims consider the Kabah the holiest site in all of Islam. When Muslims worship at the Kabah, they put on two white sheets with no seams—a sign of innocence. Then they walk around the Kabah seven times. You can see that the people in the picture are moving—they appear blurred. Finally, they touch or kiss the Black Stone embedded in the southeast side of the Kabah.

Critical Thinking Why was the Kabah important to the people of Arabia?

When he was 25 years old, Muhammad married a wealthy widow named Khadijah (kha DEE jah). Muhammad had worked for Khadijah before they got married. She had been impressed by his hard work and honesty. After their marriage, Muhammad continued to manage caravans for Khadijah. In his free time, he walked in the hills outside Mecca. Troubled by problems he saw in society, Muhammad liked to be alone to pray and think. It was during one of these trips to the hills that he heard the angel's command to proclaim the message of God.

Muhammad's Mission God said through the angel that people had abandoned the true faith. Instead of worshipping God alone, they worshipped many idols, or false gods. The angel transmitted to Muhammad the mission that God had given him. He was to pass on to the people all the messages that he would receive from God. Then the people would submit to, or agree to obey, the one true God. Muhammad would begin with the Arabs, but God's message was for the whole world.

Muhammad did as he was told. People who accepted his teachings came to be known as Muslims, which means "persons who submit." Their faith came to be known as Islam, which means "submission to God."

READ ACTIVELY

Ask Questions What do you want to know about Muhammad's work?

▶ ▼ After Mecca and Medina, Jerusalem, in the country of Israel, is the holiest city in Islam. The Shrine of the Rock (right), with its gleaming bronze dome, was built in A.D. 691 over the spot where Muslims believe Muhammad rose into heaven. The entrance to the shrine (below), is decorated with Islamic holy writings.

The Hijra: From Mecca to Medina Few Meccans listened to Muhammad. They thought his teachings about the new religion threatened their old gods. Abandoning the old gods, they thought, would end Mecca's importance as a place for worshippers.

Muhammad also taught that all people were brothers and sisters in a community established by God. This idea, too, angered the Meccans. They shouted insults at Muhammad when he preached. They threw garbage and stones at his followers. As time went on, the attacks became more and more violent. Eventually Muhammad and his followers were forced to flee the city.

People in Yathrib (YATH rub), a city north of Mecca, invited Muhammad to come to their city. They saw him as a wise man who could settle disputes in their city. Many of them also believed that Muhammad was a **prophet,** or a person who carried God's message. Muhammad seized this opportunity. In 622, he and his followers went to Yathrib.

The movement of early Muslims from Mecca to Yathrib is known as the **hijra** (HIJ rah), which means "the migration." The year of the hijra, 622, became year 1 on the Muslim calendar.

After the hijra, the name of Yathrib was changed to *Medina,* which means "city" and is short for "city of the Prophet." Medina quickly became a great Islamic center.

Expansion of Islam

Look at the map on the next page. As it shows, Islam did not remain limited to the city of Medina. In 630, Muhammad returned in triumph to Mecca. By the time of Muhammad's death in 632, Islam had spread across the Arabian Peninsula. Within the next 100 years, Islam surged west to North Africa, Spain, and southern France. It pushed east to the borders of northern India and China.

How did Islam spread so far so fast? One reason was that people did not like the nearby Byzantine and Persian empires. Their rulers were harsh and oppressive. The new religion promised a new way of life that made sense. Also, Muhammad and his people were expert traders. Merchants traveled to many parts of Asia, North Africa, and the Mediterranean Coast. They took their religion with them.

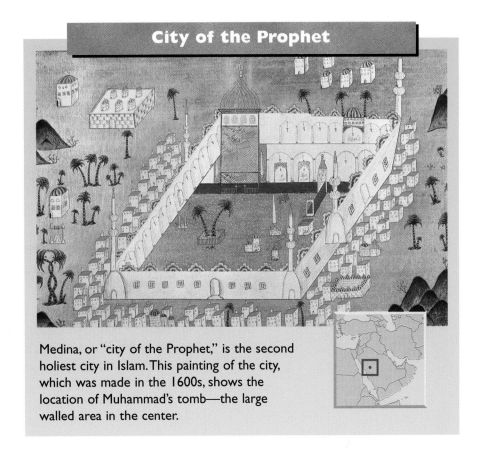

City of the Prophet

Medina, or "city of the Prophet," is the second holiest city in Islam. This painting of the city, which was made in the 1600s, shows the location of Muhammad's tomb—the large walled area in the center.

LINKS TO LANGUAGE ARTS

Muhammad and the Spider There are many legends about the time of the hijra. One of the most famous tells about a spider's role in saving Muhammad's life. When Muhammad fled from Mecca, he entered a cave to rest. After he had gone into the cave, a spider spun a web across the entrance. Muhammad's pursuers saw the web across the entrance and were convinced that he could not be in the cave. They went on and Muhammad was saved.

The Spread of Islam

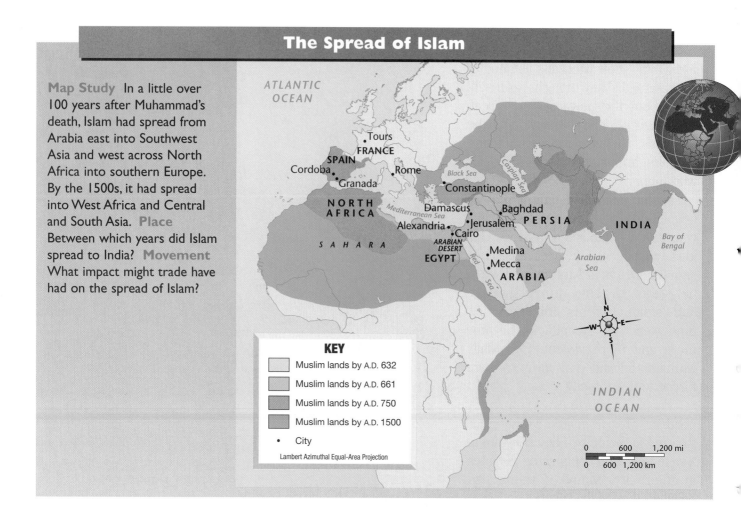

Map Study In a little over 100 years after Muhammad's death, Islam had spread from Arabia east into Southwest Asia and west across North Africa into southern Europe. By the 1500s, it had spread into West Africa and Central and South Asia. **Place** Between which years did Islam spread to India? **Movement** What impact might trade have had on the spread of Islam?

KEY

Muslim lands by A.D. 632

Muslim lands by A.D. 661

Muslim lands by A.D. 750

Muslim lands by A.D. 1500

• City

Lambert Azimuthal Equal-Area Projection

Another key reason for the spread of Islam was that Muhammad united the Arabs in his region into one community. Once they were working together, they became a powerful people. Islam respected Jews and Christians. It also recognized Abraham, Moses, Jesus, and others as earlier prophets. Under Islam, Jews and Christians were allowed to practice their own faiths.

SECTION 2 REVIEW

1. **Define** (a) nomad, (b) prophet, (c) hijra.

2. **Identify** (a) Muhammad, (b) Khadijah, (c) Mecca, (d) Medina.

3. How did the geography in which the Bedouins lived affect their lives?

4. How did Islam spread beyond Arabia?

Critical Thinking

5. **Expressing Problems Clearly** Briefly state two problems Muhammad faced in Mecca when he began teaching.

Activity

6. **Writing to Learn** You are a Bedouin herder at the time Muhammad was beginning to preach. Write a speech to deliver to fellow Bedouins. In the speech, tell why you think Muhammad's teachings will help improve your life.

The Religion of Islam

BEFORE YOU READ

Reach Into Your Background

What beliefs do you share with friends or family members? Perhaps you share beliefs about right and wrong or good and bad. In this section, you will learn about the beliefs shared by Muslims.

Questions to Explore
1. What basic beliefs do Muslims share?
2. What beliefs do Muslims share with Christians and Jews?

Key Terms
muezzin
mosque
Ramadan
hajj
Quran

Key People
Shiites
Sunnis

A muezzin (moo EZ in), a man who calls Muslims to prayer, looks out over the city and begins his call to noon prayers. The call rings out in four directions. "There is no god but God, and Muhammad is His prophet."

All over the world, faithful Muslims heed the call. Some kneel in houses of worship called **mosques** (mahsks). Others kneel outside—on the banks of the Indus River, in the Arabian Desert, or along the Mediterranean Sea. No matter where they are, the kneeling Muslims face Mecca. "There is no god but God," the faithful respond, "and Muhammad is His prophet."

Muslim Belief

This scene of prayer has been repeated around the world every day for hundreds of years. No matter where they live, Muslims share beliefs with others in the Islamic world. Their basic beliefs are expressed in what Muslims call the Five Pillars of Islam: faith, prayer, sharing, fasting, and pilgrimage. These five practices are the foundations of Islam.

▼ A muezzin calls Muslims to prayer from the top of this graceful spiral minaret in Samarra, Iraq.

21

The Five Pillars of Islam   The first pillar, faith, is based on the words of the call to prayer: "There is no god but God, and Muhammad is His prophet." This call expresses the Muslim statement of faith. The belief in one God is also the basis for the Jewish and Christian religions.

Through the second pillar, prayer, Muslims communicate with God. The muezzin calls Muslims to prayer from the minaret, or tower, of a mosque. Muslims pray five times a day—in the morning, at noon, in the afternoon, at sunset, and in the evening. The muezzin signals the various prayer times.

The third pillar is sharing. Muslims who can do so give a generous share of what they own to Muslims who are poor or sick.

The fourth pillar, fasting, occurs during a special month called **Ramadan** (ram uh DAHN). During Ramadan, Muslims fast from sunrise to sunset every day. They neither eat nor drink. In the evenings, children stay up late and join their parents in breaking the fast with a sweet, such as a few dates, and a cool drink. Then everyone sits down to an "evening breakfast."

Common Practices Other major religious groups besides Muslims practice fasting. It may be required or voluntary. Christians, for instance, may fast during the season of Lent, which honors the 40 days that Jesus fasted in the wilderness. Jews fast on several occasions. The most important is Yom Kippur, or the Day of Atonement. Hindus and Buddhists also fast to celebrate certain holy days.

▶Fasting during Ramadan is one of the five pillars of Muslim faith. These people in Cairo, Egypt, are waiting for the sunset prayer so they can break their daylong fast. In the time of the Muslim empire, people celebrated late into the night during Ramadan. Children carried small lanterns to light their way. Street magicians performed tricks, and storytellers and poets recited tales for the crowds.

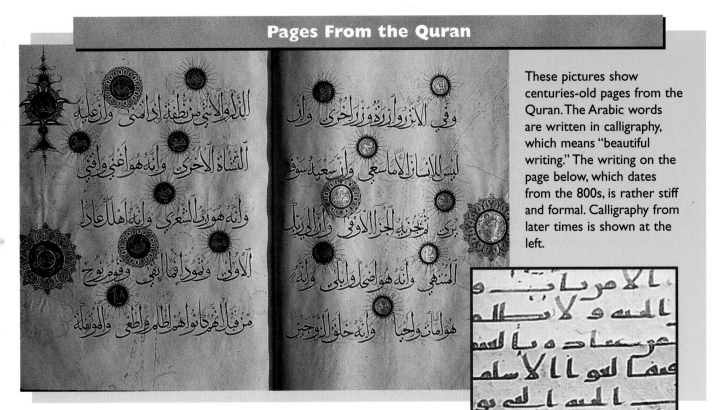

These pictures show centuries-old pages from the Quran. The Arabic words are written in calligraphy, which means "beautiful writing." The writing on the page below, which dates from the 800s, is rather stiff and formal. Calligraphy from later times is shown at the left.

The fifth pillar is the **hajj** (haj), a pilgrimage, or sacred journey, to Mecca. All Muslims who can afford to do so try to make the hajj once in their lives. In Mecca, they meet other Muslims from all over the world.

The Quran As you read about the Five Pillars, you may have gotten a sense that Islam is a not just a set of beliefs. It is a way of life. Islam is a guide to the way Muslims should live, conduct family life, and deal with others.

The things God revealed to Muhammad included the rules of Islam, which are written in a book called the **Quran** (koo RAHN). Many Muslims know the Quran by heart. Like the Torah, or Jewish holy book, and the Christian Bible, the Quran contains many kinds of writing, including stories, promises, warnings, and instructions.

Relationships Outside and Inside Islam

There is a reason for the similarity of the Quran to Jewish and Christian holy books. Muslims, like Jews and Christians, regard Adam, Noah, Abraham, and Moses as important people in their religious histories. Muhammad saw himself as the last prophet in a long line of prophets that included all of these people.

People of the Book Muhammad felt respect for Jews and Christians. He called them "people of the Book." Muslims, Jews, and Christians all practice a religion revealed in holy writings. They all believe in one single God.

Rulers of the Muslim empire saw Jews and Christians as "protected people." As long as they accepted Muslim rule, Jews and Christians were allowed to practice their religions and pursue their own business affairs. However, they had to pay a special tax called the jizyah.

Men's and Women's Roles Muhammad insisted that all Muslims were equal in spirit—whether rich or poor, men or women. This equality allowed women to have many rights in early Islamic society that they did not have in other lands. For instance, they had a right to an education and could not be married without their agreement.

Despite this type of equality, men and women had very different roles in Islamic communities. Men were more likely to be involved in life outside the home. They inherited a greater share of property after a parent died. Muslim men were expected to treat their wives kindly and to provide for them.

As Islam moved into other lands, Muslims sometimes adopted the attitudes toward women that they found in the places they conquered. In a few Muslim countries today, women must cover their faces when they go out of the house. Some Muslims find support for this in the Quran, which says that all believers, both men and women, should dress modestly.

Schism: Sunni and Shiite Muslims Earlier you read about a schism that split the Christian Church in two at the time of the Byzantine empire. A schism, or split, also occurred in Islam.

A Muslim Woman

Arabs who settled in Persia and Byzantine lands adopted the practice of secluding women in a separate part of the house. From this section of the home, women planned and oversaw the day-to-day life of the household. This painting, which was made in the late 1500s, shows a Persian woman sitting in her garden and writing. **Critical Thinking** How did the roles of Muslim men and women differ?

◄ These men and boys are worshipping at a mosque in Brunei, a small nation in Southeast Asia. Like most Muslims, they are Sunni. Only about 10 percent of all Muslims are Shiites.

In 656, Uthman (ooth MAHN), the ruler of the Muslim empire, was assassinated. His death split the Islamic world in two. Many Muslims disagreed over who should be the rightful leader of Islam. Over the next few hundred years, two main groups emerged over this disagreement.

The smaller group, the Shiites (SHEE eyets), argued that the ruler should be a direct descendant of Muhammad. They believed that Muhammad's descendants would be inspired by God, just as Muhammad had been. They also thought that this leader should tell Muslims what the Quran means.

The larger group of Muslims, the Sunni (SOON ee), disagreed. They argued that any truly religious Muslim could lead the community. They believed that no one man, not even the leader of Islam, should tell Muslims what the Quran taught. The Sunni argued that a group of Muslim scholars could best say what the holy book means.

SECTION 3 REVIEW

1. **Define** (a) muezzin, (b) mosque, (c) Ramadan, (d) hajj, (e) Quran.
2. **Identify** (a) Shiites, (b) Sunni.
3. What shared beliefs unite Muslims?
4. What do Muslims, Jews, and Christians have in common?

Critical Thinking
5. **Identifying Central Issues** One of Islam's pillars is sharing. How would sharing one's wealth help the community? What do you think would happen if people in the community did not share their wealth with people who were less fortunate?

Activity
6. **Writing to Learn** A friend has asked you to explain the Muslim religion. Write a letter describing the Five Pillars of Islam.

Reading Tables

"**A**ngie, it's your turn to take out the garbage," said Damon. His sister Angie looked surprised.

"No, it isn't!" she said. "I took it out last week."

"Maya took it out last week," Damon said. "And I took it out the week before. Now it's your turn to take out the garbage, my turn to vacuum, and Maya's turn to do laundry."

Angie shook her head. "Wait a minute, Maya did laundry last week, and you vacuumed, didn't you? You have it all mixed up."

"How are we supposed to figure this out?" said Damon. "It gets too confusing."

"We just need to keep it straight. Why don't we make a table?"

Damon nodded. "You know, that is not a bad idea, Angie! One look at a table of our chores would settle our fights."

Get Ready

Damon and Angie hit upon a good way to organize information. A simple table would keep track of who should do what chores on which days. Tables help you to organize ideas in a visual way. A table can sometimes answer a question better than a written paragraph.

You see tables all the time. Most of your textbooks include tables. You will also find them in newspapers, in magazines, and in computer programs. With tables, people can arrange ideas in a way that is easy to understand at a glance.

Chores for a Month

	Week 1	Week 2	Week 3	Week 4
Garbage	Angie	Maya	Damon	Angie
Vacuum	Damon	Angie	Maya	Damon
Laundry	Maya	Damon	Angie	Maya

Try It Out

Here is your chance to make and use a table of something you are very familiar with—weekly household or classroom chores. Make your table by following the illustration and these three simple steps.

A. Choose a topic for your table. Every table has a topic, or subject. You will make a table called *Chores for a Month*. It will show the classroom or household chores that different people have to do each week.

B. Create the columns for your table. Create the columns for your table. A table is made up of vertical columns and horizontal rows. Your table will have one column for each week of the month. The columns will be labelled *Week 1, Week 2, Week 3,* and *Week 4.*

C. Create the rows for your table. Each row lists one chore, such as emptying the wastebasket or washing the chalkboards.

D. Put the data in your table. In each cell of the table, write the name of the person or group who is to do that chore that week. To begin, put your finger on the label of the first chore, and trace the row until your finger is under *Week 1.* In that cell, write the name of the person or group who must do the first chore during the first week. Follow the same steps for the other chores and other weeks.

Now look at your completed table. You can see how easy it is to keep the chores and weeks straight.

Apply the Skill

The table below is about a much bigger topic—the Byzantine and Muslim empires. This table shows more information, but you can read it in the same way as you read the *Chores for a Month* table. Trace a row and column to their meeting point to find information. For example, if you trace the row *Location* to where it meets the column *Muslim Empire,* you will find the location of the Muslim empire. Study the table carefully to answer the questions that follow.

1 Determine the purpose of the table. What empires are being compared? How is the information in the table organized?

2 Use the table. When did the Muslim empire begin? What was the major city of the Byzantine empire? Where were the different empires located?

3 Analyze the information. How do the two empires differ? What do they have in common? Why do you think they are being compared in this table?

Byzantine and Muslim Empires

	Byzantine Empire	Muslim Empire
Time Period	A.D. 527–1453	A.D. 640–1750
Location	Bordering on the Mediterranean Sea in Southwest Asia, southeastern Europe, and northern Africa	Southwestern Asia and Northern Africa
Major City	Constantinople	Mecca
Religion	Christianity	Islam
Source of Wealth	Trade	Trade
Scientific and Mathematical Contributions	Records of Greek and Roman advances in science, mathematics, and health care	Avicenna's medical discoveries, algebra, an improved decimal system, and scientific classification

Islam's Golden Age

Reach Into Your Background

In this section, you will read about the golden, or great, years of the Muslim empire.

Think about your own life. Was there a time that was very special? What made it special?

Questions to Explore

1. What strengths of the Islamic world led to its golden age?
2. What did Islam's golden age contribute to science, mathematics, and literature?

Key Terms

caliph   tolerance
patron

Key People and Places

Omar Khayyám
Harun ar-Rashid
Maimonides
Baghdad

▼ This beautifully decorated cover of an edition of Omar Khayyám's poems has one of his most famous verses printed around the edge.

Omar Khayyám (oh mahr ky YAHM) was a skilled Muslim astronomer and one of the most famous mathematicians in the world. Khayyám was also a great poet. The series of poems he wrote in the Persian language some 900 years ago are still read today. This is one of his poems:

> "When I was a child, I sometimes
>   went to a teacher.
> And sometimes I taught myself, but
>   eventually I learned
> The limits to all knowledge: we come into
>   this world upon
> the waters, we leave it on the wind."

Do you agree with Omar Khayyám? Do you think knowledge is limited? What do you think Omar Khayyám means when he writes, "I learned/The limits to all knowledge: we come into this world upon/the waters, we leave it on the wind"?

A Baghdad Courtyard

In the 760s, the caliph al-Mansur decided to build his capital at Baghdad, a small village on the banks of the Tigris River. By 800, Baghdad was a thriving city with a huge population. Many of Baghdad's people lived in courtyard buildings like the one shown here. The courtyards allowed residents some privacy and blocked out the noise and bustle of the city.

Wise Leadership Promotes a Golden Age

The multitalented Omar Khayyám lived during Islam's golden age. Scholars see this period, from about 800 to 1100, as one of the most brilliant in world history.

Lasting works of literature, like the poetry of Omar Khayyám, were created in the golden age. Medical and mathematical knowledge expanded. Scientific experiments were made.

Why did all this happen during this time? Before a society can afford to give artists and scientists time to do their work, it needs money. And the Islamic world had plenty. The empire had grown rich from the many lands it controlled and from trade.

Find Baghdad on the map at the end of Section 2. Baghdad was the capital of the Muslim empire during Islam's golden age. You can see from the map that Baghdad, like Constantinople, was a natural center for trade.

With a finger, trace a route from India to Baghdad. Now trace a route from the Mediterranean Sea to Baghdad. Traders from all over the world brought their goods to the caliph's court. The **caliph** was the chief ruler of Islam. He was Muhammad's successor, or the person who next had the right to rule.

READ ACTIVELY

Predict Why would Baghdad's location almost guarantee that it would become a wealthy city?

Harun ar-Rashid: A Powerful Caliph   Harun ar-Rashid (hah ROO nar ash EED) became caliph of Baghdad in 786. His rule was a time of prosperity for the people, and he himself was very wealthy. For 23 years, Harun ruled the world's most glamorous court. He and his favorite subjects ate off of gold plates and drank from goblets studded with jewels.

But Harun did not use the riches of Baghdad just to have fun. He was a great **patron,** or supporter, of the arts. Harun paid many skilled writers, musicians, dancers, and artists to live in Baghdad. He lavishly rewarded those whose works pleased him. One musician is said to have received 100,000 silver pieces for a single song.

Islam's Tolerance Is Rewarded   Tolerance, or acceptance of differences, was one of Islam's major features during the golden age. Jews and Christians who accepted Muslim rule were free to practice their religions. Non-Muslims were allowed to govern their own communities. They had to pay higher taxes than Muslim subjects, and they were forbidden to carry weapons. However, they were not required to serve in the military.

In the Bazaar

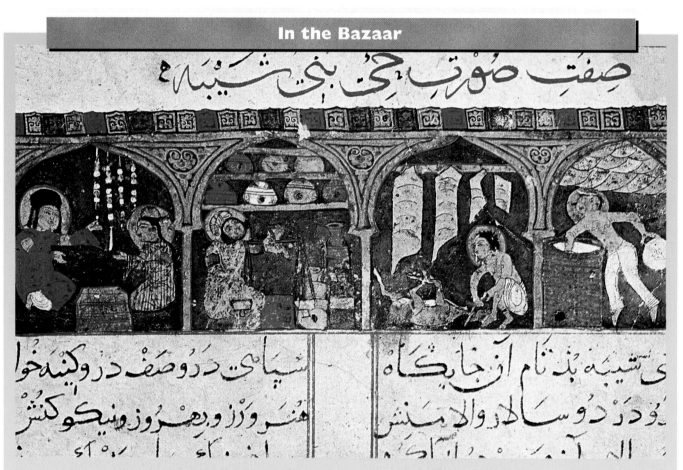

The busiest place in Baghdad was the bazaar, or marketplace. It consisted of miles of streets covered by a roof. Merchants at the bazaar sold local goods and products from all over the Muslim empire.

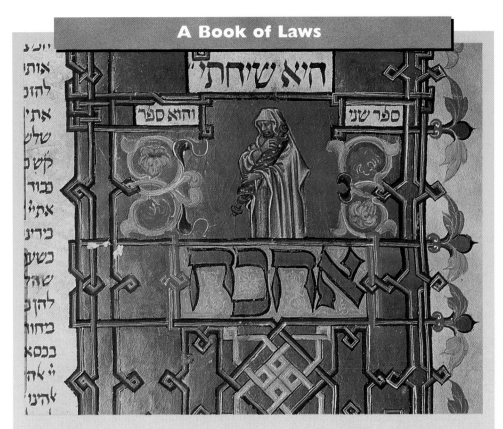

Maimonides was a religious scholar as well as a doctor and philosopher. In 1180, he completed the *Mishneh Torah,* or "Repetition of the Law." In it, Maimonides tried to classify and explain all the laws of Judaism. This picture shows the title page of an edition published in Italy. **Critical Thinking** How did Islamic attitudes toward non-Muslims help Maimonides in his work?

The Muslim empire benefited from this policy of tolerance. Jews and Christians helped to create Islam's golden age. Maimonides (my MAHN uh deez), a Jew who lived in the Muslim empire in the 1100s, is a good example of this. Maimonides was a doctor. He spent time in Spain, North Africa, and Southwest Asia. He was also a great thinker. In his book *Guide for the Perplexed,* Maimonides tried to explain how people could believe in science and religion at the same time. Today, people still study and think about his ideas.

Intellectual Achievements in the Golden Age

Muslim scholars of the golden age made lasting contributions to human understanding of the physical world. Some of these contributions to science, medicine, and mathematics are shown on the next page.

Have you ever read a book or seen a film about Aladdin and his magic lamp? This is just one of the stories gathered in *The Thousand and One Nights.* This collection of tales is made up of Indian and Persian

Math Masters How would you multiply large numbers without a number for zero? How could you talk about below-freezing temperatures without negative numbers? Early Muslim mathematicians "borrowed" the idea of zero from Indian mathematicians. A Muslim mathematician also wrote a textbook on algebra and introduced its concepts to Europeans. The work of these mathematicians enabled later scientists to make great discoveries in astronomy, physics, and chemistry.

fairy tales, Egyptian romances, and Arab legends and love stories. *The Thousand and One Nights* reached Western Europe in the early 1700s, when a French scholar translated the tales.

Muslim writers also created serious works. Poetry was particularly important in the Islamic world. Poets were treated like stars, much like popular musicians are today. You have already read a poem from one Muslim poet, Omar Khayyám.

Some people used poetry to teach ideas and beliefs. The Sufis (SOOF eez) were one group of Muslims who did this. They taught that the world will reveal its mysteries to the seeker who makes careful observations. Although some Sufis were Islamic scholars, they tried to draw close to God through prayer and a simple life. The Sufis' spiritual focus, rather than the more traditional, legal-minded approach, further enriched Muslim heritage.

Arab Contributions to Mathematics and Science

▶ The great Islamic scientist and philosopher Ibn Sina lived from 980 to 1037. He organized the medical knowledge of the Greeks and Arabs into the *Canon of Medicine*.

▲ Arab scientists were fascinated by water-driven machines. In this drawing, water falling into the cups causes the globe at the top to turn.

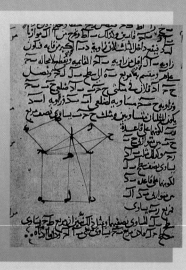

▶ Arab mathematicians invented algebra. They also studied ideas from the past, like the formula shown here. It explains how to find the length of one side of a right triangle when you know the length of the other sides.

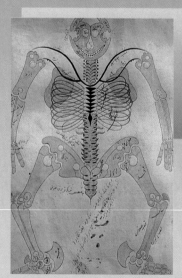

◀ Doctors studied diagrams like this one in the hospital libraries of Baghdad, Cairo, and Damascus.

A Sufi Preacher

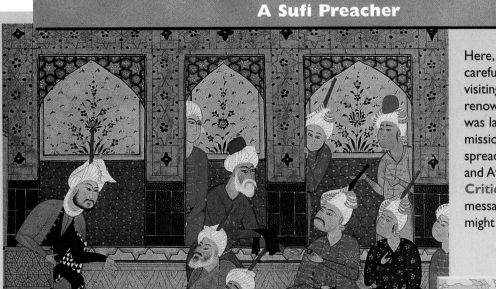

Here, a group of Muslims listens carefully to the words of a visiting Sufi preacher. Sufis were renowned for their preaching. It was largely through their work as missionary preachers that Islam spread to Central Asia, India, and Africa south of the Sahara. **Critical Thinking** What kind of message do you think the Sufi might be preaching?

The most famous Sufi poet, Jalal ad-Din ar-Rumi (juh LAHL ud DEEN ur ROO mee), founded a religious group called the Whirling Dervishes in the West. They used music and dance to communicate with God. Rumi composed the verses that appear below:

“Never think the earth [empty] or dead—
It's a hare, awake with shut eyes:
It's a saucepan, simmering with broth—
One clear look, you'll see it's in ferment [motion].”

SECTION 4 REVIEW

1. **Define** (a) caliph, (b) patron, (c) tolerance.

2. **Identify** (a) Omar Khayyám, (b) Harun ar-Rashid, (c) Maimonides, (d) Baghdad.

3. What helped bring about Islam's golden age?

4. What were some achievements in science, mathematics, and literature during the golden age?

Critical Thinking

5. **Recognizing Cause and Effect** How did the economy of the Muslim empire affect the golden age?

Activity

6. **Writing to Learn** Study the two poems you have read in this section. Then try to write a similar poem yourself. Share your poem by reading it aloud or posting it on the bulletin board in your classroom.

Review and Activities

Reviewing Main Ideas

1. What enabled the eastern part of the Roman Empire to survive after the western Roman Empire fell?

2. What contributions of the Byzantine empire affect the world today?

3. How did Mecca's location affect the culture that developed there?

4. Why did people in the former Byzantine and Persian empires adopt Muhammad's ideas?

5. What are the Five Pillars of Islam?

6. What beliefs do Muslims, Jews, and Christians share?

7. How did the Muslim empire's policy of tolerance affect the golden age of Islam?

8. Name one scientific, one mathematical, and one literary accomplishment of Islam's golden age.

Reviewing Key Terms

Use each key term below in a sentence that shows the meaning of the term.

1. strait
2. patriarch
3. schism
4. nomad
5. prophet
6. hijra
7. muezzin
8. mosque
9. Ramadan
10. hajj
11. Quran
12. caliph
13. patron
14. tolerance

Critical Thinking

1. **Drawing Conclusions** Why do you think Harun ar-Rashid spent so much money on writers, musicians, dancers, and artists?

2. **Making Comparisons** What strengths were found in both the Byzantine and Muslim empires?

Graphic Organizer

Copy the diagram onto a separate sheet of paper. Then fill in the empty circles to complete the diagram.

Muslim Empire — Contributions — Byzantine Empire

Map Activity

The Byzantine and Muslim Empires

For each place listed below, write the letter from the map that shows its location.

1. Arabian Peninsula
2. Mecca
3. Constantinople
4. Bosporus
5. Mediterranean Sea
6. Black Sea
7. Baghdad

Place Location

Writing Activity

Writing a Monologue

A monologue is a speech by one person, often spoken to oneself. Choose one of the people you have read about in this chapter. Write a monologue that describes an important moment in his or her life.

Take It to the NET

Activity Learn more about Islam and create a time line marking important events in the rise and spread of the religion. For help in completing this activity, visit www.phschool.com.

Chapter 1 Self-Test To review what you have learned, take the Chapter 1 Self-Test and get instant feedback on your answers. Go to www.phschool.com to take the test.

Skills Review

Turn to the Skills Activity.

Review the four steps for making a table. Then answer the following: (a) What is the purpose of the columns and rows in the table? (b) What are some kinds of information you might show on a table?

How Am I Doing?

Answer these questions to help you check your progress.

1. Do I understand why the Byzantine empire survived for many centuries?

2. Can I explain how the Muslim empire expanded?

3. Can I explain the basic beliefs of Islam?

4. What information from this chapter can I include in my journal?

Civilizations of Africa

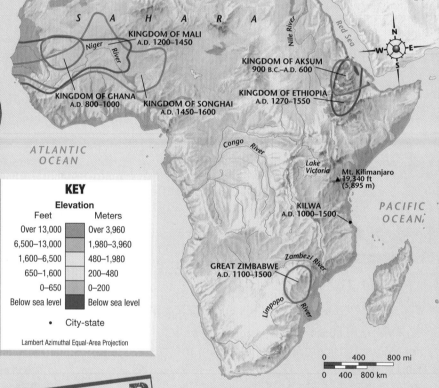

KEY

Elevation

Feet	Meters
Over 13,000	Over 3,960
6,500–13,000	1,980–3,960
1,600–6,500	480–1,980
650–1,600	200–480
0–650	0–200
Below sea level	Below sea level

• City-state

Lambert Azimuthal Equal-Area Projection

Africa was home to two of the world's earliest civilizations, Egypt and Nubia. As these glorious cultures declined, new ones were arising throughout the continent. The map shows some of the powerful kingdoms and cities of the period from 900 B.C. to A.D. 1500. To help you get to know them, do the following activities.

Study the map

Read the names of the different kingdoms on the map. Which were in the western part of Africa? Which were in the eastern part?

Recognizing names that lived on

Compare the map on this page with the political map of Africa in the Atlas at the back of this book. Which modern countries carry the names of ancient kingdoms?

The Bantu Migrations

Reach Into Your Background

Many American families move from one part of the United States to another. If you and your family were to move to another state, what would you take with you? What might be the same in your new home? What might be different?

Questions to Explore

1. What are some of Africa's major physical features?
2. What were the Bantu migrations, and how did they affect African cultures?

Key Terms
savanna
oasis
migration
clan

Key Place
Sahara

Historians know quite a lot about the history of North Africa. But historians have only a sketchy knowledge of the history of Africa south of the Sahara. For more than 2,000 years, the Sahara cut off the larger part of Africa from Europe and European historians.

Today, scientists and historians are working to piece together the history and cultural traditions of the area south of the Sahara. The task is a slow and difficult one. In many ways, it is like working to solve a puzzle. For thousands of years, the Africans seldom used materials that lasted, such as stone. The wood and clay they used to build and to keep records often disintegrated.

Even the iron tools and weapons the Africans used did not last. Iron corrodes, or rusts, fairly quickly. Since some African cultures did not have a Bronze Age during which they worked with more lasting metals, often little is left for scientists to find.

In the 1900s, scientists began to use modern techniques in their study of Africa. Some gathered stories told by traditional storytellers. These spoken histories led the scientists to new areas of exploration. Modern forms of travel also helped. Africa's physical geography was no longer the challenge it had been in the past.

▼ A modern-day griot, or storyteller, from Mali carries out his job of remembering and telling his people's history. He illustrates his story by drawing diagrams in the earth.

The Physical Geography of Africa

READ ACTIVELY

Visualize Visualize Africa's tropical savanna. What might it look and sound like?

Look at the map below. Notice that Africa's rain forests are located on either side of the Equator. Farther from the Equator, bands of grasslands curve around the rain forests. To the north and south of the grasslands are dry areas.

Africa's tropical rain forests are areas of thick vegetation. These areas receive plenty of rainfall all year. The heat and moisture support a rich environment of trees, plants, and animals.

Much of Africa to the north and south of the rain forests is tropical **savanna.** This is an area of gently rolling land covered by grasses, occasional trees, and thorny bushes. In some places, the grass is lush and tall. In others, it is short and sparse. Most of Africa's farming takes place in the savanna.

Beyond the savanna lies the desert. The Sahara—the largest desert in the world—stretches across most of North Africa. It is so big that nearly all of the United States could fit within its borders. It is a place of pale yellow to deep red sands, rocky mountains, and salt flats. There are some oases too. An **oasis** is an area of vegetation fed by springs and underground water. Oases are surrounded by desert.

Map Study If you walked either north or south from the Equator you would pass through similar natural vegetation zones. **Regions** Locate the Tropic of Cancer and the Tropic of Capricorn on the map. What kinds of vegetation are most common in this area? Look at the map again. In what areas is Mediterranean vegetation found?

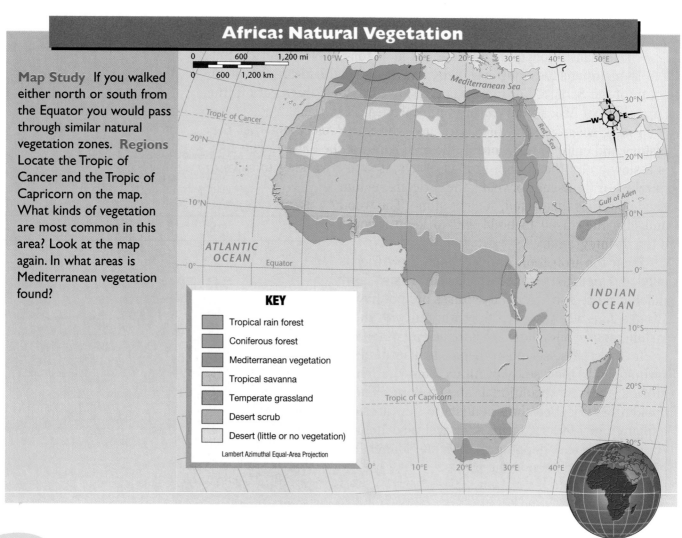

Africa: Natural Vegetation

KEY
- Tropical rain forest
- Coniferous forest
- Mediterranean vegetation
- Tropical savanna
- Temperate grassland
- Desert scrub
- Desert (little or no vegetation)

Lambert Azimuthal Equal-Area Projection

Africa's physical geography offers some dramatic sights. Giraffes graze on the plains below Kenya's 19,340-foot (5,895-m) Mount Kilimanjaro (left). Victoria Falls (right), on the Zambezi River, plunge 343 feet (105 m) and give off clouds of spray. Africans call the falls "The Smoke That Thunders."

Most of Africa is a huge plateau, edged by narrow coastal plains. In East Africa, a steep cliff marks the point where the plateau and the coastal plains meet. Rivers create great waterfalls over cliffs of the plateau. This eastern half of the continent also has huge freshwater lakes and high mountains.

The Bantu Migrations

The physical barriers formed by forests, mountains, and rushing rivers did not halt great **migrations,** or movements, of people. During these migrations, groups of Africans moved from West Africa toward the south. Look at the map on the next page and, with your finger, trace the routes of the migrations.

Among the largest population movements in human history, the Bantu (BAN too) migrations began about 2,000 years ago and went on for about 1,000 years. Bantu was the name of the family of languages that these people spoke. For this reason, we today call them Bantu-speakers. Historians have been able to figure out where the Bantu migrations started and ended by looking at where Bantu-speakers live today.

No one knows exactly why the Bantu-speaking peoples began to move from their homeland in West Africa. However, it probably had to do with population growth. The population grew so large that there was not enough land for everyone. When the land became scarce in a particular area, small groups left in search of land elsewhere.

Iron Age Farmers The practice of farming spread from Egypt to West Africa thousands of years ago. Around 400 B.C., these early African farming cultures began making iron tools. The earliest of these Iron Age settlements in West Africa is known as the Nok culture. The Nok lived in what is today northern Nigeria. Historians believe that the Nok were the first people living south of the Sahara to use iron tools.

The Bantu Migrations

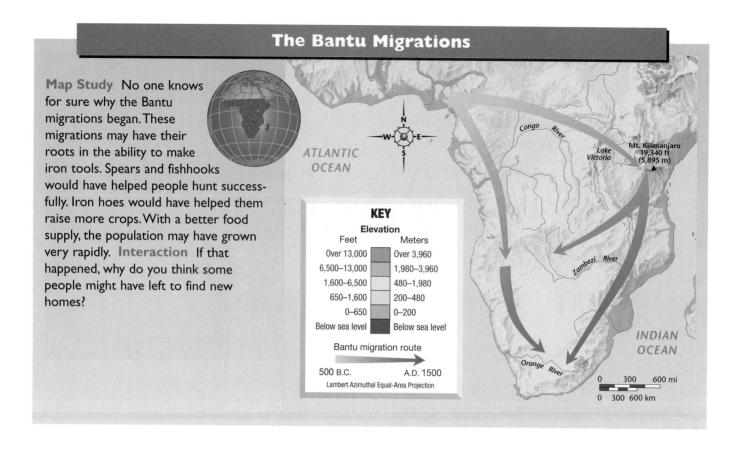

Map Study No one knows for sure why the Bantu migrations began. These migrations may have their roots in the ability to make iron tools. Spears and fishhooks would have helped people hunt successfully. Iron hoes would have helped them raise more crops. With a better food supply, the population may have grown very rapidly. **Interaction** If that happened, why do you think some people might have left to find new homes?

KEY

Elevation

Feet	Meters
Over 13,000	Over 3,960
6,500–13,000	1,980–3,960
1,600–6,500	480–1,980
650–1,600	200–480
0–650	0–200
Below sea level	Below sea level

Bantu migration route

500 B.C. ➡ A.D. 1500

Lambert Azimuthal Equal-Area Projection

ATLANTIC OCEAN

INDIAN OCEAN

Congo River

Lake Victoria

Mt. Kilimanjaro 19,340 ft (5,895 m)

Zambezi River

Orange River

Predict What kinds of changes did the Bantu-speakers make as they migrated through Africa?

Africa had always been a place where groups of people moved from region to region. Hunters and gatherers moved in search of game and other foods. Herders moved to provide their animals with fresh grazing lands. The Bantu-speakers were part of a long line of peoples to follow this tradition. It is the size of the Bantu migrations that made them so amazing.

In early times, most Bantu-speaking people were fishers, farmers, and herders. They lived in villages made up of families from the same **clan,** or group of families who trace their roots to the same ancestor. Many of these clans traced their ancestry through the mother rather than the father. For this reason, belongings and positions of power were passed on through the mother's side of the family.

The Bantu-speaking peoples moved slowly from their traditional homelands. Each generation moved a fairly short distance in the search for better farmland and more grazing lands. As they spread out from their homelands, the technology and culture of the Bantu-speakers also spread to new areas.

Bantu-Speakers Move South Often, Bantu-speakers moved into areas where other people already lived. When this happened, the Bantu-speakers sometimes joined the groups already living there. Often, they married people from the cultures they found in their new homes. Because of this, the older cultures of the area often adapted to the cultures of the Bantu-speaking peoples. At other times, the Bantu-speakers drove out the people they found in a new area. As these new areas also became crowded, some groups moved on. This process was repeated from one generation to the next for hundreds of years. In time, Bantu-speakers settled throughout Central and Southern Africa.

Learning and Teaching As the Bantu-speaking peoples migrated, they entered different environments. Often, they had to change the way they lived. For instance, they learned new ways of farming and caring for livestock.

But the people already living in these areas also learned from the Bantu-speakers. In each area they crossed, the Bantu-speaking people passed on what they had learned. They introduced new crops, such as

Cattle Herders in East Africa

Many Bantu-speakers settled in the East African highlands, where the climate was ideal for raising cattle. Today, descendants of those settlers—like these Maasai herders—still raise cattle in East Africa.

Iron tools gave the Bantu-speaking peoples more control over their environment. With strong axes, they could cut trees and clear the land. Their sharp, iron-headed spears and arrows were powerful weapons for hunting and defense. This arrowhead was made by the Hadza people of Tanzania using metalworking techniques that are centuries old. **Critical Thinking** What things, other than metalworking, did Bantu-speakers introduce to the lands they settled?

yams and bananas, to parts of Africa. They also taught people what was probably their most valuable skill—metalworking. Knowing how to make iron weapons and tools changed the way people lived throughout Africa.

As they moved through Africa, the Bantu-speakers left behind something else: their languages. Today, about 180 million Africans still speak Bantu languages. About 200 of the languages spoken in Africa south of the Sahara are related to the Bantu language family.

SECTION 1 REVIEW

1. **Define** (a) savanna, (b) oasis, (c) migration, (d) clan.

2. **Identify** Sahara.

3. Briefly describe Africa's physical geography.

4. How did the Bantu-speaking peoples change the lives of other African peoples?

Critical Thinking

5. **Identifying Central Issues** People have made important discoveries and developed new ways of doing things throughout history. Name two important contributions made by Bantu-speakers. Tell why these contributions are important.

Activity

6. **Writing to Learn** You are living in the Africa of a thousand years ago. Some Bantu-speaking people have moved into an area near your village. You have made friends with a Bantu-speaker your own age. Write a journal entry describing what your new friend has taught you about his or her people.

Kingdoms of West Africa

BEFORE YOU READ

Reach Into Your Background

How does trade affect your life? Consider the everyday things around you—the clothes you wear, the electrical appliances you use, and so on—as you think of your answer.

Questions to Explore

1. Why were gold and salt equally valuable to West African merchants?

2. How did the religion of Islam influence the empire of Mali?

Key Terms

silent barter
province

Key People and Places

Mansa Musa
Sundiata
Mali
Ghana
Tombouctou
Songhai

Five hundred slaves each carried a staff made of gold. Soldiers, with swords hanging from gold chains, rode horses decorated with gold. Hundreds of doctors, teachers, government officials, and musicians marched along. The procession included more than 60,000 people in all—and 80 camels, each loaded with 300 pounds (136 kg) of gold. This was the sight that greeted the astonished people of the city of Cairo, Egypt, one day in July 1324. It was the caravan of Mansa Musa (MAHN sah moo SAH), emperor of Mali. A hundred years later, people in the Egyptian city of Cairo still talked about Mansa Musa's amazing visit—and about the gifts of gold he handed out.

▼ Mansa Musa's fame spread well beyond Africa. This likeness of him was included on a map made in Europe in the 1300s.

Empires Built on Trade

Mali, the kingdom ruled by Mansa Musa, was just one of the rich trading empires that arose in West Africa between A.D. 800 and 1600. These empires controlled important trade routes across the Sahara, the desert that lies between North Africa and the West African coast. Merchants traveling through these empires had to pay taxes on all the trade goods they carried with them. This made the rulers of these empires rich. In return, the rulers kept peace and order throughout the land. This meant that the merchants could travel safely.

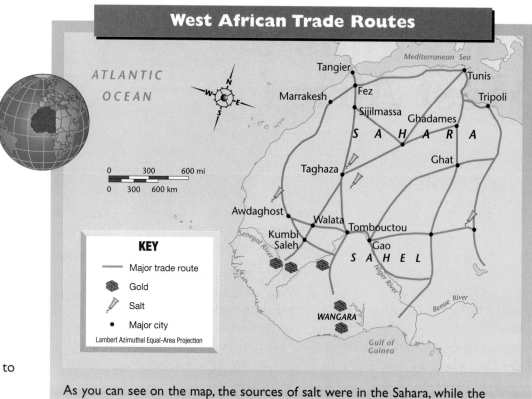

West African Trade Routes

ATLANTIC OCEAN

Mediterranean Sea

Tangier
Tunis
Marrakesh
Fez
Tripoli
Sijilmassa
Ghadames

S A H A R A

Taghaza
Ghat

Awdaghost
Walata
Tombouctou
Kumbi Saleh
Gao

S A H E L

WANGARA

Senegal River
Niger River
Benue River

Gulf of Guinea

0   300   600 mi
0   300   600 km

KEY

— Major trade route
◆ Gold
◢ Salt
• Major city

Lambert Azimuthal Equal-Area Projection

▼ Arab traders traveled to the West African trading kingdoms by camel caravan. Camels were ideally suited to survive weeks of travel across the Sahara with little or no water.

As you can see on the map, the sources of salt were in the Sahara, while the sources of gold lay far to the south in West Africa. **Location** Why were Tombouctou, Gao, and Kumbi Saleh good locations for trading cities?

Gold for Salt Gold and salt were the heart of trade in West Africa. Most of the gold came from a forested region in southern West Africa called Wangara. Most of the salt came from mines in the central Sahara.

Salt was very valuable. People needed it to flavor food and to preserve meat. Their bodies needed salt to stay healthy. In some parts of West Africa, salt was scarce, but gold was not. Therefore, salt became the chief product for which West Africans traded their gold.

Silent Barter The merchants and the Wangaran gold miners worked out a way to trade without words. It is known as **silent barter,** or trading without speaking. To *barter* means "to trade without using money." In the 900s, the Arab geographer al Masudi (al mas oo DEE) described the process of silent bartering. It began when the miners traced a boundary to mark a place to trade. The description continued:

"When the merchants reach this boundary they place their wares and cloth on the ground and then depart; and . . . the people . . . come bearing gold which they leave beside the merchandise and then depart. The owners of the merchandise then return and, if they are satisfied with what they have found, they take [the gold]. If not they go away again and the people . . . return and add to the price until the bargain is concluded."

READ ACTIVELY

Visualize Visualize two groups carrying on a trade using the system of silent barter.

Ghana's Trade Empire

The first West African trade empire founded on the gold-salt trade was Ghana. In about A.D. 300, the people of Ghana began to conquer neighboring peoples and to take control of trade routes across the Sahara.

Ghana's location was ideal. It was just north of the rich goldfields. Land routes south from the Sahara went through Ghana. Trade soon made Ghana rich. By about A.D. 800, Ghana was a major trading kingdom. Salt, cloth, and horses were exchanged for kola nuts, gold, and fine woods.

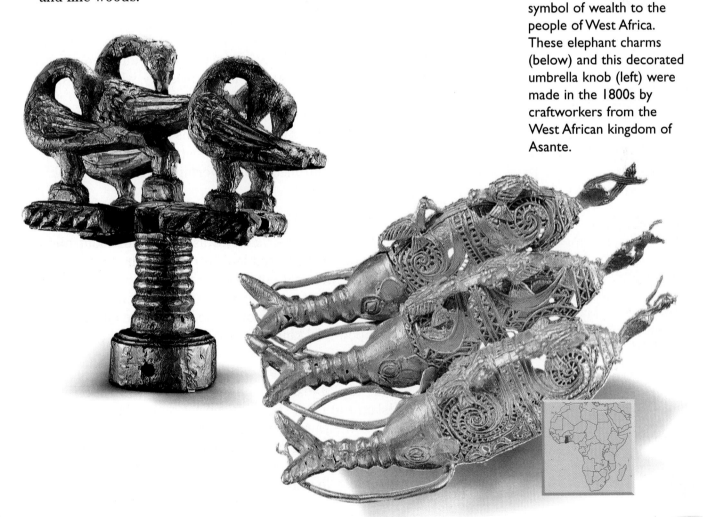

▼ Gold has long been a symbol of wealth to the people of West Africa. These elephant charms (below) and this decorated umbrella knob (left) were made in the 1800s by craftworkers from the West African kingdom of Asante.

The picture shows market day outside the Great Mosque in Djenné (jeh NAY), a city in the modern country of Mali. During the 1300s, Djenné was an important city and center of Muslim learning in the kingdom of Mali. **Critical Thinking** What do you think was the major economic activity in Djenné?

HEROES

Overcoming Obstacles
Sundiata had to overcome many difficulties in his life. As a boy, he was captured in a battle. Though his life was spared, his father, the king, was killed. Throughout his boyhood, Sundiata was lame and could barely stand, let alone walk. But he was determined to succeed in retaking his kingdom. In time, he led a revolt and took back his father's throne. Then he went on to conquer other neighboring peoples.

The kingdom's capital, Kumbi Saleh, was divided into two cities. One was the center of trade. The other was the royal city, where the king had his court and handed down his decisions.

Around A.D. 1000, the power of Ghana began to fade. Invaders from the north overran Ghana's cities. Many Ghanaians fled the area. By the 1200s, Ghana had broken into small independent states. Soon, most of the trade in the area was controlled by a powerful new kingdom, Mali.

The Empire of Mali

Mali, located in the Upper Niger Valley, was founded in about 1000. Under the leadership of Sundiata (sun JAHT ah), who came to power in 1230, Mali took control of the gold-salt trade across the Sahara. Sundiata put his people to work clearing and planting land and herding cattle. By the time he died in 1255, Mali had grown rich from trade and agriculture. It was the most powerful kingdom in West Africa.

The Rule of Mansa Musa In 1312, Mansa Musa became ruler of Mali. During his 25-year rule, he greatly expanded the empire. He also adopted Islam and made it the official religion of Mali.

A faithful Muslim, Mansa Musa went on a hajj, a journey to the holy city of Mecca. His journey brought new ties with the Muslim peoples of North Africa and Southwest Asia. It was during this pilgrimage that he made the spectacular visit to Cairo.

Mansa Musa used his new ties to make Mali a center of learning as well as of wealth. Muslim merchants who came to Mali built mosques and brought in religious leaders and scholars. The scholars taught students to read the Quran, the holy book of Islam. They also taught such subjects as arithmetic, medicine, and Islamic law.

With the help of a Muslim architect, Mansa Musa built several magnificent mosques in the city of Tombouctou (tohn book TOO). Muslim teachers and writers settled in the city, and students flocked here by the thousands. It became the leading center of learning that Mansa Musa had wanted it to be. Some merchants even grew rich buying and selling books and manuscripts.

Mali Grows Weak   While Mansa Musa ruled, Mali had many peaceful and prosperous years. But in the late 1300s, about 50 years after he died, Mali's power began to fade. Raiders attacked from the north, and fighting broke out within the empire. Many **provinces,** or small regions of the country, became independent.

Most Valued: Books! In the early 1500s, a traveler named Leo Africanus wrote about Tombouctou. It was, he said, a city of power and culture. Its king supported "countless infantry, . . . many [judges], [educated] doctors and men of religion." He continued, "[In Tombouctou] more profit is made from the sale of books than from any other merchandise."

◀ Tombouctou, pictured here, is no longer a great and powerful city. However, it still plays an important part in the West African salt trade.

Ghana, Mali, and Songhai developed in West Africa's grassland region. At the same time, other kingdoms arose in the forest lands to the south. One such kingdom was Benin (beh NEEN), which was located around the mouth of the Niger River in what today is Nigeria. The people of Benin were famous for their bronze artwork. This sculpture, which dates from the 1600s, shows the head of a Beninese princess.

Songhai

One of the provinces that broke away from Mali was Songhai (SAWNG hy). By the end of the 1400s, Songhai was the leading state in West Africa. Like the rulers of Ghana and Mali, Songhai's leaders expanded the borders of their country by conquest. With each conquest, Songhai gained control over more trade routes and sources of gold and salt.

In less than 100 years, Songhai, too, lost its power. In the late 1500s, the people of Songhai began fighting among themselves. The empire was weakened and fell easily to the guns and cannons of an army from what is now Morocco, in North Africa. The era of great trading empires in West Africa came to an end.

SECTION 2 REVIEW

1. **Define** (a) silent barter, (b) province.

2. **Identify** (a) Mansa Musa, (b) Sundiata, (c) Mali, (d) Ghana, (e) Tombouctou, (f) Songhai.

3. Why was salt so important in West Africa?

4. What important change did Mansa Musa bring to Mali?

Critical Thinking

5. **Identifying Central Issues** What did gold and salt have to do with the development of the kingdoms of West Africa?

Activity

6. **Writing to Learn** You are a foreign student at the university in Mansa Musa's Tombouctou. Write a letter to friends telling them about Mali.

Trading States of East Africa

BEFORE YOU READ

Reach Into Your Background
Trade is as important today as it was when the ancient African trading kingdoms were all-powerful. Consider things you use every day. Where were they made? How might your life be different if there were no trade among the countries of the world?

Questions to Explore
1. What cultures influenced Aksum and Ethiopia?
2. Why did so many city-states develop along the coast of East Africa?

Key Terms
city-state
Swahili

Key Places
Aksum
Ethiopia
Kilwa
Great Zimbabwe

Solomon, king of Israel, wanted to build a great temple. He sent messages to the merchants of the world saying that he would pay in gold and silver for building materials. Legends state that a merchant from the East African kingdom of Sheba took goods to Solomon and was impressed by the magnificent capital of Israel, Jerusalem. When he returned home, the merchant told his queen about the city.

The queen of Sheba wanted to see Jerusalem and Solomon for herself. She gathered a group of servants and packed gifts of gold and other precious things. Then she made the long journey to Jerusalem.

Solomon entertained the queen of Sheba and her people lavishly. Soon the queen fell in love with Jerusalem and with Solomon. She remained in Jerusalem for some time. According to legend, the child of Solomon and the queen of Sheba eventually became ruler of Sheba.

Aksum and Ethiopia

This story, told in the Bible, is one of the first references made to the kingdom of Sheba. Some historians believe that Sheba was the land we know today as Aksum. This wealthy trading state in East Africa thrived thousands of years ago.

▼ This modern painting shows the queen of Sheba meeting Solomon in Jerusalem. The emperors of Ethiopia claimed to be descendants of Solomon and Sheba.

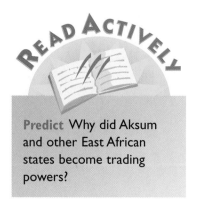

Predict Why did Aksum and other East African states become trading powers?

Wealth Through Trade Around 1000 B.C., people from Arabia sailed across the Red Sea and settled along the coast of northeastern Africa. One of the trading posts they set up along the coast was called Aksum. In 586 B.C., many Jews from Israel found refuge in Aksum when their homeland was overrun by a neighboring kingdom. In time, they mixed with the farmers already living in the area.

As the number of people in Aksum grew, so did its strength. Aksum sat on the trade route between Asia and the Mediterranean Sea. Foreign merchants came seeking such African goods as gold, ivory, and spices.

Along with their trade goods, these foreign merchants brought their ideas and beliefs to Aksum. Christianity was one such belief.

During the A.D. 300s, Aksum's king became a Christian. He soon made Christianity the official religion. This strengthened Aksum's ties with neighboring Christian traders. Over time, Christians came to Aksum from North Africa and Europe. They encouraged the people of Aksum to adopt some of the new and different forms of art, education, and literature they had brought with them.

For several hundred years, Aksum kept its control of the major trade routes linking Africa with Europe and Asia. Then, Muslim traders fought with the rulers of Aksum for control of the trade routes. They also quarreled over religion. Eventually, the people of Aksum were driven southward, away from the coast.

▶ Two important items traded at Aksum were myrrh (left) and frankincense (right). Myrrh was used in perfumes and as a medicine. Frankincense was used as a medicine and in religious services.

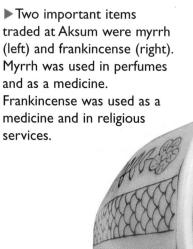

50 MEDIEVAL TIMES TO TODAY

In the 1100s, an Ethiopian ruler named Lalibela ordered his people to build a number of churches out of solid rock. Over time, 11 such churches were carved into the red stone of northern Ethiopia. The church of St. George, shown here, is 40 feet tall and shaped like a cross. **Critical Thinking** Compare the methods used to build Lalibela's churches with regular building methods.

Ethiopia   Forced into the mountains of the interior, the rulers of Aksum set up the Christian kingdom of Ethiopia. Surrounded by Muslim areas, Ethiopia was cut off from most of the rest of the Christian world. As a result, the Ethiopians developed their own very distinctive type of Christianity.

East Africa

Other trade centers developed south of Aksum, along the east coast of Africa. These trading centers were port cities. Each was a **city-state,** a city that has its own government and often controls much of the surrounding land. All thrived on trade, especially with China, India, and Southwest Asia. By 1200, there were about 30 of these city-states along the coast from what is now Somalia to Mozambique.

The City-State of Kilwa   One of the most important of the city-states was Kilwa, which was located on the coast of what is now the country of Tanzania. Kilwa was a Muslim city with orchards and fruit gardens watered by beautiful streams. The ruler of Kilwa charged duties, or taxes, on all goods that entered the port. Kilwa grew rich from these taxes and from trade.

LINKS ACROSS TIME

Prester John, the Priestly King For years, people in Europe had heard stories about a fabulously rich Christian kingdom in Africa. However, no one knew where it was. According to these stories, the kingdom was ruled by a man named Prester, or "Priest," John. By the 1400s, Portuguese ships were exploring Africa's coast. One of their tasks was to find Prester John and his kingdom. However, their search proved fruitless. Today, many people believe that Prester John's kingdom was actually Ethiopia.

▶ The ruins of Kilwa's great mosque give a hint of the splendor of this wealthy seaport. Ibn Battuta (IHB uhn bat TOO tah), a Muslim traveler from North Africa, visited Kilwa in the 1330s. He wrote that it was "one of the most beautiful and best constructed towns in the world."

Ask Questions Think of some questions you might ask about the history of the Swahili people.

The merchants of Kilwa traded with foreigners for many items. These included jewelry and cotton from India; porcelain and silk from China; and honey, wheat, rice, and other foods from Europe and Southwest Asia. For these items, the Kilwans traded gold, ivory, and iron. They also sold slaves they had captured in Africa's interior.

A New Language and Culture The people of Kilwa and the other city-states on Africa's east coast were descendants of Arabs and Bantu-speaking people. Their culture and language were called **Swahili** (swah HEE lee), which means "of the coast." Swahili is a Bantu language with borrowed Arabic words.

Beginning in the 1500s, armies from the European country of Portugal captured and looted Kilwa and other Swahili cities. Then they built forts up and down the coast and took over the trade routes on the Indian Ocean.

But the influence of Swahili culture remained. Swahili people still live along the east coast of Africa. Swahili is the official language of the modern African nations of Kenya and Tanzania, and most East Africans use it for business. Many East African cities and islands still have Swahili names.

Today, stone ruins mark the site of a once-grand city called Great Zimbabwe, or "stone house." The city included nearly 20 separate neighborhoods, set off by stone walls, and the Great Enclosure, shown here. The walls of the egg-shaped Great Enclosure are 30 feet (9 m) high and 20 feet (6 m) thick. Builders made the walls without using mortar or cement. **Critical Thinking** Why do you think the people of Great Zimbabwe built such strong walls?

Great Zimbabwe

The gold that the merchants of Kilwa and other Swahili city-states traded came from Africa's interior. Most of it was mined in the area surrounding Great Zimbabwe, a kingdom in the highlands between the Zambezi and Limpopo rivers. Great Zimbabwe was founded about A.D. 1100 by a group of Bantu-speaking people called the Shona (SHOHN uh). Most of the people were farmers and herders.

After a time, Great Zimbabwe weakened and lost power. Hundreds of years later, Europeans arrived and seized the lands where the Shona had lived. But the glory of Great Zimbabwe was not lost. Its stone ruins still stand, and its name lives on in the present-day nation of Zimbabwe.

SECTION 3 REVIEW

1. **Define** (a) city-state, (b) Swahili.

2. **Identify** (a) Aksum, (b) Ethiopia, (c) Kilwa, (d) Great Zimbabwe.

3. What cultures influenced the peoples of Aksum and Ethiopia?

4. With whom did the city-states of East Africa trade?

Critical Thinking

5. **Making Comparisons** Compare and contrast Kilwa and Zimbabwe. How were they alike? How were they different?

Activity

6. **Writing to Learn** You are a traveler visiting one of the kingdoms or city-states mentioned in this section. Write a short letter home describing some of the things you see.

Organizing Your Time

Have you ever fallen behind in your work at school? Have you wondered whether you would ever catch up? Join the club. At one time or another, most students feel this way—even the ones who seem to have no trouble. It can be hard to juggle homework, chores, after-school activities, and free time.

If you organize your time carefully, however, you can keep up with your work and activities more easily. You can learn to do this just as you learn any other skill. Organizing your time is the key to keeping up in school, keeping a good attitude, and keeping your head above water!

Get Ready

Learning to organize your time is mostly common sense. When you get a homework assignment, for example, the method below is a good one to follow.

- Find out when the assignment is due.
- Identify the steps in the assignment and how long each step will take.
- Start the assignment as early as possible.
- Arrange your time so that you have enough time to complete each step in the assignment.

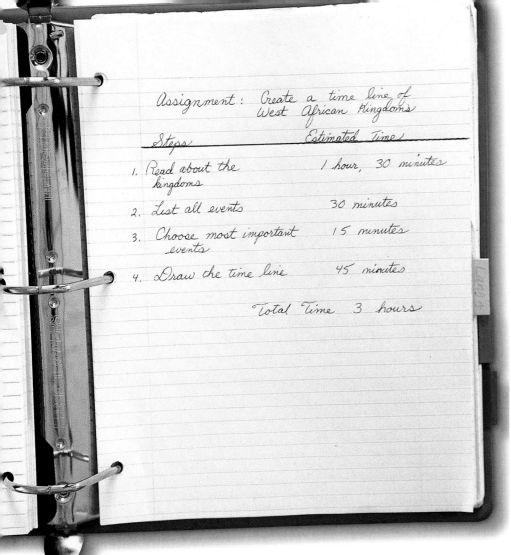

Assignment: Create a time line of West African Kingdoms

Steps	Estimated Time
1. Read about the kingdoms	1 hour, 30 minutes
2. List all events	30 minutes
3. Choose most important events	15 minutes
4. Draw the time line	45 minutes

Total Time 3 hours

◀ Here is one girl's plan for completing a homework assignment. Your plan might look different, but be sure to include the steps involved and the time you think each one will take.

Try It Out

In order to organize your time well, you must start by knowing what you have to do. For example, you need to be able to identify the different tasks that make up a homework assignment. You must also have a good sense of how long it takes to do each task. Then you can set aside the right amount of time for each part of a homework assignment. Make a plan for completing a homework assignment by following the steps below.

A. Choose a homework assignment you now have. Pick one that includes reading and writing and that is not too different from your other assignments.

B. Identify the steps of the assignment. Divide the assignment into logical parts such as reading a chapter, taking notes, and answering questions. If the assignment is to write a paper, divide the writing into the steps of the writing process.

C. Estimate how much time the assignment will take. Write down estimated times for each step and for the whole assignment. Base your estimate on your experience.

Apply the Skill

Now test your plan. Do the assignment. As you work, time yourself. Write down the actual time it takes to complete each step and compare it to your estimated time. How close was your estimate? How can this exercise help you organize your time for your next homework assignment?

CHAPTER 2

Review and Activities

Reviewing Main Ideas

1. What are the three main vegetation zones of Africa?
2. What were the Bantu migrations?
3. Why did trading empires develop in West Africa?
4. What impact did Islam have on Mali?
5. Describe the cultures that influenced the development of Aksum and Ethiopia.
6. What factors helped the ancient city-states on the coast of East Africa to thrive?

Reviewing Key Terms

Decide whether each statement is true or false. If it is true, write "true." If it is false, change the underlined term to make the statement true.

1. The vast grasslands of Africa are called <u>savannas.</u>
2. An <u>oasis</u> is a vital watering spot for desert travelers.
3. Bantu-speaking people moved south in what are known as <u>migrations.</u>
4. <u>Islam</u> refers to the language and culture of some East African people.
5. A <u>city-state</u> is a group of people with the same ancestor.
6. A <u>clan</u> is a way to trade without words.

Critical Thinking

1. **Understanding Cause and Effect** How did trade help to change cultures in West and East Africa?
2. **Making Comparisons** What did the trading empires of West Africa and the city-states of East Africa have in common? In what ways were they different?

Graphic Organizer

Copy the chart onto a separate sheet of paper. Then, in each empty oval, write an important fact about trade in early Africa.

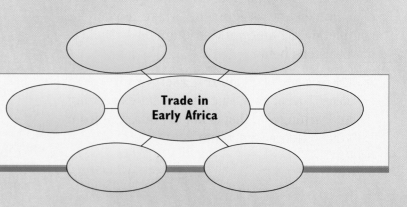

Trade in Early Africa

Map Activity

Africa

For each place listed below, write the letter from the map that shows its location.

1. Great Zimbabwe

2. Sahara

3. Tombouctou

4. Mali

5. Ethiopia

6. Ghana

7. Kilwa

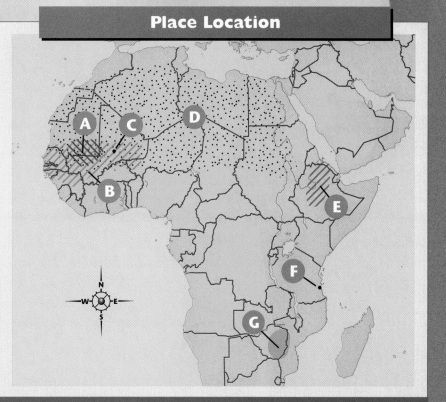

Writing Activity

Writing a Report

You are a Portuguese explorer who has visited Kilwa and several of the other port cities of Africa. Write a report to your rulers giving reasons why they may want to gain control of these cities.

Take It to the NET

Activity Explore three popular tourist attractions in Zimbabwe. Which attraction would you most like to visit and why? For help in completing this activity, visit www.phschool.com.

Chapter 2 Self-Test To review what you have learned, take the Chapter 2 Self-Test and get instant feedback on your answers. Go to www.phschool.com to take the test.

Skills Review

Turn to the Skills Activity.

Review how to organize your time. Then answer the following questions: (a) When you applied the plan to your homework, was your time estimate high, low, or just right? (b) How can this skill help you at home, at school, and at play?

How Am I Doing?

Answer these questions to help you check your progress.

1. Can I describe the physical geography of the continent of Africa?

2. Do I understand how ancient cultures in East Africa compare to cultures in West Africa?

3. Can I identify some historic events or achievements that have shaped the modern cultures of Africa?

4. What information from this chapter can I include in my journal?

The Ancient Americas

NORTH AMERICA

SOUTHWEST

Cahokia • EASTERN WOODLANDS

Mississippi River

ATLANTIC OCEAN

Gulf of Mexico

Tenochtitlán •

Caribbean Sea

MIDDLE AMERICA

PACIFIC OCEAN

Amazon River

ANDES MOUNTAINS

• Cuzco

SOUTH AMERICA

KEY

Mayas A.D. 300–900

Aztecs A.D. 1200s–1521

Incas A.D. 1400s–1535

Mound Builders 700 B.C.–A.D. 1700

Anasazi A.D. 100–1200

Pueblo 1200–Present

Lambert Azimuthal Equal-Area Projection

MAP ACTIVITIES

In ancient times, several different civilizations and cultures developed in North and South America. To help you to get to know the names and locations of these civilizations and cultures, do the following activities.

Locate a civilization
Find the areas labeled North America, Middle America, and South America. Which civilizations and cultures developed in each area?

What country is it today?
Find the locations of these civilizations and cultures on the maps in the Atlas in the back of your book. In what present-day countries were these cultures located?

Cultures of Middle America

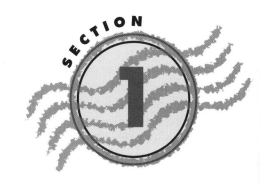

BEFORE YOU READ

Reach Into Your Background

Think about your own culture. How have your grandparents contributed to your way of life? What about your parents? What can you pass on to the next generation?

Questions to Explore
1. What did the Mayas accomplish?
2. What made the Aztecs powerful?

Key Terms
maize
slash-and-burn agriculture
hieroglyph
causeway
aqueduct
artisan

Key Places
Tenochtitlán
Lake Texcoco

In about A.D. 1325, the Aztec people of central Mexico began looking for a place to build a new capital city. Legend says that they asked Huitzilopochtli (hwits il uh PAWCH lee), their god of war, where they should build. He told them to build the city at the place where they saw an eagle perched on a cactus and holding a snake in its beak.

When the Aztecs found the sign their god had described, they were dismayed. It was such an unlikely setting for a city. The eagle was perched on a cactus growing on a rocky outcrop in a swamp. But their god had given them this sign. Therefore, they built Tenochtitlán (tay nawch tee TLAHN), the world's finest city of the time, on a swampy island at the center of Lake Texcoco.

▼ This carving shows the sign that told the Aztecs where to build their capital. Legend says that they were told to build where they saw an eagle perched on a cactus and holding a snake in its beak.

The Geographic Setting

The Aztecs were not the first civilization or culture to develop in the Americas. Many Native American peoples had lived here for thousands of years. These various peoples developed ways of life that fit their geographic setting.

The land in the Americas has great variety. Rugged mountains and highland plateaus stretch from the icy north of North America all the way down the spine of South America to the tip of the continent. Other parts of the two continents are covered by vast plains or deserts.

▼ ▶ The first people who settled the Americas lived in many different natural settings. Some groups made their homes in dense woodlands (below). Other groups settled the high plateaus of South America (right).

LINKS ACROSS TIME

Play Ball! The Mayas were enthusiastic ballplayers. On a court about the size of a football field, they played a game rather like soccer and basketball put together. The ball was a hard piece of rubber. The players could hit the ball with their elbows, wrists, shoulders, and hips but not with their hands or feet. And the ball could not touch the ground. To score, a player had to pass the ball through one of two stone hoops set high on walls.

The Americas also have many different climates. North American climates range from extreme cold in the far north to hot, almost tropical, in the south. Central and South American climates also vary, but the most common climate is tropical.

The Mayas

It was in the tropical climate of southern Mexico and Central America that one important civilization, the Mayas, developed. The Mayan way of life, which was based on farming, flourished from about A.D. 300 to 900. Today, descendants of the early Mayas still live in Mexico and Central America. Many still practice some of their ancient traditions.

A Farming Culture Mayan farmers grew many different crops, such as beans, squash, peppers, avocados, and papayas. But maize, or corn, was their most important crop. They held maize in such high regard that they worshipped a god of corn.

To plant their corn, the Mayas first had to clear the land. They cut down the trees. Then they burned the tree stumps, later using the ash as fertilizer. Finally, they planted seeds. After a few years, the soil was worn out. The Mayas then chose a new area to clear and plant. This technique is called slash-and-burn agriculture.

Religion and Cities   Crops need the sun and the rain to grow. It is not surprising then, that the Mayas worshipped the forces of nature as well as a corn god. To honor their gods, the Mayas held great festivals.

The Mayas conducted the most important of these festivals in large temples. The temples stood atop soaring pyramids in the centers of Mayan cities. Each Mayan city had one ruler, who governed the city and the area around it. Priests and nobles assisted him. These people of power and high position lived in large houses that surrounded the temples. The ordinary people lived on the outskirts of the city. Beyond the city limits lay the farms.

Mayan Achievements   Mayan priests created a calendar to plan when to hold important religious festivals. The Mayas also developed a system of writing using signs and symbols called **hieroglyphs.**

About A.D. 900, the Mayas suddenly left their cities. No one knows why. Crop failures, war, disease, drought, or famine may have killed many Mayas. Or perhaps people rebelled against their leaders. When the Mayas left their cities, their civilization declined.

LINKS TO SCIENCE

An Accurate Calendar
The Mayas were great astronomers. They watched the skies and plotted the movements of the sun, moon, and stars. Using their observations, they designed a calendar of 365 days. It had 18 "months," each of which was 20 days long. The extra five days fell at the end of the year. These were considered bad luck days.

Mayan Wall Paintings

This picture shows one of the murals, or wall paintings, found in a Mayan temple in Bonampak, Mexico. The murals were painted in the late A.D. 700s, probably to celebrate the birth of a prince. This mural portrays a battle scene. The figure on the right is wearing a jaguar headdress. The jaguar was one of the Mayan gods of the underworld. **Critical Thinking** Why do you think the Mayas included battle scenes among pictures celebrating the birth of a prince?

The Aztecs

Another ancient civilization of Middle America was that of the Aztecs. They arrived in the Valley of Mexico in the A.D. 1100s. Within 100 years, they controlled all the land in central Mexico between the Gulf of Mexico and the Pacific Ocean. In the center of their empire was Tenochtitlán, the capital they had built on Lake Texcoco.

Tenochtitlán: City in the Lake You have already read about how the Aztecs chose a spot for their capital. In spite of its swampy location, Tenochtitlán was a magnificent city. At the center was a huge square. All around it stood pyramid-temples, palaces, and large stone houses. Canals crisscrossed the city. People used the canals to transport goods and to move about the city. **Causeways,** or raised streets of hard earth, connected the city to the mainland.

As the city grew, the Aztecs realized that they needed more farmland. Their answer to the problem was to build "floating gardens." These were islands the size of football fields. The Aztecs made them by piling rich earth from the bottom of Lake Texcoco onto rafts made of wood. After a while, the roots of plants and trees grew down to the lake bottom, anchoring the rafts.

In addition, the Aztecs built **aqueducts,** pipes or channels designed to carry water from distant sources. These carried fresh springwater from the mainland to storage areas in the city.

READ ACTIVELY

Visualize Picture the city of Tenochtitlán. How would this city built in a lake look unusual?

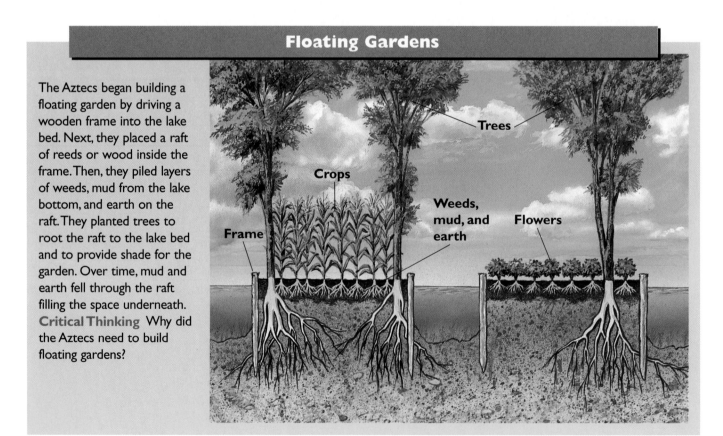

Floating Gardens

The Aztecs began building a floating garden by driving a wooden frame into the lake bed. Next, they placed a raft of reeds or wood inside the frame. Then, they piled layers of weeds, mud from the lake bottom, and earth on the raft. They planted trees to root the raft to the lake bed and to provide shade for the garden. Over time, mud and earth fell through the raft filling the space underneath. **Critical Thinking** Why did the Aztecs need to build floating gardens?

Trees

Crops

Weeds, mud, and earth

Flowers

Frame

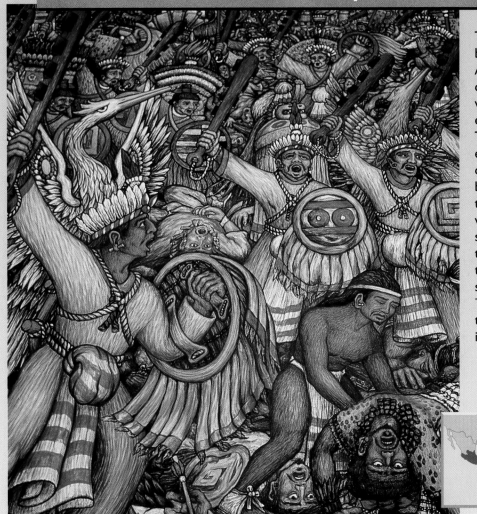

This modern painting of a battle between the Tlaxcaltecs and Aztecs illustrates an almost constant part of Aztec life—war. Most Aztec men were expected to serve as soldiers. They were well trained and well equipped. They had armor of quilted cotton, swords, and bows and arrows. After military training, young men's heads were shaved, except for a strand of hair at the nape of their necks. Only after a soldier took a captive in war could the strand be cut. **Critical Thinking** How did the Aztecs treat the people they defeated in war?

A Warlike Way of Life   Although Tenochtitlán was a peaceful place, the Aztecs themselves were a warlike people. In the 1400s, Aztec warriors began conquering the other people in the region. Soon, the Aztecs controlled a huge empire. One ruler, the emperor, ruled over all the Aztec lands.

The Aztecs forced the people they conquered to pay tributes, or taxes, in the form of food, gold, or slaves. They also took thousands of prisoners of war to serve as human sacrifices. The Aztecs believed that they had to sacrifice humans so that the sun would have enough strength to rise every day. Human blood was what gave the sun strength. If the sun did not rise, crops could not grow, and the people would starve. Priests made the offerings daily. In very bad times, members of noble Aztec families were sometimes sacrificed to please the sun god.

Because of their respect for war, it is not surprising that the upper class of Aztec society was made up of military leaders as well as members of the royal family, priests, and nobles. The next class of

The Role of Aztec Women

In these paintings, made during the 1500s, Aztec mothers teach their daughters to grind corn into flour (right and far right) and to weave cloth (right). In Aztec society, girls of 13 were expected to grind flour, make tortillas, and cook meals. By the time they became adults, they had to be skilled at weaving. Some of the cloth they wove was made into capes and used for trade. Some was used to decorate temples. The finest cloth went to make clothes for the nobles to wear. **Critical Thinking** How did the skills required of Aztec men and Aztec women differ?

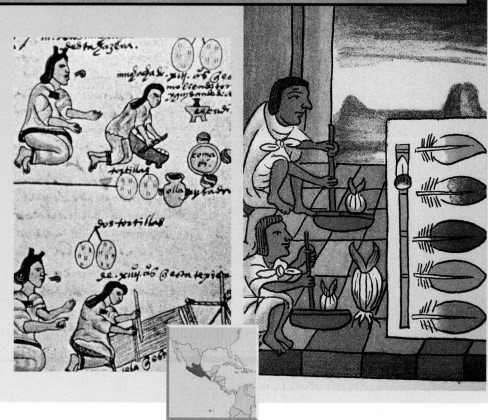

society was made up of warriors. Below them came artisans and traders. **Artisans,** or skilled workers who practice a trade, created jewelry, garments, pottery, sculptures, and other goods. Most people, however, were farmers. Slaves—most of whom were prisoners captured in battle—were at the bottom of Aztec society.

Aztecs spent much of their time in religious practices. Like the Mayas, they worshipped hundreds of gods and held many religious ceremonies. The main purpose of these ceremonies was to win the favor of the gods and bring about good crops or a victory in war.

SECTION 1 REVIEW

1. **Define** (a) maize, (b) slash-and-burn agriculture, (c) hieroglyph, (d) causeway, (e) aqueduct, (f) artisan.

2. **Identify** (a) Tenochtitlán, (b) Lake Texcoco.

3. What were some of the achievements of the Mayas?

4. What do you think made the Aztec empire strong?

Critical Thinking

5. **Making Comparisons** In what ways were the Mayan and Aztec empires alike?

Activity

6. **Writing to Learn** List the three features you found most interesting about Mayan or Aztec life. Use these to write a poem about either the Mayas or the Aztecs.

The Incas

BEFORE YOU READ

Reach Into Your Background

Throughout history, rulers have tried to promote the unity, or oneness, of their empire and their people.

Suggest two ways in which you might help bring about unity among your classmates. Name two things you could do to encourage unity in your neighborhood.

Questions to Explore

1. How did Incan rulers establish a system for effectively ruling their vast empire?

2. What were some accomplishments of the Incas?

Key Terms
quipu
terrace

Key Place
Cuzco

High in the mountains, a young boy races along a narrow stone highway. He breathes heavily, relieved that he has almost reached his goal. He lifts a conch-shell trumpet and blows. It is the signal telling the next runner to get ready.

The boy is a relay runner, chosen for his speed and endurance. The Incas depended on runners to carry messages to and from the capital at Cuzco. Like every other royal messenger, the boy knows his stretch of royal highway so well that he could run it on the darkest night.

As the runner reaches the end of his stretch of road, he passes the message to the next runner. He recites the message he memorized at the start of his run.

Securing the Empire

Incan relay runners covered a lot of territory, for the Incan empire was huge. It stretched some 2,500 miles (4,023 km) along the Andes Mountains from what is now the country of Ecuador through the

▼ An Incan relay runner announces his arrival by blowing a conch-shell trumpet.

▶ The Incas believed that gold was the sweat of the sun god and that the gleaming metal reflected the sun god's glory. All the gold belonged to the emperor. It was used only for ceremonial objects, like these decorated knives.

LINKS TO MATH

An Official Census High government officials made sure that the Incan empire ran smoothly. They decided where people would live and what kind of work they would do. They used a census, or official count of the people, to keep track of everyone in the land. Such records helped officials make sure that the people paid taxes and registered to work on public projects.

countries of Peru, Bolivia, Chile, and Argentina. But this great empire had small beginnings. In about the year 1200, the Incas settled in Cuzco (KOOS koh), a small village high in the Andes. Through wars and conquests they extended their control practically the length of this mountain range, about 2,500 miles (4,023 km). Many different peoples lived within the borders of this huge empire.

The Rule of the Incas   The Incas developed their own system of government to rule their empire. At its head was a ruler called "Sapa Inca," or "the emperor." People believed that he was descended from the sun god. He, and only he, owned the land and divided it among the people.

Incan rulers used interesting methods to unify the huge empire and its people. One ruler, for example, made the Incan language, Quechua (KECH wah), the official language of the empire. He sent people into newly conquered lands to teach Incan customs and laws and to set up schools that taught Incan religion and history.

All people were expected to pay taxes to the empire. Men had to work on public projects. They might farm land, mine gold, or build roads. Women wove cloth for government officials. Farmers and their families gave the government parts of the crops they raised. In return, the government took care of the poor, the sick, and the elderly.

Although the Incas did not have a written language, they did create an unusual system for keeping detailed records. Government officials noted information about births, deaths, taxes, and harvests on knotted strings called **quipus** (KEE poos). Every quipu had a main cord with several colored strings attached. Each color represented a different item. Knots of varying sizes stood for numbers.

A System of Roads and Bridges   To control the empire, the emperor and his officials had to know what was going on. To accomplish this, they needed a communication system—the runners. But these messengers needed roads to travel on. The Incas, therefore, built a large system of highways and bridges.

The roads served another purpose besides communication. In times of trouble, they allowed the army to travel quickly. As the soldiers traveled, they picked up supplies at stations along the way. Thus, the emperor could keep control of every part of the empire.

READ ACTIVELY

Connect Think of some ways in which you might communicate and keep records if your society had no written language.

Bridges From the Past

This rope bridge, strung across a gorge in the Andes, is similar to those used by the Incas. Incan bridges were made with strong cords of braided vines and reeds. The bridges were part of the huge road network that linked every part of the empire. Only soldiers and government officials were allowed to use this system of roads and bridges. **Critical Thinking** Why were bridges important in controlling the Incan empire?

These finely fitted granite stones are part of a building that still stands in the old Incan capital of Cuzco. Using hammers and chisels, skilled Incan stoneworkers carved 12 corners in the large stone. Then they fitted other stones around it to make a sturdy wall. If the stones of this wall were rocked by earthquakes, they simply moved, then settled back into place.

Incan Achievements

A network of roads was not the only Incan achievement. Incan engineering feats still amaze people today. For example, they changed the direction of rivers. And they were master builders.

Building With Stone   Without any of our modern power tools, Incas built magnificent bridges and huge cities. They built fortresses on mountaintops. Much of what they built is still standing.

The Incas built these fortresses and cities mainly with stone. Sometimes they chose huge stones and used them just as they came from the mountains. Other times they broke the stones into smaller blocks. To break up the stone, they cut a long groove in the surface of the rock. Then they drove stone or wooden wedges into the groove until the rock split.

When the Incas made a wall, they made sure its large, many-sided stones fit together almost perfectly. After a wall was finished, the fit was so tight that not even a very thin knife blade could be slipped between two stones. They did all this with only hammers of stone and chisels of bronze.

Many examples of Incan stonework can still be seen in the Peruvian city of Cuzco, once the capital of the Incan empire. Its ancient stone walls and buildings have withstood major storms and earthquakes for centuries.

READ ACTIVELY

Ask Questions Think of three questions you might ask about Incan building methods and achievements.

Machu Picchu (MAHCH oo PEEK choo), too, is a great example of Incan building and engineering. The Incas built this city on a high and narrow ridge between two peaks in the Andes Mountains. Using huge stone blocks from the mountaintops, they created acres and acres of buildings, walls, and plazas. They carved stairs into the face of the mountain to connect city buildings. They also cut roads into the bare rock. More than 500 years later, people still use these roads. In fact, the workers who built Machu Picchu did more than build a city. They changed the shape of the mountain landscape.

◀ ▼ The ancient city of Machu Picchu (below) is located high in the Andes about 54 miles (87 km) from Cuzco. It was home for several thousand people. It also served as a religious center. Some of the buildings located on higher ground (left) housed stones that the Incas considered holy.

69

Terrace Farming

The Incas built their terraces using stone walls. The area behind the wall was leveled out and lined with a layer of gravel to help with drainage. Then, earth was piled over the gravel. Finally, stone-lined channels were built to carry water to the terraces. These terraces in the mountains near Cuzco are still in use today. **Critical Thinking** How did the building of terraces help Incan farmers?

More Land for Farms   Because they lived among steep, dry, and rugged mountains, the Incas had little natural farmland. They did two things to increase the amount of land available for farming.

First, they built a system of canals and aqueducts. The water that flowed through this system turned dry land into fertile fields.

To make use of the land on the slopes of the mountains, the Incas built **terraces.** These steplike ledges cut into the mountainside could then be used as fields for crops. The terraces also stopped soil from being washed away by rain. Incan farming techniques such as terracing are still used in the Andes today.

SECTION 2 REVIEW

1. **Define**   (a) quipu, (b) terrace.

2. **Identify**   Cuzco.

3. What were the main features of the Incan system of government?

4. Why did the Incas build a system of roads and bridges?

5. What advances did the Incas make in building and farming?

Critical Thinking

6. **Recognizing Cause and Effect**   Why do you think that unity was an important goal of Incan rulers?

Activity

7. **Writing to Learn**   You are an explorer seeing an Incan city for the first time. Write a description of what you see. In your description, include building methods and materials, farming techniques, and other interesting points of information.

Cultures of
North America

Reach Into Your Background

In what kinds of homes do people in your part of the country live? What do these homes tell you about the environment and cultures of your area?

Questions to Explore

1. What was the role of mounds in the cultures of the Mound Builders of North America?

2. How did the environment affect the way of life of the people of the Southwest?

Key Term
pueblo

Key Place
Cahokia

ooking out of the airplane window, you see a huge earthen snake. It twists and turns across the landscape. You realize that the shape of the snake was created with mounds of dirt. What could those mounds be? It is obvious that they were formed centuries ago. Who could have made them? And why would anyone make such an effort to form a shape that could only be seen from above?

For years after they were discovered, these ancient mounds baffled scientists. Archaeologists found different kinds of mounds in other parts of the country. But nobody knew what they were or who had built them. Only now are scientists beginning to solve this ancient mystery.

▼ Monk's Mound, the largest mound in Cahokia, Illinois, measures about 1,000 feet (300 m) by 800 feet (240 m) at its base. It rises to a height of about 100 feet (30 m).

Built about 1,000 years ago, the Great Serpent Mound in Ohio is the largest image of a snake in the world. The "uncoiled" length of the serpent is about 1,300 feet (396 m). **Critical Thinking** For what purpose was the Great Serpent Mound built?

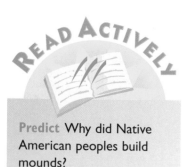

Predict Why did Native American peoples build mounds?

The Mound Builders

Separate groups of Native American peoples built different kinds of mounds. The groups were known by different names and lived at various times from about 1000 B.C. to the A.D. 1600s. Today, all of these people are known as Mound Builders.

The Mound Builders were just some of the Native Americans who lived in the region called the Eastern Woodlands. This region lies between southern Canada and the state of Tennessee, and between the Mississippi River and the Atlantic Ocean.

The Mounds of Cahokia The once-great city of Cahokia (kuh HOH kee uh) in what is now Illinois offers an example of one type of mound found in the Eastern Woodlands. Cahokia was a large city. Many of the buildings in the city were built on mounds. Some of these mounds were shaped like flat-topped pyramids. Temples for worshipping gods and buildings used for ceremonies once stood on top of these mounds. The largest mound in Cahokia has a base bigger than that of the Great Pyramid in Egypt.

Cahokia's mounds are not natural. Thousands of workers built them by moving basketfuls of dirt by hand. They accomplished all this with simple tools of wood, stone, and shell.

The Great Serpent Mound The serpent mound in Ohio served a very different purpose from that of Cahokia's pyramid mounds. This twisting, snakelike structure was a symbol of the Mound Builders' beliefs about the sun and seasons. Called the Great Serpent Mound, it is just one of many similar mounds in Ohio. When you look at these mounds from above, they are shaped like animals. Some may have served as graves for as many as 1,000 people.

Smaller mounds found near the Great Serpent Mound also hold some of the precious belongings of the Mound Builders. Researchers probing the serpent mounds have found jewelry made of shell and copper, clay statues, and other works of art. Some of these items are made from materials that are not from Ohio. Researchers, therefore, believe that the Mound Builders must have been involved in extensive trading.

▼ Native Americans of the Southwest made their pottery by hand. To make the black dye used in decorating the pottery, they boiled the roots of various plants.

People of the Southwest

The mounds of the Eastern Woodlands are truly amazing. However, they are just a small part of the fascinating story of Native Americans in North America. Other Native American groups made their homes in the rocky deserts and forested mountains of the Southwest. Today, this region includes the states of New Mexico, Arizona, Utah, and Colorado. Here, too, environment affected the Native American way of life. One present-day Pueblo elder explained it like this:

❝The story of my people and the story of this place are one single story. No man can think of us without thinking of this place. We are always joined together.❞

L·I·N·K·S

ACROSS TIME

Acequias Today's New Mexicans use an irrigation system invented by the ancient Pueblos. The region only receives between 8 and 13 inches of rain a year, but it does have rivers. People dig *acequias* (uh SAYK yuhz), or narrow, shallow ditches, from a river to the fields. Some of the water soaks the soil. The main acequia finally empties the remaining water back into the river.

▼ Modern Hopi corn dancers perform a ceremonial rain dance at a tribal gathering in the town of Gallup, New Mexico.

The Anasazi: The Ancient Ones   The Anasazi (an uh SAH zee) were among the first cultures to develop in the Southwest. The word *Anasazi* means "ancient ones." These people lived long ago and came from outside the region. Centuries ago, the Anasazi moved into the Southwest from the far north. At first, they wandered the Colorado Plateau and other nearby areas. In time, they settled and began growing corn, beans, squash, and other vegetables. They built complicated systems of canals to bring water to dry lands where they had settled. They also grew cotton and wove it into cloth, and made pottery and baskets.

By A.D. 100, permanent Anasazi villages dotted the landscape. At first, the people lived in pit houses, circular houses built partly underground. However, they found that such dwellings were not easy to protect against enemy attack. Therefore, they built some of their villages into the sides of steep cliffs. And sometimes they built villages on top of mesas, or high, flat-topped hills. These villages, called **pueblos,** were in some places as large as our high-rise apartment buildings. As many as 1,200 people might live in one village.

The Pueblo Peoples   Anasazi customs lived on among later groups we call the Pueblo people. The Pueblos used the same apartment-type villages built into cliffs. And, like the Anasazi, they were

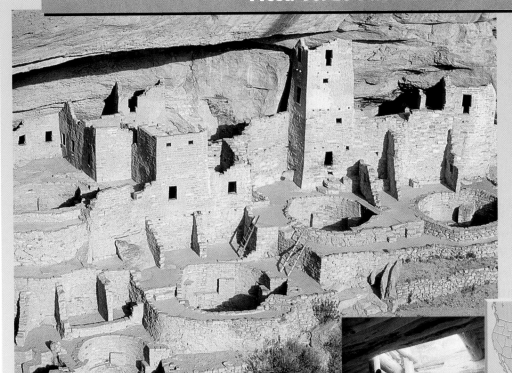

Mesa Verde Pueblo

During the 1100s, Native Americans in southwestern Colorado built these cliff dwellings at Mesa Verde (left). Families stored goods in rooms at the back of the cliff and lived in rooms near the front. They used the circular underground rooms, or *kivas*, in the foreground of the picture for religious ceremonies. People used ladders to go from level to level (below).

farmers. Their crafts included weaving, basket making, and pottery making.

The Pueblos believed in many spirits. They wanted to please these spirits, who controlled the rain that watered their plots of corn, beans, and squash. Many times during the year, men gathered in an underground room called a *kiva* to ask the spirits to send rain. They appealed to *kachinas,* or cloud spirits, by performing special rain dances.

SECTION 3 REVIEW

1. **Define** pueblo.

2. **Identify** Cahokia.

3. Why did the Native Americans of the Eastern Woodlands build mounds?

4. How did the Anasazi and Pueblo peoples use the land?

Critical Thinking

5. **Drawing Conclusions** It took a lot of time and hard work to build the mounds. What might this effort tell you about the values and beliefs of the cultures that built the mounds?

Activity

6. **Writing to Learn** Write two paragraphs telling what your life might be like if you were a teenager living in a pueblo.

Recognizing Cause and Effect

Wondering why things happen is something every human being does. Why is the sky blue? Why does the sun rise in the east? This curiosity is one reason some people become scientists or historians. Curiosity has driven us to learn how history has shaped our world. When we ask "why" about something, we are actually trying to figure out causes and effects.

Get Ready

A cause is something that makes an event or situation happen. For example, lack of sleep causes you to be tired. An effect is a result of a cause. Being tired is the effect of not getting enough sleep.

Causes and effects may be short term, such as not going to bed early enough making you tired the next morning. However, causes and effects can also be long term. For example, a war is generally the effect of many causes over a period of time.

Try It Out

To figure out causes and effects in something you are reading, it can help to look for certain words that are clues. *Because, so,* and *since* are words that can signal a cause. *Therefore* and *as a result* are some words that signal an effect.

▼ Doing a good job at school is one result of getting enough sleep every night.

Sometimes effects become causes of other effects. For example, the effect of not getting enough sleep is being tired. And being tired could cause you to not do well on a test.

You can help yourself understand cause-effect relationships by making a cause-effect diagram like this one.

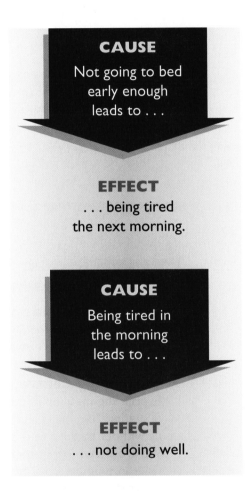

CAUSE
Not going to bed early enough leads to . . .

EFFECT
. . . being tired the next morning.

CAUSE
Being tired in the morning leads to . . .

EFFECT
. . . not doing well.

Apply the Skill

Read the paragraph at top right. Look for causes and effects. Make a cause-effect diagram if you need to. Then list the cause-effect relationships that you find in the paragraph. Remember that sometimes an effect becomes a cause of another effect.

The Need for Land

As Tenochtitlán grew, the Aztecs realized that they needed more land. They especially needed more farmland on which to grow food for the increasing number of people who lived in the city. However, Tenochtitlán was built on Lake Texcoco, and land was in short supply. The Aztecs, therefore, had to create new land. Their answer to the problem was to build "floating gardens." Using mud from the lake bottom, they built small islands about the size of football fields. After a while, the roots of plants and trees grew down to the lake bottom, anchoring the islands. The Aztecs used the islands to grow tomatoes, squash, chili peppers, and other food crops. These crops increased the food supply by a considerable amount. As a result, there was enough food to support an even larger population in Tenochtitlán.

▲ The floating gardens built by the Aztecs still exist. They are in Mexico City.

Review and Activities

Reviewing Main Ideas

1. What were the major achievements of the Mayas?

2. How did the Aztecs become powerful?

3. How did a system of roads and bridges help the Incas keep their empire together?

4. (a) Name two Incan achievements, one in building and one in farming. (b) Tell why each was important.

5. What purposes did the mounds built by the Mound Builders serve?

6. (a) Why did the Pueblos want to please the spirits? (b) What did they do to please them?

Reviewing Key Terms

Use each key term below in a sentence that shows the meaning of the term.

1. maize
2. slash-and-burn agriculture
3. hieroglyph
4. causeway
5. aqueduct
6. artisan
7. quipu
8. terrace
9. pueblo

Critical Thinking

1. **Drawing Conclusions** Why might it have been important for the Mayas to have a good calendar?

2. **Identifying Central Ideas** Explain the meaning of this quotation: "No man can think of us without thinking of this place. We are always joined together." Give an example from one of the cultures of the Southwest that supports this statement.

Graphic Organizer

Copy the chart onto a separate sheet of paper. Then fill in the empty boxes to complete the chart.

	Where They Lived	What They Were Like	Major Achievement
Mayas			
Aztecs			
Incas			
Mound Builders			
Anasazi			
Pueblo			

Map Activity

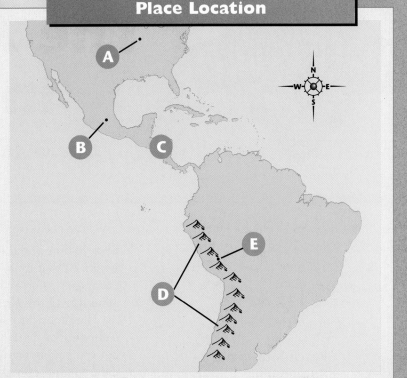

The Ancient Americas
For each place listed below, write the letter from the map that shows its location.

1. Tenochtitlán

2. Cahokia

3. Middle America

4. Andes Mountains

5. Cuzco

Writing Activity

Writing a Letter to the Editor
Assume that the government of a state wants to build an airport across land on which the Mound Builders once built a mound. Do you think the government should be allowed to destroy the mound? Why or why not? Write a letter to the editor of a newspaper explaining your reasons.

Take It to the NET

Activity Learn about an ice mummy discovered in Peru. What do the mummy and the artifacts found with it tell about the Incas? For help in completing this activity, visit www.phschool.com.

Chapter 3 Self-Test To review what you have learned, take the Chapter 3 Self-Test and get instant feedback on your answers. Go to www.phschool.com to take the test.

Skills Review

Turn to the Skills Activity.

Review the ways you can recognize cause and effect. Then complete the following: (a) What question does cause and effect answer? (b) Explain two different kinds of causes.

How Am I Doing?

Answer these questions to help you check your progress.

1. Can I describe the geographic setting of the Americas' early cultures?

2. Do I understand how cultures in the Americas compare to one another?

3. Can I identify ways in which the environment affected the lives of the early peoples who lived in the Americas?

4. What information from this chapter can I include in my journal?

FROM

The Americas in 1492

BY JAMAKE HIGHWATER

BEFORE YOU READ

Reach Into Your Background

What do you know about the year 1492? You probably know that in this year, Christopher Columbus first landed in the Americas. In this year, the colonization of the Americas began. At that time, the Europeans referred to the Americas as the New World.

The Americas may have been new to the Europeans, but the people who lived here did not think of it as new. They had entire kingdoms, languages, and religions very different from those of the Europeans.

In Mexico in 1492, the Aztecs had a great empire, ruled by the powerful Moctezuma, also known as Montezuma.

Questions to Explore

1. How does this selection help you understand life in Mexico before colonization?
2. What were some different parts of Aztec society?

The Aztec day began when the priests at the top of the great pyramids beat wooden gongs and sounded trumpets made of conch seashells. It was still dawn as the people awakened in all the houses, great and humble. Most of the homes were made of sunbaked bricks and consisted of one large family room, with the kitchen located in a separate building in the courtyard. In the first light of the day, the women fanned the coals of their cooking fires until they burst into flame. In the gardens turkeys began to strut and gobble, while in the houses there was the rumble of corn grinders. Soon there was also the rhythmic sound of the women slapping lumps of dough between their hands to make the pancake-like bread called *tlaxcalli* (or tortillas). Now all the families came together to have breakfast, a simple meal of bread and a beer-like drink called *octli*. Then, after a bath in fresh water, using a soap made from the root of the *copalxocotl* tree, they put on their sandals and tied their cloth cloaks over their shoulders and were ready for work.

Outside the city, most people worked in the fields from dawn to dusk. For their long day they packed a picnic lunch, which

tlaxcalli (tlaks KAL ee)
copalxocotl (koh puhlks un KAH tuhl)

they called *itacatl,* and then they went into the fields owned by their town or village. They grew corn, vegetables, and flowers, for which the Aztecs had a great affection. All Mexicans shared this love of gardens. The people grew flowers everywhere—in their courtyards, in broad fields along the lakes, and even on their rooftops. . . .

The common people of Mexico were born, they worked, and then they died. They had little opportunity for education or advancement. During the first years of their lives, boys were taught to carry wood and water. By the age of six, girls learned how to spin cloth and to cook. At the age of fifteen, young people who showed signs of intelligence and talent were allowed to enter the *calmecac*—a temple school where their education was entrusted to priests.

For the Aztec people of wealth and power, life was very different from the existence of the farmers and their families. They had lavish food and educational opportunities. They lived in the

great city among the splendid temples and pyramids, and they wandered among the magnificent buildings and gardens as free people.

In the main plaza at the heart of the royal city of Tenochtitlán, there was a great sea of human bodies and human baggage. Then, quite suddenly, the tangle of the crowd opened into the vast empty space at the entrance of the palace. Only men of power and rank were allowed to walk in this expansive entranceway. One by one they came to the Council Chamber of Montezuma to plead for favors or to beg forgiveness for an offense. He was more than a ruler. He was very nearly a god—so great and so holy that no one was allowed to look upon his face. He was elected from the most royal of Aztec lineages by a council of nobles, warriors, and high priests. But once he ascended to the throne, he was utterly out of reach even to those who had elected him, so vast was his power. . . .

▲ This is one artist's idea of daily life along a canal in the Aztec empire.

itacatl (it uh KAH tuhl)
calmecac (KAL muhk ak)

READ ACTIVELY

Connect How did Aztec education differ from your own?

EXPLORING YOUR READING

Look Back

1. How did the Aztec day begin? How is this similar to the way your day begins?

Think It Over

2. How did the common Aztec people live differently from the wealthy?

3. Why do you think the Aztecs honored Moctezuma in the ways that they did?

Go Beyond

4. Compare the life of Moctezuma to that of a United States president. How were the two lives similar or different?

Ideas for Writing: A Short Story

5. Write a story about a young person living in Tenochtitlán who receives a rare opportunity to see Moctezuma. What are the circumstances of the meeting? What are the young person's impressions of the great leader?

Civilizations of Asia

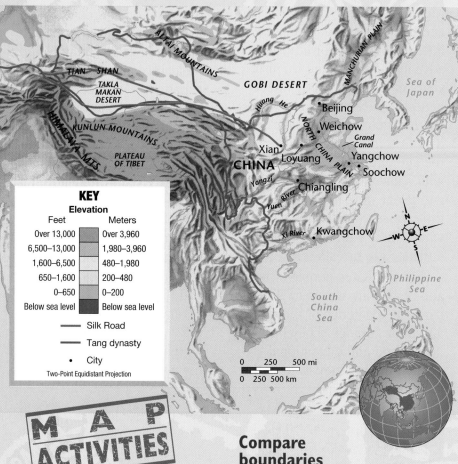

KEY
Elevation

Feet		Meters
Over 13,000		Over 3,960
6,500–13,000		1,980–3,960
1,600–6,500		480–1,980
650–1,600		200–480
0–650		0–200
Below sea level		Below sea level

——— Silk Road
——— Tang dynasty
• City

Two-Point Equidistant Projection

0   250   500 mi
0 250 500 km

MAP ACTIVITIES

Between the A.D. 600s and 900s, several great empires arose in Asia. One of the most advanced began in China. At this time, the boundaries of China were very different from what they are today. To become familiar with the Chinese empire of this time, do the following activities.

Compare boundaries

Compare the former boundaries of China during the Tang dynasty with its boundaries today. Find the present-day boundaries of China by looking at the Asia: Political map in the Atlas in the back of this book. Was China formerly larger or smaller?

Study key locations

Describe the landforms and the locations of major rivers on the map of China on this page. Where were the main cities located?

Golden Ages in China

BEFORE YOU READ

Reach Into Your Background

Suppose that future historians describe the 1900s as the "golden age" of the United States. Think about life as you know it. What do you think are the best features of the American way of life? What accomplishments of the United States do you think people in the future will remember?

Questions to Explore

1. How did the ideas of Confucius influence Chinese society during the Tang and Song dynasties?

2. Why are the years of the Tang and Song dynasties called the golden ages of China?

Key Terms

dynasty   porcelain
merit system   movable type

Key People and Places

Tang Taizong   Silk Road
Confucius   Grand Canal

Tang Taizong (tang ty zung), who ruled China from A.D. 626 to 649, fought in many battles. From the age of 16, he had been in the military. Now, late in his reign, Taizong was tired of war. He read and reread the works of Confucius (kun FYOO shus), an ancient Chinese teacher. Confucius taught that if a ruler set a good example, no one would commit crimes.

According to legend, Taizong visited a prison and saw 290 men who had been sentenced to die. It was then a Chinese custom to kill all the condemned on the same day each year. Taizong took pity on the men. He said he would allow them to go home to visit their families if they promised to return the next day. All 290 men returned. Taizong was so moved that he set them all free.

A Glorious Heritage

The Chinese often tell this story to show what a good ruler Taizong was. He tried to put into practice the teachings of Confucius, who taught about relationships among family members and among members of society. Confucius wanted to bring peace and stability to China. He believed that if all people treated each other with respect, society

▼ This painting, which dates from the 1700s, shows Tang Taizong with his pet hawk.

83

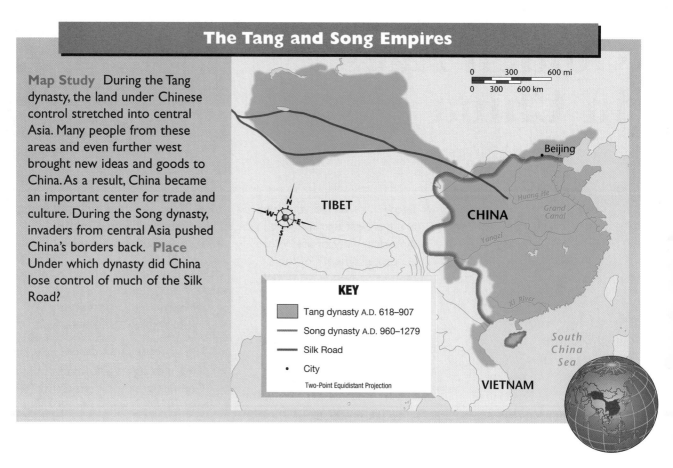

The Tang and Song Empires

Map Study During the Tang dynasty, the land under Chinese control stretched into central Asia. Many people from these areas and even further west brought new ideas and goods to China. As a result, China became an important center for trade and culture. During the Song dynasty, invaders from central Asia pushed China's borders back. **Place** Under which dynasty did China lose control of much of the Silk Road?

KEY

Tang dynasty A.D. 618–907

Song dynasty A.D. 960–1279

Silk Road

• City

Two-Point Equidistant Projection

TO LANGUAGE ARTS

Poems—and Legends Li Bo probably was the greatest poet of the Tang dynasty. He had an adventurous life—once he was even accused of treason. His poems, however, dealt with quieter subjects, such as nature and friendship. At the age of 61, while visiting relatives, he died. Soon a legend about his death spread across the country. It said that Li Bo was in a boat at night. The moon's reflection was so beautiful that he reached out to seize it, fell overboard, and drowned.

would be healthy. After Taizong's reign, many of Confucius' ideas took root in Chinese government.

Tang Taizong was the greatest ruler of the Tang dynasty. A **dynasty** is a series of rulers from one family. The Chinese give their family names first. Tang is the family name of Tang Taizong. The Tang dynasty lasted about 300 years, from A.D. 618 to 907.

The Tang dynasty united the Chinese in a large empire that reached from the Pacific Ocean to Persia. Fighting among different groups of people within the empire ended the Tang dynasty. Order was restored by the Song dynasty. The Song ruled from 960 to 1279. The map above shows the boundaries of the two dynasties.

During the Tang and Song dynasties, China entered a golden age, a time of great political and cultural achievement. The golden age of the Tang and Song dynasties happened for several reasons. One reason was the introduction of the **merit system** in hiring government officials. Under the merit system, officials had to pass tests and prove their ability to do the work. Before the Song dynasty, officials came from rich and powerful families. They were allowed to keep their positions for life even if they did not do a very good job. Hiring people based on their ability to do the job, rather than on their wealth or social position, improved the government.

The Tang and Song rulers also encouraged music, art, and fine writing. In addition, the Chinese introduced a number of key inventions during this period. During its golden ages, China became one of the most advanced and powerful empires in the world.

A Golden Age in Trade

Another reason China flourished during the Tang and Song dynasties was its trade. China produced goods that were highly prized in Southwest Asia and Europe. And its system of roads and canals helped to make travel and trade easier.

Trade Goods: Silk, Porcelain, and Tea   One of the most prized trade goods produced by China was silk. Because of its natural beauty, silk is often called "the queen of fibers." Silk comes from the cocoons of caterpillars called silkworms. For a long time, only the Chinese knew how to make silk. Even after others discovered the Chinese secret, Chinese silk was of the best quality. People in Southwest Asia and Europe were willing to pay high prices for Chinese silk.

Another prized Chinese product was porcelain, a strong and beautiful type of ceramic. Because it was first made in China, porcelain is often called "china." The Chinese developed the process for making porcelain during the Tang dynasty. They made beautiful vases, plates, cups, bowls, and figurines. For hundreds of years, the Chinese produced the best porcelain in the world.

READ ACTIVELY

Predict What products do you think China traded during its golden ages?

Tang Treasures

Europeans and South Asians paid dearly for Chinese trade goods, such as luxurious silk robes like the one worn by the woman in this illustration (left). Porcelain was another popular Chinese trade item. This man on horseback (right) shows the Tang love of green, brown, and yellow colors in ceramics. The vessel (below) shows the fine detail many Chinese porcelain-makers used. The vessel is designed to look like a well with a water jar.

▼ Most goods carried along the Silk Road were small, costly items. These included tea, pepper, jade, ivory, and porcelain—like the goose shown below.

The Chinese also discovered the use of tea. At first, tea was used as a medicine. Later, it became the custom to drink tea as a beverage. The custom spread from China to Japan and other countries. Soon tea became a major crop. Every year, much of it was shipped out of the country for sale.

Trade Routes: The Silk Road and the Grand Canal

Chinese silk, porcelain, tea, and other products traveled across roads and waterways to other countries in Asia and Europe. One important trade route was the Silk Road, which stretched all the way from China to the Mediterranean Sea. Camels, horses, and donkeys carried goods along the 4,000-mile (6,436-km) Silk Road. The Silk Road was not one long road. It was really many roads that connected with one another. Long stretches of the route crossed mountains and deserts. Travel was often difficult and dangerous, even though rest stations were built along the road. A Chinese historian described a trip through the huge Gobi Desert:

> "You see nothing in any direction but the sky and the sands, without the slightest trace of a road; and travelers find nothing to guide them but the bones of men and beasts."

Travelers on the Silk Road

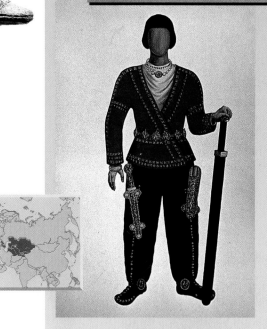

What might travelers on the Silk Road have worn? These paintings are reconstructions of clothing found in graves along the Silk Road in Central Asia. The outfits are of fine cloth decorated with gold.

Large amounts of grain and manufactured goods were also moved along a great network of rivers and canals in China. The Grand Canal connected the Huang He (HWAHNG huh) and Yangzi (YAHNG zuh). Work on the canal began in the 500s B.C. and continued for hundreds of years. The canal helped join northern and southern China. Stretching for more than 1,000 miles, the Grand Canal is still the longest canal ever built.

Printing Spreads Knowledge

During the golden ages, the Chinese developed trade products and trade routes that helped make their country rich. Chinese inventions of the period also had a great impact on their culture. The most important invention was a method of printing.

Before the invention of printing, all books were copied by hand. As a result, the number of books available was very small. The Chinese began printing in the A.D. 500s. They used blocks of wood on which they carved the characters of an entire page. Then they brushed ink over the wooden page. Finally, they laid a piece of paper over the block to make a print. Carving the pages of a book took a long time. But after the woodblocks were made, printers could make many copies of the book.

Around 1045, a Chinese printer named Bi Sheng (bee shehng) developed another method of printing using **movable type.** In this kind of printing, each character or piece of type is a separate piece. The pieces can be moved and reused. Bi Sheng made many separate characters out of clay. Then he put together the characters he needed to make the pages of a book. But the Chinese language has thousands of different characters. Most printers found woodblock printing easier and faster than the use of movable type.

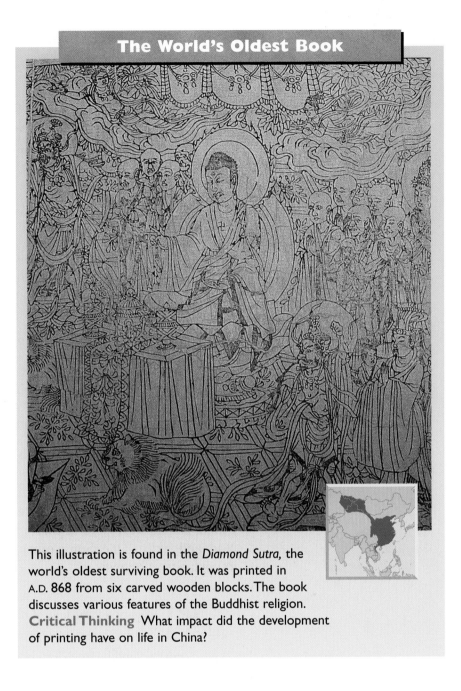

This illustration is found in the *Diamond Sutra,* the world's oldest surviving book. It was printed in A.D. **868** from six carved wooden blocks. The book discusses various features of the Buddhist religion. **Critical Thinking** What impact did the development of printing have on life in China?

READ ACTIVELY

Visualize Visualize yourself copying a whole book by hand. How long do you think it would take you?

Inventions of the Tang and Song Dynasties

The Tang and Song dynasties were a golden age for science and technology. Some developments took hundreds of years to spread to other parts of the world. The use of gunpowder and fireworks (below), for example, did not reach Europe until the late 1300s.

Invention	Date	Description
Block Printing	500s	Printers carved words onto a large wooden block. They inked the block, then pressed paper onto it to transfer the print. Many copies of the same page could be made quickly.
Gunpowder	850	The Chinese first used gunpowder to make fireworks. By about 1,000, however, they were making explosives to be used in warfare.
Smallpox Vaccine	900s	To stop the spread of smallpox, healthy people were given tiny doses of the disease. This helped them build an immunity to smallpox.
Compass	990	Sailors used the magnetic compass to navigate.
Movable Type	1045	Printers carved individual characters on small blocks. They combined the blocks to form a page. The same blocks could be reused to produce different pieces of writing.

The invention of printing helped spread knowledge throughout China. Books were sold in marketplaces. Many people learned how to read and write. One Song emperor wrote a poem telling about the importance of books:

"To enrich your family, no need to buy good land: Books hold a thousand measures of grain. For an easy life, no need to build a mansion: In books are found houses of gold."

SECTION 1 REVIEW

1. **Define** (a) dynasty, (b) merit system, (c) porcelain, (d) movable type.

2. **Identify** (a) Tang Taizong, (b) Confucius, (c) Silk Road, (d) Grand Canal.

3. What impact did the ideas of Confucius have on society during China's golden ages?

4. Identify the important accomplishments of the Tang and Song dynasties.

Critical Thinking
5. **Making Comparisons** In what ways were China's golden ages like the present times in the United States?

Activity
6. **Writing to Learn** The invention of printing made books available to many people. What would your life be like without books? Write a journal entry expressing your thoughts.

Feudalism in Japan

Reach Into Your Background

Children often play at being soldiers. You might have played such games when you were younger. But for many people, military life is not a game. It is a career. What are your impressions of the life of a soldier? Does a soldier's life interest you? Why or why not?

Questions to Explore

1. How did feudalism develop in Japan?
2. Why did the Tokugawa shoguns shut off Japan from the rest of the world?

Key Terms

samurai
daimyo
bushido
feudal system
shogun

Key People

Minamoto Yoritomo
Tokugawa Ieyasu

About 900 years ago, warriors called the **samurai** (sam uh ry) rose to fame and power in Japan. The word *samurai* means "those who serve." Samurai swore an oath to serve their leaders. They followed a code of rules. And they obeyed these rules without question. Honor meant more to a samurai than did wealth or life. A samurai would rather die than shame himself. Consider these guidelines for a samurai:

▼ Samurai warriors wore heavy armor made of small iron scales tied with silk and leather. Their face masks were designed to frighten enemies and to withstand spear thrusts.

“The way of the warrior is something you must [think about] in every detail, day and night, on the assumption that you may not be able to live through the day. You may win or lose, depending on the circumstances. But you can't shame yourself. . . . An accomplished warrior doesn't think whether he's going to win or lose, but dashes into the place of death with single-minded determination.

A samurai must be careful about everything and try not to show any weakness.

Surrendering is something a samurai never does, be it for deceiving the enemy or for the emperor.”

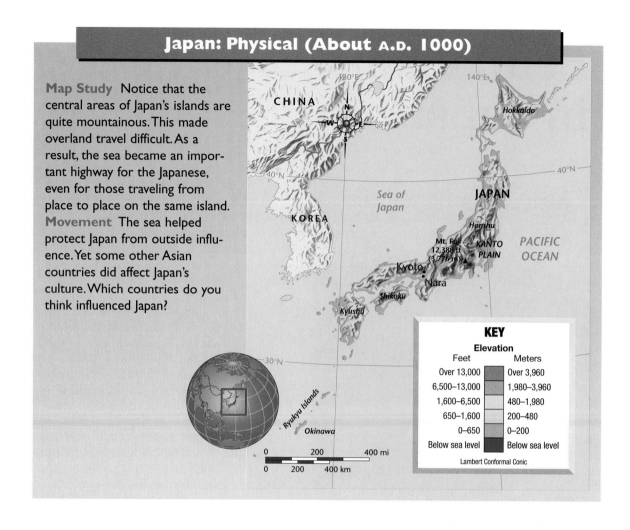

Japan: Physical (About A.D. 1000)

Map Study Notice that the central areas of Japan's islands are quite mountainous. This made overland travel difficult. As a result, the sea became an important highway for the Japanese, even for those traveling from place to place on the same island. **Movement** The sea helped protect Japan from outside influence. Yet some other Asian countries did affect Japan's culture. Which countries do you think influenced Japan?

KEY

Elevation

Feet	Meters
Over 13,000	Over 3,960
6,500–13,000	1,980–3,960
1,600–6,500	480–1,980
650–1,600	200–480
0–650	0–200
Below sea level	Below sea level

Lambert Conformal Conic

A Country of Islands

Today the way of life of the samurai seems strange to most people outside Japan. But life in Japan 900 years ago was unusual in many ways. One reason Japan was so different is its unusual geography.

Study the map of Japan on this page. Japan is a group of mountainous islands in the Pacific Ocean about 100 miles (160 km) across the water from Korea. It is about 500 miles (800 km) from China. For centuries, the sea protected Japan from invaders. But the sea also served as a highway for the Japanese. It served as a link between their own islands. In this geographic setting, the Japanese developed a distinctive way of life.

The Rise of the Samurai

Why were warriors so important in Japan if the sea kept the country safe from invaders? Against whom were the Japanese fighting? The answer is that they fought with each other as different groups tried to gain power.

Feudalism Develops in Japan To understand the Japanese system of government, you have to go far back in history. For centuries, emperors ruled Japan from the city that is now called Kyoto. Over time,

READ ACTIVELY

Predict What do you think a samurai's responsibilities were?

wealthy families created large private estates in the country and gained much power. Between 1000 and 1200, the emperor lost more and more power. Estate owners, called **daimyo** (dy myoh), became more independent. They hired bands of samurai to protect them and the peasants who farmed their land from rival daimyo.

As the daimyo gained power, a new political and military system developed in Japan. Under this system, the daimyo and the samurai were closely connected. The samurai promised to obey and to be loyal to their daimyo. They followed a set of rules for warriors called **bushido** (boo shee doh). These rules stressed honor, discipline, bravery, and simple living. A samurai's loyalty to his daimyo was stronger than his loyalty to his own family. He was expected to gladly give his life for his lord.

This system of government, in which less powerful people promise loyalty to more powerful people, is called a **feudal system.** Think of a feudal system as a kind of pyramid. At the bottom of the pyramid were many poor and powerless people, the peasants. Then came more powerful people. In Japan, these were the samurai. Next came local lords—the daimyo. Then came the most powerful lord in Japan, the **shogun** (shoh gun), or great general.

Waiting to See the Shogun

The shogun expected loyalty from the daimyo. In return, the shogun did not interfere in the way the daimyo ruled their own lands. Here, a group of daimyo wait to see the shogun. **Critical Thinking** Why was it important for the shogun to have the loyalty of the daimyo?

TO
LANGUAGE ARTS

Lady Murasaki's Novel In the early 1000s, Lady Murasaki Shikibu wrote *The Tale of Genji*, the first novel ever written. It begins with the life and loves of Prince Genji (gehn jee). Then it tells about his children and grandchildren. Lady Murasaki describes court life in great detail. Her characters are complex and true to life. Some people consider *The Tale of Genji* as the best Japanese novel ever written.

Shoguns Gain Control The first shogun did not take power in Japan until 1192. All through the 1100s, Japan was torn by war as samurai armies battled one another. Two powerful families—the Minamoto (mee nah moh toh) and the Taira (ty rah)—fought for control of the country. In 1185, the Minamoto family won. Yoritomo (yor ee toh moh), the head of the Minamoto family, made himself the ruler of the country.

In 1192, the emperor of Japan named Yoritomo shogun. Shoguns ruled Japan in the emperor's name until 1867. The emperor held a position of honor but had no real power. Japan's period of military rule lasted almost 700 years.

Some of Japan's shoguns had problems uniting the country's many daimyo and their samurai bands. During the rule of weak shoguns, local samurai bands were always at war.

Isolation for Japan

Within a century after shogun rule started, Japan was threatened by an attack from the Mongols. The Mongols came from a country called Mongolia, north of China. Under their fierce and brilliant leader, Kublai Khan (KOO bluh kahn), the Mongols had already conquered China. Kublai Khan twice tried to take over Japan. He failed both times.

Kublai Khan

This picture is of the great Chinese leader, Kublai Khan. He ruled a huge empire, but he wanted more. In the late 1200s, he decided to invade Japan. In 1274, his invasion fleet got only as far as the island of Kyushu. A violent storm frightened the sailors back to China. When Kublai Khan tried again in 1281, another violent storm destroyed his ships. The Japanese called this storm *kamikaze* (kah muh kah zee) or "divine wind."

The Arrival of Europeans For nearly 300 years after the Mongols were beaten, few foreigners came to Japan. Then, in 1543, some Portuguese sailors were blown off course and landed in Japan. The Japanese showed great interest in the guns that the Portuguese carried. In the years that followed, many European traders and Christian missionaries arrived. A lively trade developed, and thousands of Japanese became Christians.

The Tokugawas Cut Off Japan
The European influence in Japan did not last long. In 1603, Tokugawa Ieyasu (toh koo gah wah ee yay ah soo) became shogun. Ieyasu was determined to bring order to the country. He wanted to end the fighting among warring samurai bands. Ieyasu divided Japan into about 250 regions, each headed by a daimyo. The daimyos promised to serve the shogun and swore loyalty to him.

Ieyasu feared that Europeans might try to conquer Japan. He and the Tokugawa rulers who followed him isolated Japan from Westerners. The shoguns outlawed Christianity and forced Europeans to leave the country. They banned most foreign travel and trade. They closed Japanese ports to outsiders. They stopped the building of large ships that could travel great distances.

In effect, they closed Japan to the outside world. Shut off from others, the Japanese continued their own distinctive culture. Their isolation lasted for 250 years, until 1853.

▼ One distinctive feature of Japanese culture is a form of theater called *no*. In this drama, dancers in colorful robes tell folk stories, moving to the slow music of chants, flutes, and drums.

SECTION 2 REVIEW

1. **Define** (a) samurai, (b) daimyo, (c) bushido, (d) feudal system, (e) shogun.

2. **Identify** (a) Minamoto Yoritomo, (b) Tokugawa Ieyasu.

3. Describe the feudal system in Japan.

4. What measures did the Tokugawas take to close Japan off to other countries?

Critical Thinking

5. **Recognizing Cause and Effect** The warrior class in feudal Japan included about 5 of every 100 Japanese. How does this help explain why warfare was so common?

Activity

6. **Writing to Learn** What if you could interview a samurai from feudal Japan? Write five interview questions that you would ask about his life or about bushido.

The Great Mughal Empire in India

BEFORE YOU READ

Reach Into Your Background

What qualities do you respect in a leader? Think about

American presidents. Which ones do you think were great leaders? Why?

Questions to Explore

1. What impact did Mughal rule have on India?
2. Why is Akbar considered one of the world's great rulers?

Key Terms

Hinduism   sultan
caste system

Key People and Places

Tamerlane   Shah Jahan
Babur   Delhi
Akbar   Taj Mahal

Even before he invaded India, people had heard of the Mongol conqueror Tamerlane (TAM ur layn). Throughout Asia and the Middle East, he had destroyed entire cities and killed all the people.

Tamerlane's campaign into India was no different. In 1398, he invaded the country and destroyed fields and crops as well as towns. At the city of Delhi, Tamerlane quickly defeated the Indian army. Then he left the city a mass of ruins. His troops took everything of any value. They killed most of the people. Those they did not kill they took as slaves. After the destruction, it was reported that "not a bird on the wing moved for two months."

The Muslim Invasion of India

The Mongols were not the first to invade India. Long before the Mongols came, India's great wealth had tempted many groups.

Seeking India's Wealth India had always been called a land of riches. In northern India, a great civilization flowered during the Gupta (GOOP tuh) dynasty, from 320 to about 540. The Gupta dynasty built beautiful cities and traded in jewels and spices. The people in the Gupta empire practiced **Hinduism,** a religion and a way of life that developed in India over a long period of time.

▼ The people of Asia feared Tamerlane because of his ferocity in battle.

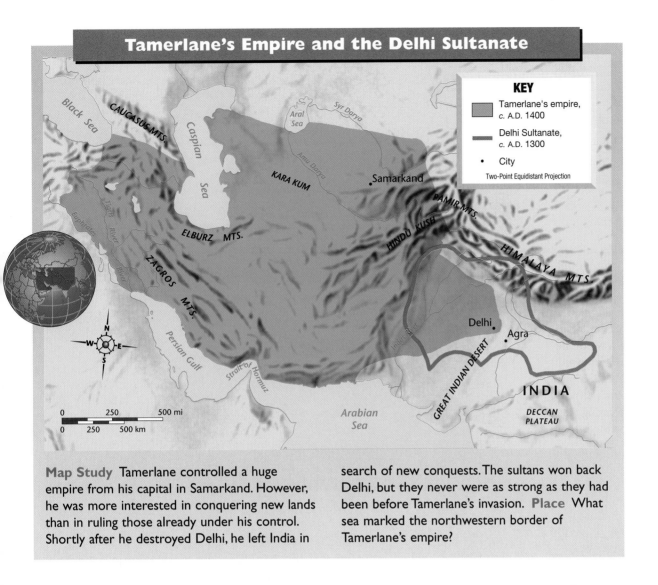

Tamerlane's Empire and the Delhi Sultanate

KEY

Tamerlane's empire,
c. A.D. 1400

Delhi Sultanate,
c. A.D. 1300

• City

Two-Point Equidistant Projection

Map Study Tamerlane controlled a huge empire from his capital in Samarkand. However, he was more interested in conquering new lands than in ruling those already under his control. Shortly after he destroyed Delhi, he left India in search of new conquests. The sultans won back Delhi, but they never were as strong as they had been before Tamerlane's invasion. **Place** What sea marked the northwestern border of Tamerlane's empire?

Hindus accepted many gods, but believed that all these gods were just different aspects of one supreme being. They also believed that each person must search for his or her own religious truth. And Hindus believed that social classes were part of the natural order of the universe.

The Hindu **caste system,** a strict system of social classes, controlled every part of everyday life. Caste determined people's jobs. At the top of the caste system were the priests, teachers, and judges. Next came the warriors. Then came a social group made up of farmers and merchants. The fourth class was made up of craftworkers and laborers. Finally there was a group of poor and powerless people called the "Untouchables." Though this unequal system was hard on the lower classes, it brought India stability. During the Gupta dynasty, India entered a golden age.

But India's golden age came to an end as different groups attacked the empire. Muslim invaders poured into India. From 1206 to 1526, the Muslims controlled an empire that covered much of what is now India, Bangladesh, and Pakistan. A **sultan,** or Muslim king, ruled the empire. Because its capital was at Delhi, the empire was called the Delhi Sultanate.

LINKS TO LANGUAGE ARTS

Common Ground The Hindu sacred books were written in a language called Sanskrit. It may be one of the world's oldest languages. Sanskrit influenced many other languages in the world, such as ancient Greek and Latin. Today, words with ancient Sanskrit roots exist in most modern European languages. *Mother* and *father,* for example, have Sanskrit roots.

Paramita Hazra
age 11
India

In this painting, the artist shows a scene from everyday life in her village. In many rural areas in India, people follow ways of life similar to those followed by people in the 1500s and 1600s. **Critical Thinking** What in the painting illustrates traditional ways?

Unlike earlier conquerors, the Muslims did not become a part of Hindu society. Muslim culture was based on ideas that were very different from those of Hindu culture. These differences caused conflicts between Hindus and Muslims. Religious differences still divide Hindus and Muslims in India today.

The Invasion of the Mongols It was the Delhi Sultanate that Tamerlane, who was also a Muslim, invaded. But Tamerlane cared little about ruling India. He mainly wanted the country's riches. From Delhi, his soldiers carried off more pearls, rubies, diamonds, and golden dishes than they could count. They also took hundreds of slaves. Shortly after Tamerlane's troops left, the sultan regained Delhi. But the empire split apart into smaller kingdoms.

A descendant of Tamerlane, a Turkish prince named Babur (BAH boor), later took advantage of the disorder in northern India. In 1526, he attacked the sultan's army. Babur's troops were outnumbered almost 10 to 1. And while the sultan's forces had 100 elephants, Babur's troops had none. But Babur's troops were better fighters, and they had cannons. They defeated the sultan, and Babur went on to conquer most of northern India. He founded the brilliant Mughal (MOO gul) empire, which lasted into the 1700s.

The Mughal Empire

Mughal is another word for "Mongol." Like Babur, the Mughal emperors were Muslims. But the people they ruled were mostly Hindus. Under earlier Muslim rulers, Indian society had remained divided by religion. But Babur's grandson, Akbar (AK bar), persuaded Hindus and Muslims to live more peacefully together.

Akbar, the Greatest Mughal Emperor   Akbar was only 13 years old when he came to power. As he grew up, he became a talented soldier and greatly expanded the empire. He also ruled well. Akbar realized that the best way to make the empire peaceful was to be fair to people of different religions. Unlike earlier Muslim rulers, he allowed Hindus to practice their religion freely.

Akbar divided the empire into provinces. He gave government jobs to qualified people, whatever their religion. Hindu warriors served as generals, governors, administrators, and clerks. Akbar also ended unfair taxes on non-Muslims. And he regularly brought together scholars of different religions for discussion. Akbar searched for religious truth and listened to differing viewpoints.

The Games We Play
Parcheesi, a popular board game, originated in India. Akbar loved the game. He had workers cut the design of the board into the pavement of one of his courtyards. Then he would play the game—using servants from the palace as the playing pieces!

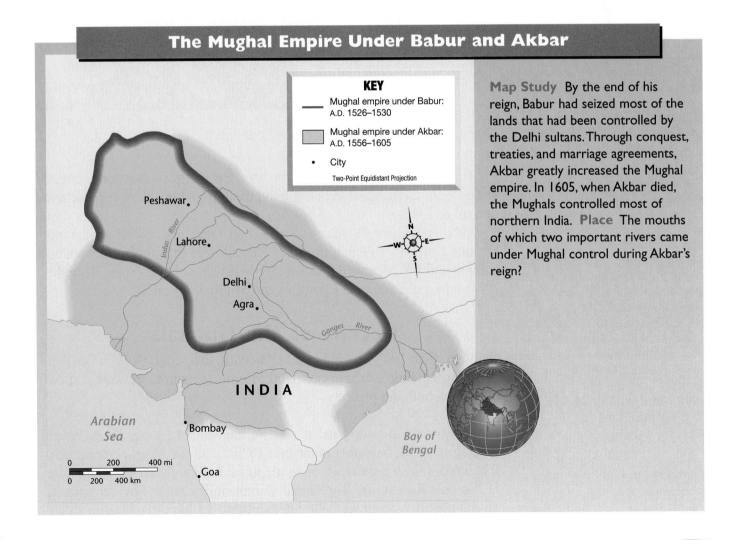

The Mughal Empire Under Babur and Akbar

KEY

— Mughal empire under Babur: A.D. 1526–1530

▢ Mughal empire under Akbar: A.D. 1556–1605

• City

Two-Point Equidistant Projection

Peshawar
Lahore
Delhi
Agra
Indus River
Ganges River

INDIA

Arabian Sea
Bombay
Bay of Bengal
Goa

0   200   400 mi
0   200   400 km

Map Study By the end of his reign, Babur had seized most of the lands that had been controlled by the Delhi sultans. Through conquest, treaties, and marriage agreements, Akbar greatly increased the Mughal empire. In 1605, when Akbar died, the Mughals controlled most of northern India. **Place** The mouths of which two important rivers came under Mughal control during Akbar's reign?

In this painting, made around 1600, Akbar (sitting in right center) receives visitors to the splendid palace. Akbar loved the arts, and the artists who worked at his court made beautiful miniature paintings like this one. The paintings showed court celebrations, battles, gardens, and often Akbar himself. **Critical Thinking** What does this painting tell you about the artist's attitudes toward nature?

The emperor also supported the arts. He set up studios for painters at his court. He supported poets, even though he himself never learned to read and write.

Akbar ruled for 49 years. During that time, his way of governing became firmly established in India. This allowed the empire to develop and expand for 100 more years under less-talented emperors. Because of his wise rule, Akbar is known as the Mughals' greatest leader.

Decline of the Mughals

More than 100 years after Akbar's death, the Mughal empire began to fall apart. Rulers began to spend too much money on wars and on expensive building projects.

Reign of Shah Jahan The grandson of Akbar, Shah Jahan (shah juh HAHN), became emperor in 1628. Of all the Mughal emperors, Jahan spent the most money on extravagant buildings. The most famous of his buildings is the Taj Mahal (tahzh muh HAHL). This "dream in marble," as one observer called it, is a tomb for Mumtaz (muhm TAHZ)

Visualize Suppose that you wanted to build a monument in honor of someone you love. Visualize what the monument would look like.

Mahal, the emperor's wife. When she died at age 39, Shah Jahan was overcome with grief. The two had been constant companions. She even went on his military campaigns. He had asked her opinion on many issues. After she died, Jahan set out to build her a tomb "as beautiful as she was beautiful."

To build the Taj Mahal, Jahan called together 20,000 craftworkers and laborers from all over India, Asia, and Europe. Working for 22 years, they built this stunning monument in Agra in northern India.

The Empire Declines The cost of Shah Jahan's building projects was enormous. Added to the cost of his wars, they drained the empire of money. Shah Jahan's son, Aurangzeb (OR ung zeb), spent still more money in expensive wars. He also reversed Akbar's policies toward Hindus. Aurangzeb tried to force Hindus to convert to Islam, and he began to tax them again. Many Hindus rebelled.

Fighting the rebels cost still more money. After Aurangzeb's death in 1707, the empire split into many small kingdoms.

▲ Many people feel the Taj Mahal in Agra, India, is the grandest example of the Mughal architecture.

SECTION 3 REVIEW

1. **Define** (a) Hinduism, (b) caste system, (c) sultan.

2. **Identify** (a) Tamerlane, (b) Babur, (c) Akbar, (d) Shah Jahan, (e) Delhi, (f) Taj Mahal.

3. What did the Mughal rulers achieve in India?

4. In what ways did Akbar prove himself a wise ruler?

Critical Thinking

5. **Expressing Problems Clearly** Summarize some of the reasons for the downfall of the Mughal empire.

Activity

6. **Writing to Learn** Suppose Akbar is a leader under a system of government like the United States government. He is running for reelection. You are his campaign manager. Write a short speech stating why voters should reelect him.

SKILLS ACTIVITY

Assessing Your Understanding

What does a good grade mean? Among other things, it means that your teacher believes that you understand an assignment. For example, you get a good grade on a test when you understand the subject well enough to answer most of the questions correctly. You get a good grade on a paper when you understand your topic well enough to write about it clearly and completely.

How do you know whether you understand something or not? Sometimes you might think you understand an assignment but later find out that you have made some mistakes. Assessing, or measuring, how well you understand something is a skill itself.

Get Ready

Suppose you have an assigned reading in a textbook. When you finish a section, you should stop to assess your understanding of the text. If you find that you understand it perfectly, then you can move on. However, if you realize that there is something you do not understand, then stop. Think about how you can begin to figure out what you have missed.

Why was I given this assignment?

What are the main ideas of the assignment?

Try It Out

How do you measure your understanding? Take a self-survey. Choose one reading assignment you completed recently. Review the selection, and then think about it as you read and answer each question below.

A. Why were you given this assignment?

B. What are the main ideas of the assignment?

C. How does this assignment relate to what you already know?

D. How could you use the information from the assignment in the future?

If you answered all four questions with confidence, then you probably understood the reading well. If you are not so sure about any of your answers, review the assignment with the questions in mind.

Apply the Skill

Practice assessing your understanding with the short reading assignment in the box. Read the assignment, then complete the activities that follow.

Answer the following questions.

1 Why were you given this assignment?

2 What is the main point of the selection?

3 How does knowing about Sui Wendi relate to what you already know about Chinese history?

4 How can you use the information in the selection as you learn more about China?

Think of ways to improve your understanding. List at least three things you can do to better understand the reading assignment.

Sui Wendi

From A.D. 581 to 604, a man named Sui Wendi (originally named Yang Chien) ruled China as emperor. Sui Wendi unified China after it had been divided for about 300 years. Long after his death, China has remained united and powerful. The people of China, who are about one fifth of the world's population, have probably suffered fewer wars than many other peoples.

Yang Chien was born in 541 to a powerful family in northern China. He worked for the emperor of the northern Chou dynasty. He quickly became a valued official. He helped the emperor gain control of most of northern China. Shortly after the emperor's death, Yang Chien became emperor himself. He took the new name Sui Wendi.

As emperor, Sui Wendi wanted to rule more than northern China, so he invaded southern China. In 589, he became ruler of all of China. He built a new capital city for his empire. He also began reconstruction of the Grand Canal. This canal now connects the Yangzi and the Huang He, which are the two greatest rivers in China.

Sui Wendi also reformed the ways in which government officials were chosen. His civil service tests and other new rules helped to create a talented and skilled group of officials. Unlike officers in earlier times, these came from all social classes.

This cautious but strong leader ruled until his death in 604. His political and military actions had long-lasting effects in Chinese history.

Review and Activities

Reviewing Main Ideas

1. How were Confucian ideas put into practice during the Tang and Song dynasties?
2. Describe the achievements of the Tang and Song dynasties.
3. How did feudalism work in Japan?
4. Why did the Tokugawa shoguns refuse to let Japan stay in touch with the rest of the world?
5. How were the Mughal rulers different from earlier Muslim rulers of India?
6. Describe how Akbar ruled India.

Reviewing Key Terms

Match the definitions in Column I with the key terms in Column II.

Column I

1. class of warriors in feudal Japan
2. set of rules for Japanese warriors that stressed honor, discipline, bravery, and simple living
3. series of rulers from one family
4. strict system of social classes among Hindus
5. government system in which less powerful people promise to be loyal to more powerful people

Column II

a. dynasty
b. samurai
c. bushido
d. feudal system
e. caste system

Critical Thinking

1. **Making Comparisons** In which ways were Tang Taizong of China and Akbar of India alike as rulers?
2. **Drawing Conclusions** Europeans took over the land that eventually became the United States. Considering this, do you think the Tokugawa shoguns were right in thinking that Europeans might try to take over Japan? Explain your answer.

Graphic Organizer

Copy the chart onto a separate sheet of paper. Complete the chart by describing important characteristics or accomplishments of each civilization.

Civilization	Description
Tang and Song Dynasties	
Feudal Japan	
Mughal Empire	

Map Activity

Asia

For each place listed, write the letter from the map that shows its location.

1. China during the Tang dynasty
2. Silk Road
3. Grand Canal
4. Japan
5. Mughal empire
6. Delhi

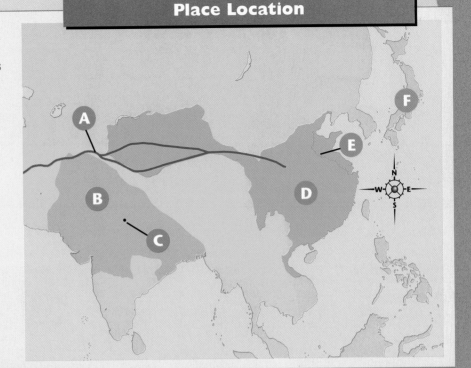

Writing Activity

Writing a Story

Bushido required that samurai show complete loyalty to their daimyo. A samurai's family took second place behind his daimyo. Write a brief story that illustrates a samurai's loyalty to his daimyo.

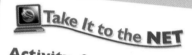

Take It to the NET

Activity Study Chinese culture by reviewing Chinese literature and art. For help in completing this activity, visit www.phschool.com.

Chapter 4 Self-Test To review what you have learned, take the Chapter 4 Self-Test and get instant feedback on your answers. Go to www.phschool.com to take the test.

Skills Review

Turn to the Skills Activity.

Review the four questions for assessing how well you understand something you have read. Explain what steps you might take if you could not answer all the questions.

How Am I Doing?

Answer these questions to check your progress.

1. Can I describe the accomplishments of the Tang and Song dynasties?
2. Do I understand how feudalism developed in Japan and why the shoguns cut off Japan from the world?
3. Can I tell how Mughal rule affected India and why Akbar was a great ruler?
4. What information from this chapter can I include in my journal?

CHAPTER 5

Europe in the Middle Ages

KEY
• City
Lambert Azimuthal
Equal-Area Projection

MAP ACTIVITIES

About 800 years ago, Europe was made up of many separate kingdoms and states. These are labeled on the map above. To begin your exploration of Europe during this time, do the following activities.

Study the map
Read the names of the different kingdoms shown on the map. Which names are familiar? Which names are not familiar?

Plan a trade route
Trace the route that a merchant ship might have taken between Venice and Barcelona. Which kingdoms would it pass? Through which bodies of water would it sail?

Feudalism: A System for Living

BEFORE YOU READ

Reach Into Your Background

Have you ever ridden a local bus? Have you used public parks? If so, you have used services provided by your local government. Do you think your community does a good job providing services that people need? Why or why not?

Questions to Explore

1. How did feudalism protect people during the dangerous times of the early Middle Ages?

2. What was life like on a medieval manor?

Key Terms

Middle Ages
medieval
feudalism
vassal
manor
self-sufficient
serf

Key People and Places

Charlemagne
Gaul

As darkness fell, a young man prepared for a special ceremony. The next day he would stop being a squire, or knight-in-training, and become a real knight. It was a big step up in life.

The squire put on a white tunic and red and black cloaks. Then he walked to the church, where he spent the night alone, praying. The next morning he entered the castle courtyard, where knights and ladies had gathered. His lord presented him with his sword, spurs, and shield. The squire knelt. Then he felt the lord's sword lightly tap him on each shoulder. "In the name of God, Saint Michael, and Saint George, I call you a knight," declared the lord. "Be loyal, brave, and true."

The young man had become a knight, an important person in European society. Before all else, a knight was expected to be loyal and true to the lord who knighted him. His lord, in turn, was loyal to a more powerful lord. That lord might be loyal to a king. A thousand years ago, governments in Europe depended on each person's loyalty to those who had more land and wealth. Each knight and lord was also supposed to watch over the people in his care, who were less powerful.

▼ This picture shows a squire being knighted. He receives his broadsword and other weapons from his lord.

Medieval Times

This kind of government came about because it filled the needs of communities for protection during the Middle Ages. What are the Middle Ages? Historians usually say that ancient times lasted until about A.D. 500. They say that modern times actually started about A.D. 1500. The years in the middle, between ancient times and modern times, are called the **Middle Ages.** This part of history is sometimes called **medieval** (mee dee EE vul) times. *Medieval* means "from the Middle Ages."

The Collapse of the Roman Empire In ancient times, the Roman Empire protected much of Western Europe. When it no longer had an army strong enough to defend its borders, the empire became weaker. In wave after wave, invaders claimed parts of the empire. They destroyed towns and cut off trade routes. They kept their own languages and laws. By doing this, the invaders broke the bonds that

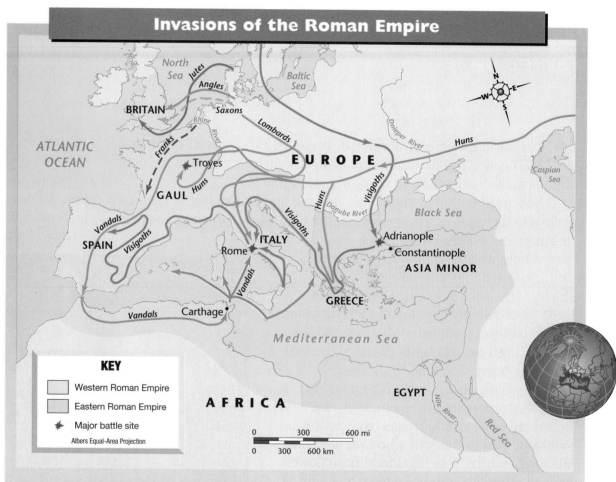

Invasions of the Roman Empire

KEY

Western Roman Empire

Eastern Roman Empire

★ Major battle site

Albers Equal-Area Projection

Map Study At the height of its power, the Roman Empire included the lands around the Mediterranean Sea and much of Western Europe. In the late A.D. 200s, an emperor divided it to make it easier to rule. The western part went into decline. From the 300s to the 500s, peoples from northern and eastern Europe invaded and took control of much of the eastern empire. **Movement** Which groups of invaders attacked Rome?

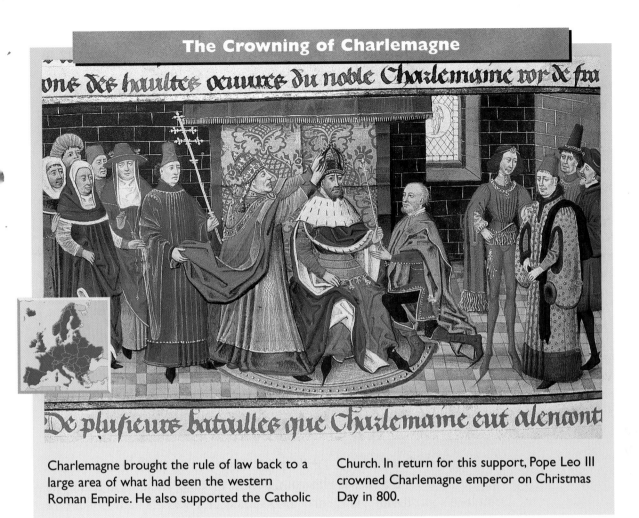

The Crowning of Charlemagne

one des haultes oeuures du noble Charlemaine roi de fra

De plusieurs batailles que Charlemaine eut alencont

Charlemagne brought the rule of law back to a large area of what had been the western Roman Empire. He also supported the Catholic Church. In return for this support, Pope Leo III crowned Charlemagne emperor on Christmas Day in 800.

had held the Roman Empire together. Even reading and writing were in danger of vanishing, because many invading groups could not do either.

Charlemagne's Empire As time went on, the invading groups set up small kingdoms throughout Europe. One group, the Franks, claimed the area called Gaul, which is now the country of France. In 768, a skilled military leader named Charlemagne (SHAR luh mayn) became king of the Franks. He soon expanded his kingdom into an empire by conquering much of Western Europe.

During his rule of more than 45 years, Charlemagne worked to keep Western Europe united. He also established schools to promote learning and culture. The rulers who came after Charlemagne were weak. They could not defend his empire against new waves of invasions. By the end of the 800s, Charlemagne's empire had fallen apart.

▲ Some people believe this gold crown set with jewels was worn by Charlemagne.

Feudalism: A Basis for Government

Perhaps the fiercest attacks against Charlemagne's empire were made by the Vikings. These tough warriors came from northern Europe, where Denmark, Sweden, and Norway are now. Their attacks began around 800 and continued for about 300 years. Relying on

Vikings in America Vikings looked beyond Europe for conquest. They went into North Africa. They traveled westward to Greenland and beyond. *Saga of the Greenlanders*, a Norwegian saga, describes a journey to lands west of Greenland. The storyteller gives clues about the location of Vinland, a settlement founded in this new land. Historians who have worked with these clues think that Vinland was probably somewhere in what is now Newfoundland, Canada.

▼ Knights carried colorful coats of arms into battle. They knew the coats of arms so well, they could identify each other at a glance.

surprise, the Vikings looted towns and murdered the people living in them. The people of Europe had to find a way to defend themselves against the Vikings. Slowly they worked out a new system of government that could protect small towns and entire kingdoms.

Creating Order   The medieval power system was constructed like a pyramid. The people at the top of the system had the most power. They were kings and queens. Next in power were nobles, then knights, and finally peasants. This system is called **feudalism.**

In medieval Europe, power belonged to those who controlled the land. A landowner gave a share of land, called a *fief* (feef), to another man who promised to be loyal to the landowner, to follow his laws, and to fight for him. In this system, the landowner was called a lord, and the man who promised to be loyal to him was his **vassal.** A vassal could also be a lord. However, he had much less power than the great lord to whom he swore loyalty.

The agreement between lord and vassal was begun in a solemn ceremony. Like a new knight, the vassal knelt before the lord and swore to be loyal. The lord, in turn, promised to treat the vassal with honor. Then the lord gave the vassal a handful of dirt or some other symbol of the fief he was to receive.

Feudal Duties   A lord's chief duty was to protect his vassals and their lands. If a vassal with young children died, the lord became the children's protector. The lord also asked his vassals' advice before making laws or going to war.

Vassals had other duties besides serving in the lord's army. When the lord called them, they had to appear at a special gathering called the lord's court. They also had to make special payments of money or goods to the lord when his oldest daughter married or when his oldest son became a knight.

Women of noble class also played an important part in feudal society. Like the men in her family, a noblewoman was often sent to friends or relatives for training. After her training was finished, she took her place as lady of the household. She managed the household, performed necessary medical tasks, and supervised servants. When her husband or father was off fighting, she often served as "lord of the manor."

Peasants and Manors

A lord might rule over one manor or many. A **manor** was a large estate that often included a village as well as farmlands inhabited by peasants. The manor was very important in the feudal system, since a lord depended on the wealth his manor provided.

A Medieval Manor

The most important building on a manor was the lord's house, or the manor house. It was surrounded by a fence or wall for protection. Beyond the lord's house lay the village. It consisted of a church, peasants' homes, a blacksmith's shop, a mill for grinding grain into flour, and other workplaces. The fields outside the village where crops were grown were part of the manor, too. **Critical Thinking** Why could a manor be called self-sufficient?

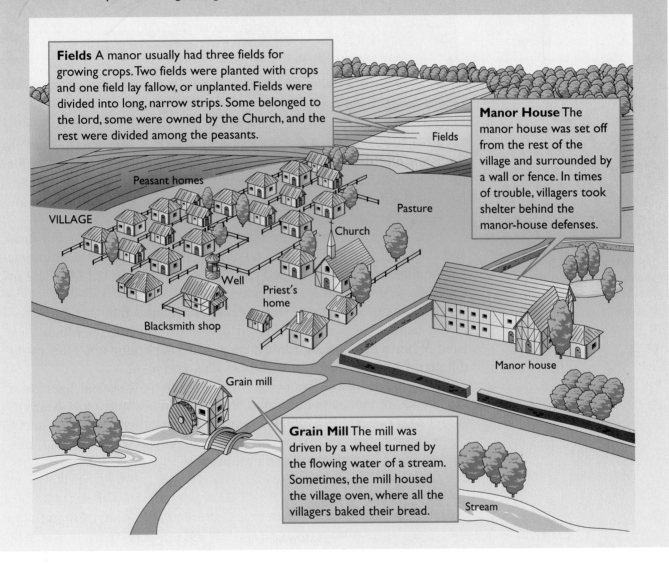

Fields A manor usually had three fields for growing crops. Two fields were planted with crops and one field lay fallow, or unplanted. Fields were divided into long, narrow strips. Some belonged to the lord, some were owned by the Church, and the rest were divided among the peasants.

Manor House The manor house was set off from the rest of the village and surrounded by a wall or fence. In times of trouble, villagers took shelter behind the manor-house defenses.

Grain Mill The mill was driven by a wheel turned by the flowing water of a stream. Sometimes, the mill housed the village oven, where all the villagers baked their bread.

Fields

Peasant homes

VILLAGE

Pasture

Church

Well

Priest's home

Blacksmith shop

Grain mill

Manor house

Stream

A Complete Community The illustration above shows the plan of a typical manor. The manor was governed by the lord. He made the rules and acted as judge. He also chose officials to manage the farming and other daily work. Since the manor was often far from towns and villages, its residents had to be **self-sufficient,** or able to supply their own needs, including food, shelter, and clothing. While most peasants were farm laborers, the manor would also have a carpenter, a shoemaker, a metalworker called a smith, and other skilled workers.

▶ This illustration, made in France during the 1400s, shows the kinds of work peasants had to do on a manor. These tasks included plowing, sowing seeds, pruning trees, and tending sheep.

Visualize Picture in your mind the inside of a peasant's hut.

The Lives of the Peasants and Serfs   The peasants did all the labor on the manor. They farmed the lord's fields to raise food for his household. In return, each peasant family could farm a small strip of land for itself. However, the family still owed the lord a part of the fall harvest.

Peasants lived in one-room huts with just a single window. For heat and cooking, they built a fire on the dirt floor. Without a chimney, smoke filled the dark, cramped interior before drifting out of a hole in the roof.

In most cases, peasants were **serfs.** This means that they belonged to the land. They were considered part of the manor on which they lived. When a noble was given a manor, its serfs became his. They could not marry or leave the manor without his agreement.

Although serfs were property, they were not quite slaves. A serf who saved enough money to buy a plot of land could become a free peasant. A serf who escaped to a city and managed to live there for a year and a day without being caught also became free. As you will soon read, this custom had a big effect on medieval Europe.

SECTION 1 REVIEW

1. **Define**   (a) Middle Ages, (b) medieval, (c) feudalism, (d) vassal, (e) manor, (f) self-sufficient, (g) serf.

2. **Identify**   (a) Charlemagne, (b) Gaul.

3. (a) How did feudalism benefit the wealthy and powerful? (b) How did it affect the poor?

4. Describe the life of a peasant on a medieval manor.

Critical Thinking

5. **Identifying Central Issues**   Was feudalism the best way of providing protection for the poor? Give reasons for your answer.

Activity

6. **Writing to Learn**   You are a medieval lord. List the various tasks you might perform in this position. Which tasks do you think you would like? Which do you think you would dislike? Explain your answers.

The Rise of Cities

BEFORE YOU READ

Reach Into Your Background

Think about the jobs the people in your community do.

How did they train for these jobs? Keep your answers in mind as you read this section.

Questions to Explore

1. How did the Roman Catholic Church influence life in the Middle Ages?

2. How did the growth of trade affect life in the Middle Ages?

Key Terms

clergy
excommunicate
guild
apprentice
chivalry
troubadour

A city's buildings tell a lot about what the city's people value and believe in. In modern times, for example, skyscrapers make a statement about the importance of big business in today's society.

Medieval cities also had buildings that soared above the rest. These buildings, however, had nothing to do with business. The grandest building in any medieval city was almost always a cathedral—an especially large church. It made a statement about the importance of religion.

The word *religion* in Europe in the early Middle Ages usually referred to the largest and most powerful religious organization of the time, the Roman Catholic Church. It had so much more influence than other religions that it was usually called simply "the Church."

The Church in the Middle Ages

Why was the Church so powerful? During the Middle Ages, life was short and hard for many people. They were comforted by the Roman Catholic belief that they could enjoy the rewards of heaven after death if they lived good lives. The **clergy,** the men who performed the services of the Church, helped people follow Church rules about how to live. The clergy performed marriages and funerals. They blessed the sick

▼ The cathedral in Aachen, Germany—the burial place of Charlemagne—was built in the late 700s. The large section on the right was added in the 1300s.

In this painting, made in Spain in the 1200s, a priest (on the left, holding a jug) performs a baptism. This ceremony symbolically washed away the man's sins and signaled the start of his new life in the Church. The clergy were deeply involved in people's lives, from birth to death. **Critical Thinking** How did services like baptisms and funerals help add to the Church's influence?

LINKS TO ART

Glass for the Glory of God The grandeur of cathedrals was increased by the use of stained glass in windows. Richly colored pieces of glass were pieced together by craftworkers to show scenes from the Bible. The windows took many years to create and were very expensive. Rich nobles and merchants gave money to the Church to pay for these windows. Their gifts to the Church were meant to show that they were good Christians and that they deserved to go to heaven.

and the dying. The clergy also listened when believers came to church to confess their wrongdoings. In the name of God, the clergy then forgave the believers for the wrongs to which they had confessed.

The Church in Everyday Life The Church was also powerful because it took on many of the jobs government does today. In the United States, leaders have always been careful to keep government and religious organizations separate. For example, the government is not allowed to adopt a national religion or to support the activities of any religion. Nor are religious organizations allowed to run the government.

In the Middle Ages, the Church made laws and set up courts to enforce them. It gained great wealth by collecting taxes. It also took fiefs from lords in exchange for services performed by clergy. These Church lands were farmed by men and women who dedicated their lives to serving the Church. The men were called monks, and the women, nuns. These monks and nuns developed better ways of growing crops and tending livestock. In this way, the Church helped to improve the economy of the Middle Ages, which was based on farming.

The Church as Peacekeeper High Church officials also exercised great political power as advisors to kings. The Church helped limit warfare among feudal lords. When a lord rebelled, the Church could threaten to **excommunicate** him, or prevent him from taking part in Church life. A lord seldom ignored this threat, because if he were excommunicated, no one would associate with him.

Towns Grow as Trade Revives

By about A.D. 1000, the strong governments created by the Church and powerful lords had restored some order in Europe. This order meant that populations could grow. Many manors became crowded. Providing food and clothing for everyone who lived on the manor became difficult. Many lords gladly allowed peasants to buy their freedom. These farmers and craftworkers set up small communities outside the manor. As more people moved to them, these communities grew into towns.

The Rise of a Merchant Class Many peasants who left the manor to work in towns saw their lives improve. They made enough money to pay for more than their basic needs. Some even became members of the merchant class, a group between nobles and peasants. The merchant class included merchants, traders, and craftspeople. Serfs still bound to the manor heard these success stories and longed to move to the towns. Some saved their money and bought their freedom. Others simply ran away.

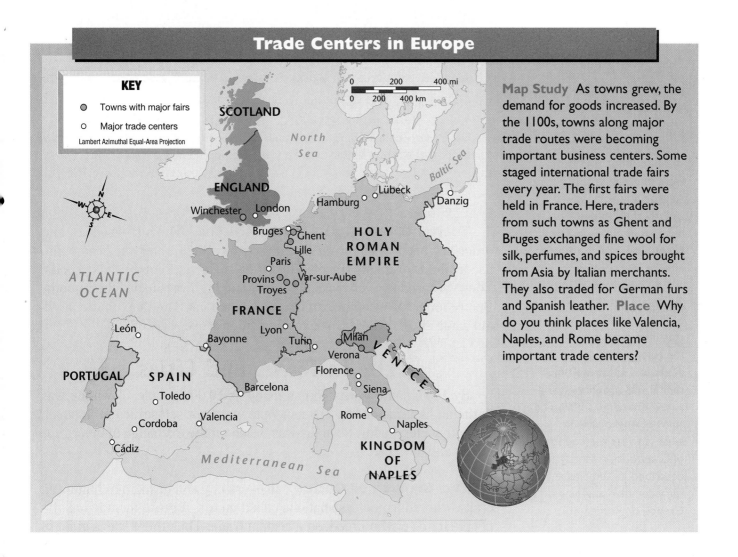

Trade Centers in Europe

KEY
● Towns with major fairs
○ Major trade centers
Lambert Azimuthal Equal-Area Projection

Map Study As towns grew, the demand for goods increased. By the 1100s, towns along major trade routes were becoming important business centers. Some staged international trade fairs every year. The first fairs were held in France. Here, traders from such towns as Ghent and Bruges exchanged fine wool for silk, perfumes, and spices brought from Asia by Italian merchants. They also traded for German furs and Spanish leather. **Place** Why do you think places like Valencia, Naples, and Rome became important trade centers?

Most medieval towns had a market where local and foreign goods were sold. This scene shows grocers at work. Carpenters, barbers, butchers, bakers, and other tradespeople also might have stalls at the market. **Critical Thinking** How are medieval markets similar to the places you shop? How are they different?

LINKS ACROSS THE WORLD

Angkor: An Asian Capital
When London and Paris were growing into cities, Angkor (AN kor) was already the capital of a huge empire in Asia. The Hindu rulers of the Khmer empire founded Angkor in A.D. 802. For more than 300 years, the city grew. Each ruler built more magnificent temples than the ruler before him. Then, in about 1431, the Khmer capital was abandoned and a new capital was built. The ruins of Angkor are in what is today the country of Cambodia. Visitors have described its temples as "grander than anything in Greece or Rome."

Towns Grow Along Trade Routes   The increased law and order in Europe also meant that trade routes and waterways came into use again. Merchants traveled to Africa and Asia to buy valued goods. They gathered at river crossings and along highways to sell their goods. Before long, towns sprang up in these locations. The map on the previous page shows where these trading cities arose.

Life in Towns and Cities

By 1400, some towns had as many as 10,000 people. Town life was not at all like manor life. Townspeople were not self-sufficient. Instead, like our society today, town life was based on the exchange of money for goods and services.

The Growth of Guilds   In every city and town, merchants and craftworkers formed associations called guilds. A **guild** included all the people in town who practiced a certain trade. Thus there was a guild of weavers; another of grocers; and another of masons, or people who worked with stone. Each guild made rules to help its members earn good wages. The guilds set prices and prevented outsiders from selling goods in town. They also set standards for the quality of goods. Those who belonged to guilds paid dues. This money was used to help needy members, or to support the families of members who had died.

Women also worked actively in the guilds. Girls became apprentices in guilds for weaving, papermaking, surgery, and so on. An **apprentice** is an unpaid worker being trained in a craft. Women often joined the same guild as their fathers or husbands. Because they were familiar with the family craft, they often kept the shops in which finished goods were sold.

Between the ages of 8 and 14, a boy who wanted to learn a certain craft became an apprentice. He lived and worked in the home of a guild master. After seven years, the boy became a journeyman. He traveled from town to town, working with different masters. In time, guild officials examined the journeyman's work. If it met their standards, he could join the guild.

Overcrowding and Disease Organizing guilds helped medieval people improve their lives. Yet there was much they did not know about making healthy cities. Cities often had walls for protection,

READ ACTIVELY

Connect How is your education different from that of a guild apprentice?

A Master and His Apprentice

At the left of this picture, an apothecary, or maker of medicines, checks his books. In the center, his apprentice weighs out a prescription for a customer. On the right, a worker, possibly a journeyman, grinds powders with a mortar and pestle. Journeymen often were not well paid. Also, it might take them several years before they could win acceptance into a guild and become masters themselves. **Critical Thinking** Why do you think the guild system was set up?

so space in them was limited. Houses were crowded together, streets were filthy with waste thrown from windows, and sicknesses spread quickly.

One disease, the Black Death, wiped out a third of Europe's population—that's one out of every three people—in just four years. The Black Death was another name for bubonic plague, a disease spread by fleas on rats. By the time victims noticed the swellings and black bruises that were symptoms of the disease, it was too late. Death usually followed quickly. As one French clergyman wrote, "He who was well one day was dead the next." At its height, the Black Death claimed 800 people each day in the city of Paris. It would take centuries for people in Europe to begin to make their cities clean, healthy places to live.

▼ This 1300s painting shows the people of Tournai, a city in what today is Belgium, burying victims of the Black Death. About 25 million Europeans were killed by the bubonic plague.

Medieval Culture and Learning

Despite the hardships, medieval life was not all a struggle for survival. The growing cities attracted traveling scholars, and young men flocked to cathedral schools to hear their lectures. By 1200, many cathedral schools had become universities with full-time scholars. Students studied subjects such as grammar, reasoning, and mathematics. Some even went on to higher studies in philosophy, law, or medicine.

Writing about chivalry blossomed in the Middle Ages. **Chivalry** was the name for the noble qualities knights were supposed to have. A knight was supposed to be brave and loyal and do heroic deeds to win the love of a worthy woman. Traveling performers called **troubadours** (TROO buh dorz) wandered from place to place singing about the chivalrous deeds performed by knights for their ladies.

SECTION 2 REVIEW

1. **Define** (a) clergy, (b) excommunicate, (c) guild, (d) apprentice, (e) chivalry, (f) troubadour.

2. Why was the Church so important to people during the Middle Ages?

3. What major changes took place in medieval society as trade became more important?

Critical Thinking

4. **Drawing Conclusions** (a) What might a serf gain by escaping to town? (b) What would the serf lose?

Activity

5. **Writing to Learn** Do you think a young person should be expected to start learning a trade between the ages of 8 and 14? Write a paragraph expressing your views. Give reasons for your answer.

The Crusades

Reach Into Your Background

In this section, you are going to read about wars fought over religion and resources.

Think of other reasons why people go to war. Do you accept these reasons? Why or why not?

Questions to Explore

1. Why did the Crusades take place?
2. How did the Crusades cause lasting changes in Europe?

Key Term
Crusades

Key People and Places
Pope Urban II
Peter the Hermit
Saladin
Holy Land
Jerusalem

On November 18, 1095, a crowd gathered in the French town of Clermont to hear an urgent message from Pope Urban II:

> "You common people who have been miserable sinners, become soldiers of Christ! You nobles, do not [quarrel] with one another. Use your arms in a just war! Labor for everlasting reward."

▼ This picture shows Pope Urban II calling for a crusade to the Holy Land.

The war to which Pope Urban II called the people of Europe was in Palestine, a small region on the eastern shore of the Mediterranean Sea. Jews, Christians, and Muslims called this place the "Holy Land." To all three religions it was sacred. Now, said the Pope, the Holy Land had fallen to an enemy. Christians must win it back.

Causes of the Crusades

Over the next 200 years, the Church launched eight bloody wars to capture Palestine. These wars are called the **Crusades.** The word comes from *crux,* the Latin word for "cross." Crusaders, from knights to peasants, carried the Christian cross into battle against the enemy, the Fatimid dynasty and later, the Seljuk (SEL jook) Turks. Under the

Huge armies of crusader knights sailed to Palestine hoping to drive the Muslim Turks from the Holy Land.

This container, called "The Right Arm of Saint Louis," held the remains of Louis IX of France. He led a crusade to the Holy Land in 1248.

Fatimid caliph al-Hakim, the Christians and Jews were treated harshly and many churches were destroyed. The Fatimids had many enemies, among whom were the Seljuks, who eventually gained control of the Holy Land.

The Rise of the Turks The Seljuks, a Turkish ethnic group, came from Central Asia. They moved into Southwest Asia, where they became Muslims. By 1071, the Turks had invaded and captured much of the Byzantine empire. Then they took the sacred city of Jerusalem from the Byzantines.

The Byzantine emperor in Constantinople asked Pope Urban II to send knights to fight the invaders. The pope agreed.

Attacks on Pilgrims Since about A.D. 300, European Christians had been traveling to Jerusalem. These people were pilgrims—people who journey to a sacred place. When the Turks took over Palestine, they turned the pilgrims away. Some were attacked and murdered. The violence occurred even though Islamic teaching states that Jews and Christians are fellow believers in God. The Turks' attacks gave the pope a religious reason to call Christians to action.

Land, Trade, and Wealth The Church had other reasons for launching the Crusades. Europeans wanted not only Palestine's holy sites, but control of its key trade routes between Africa, Asia, and Europe as well. The map on the next page shows Palestine's ideal location lying close to three continents.

The Church also had its eye on the rich empire of the Byzantines. Although Pope Urban II had agreed to help the Byzantine emperor, the two were rivals. The pope hoped to weaken the Byzantine empire and control its wealthy trade routes. This possibility encouraged European merchants to join the crusaders.

A Series of Crusades

Urban II's best hope for reopening the Holy Land rested with the lords and their trained, experienced knights. But before the lords could assemble armies, a band of common people set out to fight the Muslims.

Peter the Hermit and the People's Crusade   In 1096, before the First Crusade, Peter the Hermit, a small, ordinary-looking man who wore monk's robes, gathered an army of common people. In some cases, whole villages packed up and followed him.

Peter, however, had no experience in organizing such a large group. As more people joined, food became scarce. Crusaders broke away to loot towns. Many died when local troops fought back. Others were taken prisoner.

READ ACTIVELY

Visualize Visualize a day's march as you follow Peter.

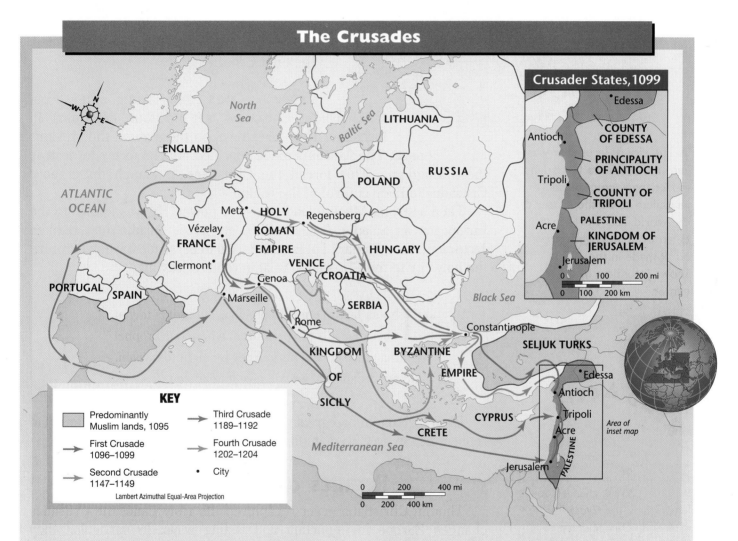

The Crusades

Crusader States, 1099

KEY

- Predominantly Muslim lands, 1095
- → First Crusade 1096–1099
- → Second Crusade 1147–1149
- → Third Crusade 1189–1192
- → Fourth Crusade 1202–1204
- • City

Lambert Azimuthal Equal-Area Projection

0   200   400 mi
0   200   400 km

Map Study In 1099, after the First Crusade, the crusaders set up four separate states in the Holy Land. These states are shown in detail on the inset map. Later crusades—including several not shown on the map—were launched to protect the crusader states. Even so, by the late 1200s, Muslim forces had retaken all of the Holy Land. **Movement** In which crusade did crusaders travel to the Holy Land mostly by sea? Which crusade did not reach the Holy Land? Where did it end?

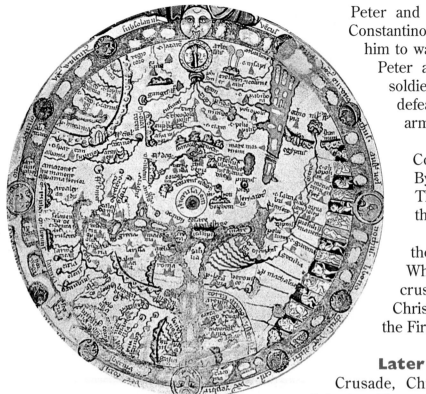

Peter and the rest of his army went on to Constantinople. The Byzantine emperor advised him to wait for help from an army of knights. Peter agreed, but his army rebelled. His soldiers attacked the Turks, who easily defeated them. Only a small part of his army survived.

At last, armies of knights arrived in Constantinople. They treated the Byzantines badly, killing and looting. The Byzantines regretted asking for their help.

Joined by the last of Peter's army, the knights captured Jerusalem in 1099. While taking control of the city, the crusaders killed 10,000 of its Muslim, Christian, and Jewish inhabitants. This was the First Crusade.

▲ The city of Jerusalem was very important to Christians. In fact, many considered Jerusalem to be the center of the world. This world map, taken from an English prayer book made in the 1200s, shows Jerusalem in the center.

Later Crusades After the First Crusade, Christians set up four kingdoms in Palestine. They are shown on the map on the previous page. The Muslims made repeated attacks to try to destroy these kingdoms. This forced the Christians to launch three more Crusades to keep control of the region.

Then a strong Muslim leader rose to power. He was known to the Europeans as Saladin (SAL uh din). By 1187, Saladin had retaken Jerusalem. King Richard I of England tried to persuade Saladin to return the holy city to the Christians. Saladin refused, saying:

READ ACTIVELY

Predict What changes do you think the Crusades made in European life?

66To us Jerusalem is as precious . . . as it is to you, because it is the place from where our Prophet [Muhammad] made his journey by night to heaven. . . . Do not dream that we will give it up to you.99

Even so, Saladin had great respect for King Richard. So he agreed to reopen the city to Christian pilgrims.

Results of the Crusades

Though Christians never recaptured the Holy Land, the Crusades changed Europe in important and lasting ways. In particular, they increased trade and made the use of money more common.

For much of the Middle Ages, most people tended not to use money. Instead they exchanged services for land or protection. But crusading nobles needed to buy armor and supplies. They raised money by letting individuals, and also whole towns that were built on their lands, buy

The Beginnings of Banking

As the use of money grew, so did the banking industry. The earliest European banks were set up in the great Italian trade cities, such as Florence, Siena, and Venice. This picture shows Italian bankers taking deposits and issuing loans. **Critical Thinking** How did the Crusades contribute to the growth of banking?

An Expanded World
During the Crusades, European Christians learned much about the world outside Europe. They came into contact with new people, places, and ideas. They came to understand that millions of people lived in regions they had not even known existed. Some Europeans traveled to far-off places. Most of these travelers were either traders or priests hoping to convert people to Christianity. Francesco Pegolottia (frahn CHAY scoh pay goh LAWT tee uh), a merchant from Florence, Italy, was one of these travelers. His book, *Merchant's Handbook,* was a valuable manual about trading with Asia.

their freedom. In this way, feudalism grew weaker, towns became more important, and money came into widespread use.

During the Crusades, European ships carried armies and supplies across the Mediterranean Sea. These ships returned from the Holy Land with rugs, jewelry, glass, and spices. Soon, these goods were in great demand. Thus, the Crusades helped trade grow during the later Middle Ages.

SECTION 3 REVIEW

1. **Define** Crusades.

2. **Identify** (a) Pope Urban II, (b) Peter the Hermit, (c) Saladin, (d) Holy Land, (e) Jerusalem.

3. (a) Why did Pope Urban II launch the Crusades? (b) What were some other reasons for the Crusades?

4. How did the Crusades lead to economic changes in Europe?

Critical Thinking

5. **Recognizing Cause and Effect** What problems led the crusaders to fail?

Activity

6. **Writing to Learn** Were Peter the Hermit and his peasant crusaders determined and brave, or just foolish? Write a newspaper editorial on this question. Give reasons for your opinion.

Using Route Maps

ichaela sat at the dining room table with her schoolbooks. Her grandmother looked up and said, "What have you got there?"

"Gram, have you ever heard of the Children's Crusade?" Michaela asked.

"Oh, yes," Gram answered. "They were the French and German children who made a pilgrimage to Jerusalem in the Middle Ages."

"They never made it across the Mediterranean Sea," Michaela said. "But they traveled all the way from France and Germany. I wonder if they had to cross the Alps!"

"Do you have a map of the route they took?" asked Gram.

"No, just a map of Europe. Isn't that enough?"

Get Ready

When people move from one place to another, they follow a certain route. Many journeys have played important roles in history, and historical route maps show the paths of such journeys. A route map shows exactly where people went and how they got there.

A route map can show many of the same things you find on other maps, such as political borders, major landforms, and bodies of water. It also includes common map features such as a title, key, scale, compass rose, and labels. On every route map, a line shows the path of the journey.

Try It Out

To understand how to use route maps, make one of your own. You will need a sheet of paper, colored pencils, a map of your community, and a ruler.

A. Make a map. Draw a simple map of the area that includes your school and your home.

B. Add symbols. Mark the location of your school and your home with appropriate symbols. Identify the symbols in a map key.

C. Add routes. Using a colored pencil, draw a line to show the route you take from home to school. Use a different color to draw a line that shows another route, such as your path to visit a friend. In the map key, indicate the meanings of different colored lines.

Apply the Skill

Now that you have practiced with a modern route map of an area close to home, you have the skills you need to read a route map of a long-ago journey.

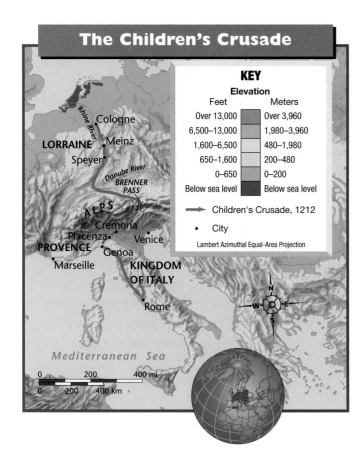

The route map below shows the path of the Children's Crusade. For background on the Crusade, read the selection in the box. Then use the information and the map to complete the activities.

The Children's Crusade

In the year A.D. 1212, thousands of young people from Germany and France began a journey to Jerusalem. The crusaders, aged 10 to 18, believed that because they were poor and faithful, God would help them capture the holy city. The children also believed that God would part the Mediterranean Sea, letting them cross to Jerusalem.

The long march took its toll on the children. Many starved to death. Others froze. When they reached the sea at Genoa and the miracle parting did not happen, many turned back. Others managed to find places on ships but were lost in storms or captured when they landed. Some almost made it as far as Rome.

1 **Become familiar with the map.** What is the map's title? Where did the Children's Crusade take place? What does the map key show?

2 **Understand the routes shown.** How is the route of the crusaders shown? Where did the crusaders begin their journey? What was their goal? Did their route take them across rivers? Across mountains? How can you tell? Where did their journey actually end?

3 **Draw conclusions.** How do you think the journeys might have affected the children? What difficulties may they have faced?

Kings and Popes

Reach Into Your Background

Nations came into being in Europe as the Middle Ages came to an end. The people of the United States come from many different backgrounds.

Sometimes we feel divided by our differences. Still, as citizens of the United States we have much in common. What makes us feel like one nation?

Questions to Explore

1. Why did kings and popes come into conflict in the Middle Ages?
2. What events made nations out of the kingdoms of Europe in the late Middle Ages?

Key Terms
nation
the Magna Carta
Parliament

Key People and Places
Pope Gregory VII
King Henry IV
King John
Joan of Arc
Runnymede
Orléans

▼ King Henry IV kneels before Pope Gregory VII and asks for his forgiveness. Countess Mathilde, shown on the right, arranged for the two men to meet.

The king regretted disobeying the pope. For three days, he waited outside the gates of the castle where Pope Gregory VII was staying. Barefoot in the winter cold, the king begged forgiveness for the mistake he had made. Would the pope forgive Henry IV of Germany?

In the Middle Ages, kings and popes often quarreled over who should pick Church officials called *bishops*. Since bishops were part of the Church, popes claimed the right to choose them. Kings also wanted this right because bishops often controlled large areas of their kingdoms.

This was the power struggle that caused Henry IV to beg for the pope's forgiveness. King Henry had been choosing bishops even though Pope Gregory VII had ordered him not to. In response, Gregory excommunicated the king and declared that his people no longer had to obey him.

Henry traveled to Gregory to beg for forgiveness. After three long days, the pope gave in. He allowed Henry to rejoin the Church.

◀ During the Middle Ages, many wealthy nobles lived in luxury. At dinner time, they might be waited on by 10 or more servants. These nobles were so rich and powerful that they rivaled kings. With the decline of feudalism, however, kings gained more power.

Nation Building Begins

Pope Gregory made a great mistake in treating King Henry IV in this way. In 1081, Henry invaded Italy, where the pope lived. By 1084, Henry had replaced Gregory with a new pope. Gregory was sent into exile and died far from his home. Henry IV's success in overthrowing Pope Gregory VII was a hint of things to come. As kings gained power, they dared to put their own wishes before those of the Church.

The Decline of Feudalism   When the 1200s began, Europe was still a feudal society. For most people, the only important authority was the local lord. He protected them from invaders and made the laws, just as our government does today.

While there were kings who reigned over kingdoms, their power was far from complete. The wealthiest lords also had great influence. Many of them saw themselves as nearly the king's equal. In fact, it was not unusual for a noble to have more land, vassals, and knights than his king.

In time, kings gained power as different forces weakened feudalism. The Crusades, for example, did much to weaken nobles. Many gave up land to raise money to join the Crusades. Other families lost their land when kings claimed the estates of nobles who died in the Crusades. Kings also began to support the new towns in exchange for money. They agreed to protect towns and made laws to help towns grow rich. Then, with the money paid by townspeople, kings hired armies and used them to attack troublesome nobles.

In these ways, kings became the main authority in their kingdoms. Gradually their kingdoms began to be real nations. A **nation** is a community that shares a government. A common language and culture are other things that sometimes unite the people of a nation.

England Becomes More United

On June 15, 1215, about 2,000 English nobles gathered at Runnymede, a meadow along the Thames River in England. Dressed in armor and carrying banners, they had marched from London, a short distance away. Now they prepared to meet with King John.

This was an unusual meeting. The king had not called it. The nobles were the ones who had demanded the meeting. King John, who once had had enormous power, had been forced to attend.

Predict What could have caused King John to attend the meeting at Runnymede?

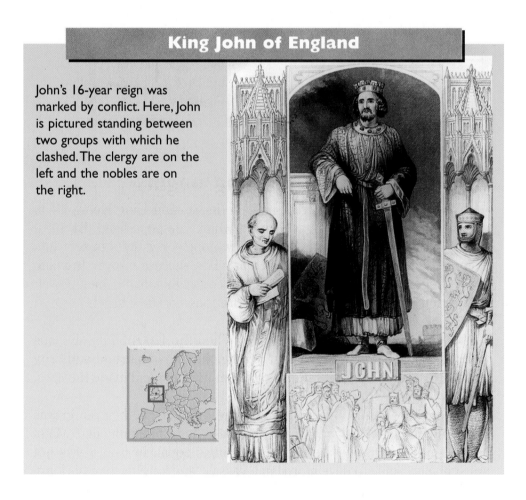

King John of England

John's 16-year reign was marked by conflict. Here, John is pictured standing between two groups with which he clashed. The clergy are on the left and the nobles are on the right.

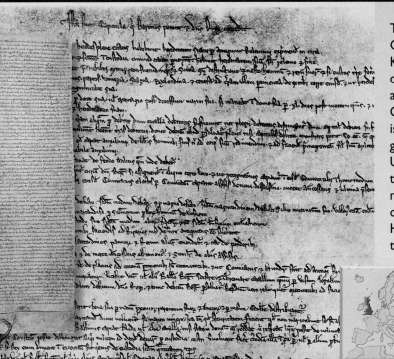

This shows a copy of the Magna Carta made many years after King John's reign. The original document, with John's seal attached, is shown in the inset. On the surface, the Magna Carta is simply a list of the nobles' grievances against King John. Underlying this list, however, is the principle that the government may not interfere with the rights of individuals. **Critical Thinking** How did the Magna Carta limit the power of English monarchs?

King John Gets Into Trouble   When John had become king of England in 1199, he quickly moved to increase his wealth and power. He taxed people heavily. He jailed his enemies unjustly and without trial. Even the most powerful nobles were hurt by John's unfair actions.

John also clashed with the pope by objecting when a man he did not like was made bishop. He seized Church property. The pope struck back by excommunicating John and declaring that he was no longer king.

The Magna Carta   John was now at the mercy of the nobles and clergy he had angered with his earlier actions. Now that he was in trouble with the pope, the nobles and clergy struck back. With the bishops' help, the nobles made a list of demands and called John to Runnymede. There he put his royal mark on their document, which was called the **Magna Carta** (MAG nuh KAR tuh), or the "Great Charter." Once John's mark was on the paper, it became law.

The Magna Carta limited a king's power over the nobles. The king could no longer jail nobles without just cause, nor could he tax them without their agreement. The Magna Carta also paved the way for the first **Parliament,** a council that would advise the English king in government matters.

In some ways, the Magna Carta made King John and the kings who followed him more powerful. Because nobles had a say in government, England became more united behind its royal ruler. It became a true nation instead of a quarreling collection of feudal fiefs.

LINKS ACROSS THE WORLD

The Declaration of Independence More than 500 years after King John signed the Magna Carta, another group demanded their rights. British colonists in North America thought that they were being treated unfairly. They complained about unfair taxation. When Parliament and the king refused to listen to their demands, the colonies declared their independence from Britain. The ideas in the Declaration of Independence are largely based on the laws and ideas that grew out of the Magna Carta.

The Hundred Years' War

The idea of nationhood was taking hold all over Europe in the late Middle Ages. In Spain, for example, a royal marriage united the king and queen of the two largest kingdoms. In Russia, Moscow's rulers were expanding their territory and their power over other princes. The new nations did, however, have many growing pains.

England and France at War   One of the difficulties these young nations had was conflict with one another. In particular, England and France often clashed. One conflict between them led to the Hundred Years' War, which lasted from 1337 to 1453.

The English king owned and controlled a large amount of land in France. In 1328, the French king died and Edward III, who was king of England, decided he should become the new king of France. The French nobles did not agree. Determined to get his way, Edward III invaded France. Many bloody battles were fought, but nothing was settled. England won most of the battles, but the French continued to fight. The war dragged on, fought by one king after another.

Joan of Arc's Victory   England continued to gain ground in the war until 1429. Then a 17-year-old peasant girl named Joan of Arc joined the French army. Deeply religious, Joan believed that God had called her to lead the French forces at the battle of Orléans (OR lay ahn). She met with the young French king and convinced him that she should

An English Victory

This battle of the Hundred Years' War took place in 1346 at Crécy (kray SEE), France. Archers armed with longbows enabled the English, at the left, to defeat a bigger French force, at the right. An English archer using a longbow could hit a target 300 yards (274 m) away. He also could fire five arrows in the time it took a French archer, who was armed with a crossbow, to shoot just one. In the Battle of Crécy, English archers killed half the French force, including about 1,500 knights.

This picture, dating from the 1400s, shows Joan of Arc's first meeting with the French king. In several battles in 1429, Joan defeated the English army and broke its spirit. To this day, the French consider Joan of Arc a heroine.

command his army. Then she went on to Orléans. There the French greeted her with hope and curiosity. One person who was there said:

> "People could not weary of seeing her, and it seemed to all a great marvel that she could sit on her horse with such ease and grace. And in truth she bore herself as highly in all ways as a man-at-arms who had followed the wars from his youth."

Under Joan's command, the French defeated the English at Orléans. She then led her forces to victory in four other battles. In 1430, Joan was taken prisoner by the English, tried as a witch, and burned at the stake. Her death came too late to help England's cause. It did not help England recover from its string of losses. By 1453, France had reclaimed all but a small portion of its lands. With the English troops in retreat, the French were on their way to becoming a strong and united nation.

SECTION 4 REVIEW

1. **Define** (a) nation, (b) the Magna Carta, (c) Parliament.

2. **Identify** (a) Pope Gregory VII, (b) Henry IV, (c) King John, (d) Joan of Arc, (e) Runnymede, (f) Orléans.

3. What caused struggles between kings and popes in the Middle Ages?

4. Describe some events that helped European kingdoms become nations in the late Middle Ages.

Critical Thinking

5. **Understanding Cause and Effect** Explain how the actions taken by England's King John led to the creation of the Magna Carta.

Activity

6. **Writing to Learn** Suppose that you are a French soldier preparing for the battle of Orléans. Describe your reaction to the news that a young peasant girl, Joan of Arc, is your new commander.

Review and Activities

Reviewing Main Ideas

1. (a) Why did the people of the Middle Ages need protection? (b) How did the feudal system provide this protection?

2. How was work divided among the people who lived on a medieval manor so that they could meet their own needs?

3. Describe what the clergy did during the Middle Ages.

4. (a) What caused towns to spring up during the Middle Ages? (b) What role did guilds play in a town?

5. (a) Why did the Church call for people to fight in the Crusades? (b) Why were merchants interested in the Crusades?

6. How did the Crusades lead to the weakening of feudalism?

7. Why did kings quarrel with popes over the appointment of Church officials?

8. How did the growing importance of kings help nations become stronger in Europe in the Middle Ages?

Reviewing Key Terms

Use each key term below in a sentence that shows the meaning of the term.

1. Middle Ages
2. feudalism
3. vassal
4. manor
5. self-sufficient
6. serf
7. clergy
8. excommunicate
9. guild
10. apprentice
11. chivalry
12. nation
13. Parliament

Critical Thinking

1. **Recognizing Cause and Effect** Provide evidence to support this statement: "As order was restored in Europe, the feudal system grew weaker."

2. **Making Comparisons** Compare a manor peasant to a guild master's apprentice. How were their lives similar? How were they different?

Graphic Organizer

Copy the chart onto a sheet of paper, then fill in the empty boxes to complete the chart.

	Place in Medieval Society	Role in Crusades	Role in Rise of Cities
Church			
Kings			
Nobles			
Peasants			
Merchants			

Map Activity

Europe and the Holy Land

For each place listed below, write the letter from the map that shows its location.

1. England

2. France

3. Jerusalem

4. Mediterranean Sea

5. Rome

6. Constantinople

Writing Activity

Write a Letter

In this chapter, you have met medieval people from all walks of life. Suppose that you could interview one of these people, famous or unknown, to find out more about his or her life. Write a letter in which you introduce yourself to this person and ask for an interview. Be sure to explain why the person's life interests you, and what you want to learn by interviewing him or her.

Take It to the NET

Activity Take a tour through the Middle Ages to learn more about the Crusades and daily life in medieval times. For help in completing this activity, visit www.phschool.com.

Chapter 5 Self-Test To review what you have learned, take the Chapter 5 Self-Test and get instant feedback on your answers. Go to www.phschool.com to take the test.

Skills Review

Turn to the Skills Activity.

Review how to use route maps. Then answer the following questions: (a) How does a route map differ from other maps? (b) Why is the map key important?

How Am I Doing?

Answer these questions to help you check your progress.

1. Can I describe the feudal pyramid and the manor system of medieval Europe?

2. Can I explain why medieval cities developed and describe what they were like?

3. Do I understand the causes and effects of the Crusades?

4. Do I know how medieval kingdoms grew into strong nations?

5. What information from this chapter can I include in my journal?

Of Swords and Sorcerers

FROM THE ADVENTURES OF KING ARTHUR AND HIS KNIGHTS BY MARGARET HODGES AND MARGERY EVERNDEN

BEFORE YOU READ

Reach Into Your Background

How should a good and just ruler behave? What traits should a king or queen have? What do you admire in people who lead others?

People have read and enjoyed the stories of King Arthur for hundreds of years. To many, he symbolizes the virtue and justice of a good ruler. According to legend, he was loved and respected by all of his people.

Legends about King Arthur exist in many forms, and stories about him have been written and rewritten in several languages. The following selection is one tale of Arthur's meeting his friend Pellinore and finding his sword named Excalibur.

Questions to Explore

1. Why did King Arthur's subjects consider him such a good king?
2. Who is Merlin? What role does he play in this story?

---

petty *adj.*: unimportant; of low rank

fealty *n.*: loyalty to a feudal lord

gimlet *adj.*: having a piercing quality

malice *n.*: mean wish to damage or hurt someone

No king before Arthur had been able to unite the realm and rule it. This Arthur did. Lightnings and thunders surrounded him as he fought. In twelve great battles he defeated petty kings who had been constantly at war, laying waste all the land. The last to surrender was Arthur's own brother-in-law, King Lot of Orkney. When Lot laid down his arms and swore fealty to Arthur, he sent his sons to become knights at Camelot.

One son was Gawain, handsome and strong, whom Arthur called Gawain the Courteous. Another was Mordred, whose foxy smile and gimlet eyes concealed malice and a thirst for power. Gawain took the vows of knighthood in good faith, but Mordred's vows were insincere, and he soon began listening at the castle doors in hope of ferreting out secrets that might damage the court and someday play into his own hands. He saw that the time to strike

◀ The Round Table of King Arthur and his knights.

had not yet come. The powers of heaven and earth all seemed to be on Arthur's side. The people loved him, and Camelot was in its glory.

Now there came a day when Arthur rode with Merlin seeking adventure, and in a forest they found a knight named Pellinore, seated in a chair, blocking their path.

"Sir, will you let us pass?" said Arthur.

"Not without a fight," replied Pellinore. "Such is my custom."

"I will change your custom," said Arthur.

"I will defend it," said Pellinore. He mounted his horse and took his shield on his arm. Then the two knights rode against each other, and each splintered his spear on the other's shield.

"I have no more spears," said Arthur. "Let us fight with swords."

"Not so," said Pellinore. "I have enough spears. I will lend you one."

Then a squire brought two good spears, and the two knights rode against each other again until those spears were broken.

"You are as good a fighter as ever I met," said Pellinore. "Let us try again."

Two great spears were brought, and this time Pellinore struck Arthur's shield so hard that the king and his horse fell to the earth.

Then Arthur pulled out his sword and said, "I have lost the battle on horseback. Let me try you on foot."

Predict Who will win the fight?

▶ Several suits of armor perhaps similar to those of the knights of the Round Table.

READ ACTIVELY

Ask Questions What more would you like to know about King Arthur?

wrath *n.:* great anger or rage
hermit *n.:* person who lives alone and away from others
salve *n.:* an oily substance used as medicine on the skin

Pellinore thought it unfair to attack from his horse, so he dismounted and came toward Arthur with his sword drawn. Then began such a battle that both were covered with blood. After a while they sat down to rest and fought again until both fell to the ground. Again they fought, and the fight was even. But at last Pellinore struck such a blow that Arthur's sword broke into two pieces. Thereupon the king leaped at Pellinore. He threw him down and pulled off his helmet. But Pellinore was a very big man and strong enough to wrestle Arthur under him and pull off the king's helmet. All this time Merlin had watched, silent, but when he saw that Pellinore was about to cut off Arthur's head, he interfered.

"Do not kill this man," he said to Pellinore. "You do not know who he is."

"Why, who is he?" said the knight.

"It is King Arthur," said Merlin.

When he heard this, Pellinore trembled with fear of the royal wrath, for he would not knowingly have fought against the king. Then Merlin cast a spell of sleep on Pellinore so that he fell to the earth as if dead.

"Alas," said Arthur, "you have killed the best knight I ever fought."

"Have no fear," said Merlin. "He will awake in three hours as well as ever he was."

Then he mounted Pellinore's horse and led Arthur to a hermit, who bound up the king's wounds and healed them with good salves, so that he might ride again and go on his way.

But Arthur said, "I have no sword."

"Never fear," said Merlin. "Not far away is a sword that can be yours." So they rode on until they came to a broad lake of clear water. Far out in the middle of the lake Arthur saw an arm clothed in shining white and holding a noble sword, its golden hilt richly set with jewels.

"Lo," said Merlin, "yonder is the sword Excalibur."

Then they saw a lady floating toward them as if she walked on the water. Her garments were like a mist around her.

"That is the Lady of the Lake," said Merlin. "Within the lake is a rock, and within the rock is a palace, and within the palace lives this lady with many other ladies who serve her. She is called Vivien. Speak to her as a friend, and she will give you that sword."

So, when she had come close, Arthur said to her, "Lady, I wish that sword were mine, for I have no sword."

"It shall be yours," said the lady, and she showed Arthur a little boat lying at the edge of the lake. "Row out to the sword," she said. "Take it with its scabbard." Then she disappeared. Arthur and Merlin rowed out into the lake, and Arthur took the sword from the hand that held it. And the arm and the hand vanished under the water.

Arthur and Merlin rowed to shore and went on their way, and whenever Arthur looked on the sword, he liked it well.

"Which do you like better?" asked Merlin. "The sword or the scabbard?"

"I like the sword better," said Arthur.

"The scabbard is worth ten such swords," said Merlin, "for while you wear the scabbard, you will never lose blood, no matter how sorely you are wounded."

So they rode back to Arthur's court, and all his knights marveled when they heard that the king risked his life in single combat as his poor knights did. They said it was merry to be under such a chieftain.

READ ACTIVELY

Visualize Picture the Lady of the Lake as she floats across the water.

scabbard *n.*: a case or cover for a sword or dagger
chieftain *n.*: the head of a clan; leader of many people

EXPLORING YOUR READING

Look Back
1. Why did Arthur fight Pellinore?
2. What gift does Arthur receive at the end of the story?

Think It Over
3. Describe how Arthur and Pellinore fight.

4. How do you think the fight would have ended if Merlin had not interfered? Why do you think so?
5. How do Arthur's subjects feel about him? What did his knights think when they heard about his fight with Pellinore?

Go Beyond
6. What qualities does Arthur have that make him a good ruler? What kind of a ruler do you think he would be in today's world? Why?

Ideas for Writing: Poem
7. Many characters in myths and legends have tools or weapons that protect them or give them special powers. Write a poem about a character who receives one such tool. What are its powers? How does it help your character?

CHAPTER 6

A New Age in Europe

SECTION 1
The Renaissance and Reformation

SECTION 2
The Age of Exploration

SECTION 3
The Age of Powerful Kings

SECTION 4
Conquests in the Americas and Africa

PICTURE ACTIVITIES

The late 1400s began an age of great change in Europe. One aspect of this change was a new sense of curiosity about other lands. The picture above shows a replica, or exact copy, of one of the ships commanded by Christopher Columbus when he crossed the Atlantic Ocean to the Americas in 1492. To learn more about exploration and other changes of this period, do the following activities.

Study the picture
What do you notice about the design of the ship that might make it suitable for undertaking long ocean voyages? What kind of storage areas do you think the ship has?

Make connections
What do you think might cause people to set out on a voyage into the unknown? Would you make such a trip? Why or why not?

The Renaissance and Reformation

Reach Into Your Background

What do you do when you think of or hear about an interesting new idea? You probably share it. Maybe you share it by telling someone else about it. During the Renaissance and Reformation, many people in Europe had new ideas they wanted to share.

Questions to Explore

1. Why did the Renaissance begin in northern Italy rather than in northern Europe?
2. Why did many northern European leaders want to adopt Protestant religions?

Key Terms

Renaissance
perspective
Reformation
indulgence
Protestant

Key People and Places

Leonardo da Vinci
Michelangelo
Martin Luther
Florence

Have you ever wanted to fly like a bird? Leonardo da Vinci (lee uh NAR doh duh VIN chee) did. This brilliant artist and scientist who lived about 500 years ago thought that people could learn to fly. He studied birds and bats, as well as winged toys and seeds, to learn about flying.

Leonardo never built a working airplane. But, as you can see from his drawings, he drew plans for one. He also made drawings of what looked like early examples of a parachute and a helicopter.

Leonardo was just one of many gifted Europeans who lived between 1300 and about 1600. This was the time of the **Renaissance** (REN uh sahns), or rebirth of learning in Europe. Toward the end of the Middle Ages, people again became deeply interested in art,

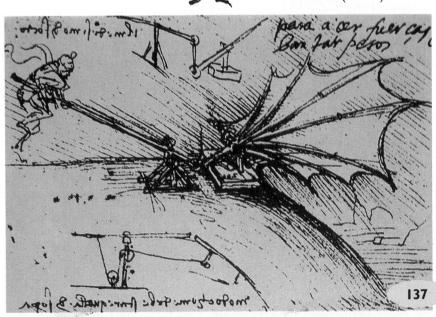

▼ Leonardo's drawing of a parachute (left) looks very much like the real thing. He used what he had learned about bat wings in this idea for a flying machine (below).

137

FIORENZA

▲ The city-state of Florence on the Arno River was an important center of the Renaissance in Italy. Its artists and poets were supported by the city's wealthy merchants and bankers.

ACROSS THE WORLD

Building on the Past
People during the Renaissance did not work in isolation. Often, they built upon ideas and methods brought to Europe from other parts of the world. The learning that was carried to Spain by the Muslims of North Africa was an important part of this exchange. For example, the Muslims reintroduced the works of Aristotle and other Greek thinkers and scientists to Europe.

literature, science, and many other subjects. People changed the way they saw themselves and their world. The Renaissance began in northern Italy and spread to the rest of Europe.

The World That Made Leonardo

Italy, where Leonardo lived, was an unusual place. During the Middle Ages, life in Italy was easier than in much of the rest of Western Europe. People in northern Europe were threatened by war and disease. They depended on the protection of the clergy and local lords, who were controlled by popes and kings.

But in northern Italy people lived in city-states, or cities that had self-rule. The lives of these people were not as closely controlled by popes and kings. Instead, power was held by wealthy merchants. These merchants controlled European trade with Asia. Muslim traders brought precious goods like silk and spices from the East to the Mediterranean. From here, Italian merchants transported the goods throughout Europe, reselling them at top prices.

Because of their wealth from trade, some northern Italians had more time to think, to read, and to create and enjoy art. In the world of Renaissance Italy, artists competed for fame and money like athletes of today. Wealthy and powerful families sponsored artists and art schools. Because they were proud of their cities and their families, the wealthy built fine homes. Many were religious people who expressed their love of God by spending money to build and decorate churches. Others hoped that offerings of beautiful works of art would lead God to forgive their sins. Some popes sponsored the arts because they hoped to inspire loyalty to the Church.

The Renaissance Artist

From its birthplace in northern Italy, the Renaissance spread to other European lands. After all, Italian artists had much to teach other Europeans. They had studied and copied the classical art of ancient Greece and Rome. Like the artists of these two civilizations, they wanted to show things as they really were.

Techniques Used by Artists To better understand how to draw and paint people, Italian artists studied the bones, muscles, and organs of the body. They used **perspective** in their paintings. This is the technique of showing objects as they appear to the eye. One of the ways they did this was to make distant objects smaller in relation to closer objects. This made scenes in their paintings look as they appeared to the human eye. In addition, they used light and shadow to make the things they painted look solid.

Michelangelo and the Sistine Chapel Michelangelo (my kul AN juh loh) was one of these artists. Sponsored by Lorenzo de Medici (loh RENT soh duh MED uh chee), a wealthy citizen of Florence, and others, Michelangelo began his career as a sculptor. He carved marble so that it looked like flowing cloth, rippling muscle, and twisting hair. But his most famous work is a painting, not a sculpture. Actually, it is many paintings. Together these paintings cover the ceiling and walls

▼ This statue of the Virgin Mary holding the body of her son, Jesus, in her arms, still brings an emotional response from visitors to St. Peter's Church in Rome. Michelangelo created it in 1499, when he was in his early 20s.

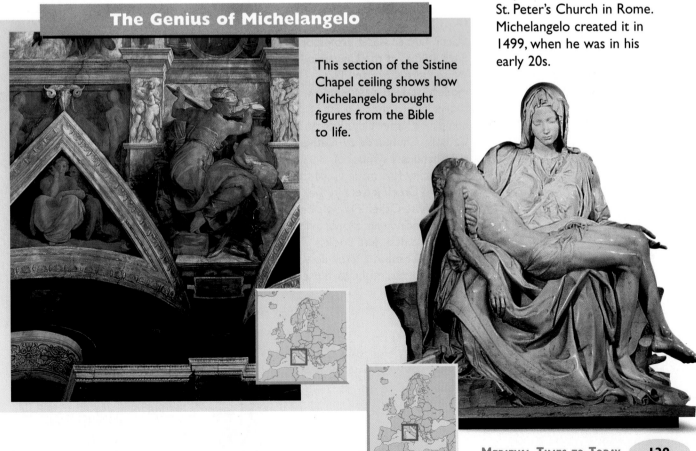

The Genius of Michelangelo

This section of the Sistine Chapel ceiling shows how Michelangelo brought figures from the Bible to life.

of the Sistine Chapel in the Vatican in Rome, Italy. Michelangelo did these paintings for Pope Julius II. See the picture on the previous page for a view of the Sistine Chapel ceiling.

It took Michelangelo about four years to finish painting the Sistine Chapel. He worked on scaffolding, or a framework, 80 feet (24 m) above the ground. Much of the time he painted lying on his back. Sometimes he stood for hours with his arm up in the air and his neck bent backward.

The pope was angry because the work took so long. Once he even hit Michelangelo with his cane and threatened to push him from the scaffolding. But Michelangelo kept working. When he finished, viewers were amazed. Michelangelo had used his artist's understanding of bone and muscle to bring scenes from the Bible to life in paint.

The Reformation

Michelangelo's work showed the great power of the Roman Catholic Church in his time. But not everyone was happy with the Church. In 1517, five years after Michelangelo finished painting the Sistine Chapel, a German monk named Martin Luther sharply criticized the Church. Luther nailed a list of his complaints on the door of a church in Wittenberg, Germany. This act changed the religion of his times. The change he caused was called the **Reformation** because it was meant to reform, or improve, religious customs.

Martin Luther Speaks Out

Martin Luther was a professor of Bible studies at the University in Wittenberg, Germany. This modern stained-glass window shows him nailing up a list of complaints against the Roman Catholic Church. Below Luther's right hand is a symbol of Christianity. It is made up of the first two Greek letters in the word *Christ*. Other symbols on the window include an ink pot with a quill pen, a desk, and books. **Critical Thinking** Why do you think the artist might have used these symbols?

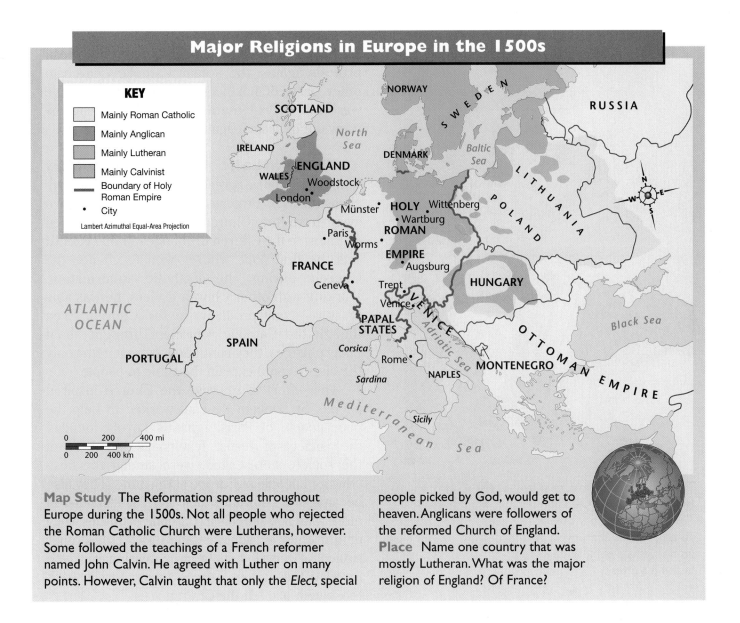

Major Religions in Europe in the 1500s

KEY

- Mainly Roman Catholic
- Mainly Anglican
- Mainly Lutheran
- Mainly Calvinist
- ━━━ Boundary of Holy Roman Empire
- • City

Lambert Azimuthal Equal-Area Projection

NORWAY
SWEDEN
RUSSIA
SCOTLAND
North Sea
IRELAND
Baltic Sea
DENMARK
LITHUANIA
ENGLAND
WALES
Woodstock
London
Münster
HOLY • Wittenberg
• Wartburg
ROMAN
Paris
Worms
EMPIRE
FRANCE
• Augsburg
Geneva
Trent
HUNGARY
Venice
VENICE
ATLANTIC OCEAN
Black Sea
PAPAL STATES
Adriatic Sea
SPAIN
OTTOMAN EMPIRE
PORTUGAL
Corsica
Rome
MONTENEGRO
Sardina
NAPLES
Mediterranean Sea
Sicily

0 200 400 mi
0 200 400 km

Map Study The Reformation spread throughout Europe during the 1500s. Not all people who rejected the Roman Catholic Church were Lutherans, however. Some followed the teachings of a French reformer named John Calvin. He agreed with Luther on many points. However, Calvin taught that only the *Elect*, special people picked by God, would get to heaven. Anglicans were followers of the reformed Church of England.

Place Name one country that was mostly Lutheran. What was the major religion of England? Of France?

The Protestant Reformation Luther's beliefs were very different from those of the pope. According to Luther, people did not need bishops and popes to tell them what God wanted them to do. Belief in God, not obedience to the Church, was the key to getting into heaven.

Luther especially disliked the way the Church raised money by selling **indulgences,** official pardons given by the pope. If people committed a sin, they could pay money to the Church for an indulgence and be forgiven. Luther believed that the Church did not have the power to do this.

In Germany, princes and nobles who disliked the power of the pope quickly accepted Luther's ideas. These rulers wanted to collect their own taxes and make their own laws. They wanted the same powers enjoyed by the leaders of Italy's city-states. By the time Luther died, most of what is now northern Germany was Lutheran. That is, people there believed in Luther's ideas about how to be a Christian, not in the ideas of the Roman Catholic Church.

The words in the book held by Ignatius Loyola are the Latin for "To the greater glory of God." To achieve this aim, Loyola gave up his life as a noble in Spain to become a priest.

People with views similar to Luther's spread protests against the Roman Catholic Church to other parts of northern Europe. These people were called **Protestants** because their religions grew out of protest against Roman Catholicism.

The Catholic Reformation Many Roman Catholics agreed with some of the criticisms made by Protestants. But they did not turn away from the Church. Instead, they worked from inside the Church to change it. Pope Paul III was the first pope who worked to change the Church during the Catholic Reformation. Working with other Church leaders, he was able to solve many problems in the Church. Even though the Catholic reformers brought about many changes, they continued to preach that only the clergy could explain the Bible to people.

This effort to improve the Church inspired people. St. Vincent de Paul worked to help the poor people of Paris. Ignatius Loyola founded the Society of Jesus. Jesuits, as members of the society were called, were among the best-educated people of Europe at this time. They also became well known for their work as teachers. In more than 500 schools in Catholic countries, they taught children about religion as well as other subjects. Many Jesuits became missionaries who traveled throughout Europe trying to win back those who had left the Church.

SECTION 1 REVIEW

1. Define (a) Renaissance, (b) perspective, (c) Reformation, (d) indulgence, (e) Protestant.

2. Identify (a) Leonardo da Vinci, (b) Michelangelo, (c) Martin Luther, (d) Florence.

3. What conditions in northern Italy led to the Renaissance?

4. Why did kings and nobles in northern Europe want to break away from the Roman Catholic Church?

Critical Thinking

5. Identifying Central Issues Why do you think people were so astonished by Michelangelo's work in the Sistine Chapel?

Activity

6. Writing to Learn You are a Catholic who thinks that your Church needs to reform. Write a letter to a friend explaining why changes are needed.

The Age of Exploration

Reach Into Your Background

Think about a time when you traveled to a new place, alone or with your family. Perhaps you asked directions before you went. Maybe someone looked at a map. Did you get lost? Did you see things that surprised you?

Questions to Explore

1. How did Portugal lead the way in European exploration of the world outside Europe?
2. How did other explorers help Europeans learn about new lands?

Key Terms

navigator
caravel
astrolabe
circumnavigate

Key People and Places

Henry the Navigator
Ferdinand Magellan
Cape Bojador
Strait of Magellan

Look at the map on this page. It was drawn in the 1470s by an Italian mapmaker. Europe, Asia, and Africa cover the whole map. The Americas are nowhere to be seen.

At this time, Europeans had done little exploring beyond their own shores. In fact, the vast majority of Europeans never left their own town or village. They had very little knowledge of, or interest in, other lands. With the new spirit of curiosity of the Renaissance, however, their attitudes began to change.

Europe Expands Its Horizons

By the early 1400s, people in many European countries had grown tired of paying high prices to Italian merchants for Asian goods. They wanted to gain control of the rich trade with the East themselves. They realized that to do this they would have to find a new trade route to Asia.

▼ This map is from one of the world's oldest printed atlases.

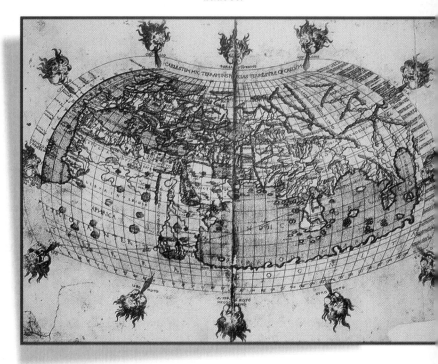

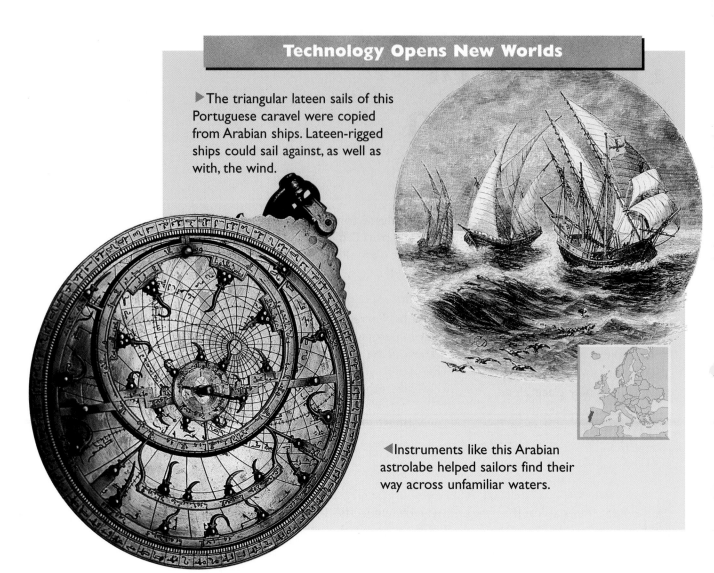

▶The triangular lateen sails of this Portuguese caravel were copied from Arabian ships. Lateen-rigged ships could sail against, as well as with, the wind.

◀Instruments like this Arabian astrolabe helped sailors find their way across unfamiliar waters.

Portugal Takes the Lead Find the political map of Europe in the Atlas at the back of your book. Notice that Portugal is located where the southwestern tip of the continent juts out into the Atlantic Ocean. Would it surprise you to learn that a country with this location has had a long history of seafaring? Portuguese sailors used their great experience on the seas to lead the way in the search for the new trade route.

The success of the Portuguese was due, in large part, to Prince Henry, the son of Portugal's king. In 1419, he opened a school. He invited mapmakers, shipbuilders, and **navigators,** or expert sailors, from all over the country to attend. Although Prince Henry himself did not go exploring, his work won him the title of Henry the Navigator.

Under Prince Henry's leadership, the Portuguese made many advances. His shipbuilders designed a ship called a **caravel.** It was larger, stronger, easier to steer, and much faster than other types of ships. Portuguese sailors also became expert at navigation. They used the compass to find out which direction they were traveling. They measured their latitude, or distance north or south of the Equator, with an **astrolabe** (AS troh layb). They gathered all the information they could from other sailors to make new, more detailed charts and maps of the Atlantic.

Prince Henry thought that his sailors might find a route to Asia if they sailed south along the western coast of Africa. While they searched, they could build trading ties with the Africans they met. They could also convert these people to Christianity.

His sailors, however, were unwilling to sail beyond Cape Bojador (BAHJ uh dor). They feared what they might find beyond this small bulge in the coastline of what today is known as the western Sahara. Perhaps they would be attacked by great sea monsters. Or they might be lost forever in what Arab sailors called the "Green Sea of Darkness." Finally, one brave sailor, Gil Eanes (gil YAH neesh), did lead his crew beyond the cape. When he returned safe and sound, the others realized that their fears were unfounded.

Portuguese ships then pushed farther south along Africa's west coast. As they sailed, Portuguese sea captains gathered information on winds, currents, and coastlines. They set up trading posts, bringing such goods as gold and ivory back to Portugal. Finally, in 1497, a Portuguese captain named Vasco da Gama (VAS koh duh GAH muh) rounded the southernmost tip of Africa. From here, he sailed along the eastern coast of Africa and then across the Indian Ocean to India. He returned with a cargo of spices and precious stones. The Portuguese had set up their trade route to Asia.

READ ACTIVELY

Connect The early explorers helped people expand their understanding of the world. What kinds of explorations are people making today to help expand our understanding?

Christopher Columbus

On his first voyage across the Atlantic, Christopher Columbus commanded a fleet of three ships and a crew of about 90 sailors. The journey from Spain to the Americas took more than eight weeks to complete. Below is a copy of the first page of a letter Columbus wrote to King Ferdinand describing the voyage.

145

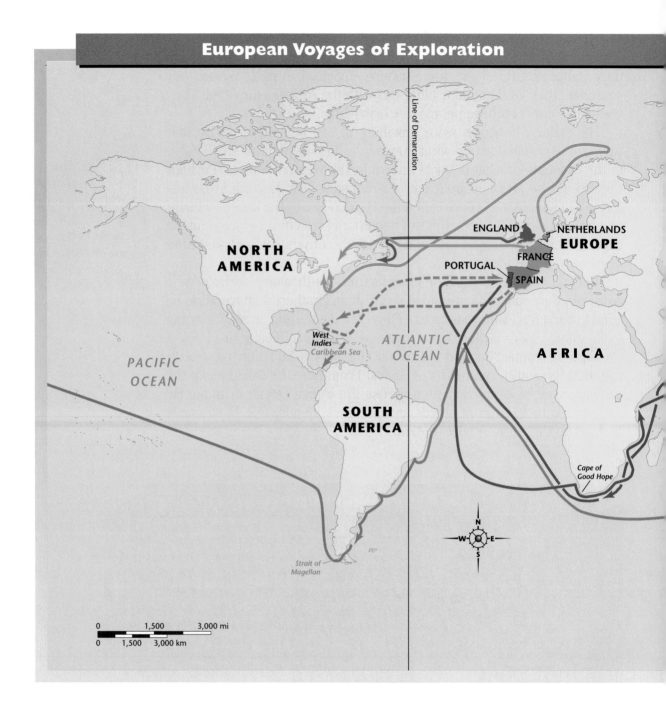

Spain's Contribution The Portuguese sailed east to find their route to Asia. An Italian sea captain named Christopher Columbus was convinced that he could reach India by sailing west, across the Atlantic.

Columbus, like many others of his time, accepted that the world was a sphere. Therefore, it made sense to him that a ship sailing west would eventually reach Asia. It made sense to Queen Isabella and King Ferdinand of Spain, too. The thought of the great riches to be gained convinced them to support Columbus's voyage.

What Columbus did not know was that two huge continents lay between Europe and Asia. Thus Columbus reached the Americas, not Asia. Soon, both Spain and Portugal would begin to carve empires out of these continents. In time, other European countries would join them.

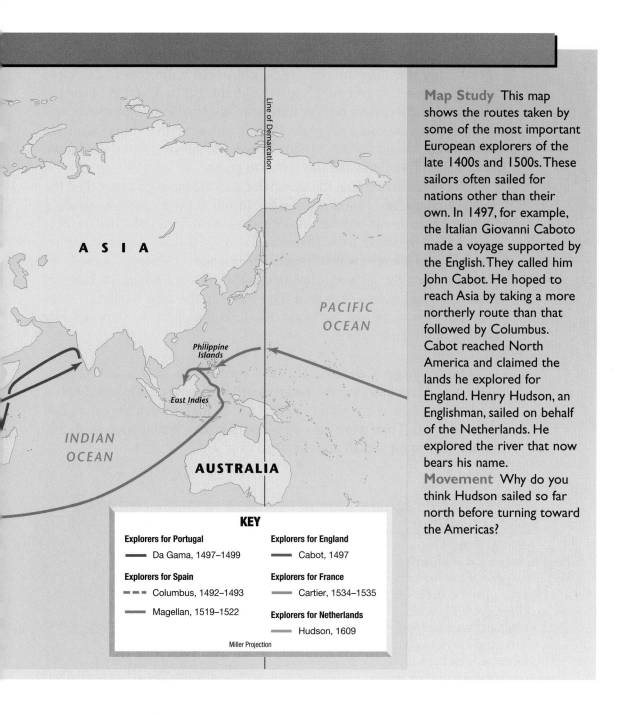

Map Study This map shows the routes taken by some of the most important European explorers of the late 1400s and 1500s. These sailors often sailed for nations other than their own. In 1497, for example, the Italian Giovanni Caboto made a voyage supported by the English. They called him John Cabot. He hoped to reach Asia by taking a more northerly route than that followed by Columbus. Cabot reached North America and claimed the lands he explored for England. Henry Hudson, an Englishman, sailed on behalf of the Netherlands. He explored the river that now bears his name.
Movement Why do you think Hudson sailed so far north before turning toward the Americas?

KEY

Explorers for Portugal	**Explorers for England**
——— Da Gama, 1497–1499	——— Cabot, 1497
Explorers for Spain	**Explorers for France**
- - - Columbus, 1492–1493	——— Cartier, 1534–1535
——— Magellan, 1519–1522	**Explorers for Netherlands**
	——— Hudson, 1609

Miller Projection

Magellan Sails Around the World

Even after Columbus reached the Americas, Europeans did not understand how large the Earth was. They believed that Japan, which they called Cipango (sib PANG goh), was separated from the Americas by only a narrow channel of water. The Portuguese sailor Ferdinand Magellan (FUR din and muh JEL un) was eager to cross that channel.

Magellan Sets Out Magellan was an officer in the Portuguese navy. However, the Portuguese king would not support his journey. Magellan then convinced the Spanish king to back him. Like Columbus, Magellan was mistaken about how far he would have to go.

Magellan set sail in 1519 with five ships and a crew of about 250 men. Shortly after reaching the coast of South America, the crews of three of the ships refused to sail on. They were afraid that they would never see home again unless they returned the way they had come. Magellan was convinced that he could not make the trip unless all five ships sailed. He needed every sailor and every ship in order to survive, so he used force as well as skill to persuade the crews to go on.

After much searching, the sailors located the passage now called the Strait of Magellan. Ships must pass through these narrow, twisting passages near the tip of South America to get from the Atlantic Ocean to the Pacific Ocean. It took Magellan 38 days to sail through. Strong currents and fierce winds made the journey difficult. Sometimes Magellan thought he was moving rapidly forward when, in fact, his ships were almost at a standstill. The winds in the sails made the ships look like they were making progress while the currents were actually holding them back.

The Voyage Continues   But even before they sailed through the straits, Magellan's crews made a terrible discovery. They had only a third as much food and water as they had thought. Their suppliers had cheated them. They were also unaware that they would soon be facing an ocean far bigger than any they had ever seen.

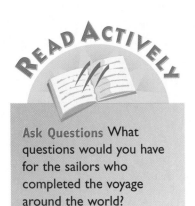

Ask Questions What questions would you have for the sailors who completed the voyage around the world?

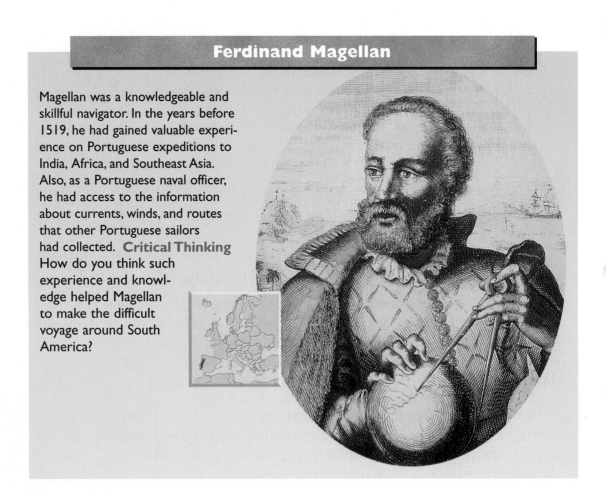

Ferdinand Magellan

Magellan was a knowledgeable and skillful navigator. In the years before 1519, he had gained valuable experience on Portuguese expeditions to India, Africa, and Southeast Asia. Also, as a Portuguese naval officer, he had access to the information about currents, winds, and routes that other Portuguese sailors had collected. **Critical Thinking** How do you think such experience and knowledge helped Magellan to make the difficult voyage around South America?

◄ Here, Magellan's ships round the southern tip of South America. Magellan named the area *Tierra del Fuego* (tee EHR uh del FWAY goh), or "Land of Fires," because his sailors saw many fires on land.

With one third of the food they had thought they needed, they continued on a journey that would be much longer than they had expected. The crews had to live on short rations. Some men starved to death or died of disease. Those who lived ate biscuits full of worms. They soaked and cooked the ox hides they had used to cover equipment on the ship. Some even ate sawdust.

Magellan's skill as a sailor took them across the Pacific Ocean. But Magellan did not live to return to Spain. He unwisely became involved in local politics in the Philippines, islands off the coast of Asia. In the spring of 1521, Magellan was killed in battle by a Philippine ruler. More than three years after leaving home, one ship returned to Spain. Of the roughly 250 sailors who had set sail with Magellan, only 18 returned. They were the first people to **circumnavigate,** or sail around, the world.

SECTION 2 REVIEW

1. **Define** (a) navigator, (b) caravel, (c) astrolabe, (d) circumnavigate.
2. **Identify** (a) Henry the Navigator, (b) Ferdinand Magellan, (c) Cape Bojador, (d) Strait of Magellan.

3. What did Henry the Navigator do to make Portugal a leader in exploration?
4. (a) Name two explorers who sailed for the monarch of Spain. (b) Explain what they accomplished.

Critical Thinking
5. **Identifying Central Issues** What special characteristics do you think an explorer needs? Explain your answer.

Activity
6. **Writing to Learn** You are a member of Ferdinand Magellan's crew. Write a journal entry about sailing across the Pacific Ocean for the first time.

The Age of Powerful Kings

BEFORE YOU READ

Reach Into Your Background

There was a time when kings and queens had the power to tell everyone else what to do. Have you ever dreamed of having such power? Have you ever wondered what it would be like to have all your commands obeyed? To have your wishes fulfilled?

Questions to Explore

1. How did the idea of divine right help make kings more powerful?
2. What actions did the rulers of Europe take to increase their power after the Middle Ages?

Key Terms
democracy
divine right
absolute monarch

Key People and Places
Louis XIV
Cardinal Richelieu
Peter the Great
Versailles

▼ This picture shows Louis XIV and his dinner guests surrounded by servants.

Louis XIV, king of France, was ready for his dinner. He would be eating alone this night. That did not mean he would be by himself. It only meant that he would be the only one eating. Although the meal had just begun, a crowd of servants already surrounded him. It was time for his meat to be brought from the kitchen. Two guards entered first. They were followed by ushers, gentlemen-in-waiting, the keeper of the king's china, and more guards. Somewhere in the crowd were the officers of the food department who actually carried the meat. In all, it required 15 people to bring the meat to Louis.

Louis asked for a drink. "Drink for the King!" cried the gentleman cupbearer. Then he turned to the chief cupbearer, who handed him a gold tray with a glass and drinks. The gentleman cupbearer, the chief cupbearer, and the chief cupbearer's attendant walked to the table. They bowed to the king, and presented the tray. The king helped himself. The gentleman cupbearer bowed to Louis and returned the tray to the chief cupbearer, who took it away. Before the king finished his meal, some 500 people would have helped to prepare and serve it.

Louis XIV was shorter than average. To make himself look taller and more powerful, he wore high-heeled shoes and tall wigs. The rich robe that he wears in this portrait is embroidered with golden fleur-de-lis (flur duh LEE) symbols. This flower-like design was the mark of French royalty. This sun symbol (below) was specially designed for Louis. **Critical Thinking** What qualities of Louis' character do you think are shown by his clothes and his specially-designed sun symbol?

The Age of Absolute Rule

Why did Louis XIV have so many people waiting on him? What right did he have to all this service? Was it just because he was the leader of France? Stop and think for a minute. What gives our government the right to lead us? We, the people, give our government that job—because we live in a democracy. In a **democracy,** the people elect representatives to govern. They choose the government. Yet not all governments are democracies.

The Divine Right of Kings   France was not a democracy in the 1600s. The people did not choose their king. They believed that God chose the king, and that the king was God's representative. The king's right to rule was divine—that is, it was thought to come directly from God. This idea is called the **divine right** of kings, and many Europeans believed in it 400 years ago.

The Growth of Absolute Monarchy   King Louis XIV was an **absolute monarch.** He had absolute, or complete, power over every part of life in his kingdom. Absolute monarchs did not share power with nobles or parliaments or the people. Louis was so powerful that he became known as the "Sun King." Just as the sun was the center of the solar system, Louis was the center of the French nation.

It is amazing to think of one person being so powerful. It took a long time for the French kings to gain absolute power. King Louis was as powerful as he was because other kings had gradually taken power away from the nobles. This process had been going on for 150 years.

Absolute Rule in France

Before Louis became king, Cardinal Richelieu (RISH loo) had served as chief minister to Louis' father, Louis XIII. For 18 years, Richelieu worked to increase the power of France and the French king. To do this, he had to destroy the power of the nobles. He allowed wealthy merchants to buy titles of nobility. Then he stripped the old nobles of some of their rights. He also started businesses for the French government. These businesses earned a great deal of money for the crown. Altogether these changes made the nobles weaker and the king wealthier and more powerful.

Louis XIV came to the French throne in 1643, a year after Richelieu's death. As Louis was only four years old, another French Church official, Cardinal Mazarin (maz uh RAN), ruled for him. When Mazarin died in 1661, Louis was glad to be rid of him. He wanted power all to himself. He took steps to further weaken the nobles. He also reduced the power of the Church. "I am the state," he declared.

Life at the Sun King's Court   One way in which Louis showed his power was with his lifestyle. He lived in incredible luxury at Versailles (vur SY), his huge palace outside Paris.

LINKS TO ART

Court Dress Nobles at Versailles dressed as though they were always on stage. Gentlemen wore richly embroidered jackets that reached to their knees. Wide sleeves showed that they had money to spend on costly fabrics. Ladies wore dresses with trains that might be 40 feet (12 m) long. The most important item was the wig. Men wore fancy, oversized wigs. Women's wigs were piled high, and trimmed with lace, ribbons, and even real birds' nests.

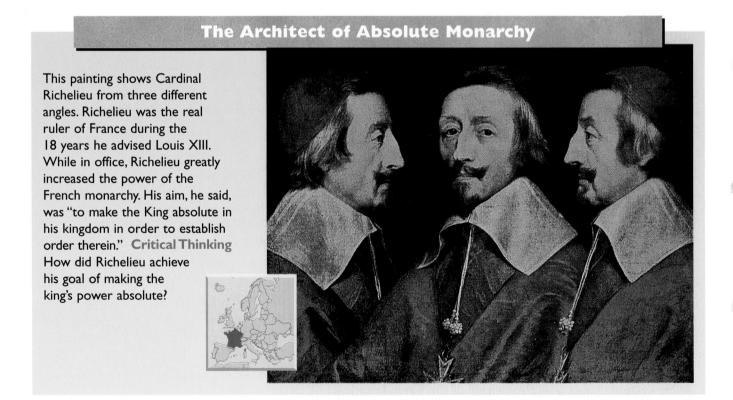

The Architect of Absolute Monarchy

This painting shows Cardinal Richelieu from three different angles. Richelieu was the real ruler of France during the 18 years he advised Louis XIII. While in office, Richelieu greatly increased the power of the French monarchy. His aim, he said, was "to make the King absolute in his kingdom in order to establish order therein." Critical Thinking How did Richelieu achieve his goal of making the king's power absolute?

Some 30,000 laborers worked 40 years to complete his magnificent estate. Many nobles lived at Versailles with Louis. Having the nobles at Versailles made it easier for Louis to keep an eye on them. If he had left them on their estates, they might have been a threat to his power. To keep them satisfied, Louis gave huge parties with lots of entertainment. He treated them well and, for the most part, left them free from paying taxes. This made the nobles forget that they were little more than the king's prisoners.

All of this luxury and entertainment cost a great deal of money. As you have just read, the nobles rarely were taxed. Most merchants and craftspeople also managed to avoid taxes. That meant that the poorest and weakest people—the peasants—in France paid for the luxury of Louis XIV's court.

France at War Louis' aim was to make France the greatest nation in Europe. To do this, he encouraged the growth of industry. He also supported efforts to build an empire in Asia and the Americas. He went to war to gain new territories. From 1667 until 1713, France was almost constantly at war with other European countries.

All of these wars took their toll. They cost huge sums of money. They won France little in the way of more land or power. By the time Louis died in 1715, France had huge debts. Even the silverware collection at Versailles had been sold to help pay for France's wars.

▼ Today, the Palace of Versailles and its gardens still attract countless tourists. This sculptured candleholder (shown in oval) is one example of the magnificent decorations found inside the palace.

European Monarchs Gain Power

Louis XIV was not the only powerful ruler in Europe. Many years before Louis XIV, there were King Ferdinand and Queen Isabella of Spain. When they married, they joined their separate kingdoms into one and built up Spain's army. They used their powerful military and courts to strengthen Catholicism throughout Spain, and they expelled the Jews and the Moors. The Moors were the descendants of North African Muslims who had occupied Spain in the A.D. 700s and had built a flourishing civilization known as Andalus. Ferdinand and Isabella also supported voyages of exploration. These voyages resulted in the building of a huge empire in the Americas.

Peter the Great became czar of Russia in 1682, when he was 10 years old. However, he did not actually rule Russia until he reached the age of 17. For the next 36 years, he modernized the Russian army and navy and improved Russian farming and industry. He expanded Russia's territory, adding land with ports so Russia could trade by sea.

Like Louis XIV, Peter the Great limited the power of the nobles to strengthen his own position. And, also like Louis, Peter the Great lived in a magnificent palace that he built to show the rest of the world his wealth and power.

▼ When they married, Ferdinand of Aragon and Isabella of Castile united their two Spanish kingdoms. Castile means "country of castles." Isabella's favorite castle was this one, Alcazar, in the city of Segovia.

In 1703, Peter the Great of Russia founded the city of St. Petersburg. He called the city his "window to the West." He wanted to make Russia more like Western Europe. The Winter Palace, shown here, was not completed until after his death. However, as Peter hoped, it echoed the splendor of Louis XIV's palace at Versailles. The Winter Palace is now a museum housing world-famous paintings and sculptures. **Critical Thinking** Why do you think Peter the Great wanted to build a splendid palace like Versailles?

In England, kings and queens had to share power. Although English monarchs like Henry VII and Elizabeth I did strengthen the power of monarchs, the nobles of England held power through Parliament. This power had been given to them by the Magna Carta. When Charles I came to power, he claimed that he could ignore Parliament because he ruled by divine right. Parliament did not agree. War broke out, and Charles I was executed in 1649. Future English monarchs found that they could rule only if they accepted limitations on their power.

SECTION 3 REVIEW

1. **Define** (a) democracy, (b) divine right, (c) absolute monarch.

2. **Identify** (a) Louis XIV, (b) Cardinal Richelieu, (c) Peter the Great, (d) Versailles.

3. What do you think Louis XIV meant when he said "I am the state"?

4. Which groups did European monarchs weaken to make themselves more powerful?

Critical Thinking

5. **Distinguishing Fact From Opinion** Is the following sentence fact or opinion? "Louis XIV made France the greatest nation in Europe." Explain your answer.

Activity

6. **Writing to Learn** Write a description of a day at Versailles as it might appear to a noble. Then write a description of how the day might look to a peasant.

Conquests in the Americas and Africa

Reach Into Your Background

Los Angeles, California; Santa Fe, New Mexico; El Paso, Texas—you have heard the names of these American cities before. Maybe you have visited

one. Or perhaps you live in one. These cities have Spanish names. Some of the old buildings in these cities look like buildings in Spain. The first Europeans to explore and settle California, New Mexico, and Texas were from Spain. They left their mark on the language and culture of the people who live there today.

Questions to Explore

1. How did Spain build an empire in the Americas?

2. How did the Atlantic slave trade affect Africa?

Key Terms
encomienda
conquistador

Key People and Places
Moctezuma
Hernán Cortés
Malinche
Francisco Pizarro
Tenochtitlán

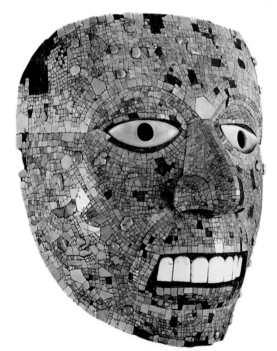

▼ This mask of Quetzalcoatl was made with many small pieces of stone.

About a hundred years before Louis XIV ruled France, another king had sat down to a splendid dinner. Moctezuma (mahk the ZOOM uh) was the ruler of the powerful Aztec empire in the Valley of Mexico. Like Louis, Moctezuma was usually the only one who ate at his dinners. Also like Louis, he was not alone. More than 400 people brought him his food. After his servants had put down the food, Moctezuma looked over the huge selection and chose the foods he wanted. Then servants drew a wooden screen around him to protect him from onlookers. His food was served by his personal servants.

Moctezuma was powerful. But he and other Aztecs believed that the gods were still more powerful. An ancient Aztec legend said that long ago the Aztecs had disobeyed the gods. It said that someday the white-skinned god Quetzalcoatl (ket sahl koh AHTL) would come from the east to punish them.

In 1519, it seemed to happen. Moctezuma and the Aztecs heard about a group of pale-skinned men who had landed on the coast. The Aztecs wondered if these men could be Quetzalcoatl and his followers.

This painting of the Aztec capital, Tenochtitlán, was made by the Mexican artist Diego Rivera in the 1940s. It is one of a series of murals, or wall paintings, on Mexican history that Rivera painted in the National Palace in Mexico City.

The Conquest of the Aztec Empire

The leader of the pale-skinned men was the Spaniard Hernan Cortés (hur NAN kor TEZ). Soon after landing in present-day Mexico, he met a Native American woman named Malinche (mah LIHN chay). She told him stories about the wealth of the Aztecs. Cortés, who was searching for gold, was intrigued. When Malinche told him about the hatred many of the native peoples had for the Aztecs, Cortés began to plan.

He asked other Native American peoples to help him against the Aztecs. At first he had little success. But Malinche, who could speak several native languages, helped to persuade these Native Americans to join with Cortés against the Aztecs.

The Conquest Begins When Cortés arrived in Tenochtitlán (tay nawch tee TLAHN), the Aztec capital, Moctezuma welcomed him. The Aztecs were afraid that Cortés might be the returning Quetzalcoatl, so they treated him and his men as honored guests. But the Spaniards knew that they were surrounded by danger.

LINKS TO ART

City of Dreams: Tenochtitlán "When we saw the many cities and villages built both on the water and on dry land ... we could not resist our admiration. . . because of the high towers [pyramids], and other buildings of masonry. . . ." This is how Bernal Diaz, a soldier with Cortés, described the Aztec capital. At the time of the Spaniards' arrival, Tenochtitlán was 10 times larger than the largest city in Spain. Within a few years it was gone, totally destroyed by the Spanish conquerors.

Cortés tried to convince Moctezuma to surrender to Spain. After several months, Moctezuma agreed. The peace was a short one, however. Spanish soldiers killed several Aztecs. Then the Aztecs began to fight the Spaniards. The battle was fierce and bloody. Moctezuma was killed. Cortés and his army barely escaped.

With the help of Native American allies, Cortés surrounded and attacked Tenochtitlán. In 1521, the Aztecs finally surrendered. By then, about 240,000 Aztecs had died, and 30,000 of Cortés's allies had been killed. Tenochtitlán and the Aztec empire lay in ruins.

After the Conquest Cortés then took control of the land, which he called New Spain. He built his new capital, Mexico City, on the site of Tenochtitlán.

Like most Europeans, Cortés tried to make life in New Spain like that in his home country. He imported European plants and farm animals such as sugar cane, barley, wheat, cattle, pigs, and chickens. He also introduced a new economic system, the encomienda (en KOH mee en duh), to Mexico. In this system, the Spanish king gave settlers large areas of land. Along with each piece of land, the new Spanish landlord received the labor of the Native Americans who lived on it. In return, the landlords were supposed to protect the Native Americans. They were also expected to persuade the Native Americans to adopt the Roman Catholic faith. The landlords also were supposed to allow the Native Americans to work their own plots of land to grow food. The encomienda

Cortés the Conquistador

Hernán Cortés, pictured here, was the first of the Spanish conquistadors (kon KEES ta dorz), or conquerors. The Spanish king gave conquistadors the right to hunt for treasure in the Americas. Not content with conquering the Aztec empire, Cortés led an expedition to Central America. However, he found no treasure there. **Critical Thinking** The conquistadors had to pay for their own expeditions. Why do you think they were willing to risk losing everything on expeditions to the Americas?

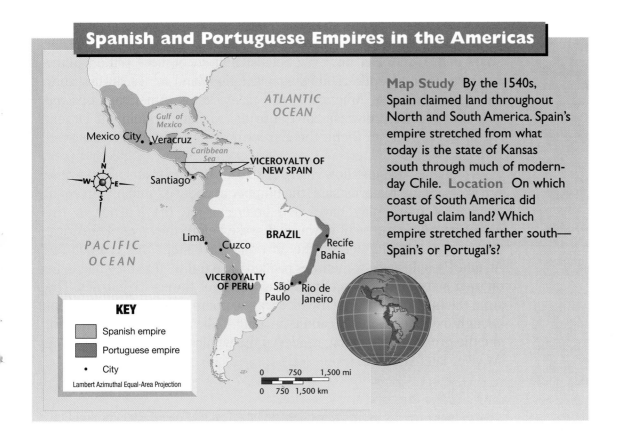

Spanish and Portuguese Empires in the Americas

Map Study By the 1540s, Spain claimed land throughout North and South America. Spain's empire stretched from what today is the state of Kansas south through much of modern-day Chile. **Location** On which coast of South America did Portugal claim land? Which empire stretched farther south—Spain's or Portugal's?

system was meant to be like the medieval manor system. In reality, it became a kind of slavery. Many Native Americans were worked to death.

In the years after the fall of the Aztecs, Cortés and other Spanish **conquistadors** (kon KEES ta dors), or conquerors, traveled throughout Central and South America and parts of the Caribbean. They claimed the land and the people who lived on it for Spain and the Roman Catholic Church. Francisco Pizarro, for example, conquered the Incan empire in 1533.

Amazingly, Pizarro managed to take control of an empire of some 12 million people with an army of about 200 soldiers. How was this possible? First, a war was raging in the empire. Some of the people rebelling against Incan rule sided with Pizarro. Further, European diseases like smallpox had killed thousands of people in the region. Many of those who had survived the disease were too sick to fight.

Europeans and Africans Clash

Europeans were looking for riches in other lands as well. Once the Portuguese had opened up the coast of West Africa to trade, sailors from other European countries followed. British, French, and Dutch ships visited Africa to trade for gold, ivory, and pepper. Occasionally, they traded for enslaved people as well. One British ship brought five enslaved Africans to England in the 1540s. No one would buy them, so they were taken back to Africa. Europe did not offer a big market for slavery. At this time, Europe had enough cheap labor. It did not need more workers.

Disease in the Americas
Many of America's native peoples were killed by Europeans without ever going into battle. The Europeans brought new diseases to the Americas—diseases against which the Native Americans had no built-up immunity. Smallpox and measles killed thousands. The Aztec and Incan empires were greatly weakened by diseases that swept through their populations. The same thing happened in North America.

Slavery Comes to the Americas There was a market for slaves in the Americas, however. Spanish and Portuguese settlers in the Americas wanted workers for their plantations and mines. At first they had enslaved Native Americans. But many Native Americans became sick and died from diseases or the brutal working conditions. Others ran away. To replace them, the Europeans began importing enslaved Africans.

No one is sure just how many enslaved Africans were taken to the Americas. Some historians put the number at about 12 million. An equal number or more may have died before or on the journey to the Americas. Some were cut down by disease before they even left Africa. Others got sick and died on the crowded slave ships that crossed the Atlantic. People were sometimes packed in so tightly that they had to lie on their sides, cupped together like spoons, for the entire journey. The air in the holds where they traveled was so poor that there was often not enough oxygen to keep a candle burning. "The shrieks of the women, and the groans of the dying, rendered the whole a scene of horror," one survivor later recalled.

Plan of a Slave Ship

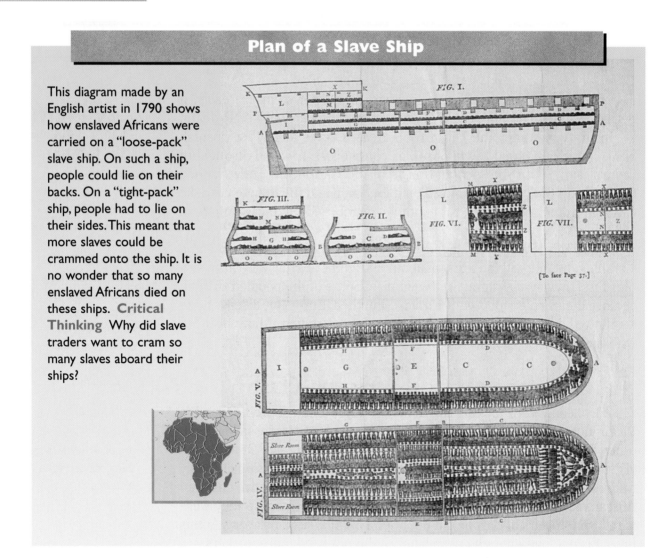

This diagram made by an English artist in 1790 shows how enslaved Africans were carried on a "loose-pack" slave ship. On such a ship, people could lie on their backs. On a "tight-pack" ship, people had to lie on their sides. This meant that more slaves could be crammed onto the ship. It is no wonder that so many enslaved Africans died on these ships. **Critical Thinking** Why did slave traders want to cram so many slaves aboard their ships?

The Slave Trade

A European slave trader pays an African for some enslaved men on the coast of West Africa in the early 1800s. **Critical Thinking** What impact do you think the slave trade had on Africa?

Effects of Slavery   The slave trade created a disaster for Africa. European slavers lured Africans into wars against their neighbors. They even provided them with guns and other deadly weapons. Then the slavers bought men, women, and children captured in the wars. These wars guaranteed the slavers a steady supply of people to buy.

Europeans wanted the youngest and healthiest Africans to provide free labor for the Americas. But the loss of so many of its best people and other problems created by the wars caused Africans to suffer for centuries. Even after the slave trade ended in the late 1800s, its effects continued to be felt.

SECTION 4 REVIEW

1. **Define** (a) encomienda, (b) conquistador.

2. **Identify** (a) Moctezuma, (b) Hernán Cortés, (c) Malinche, (d) Francisco Pizarro, (e) Tenochtitlán.

3. How were Cortés and Pizarro able to conquer great empires with only small numbers of Spanish soldiers?

4. What impact did the slave trade have on Africa?

Critical Thinking

5. **Recognizing Cause and Effect** How did the arrival of the Europeans affect the Aztec and Incan empires?

Activity

6. **Writing to Learn** Write two paragraphs, one from the viewpoint of an Aztec soldier defending Tenochtitlán, the other from the viewpoint of one of Cortés's soldiers.

SKILLS ACTIVITY

Distinguishing Fact From Opinion

You have probably heard people say things like these:

"The fact of the matter is. . . ."

"Let's look at the facts."

"That's just your opinion."

"Well, in my opinion. . . ."

Just what is the difference between a fact and an opinion? Distinguishing between them can help you better understand what you read and hear. Knowing the difference can help you make good decisions.

Get Ready

How do facts and opinions differ? Facts are statements that can be proved true. Opinions are personal beliefs. For example, it is a fact that the Earth is round. This has been proved by people who have traveled all the way around the Earth. The shape has been seen by astronauts looking at the Earth from outer space. It is an opinion that the Earth is beautiful. People may believe that, but no one can prove that it is true.

You will often need to make judgments or decisions based on facts, and you must be able to recognize them. How can you tell facts and opinions apart? It's as simple as 1-2-3!

1 Facts can be proved true.

2 Opinions usually cannot be proved true.

3 Opinions often include words and phrases such as "I think," "I believe," or "should," and adjectives such as "great" or "terrible."

Try It Out

Learn to distinguish facts from opinions by playing a simple game. You will need note cards, two pens, and a partner.

Front

Potatoes grow under ground.

Back

Fact

A. **Make game cards.** Give 10 note cards to your partner and keep 10 for yourself. Each of you should then write one fact or one opinion on each of your note cards. For example, "It snowed last week" would be a fact. "We had wonderful weather last week" would be an opinion. Make sure that all of your facts can be proved. On the back of each card, identify your statement as a fact or an opinion. Do not let your partner see these answers!

B. **Play the game.** Shuffle your cards and give them to your partner face up. Challenge him or her to identify each sentence as a fact or opinion. Award one point for each correct answer. Give a bonus point if your partner can explain how the statement could be proved true if it is a fact or how your partner knew it was an opinion.

C. **Switch the cards.** Now try your hand at identifying your partner's facts and opinions. Compare scores. Who won?

Apply the Skill

Now look at some facts and opinions about explorers. Read the 10 statements in the box. Use the three qualities of facts and opinions explained in Get Ready. Identify each statement as a fact or an opinion. If it is a fact, explain how it could be proved true. If it is an opinion, tell how you know it is an opinion.

Statements About Explorers

1. Columbus was the greatest explorer in history.

2. It would have been better if European explorers never came to the Americas at all.

3. Vasco da Gama sailed around the Cape of Good Hope to India.

4. Vasco Balboa sighted the Pacific Ocean.

5. Ponce de León was foolish to search for the Fountain of Youth.

6. America is named for the explorer Amerigo Vespucci.

7. Francisco Pizarro came from Spain.

8. John Cabot was a very handsome man.

9. Hernando de Soto and his army traveled through what is today Georgia, South Carolina, North Carolina, Tennessee, Alabama, Mississippi, Arkansas, and Louisiana.

10. Explorers have changed the world more than any other group of people.

Back

Opinion

Front

Potatoes are delicious with sour cream and butter.

Review and Activities

Reviewing Main Ideas

1. List reasons why Italian merchants supported the work of artists during the Renaissance.
2. Why did many princes in Germany adopt the ideas of Martin Luther?
3. Why were instruments like the compass and astrolabe so important to European explorers?
4. Why did European nations support voyages of exploration?
5. Why did the people of France feel that they could not challenge the demands of King Louis XIV?
6. What did European monarchs do to take more power for themselves?
7. How did the Spanish go about building an empire in the Americas?
8. Why was the slave trade a disaster for Africa?

Reviewing Key Terms

Match the definitions in Column I with the key terms in Column II

Column I

1. a ruler who has total power over every aspect of life in a country
2. the rebirth of learning in Europe
3. the belief that a king rules by the will of God
4. a type of ship developed in the 1400s that was stronger and easier to sail than other ships
5. a system in which people govern themselves, choosing their own government
6. the painting technique that makes objects in the distance look smaller relative to objects in the foreground
7. a new, great change in religion intended to reform religious customs
8. an instrument for measuring latitude

Column II

a. Renaissance
b. city-state
c. perspective
d. Reformation
e. astrolabe
f. caravel
g. democracy
h. divine right
i. absolute monarch

Critical Thinking

1. **Recognizing Cause and Effect** How did the development of empires in the Americas affect trade between European countries and Africa?
2. **Expressing Problems Clearly** Why did Peter the Great want seaports for his country?

Graphic Organizer

Copy the chart onto a separate sheet of paper. Under each heading, list the names of two people connected with the change given.

Renaissance	Reformation	Exploration	Absolute Monarchy	Conquest of the Americas

Map Activity

European Empires in the Americas
For each place listed below, write the letter from the map that shows its location.

1. Atlantic Ocean

2. North America

3. Pacific Ocean

4. Portuguese empire

5. South America

6. Spanish empire

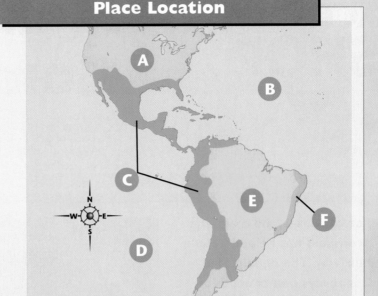

Writing Activity

Writing a Tour Plan
Your school's history club is planning a summer study tour of Europe. Choose four to six places you think should be included on the tour. Discuss what might be seen in these places and explain why they are important to understanding the history of the period covered by this chapter.

Take It to the NET

Activity Explore the explosion of art and science in the Renaissance. What expression of creativity during this time do you find most interesting? For help in completing this activity, visit www.phschool.com.

Chapter 6 Self-Test To review what you have learned, take the Chapter 6 Self-Test and get instant feedback on your answers. Go to www.phschool.com to take the test.

Skills Review

Turn to the Skills Activity.
Review how you can distinguish fact from opinion. Then answer the following questions: (a) What are some fact and opinion language clues? (b) In making a decision, would you base it on facts or opinions? Why?

How Am I Doing?

Answer these questions to help you check your progres.

1. Can I name some changes that the Renaissance and the Reformation brought to Europe?

2. Do I understand the importance of European exploration and how it affected the lives of people in Europe, Africa, and the Americas?

3. Can I explain how absolute monarchs gained power in Europe?

4. What information from this chapter can I include in my journal?

Making a Compass

For centuries, the magnetic compass has helped people find their way. The needle of a compass always points north or south. If you know where either north or south is, you can always find the three other directions.

The compass once looked quite different than it does today. Often, people simply used a piece of magnetized iron attached to a piece of cork floating in a bowl of water. Although such compasses were simple, they worked well.

▲ An antique pocket compass.

Purpose

In this activity, you will create your own compass. By observing how the compass acts, you can learn something about the forces that make it work.

Materials

- a small bowl
- enough water to fill the bowl
- a small flat cork disk, $\frac{1}{2}$ to $\frac{3}{4}$ inches across
- a sewing needle
- a bar magnet about 3 inches long

Procedure

In order to understand how a compass works, you must first know that the Earth has its own magnetic field. This magnetic field has two poles. That means it is strongest at its two opposite ends. The Earth's magnetic poles are very close to the Earth's North Pole and South Pole.

Bar magnets also have north and south magnetic poles. If allowed to move freely, any bar magnet will be drawn by the currents of the strongest nearby magnetic field. It will move so that its poles match the poles of that magnetic field. Before you begin making your own compass, read the steps on the next page.

STEP ONE

Prepare your materials. Fill the bowl with water. Dunk the cork disk in the bowl of water, wetting it completely. Then let it float in the center of the bowl.

STEP TWO

Build your compass. Rub the needle several times across the magnet, from one end to the other. When you do this, the needle itself becomes a weak magnet. Immediately lay the needle flat in the center of the cork disk. You might need to nudge the cork so that it stays near the center of the bowl. Then watch carefully. What happens?

You may need to repeat rubbing the needle, especially if the needle accidentally gets wet. Dry it off, then rub it on the magnet again.

STEP THREE

Test your compass. Turn the cork about one quarter turn and let go. What happens? Next, slowly and carefully rotate the bowl of water. What does the cork do?

Observations

1. What happened when you placed the needle on the cork disk?

2. Did the needle move immediately to one position, or did it seem to sway and hesitate?

3. What happened to the needle when you changed its position or the position of the bowl?

ANALYSIS AND CONCLUSION

1. Why do you think the needle always points in one direction?

2. Why is it necessary for a compass needle to float and move freely?

Changes in the Western World

PICTURE ACTIVITIES

The picture above shows a group of French citizens storming the Bastille (bas TEEL), a prison in Paris, France. This event, which took place on July 14, 1789, was the first violent act in the revolt that brought down the French monarchy. The period from the late 1700s to 1900 saw many such changes in the Western world. To begin your study of this period, do the following activities.

Study the picture
Look at the Bastille, the large building in the left background of the picture. Write a sentence describing the building.

Describe the action
Write a caption for this picture that describes the action. Which is the group of French citizens? Which is the group of soldiers?

Limits on Monarchs

BEFORE YOU READ

Reach Into Your Background

Have you ever heard people talk about having a right to do something? Think about the rights people in the United States have. Which rights do you think are important? How did people get these rights?

Questions to Explore

1. Why was the Elizabethan Age a glorious time for England?
2. How did England turn away from absolute monarchy in the 1600s?

Key Terms

civil war
revolution
bill of rights
constitutional monarchy

Key People

Henry VIII
Elizabeth I
William and Mary

Most kings wanted sons to rule after them. They felt that their kingdoms would be more secure with a male on the throne. That is one reason why King Henry VIII of England married six times. He kept hoping for a son who would be king after him.

Each of Henry's six marriages was made to strengthen his ties to a powerful family. When Henry's first wife, Catherine of Aragon, did not produce a son, Henry decided to divorce her. The Roman Catholic Church did not allow divorce. Nor would the pope give Henry special permission to end his marriage. Henry, therefore, broke away from the Church and started a new Protestant church, the Church of England. He named himself head of the new church. Then he ended his marriage to Catherine.

Henry finally did have a son, Edward, who became king but died at age 16. What happened after Edward's death would probably have amazed Henry. One of Henry's daughters, Elizabeth, became the most powerful and successful ruler England had ever known.

Elizabethan England

When Elizabeth I became queen in 1558, she suddenly found herself in a position of great power. Her grandfather, Henry VII, had ended the battling among

▼ King Henry VIII was ambitious and sometimes cruel. He hated to be refused anything he wanted.

the armies of local lords. He had made sure that England's monarch would be more powerful than any of the nobles. Her father's break with the Roman Catholic Church also gave the monarch greater power.

The Young Elizabeth   Like her father, Elizabeth was determined and intelligent. As a young woman, she enjoyed music. She loved horseback riding and other sports. Elizabeth also knew several foreign languages. She spoke French and Italian. She read Greek and Latin. Unlike Henry, however, Elizabeth was fair, and she was grateful to those who helped her. Also unlike her father, who married so often, Elizabeth never married. She knew that if she married she would lose her power to her husband.

Elizabeth was also wise enough to get the support of the English people. After she became queen, she traveled throughout the English countryside. She let her people get to know her, and she got to know them. Her plan to win support from the people was a success. The English people came to love and admire their queen.

Elizabeth ruled for 45 years. Those years made up one of the most glorious periods of England's history.

Elizabeth's Monarchy   Elizabeth continued the work of strengthening England. She did this in two ways. First, she prevented war at home. She cleverly found ways to prevent religious wars between Catholics and Protestants in England. The second thing she did to

Connect Think of some leaders you admire. What qualities do you admire in them?

Elizabeth I of England

With her red hair, Elizabeth I reminded her people of her father. But she turned out to be a far wiser and stronger ruler than Henry VIII. She cleverly used the possibility of marriage to keep the peace. Her Catholic subjects were loyal because they thought she might marry one of their faith. For the same reason, Catholic rulers in Europe were unwilling to go to war with England. At the same time, her Protestant subjects hoped she would marry a Protestant. **Critical Thinking** Why might it be a disadvantage for rulers not to marry?

William Shakespeare and the Globe Theater

The plays of William Shakespeare (pictured below) were written and performed during the reign of Elizabeth 1. Actors performed the plays at the Globe, an outdoor theater on the south side of the Thames River in London. In the mid-1990s, a replica of the Globe was built on its original site (left).

strengthen England was to go to war with Spain, a rival European power. When Catholic Spain sent a huge fleet to invade Protestant England, Elizabeth sent out her ships to fight off the Spaniards. After the battle, most of the Spanish ships were destroyed in a terrible storm. England was then left with the most powerful navy in the world.

This strong navy allowed England to become a leader in exploration. Sir Francis Drake, a famous English sea captain, sailed around the world. He also delighted Elizabeth by leading pirate attacks on Spanish ships carrying treasure from the Americas. Another Englishman, Sir Walter Raleigh, set up the first English settlement in North America.

Drake and Raleigh were two among many who added to the glory of the Elizabethan Age. It was a golden age for science, art, and writing. Perhaps the greatest writer in the English language, William Shakespeare, began his career during Elizabeth's rule. His works include such plays as *Hamlet, King Lear, Romeo and Juliet,* and *A Midsummer Night's Dream.*

Conflict Between Monarch and Parliament

Even as Elizabeth worked to increase the strength of England, she understood that her power was not absolute. The Magna Carta had put limits on the powers of English rulers. Shortly before she died, Elizabeth told Parliament, a council that advised the monarch: "Though

ACROSS TIME

The Globe Shakespeare's theater in London was called the Globe. It was 3 stories high and had 20 sides, so it was almost round. Inside, the stage was against one wall. Seats for playgoers ran along the other walls. People also stood in the area in front of the stage. Wealthy young people often paid extra to sit on the stage so everyone could see them. The Globe has been rebuilt on its original site in London so people can experience Shakespeare's plays in their original setting.

Predict What do you think happened in England after Queen Elizabeth's death?

God hath raised me high, yet this I account the glory of any crown, that I have reigned with your loves." Elizabeth knew that she ruled with the approval of Parliament and the people.

Elizabeth died in 1603 without heirs. Her closest living relative was James Stuart, king of Scotland, England's northern neighbor. He was offered the crown and became James I of England. Eventually, England and Scotland were joined as the nation we now call Great Britain.

Civil War Breaks Out James believed that he was king by divine right. That is, his power to rule came from God. He also believed that his power was absolute. For long periods of time, he governed without Parliament. His son, Charles I, continued this practice, ruling without Parliament for 11 years.

When Parliament did meet again, it passed laws to limit Charles's power. Angered by this, Charles tried to arrest Parliament's leaders. As a result, war broke out between the king and Parliament. This was a **civil war,** a battle for power between two groups within one country. The English civil war eventually led to the death of Charles I. He was beheaded in 1649. The war actually was a **revolution,** or a sudden change in the way people think or in the way they are ruled.

A King Condemned to Death

During the English civil war, Charles I was supported by the nobility, upper classes, and the clergy. Against him were Parliament, merchants, and the Puritans—Protestants who wanted to make religion simpler. Here, Charles is shown after being found guilty of treason. Below is Charles's death warrant signed by members of Parliament. **Critical Thinking** Why do you think Charles chose to fight rather than share power with Parliament?

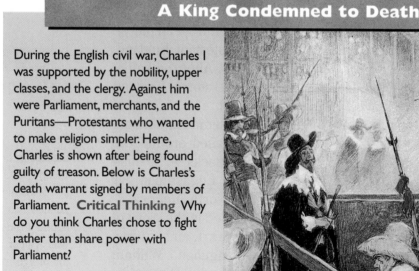

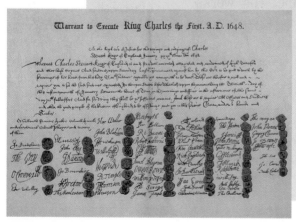

The Monarchy Is Restored

For the next 11 years, Britain was ruled by the people. Then, in 1660, the English brought back the government of kings. The next two monarchs, Charles II and James II, both had disagreements with Parliament. James II also tried to make Britain a Catholic country once again.

Several English leaders looked for a new ruler. They believed that the king had to be Protestant and that he had to respect Parliament. In 1688, they invited the Dutch prince William of Orange "to rescue the nation and the religion." William seemed the obvious choice because his wife was Mary, the daughter of James II. Unlike her father, Mary was a Protestant.

William and Mary's armies quickly drove James out of the country. In what is now called the Glorious Revolution, Parliament officially offered the throne to these new rulers. There was, however, one condition. They had to accept a statement called the Declaration of Rights, which later became the British Bill of Rights. A **bill of rights** is a summary of all the rights held by a people under their government.

Under the English Bill of Rights, all laws had to be approved by Parliament. William and Mary agreed, making Britain a **constitutional monarchy,** a government in which the monarch's power is limited by a set of laws. To this day, Britain remains a constitutional monarchy.

Ruler But Not King

Oliver Cromwell was a leader of Parliament's forces during the civil war. After the war, some of his advisers urged him to take the throne. He refused. Instead, he worked to build a government in which Parliament was supreme. He was a very religious man who believed that everything he did was guided by God. **Critical Thinking** What did Charles I and Cromwell have in common?

SECTION 1 REVIEW

1. **Define** (a) civil war, (b) revolution, (c) bill of rights, (d) constitutional monarchy.

2. **Identify** (a) Henry VIII, (b) Elizabeth I, (c) William and Mary.

3. List two accomplishments of Elizabeth I's rule.

4. What brought about the English civil war?

Critical Thinking

5. **Identifying Central Issues** Why did Parliament insist that William and Mary agree to the Declaration of Rights before allowing them to take the throne?

Activity

6. **Writing to Learn** Make a list of the rights that you think prevent one person from gaining too much power in the United States.

The Enlightenment

Reach Into Your Background

How do you conduct experiments in science class? You probably try things out, observe what happens, and then note your observations. In this section, you'll learn when and how this way of studying science developed.

Questions to Explore

1. How did new ways of thinking change how people approached science?

2. How did new ways of thinking change how people looked at their governments?

Key Terms

Enlightenment
scientific method
natural law
colony

Key People

Galileo Galilei
Isaac Newton
John Locke
Thomas Jefferson

▼ The Italian scientist Galileo was the first person to study the sky through a telescope.

The whole room was silent. Members of the court leaned forward, waiting for Galileo Galilei (gal uh LAY oh gal uh LAY ee) to respond to the question. Did the great Italian scientist really believe that the Earth moved around the sun?

This was an important question in 1633. The Roman Catholic Church taught that God had made the Earth the center of the universe. If that was true, everything—sun, planets, and stars—moved around the Earth. In the 1500s, a Polish astronomer, Nicolaus Copernicus (koh PUR nuh kuhs), had claimed that this was wrong. He had said that the Earth moved around the sun.

Galileo had quietly supported the ideas of Copernicus. Now the Church court was asking Galileo what he really believed. He knew that he could be put to death if he disagreed with the Church. So he told the court that, in fact, the Earth did not move. He did not say what he truly believed.

As Galileo was being led away, he is said to have muttered something to himself about the Earth. "Nevertheless, it does move," he said.

The Age of Reason

The **Enlightenment** was a period of revolution, a time that saw a major shift in the way people thought. People of the Enlightenment had great confidence in the power of reason. They used reason to shine a new "light" on traditional ideas and redefined their society. The Enlightenment affected politics, art, literature, science, and religion. Many of the new ways of thinking can be traced to the Scientific Revolution of the 1500s and 1600s.

The Scientific Revolution   For hundreds of years, people made their ideas about science fit their religious beliefs. During the Renaissance this began to change. Scientists like Copernicus and Galileo began to look at how the universe really worked. They observed things first, and then drew conclusions based on what they had seen. They used reason to explain the physical world around them.

Galileo's observations led him to new thoughts about objects and the speed at which they fall. You might think that heavier objects fall faster than lighter ones. However, that is not true. Galileo proved that objects fall at the same speed. According to legend, he dropped a light object and a heavy object from a tower at the same time. They landed in the same instant. His observations led him to realize that the old ideas about falling objects were wrong.

He also used a new scientific tool, the telescope, to examine planets. He eventually proved that the Earth was not the center of the universe. For him, observation was more important than old ideas that fit with traditional beliefs.

READ ACTIVELY

Visualize Visualize someone dropping a tennis ball and a bowling ball from the top of a tower, both at the same time. Will the two objects land at the same time? Why or why not?

A New View of the Universe

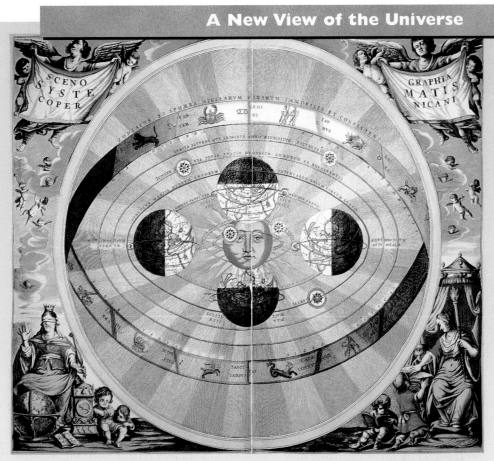

In 1543, Copernicus published his ideas on the nature of the universe. He said that the sun was the center of the universe and all the other planets, including the Earth, moved around it. This map, which was published nearly 120 years later, shows the Copernican view of the universe.
Critical Thinking Why do you think that Copernicus' ideas on the universe were referred to as the Copernican Revolution?

Achievements of the Scientific Revolution

Chart Study Many of the scientists listed here met with opposition when they first published their new ideas. Copernicus, for example, was accused of destroying "the whole art of astronomy." Later scientists, however, understood the importance of these contributions. Isaac Newton commented: "If I have seen farther than others, it is because I have stood on the shoulders of giants."
Critical Thinking What do you think Newton meant by this statement?

Discipline	Date	Contributions
Medicine	1543	Andreas Vesalius published *On the Structure of the Human Body*. His book gave the world the first accurate descriptions of the human body.
	1628	William Harvey described how blood circulates through the body. He was the first physician to use medical experiments.
Chemistry	mid- to late 1600s	Robert Boyle described the basic makeup of all matter. For centuries, people had believed that matter was made up of earth, water, air, and fire.
Astronomy	1543	Nicolaus Copernicus shocked Europe by saying that the Earth and other planets moved around the sun. Until that time, people had believed that the sun, stars, and planets circled the Earth.
Scientific Thought	early 1600s	Philosophers offered new ways to study the world. Francis Bacon stressed the importance of experiment and observation. René Descartes believed that human reasoning leads to understanding.

The Scientific Method Galileo and other scientists of the Renaissance were developing a new way of learning about the world. Today, it is called the scientific method. In this approach, scientists perform experiments under conditions they control. Then, the scientists record what they have seen. Next, they examine their results. Finally, they decide what the facts are, based on what they have seen. If an experiment is done well, other scientists will be able to do it and get the same results.

New Political Ideas

The ideas of the English scientist Isaac Newton led other thinkers to apply reason to the laws governing society. In the late 1600s, Newton began to ask bold new questions. What, he asked, caused the planets to circle the sun? Studying such questions led Newton to realize that there are natural laws, or forces that rule the behavior of the universe. Newton's observations led him to develop laws of motion and of gravity. He was able to describe these laws using mathematics.

Another Englishman, John Locke, questioned the way society and government worked. Locke looked at human society and tried to figure out its natural laws. In other words, he applied Newton's ideas to society.

A New View of Government   Locke and other thinkers came to believe that there are, indeed, natural laws that govern human behavior. Government, they said, should be based on these natural laws. Locke argued that nature had meant human beings to be free. In other words, people had the right to be free. They also had the right to live and the right to own property. If a government took these rights away, it was not acting properly.

Locke went even further. He said that government was based on an agreement between rulers and the people. Rulers should rule only as long as they have the support of the people. If a ruler were to break the agreement by taking away people's rights, people had a right to change the government.

The Impact of Locke's Ideas   These were startling ideas. Locke was saying that rulers like those of France, Spain, and Russia should not have absolute, or total, power. Instead, he suggested, rulers had responsibilities toward those they ruled. This was shocking to people who thought that kings ruled by divine right.

People in many countries read books, pamphlets, and newspapers about the new ideas. They began to wonder whether their governments were acting as they should.

READ ACTIVELY

Predict How do you think John Locke's ideas affected the history of the United States?

A Coffee-House Speech

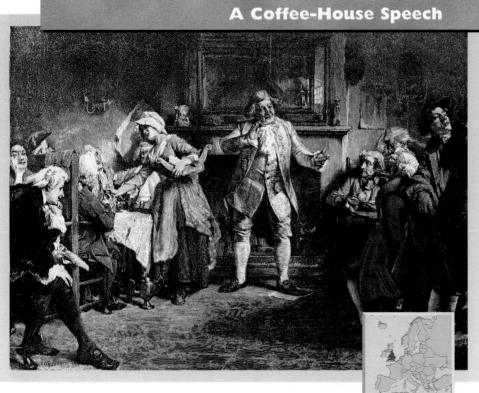

Coffee came to Europe from Southwest Asia in the 1500s. By the mid-1600s, coffee houses had grown up all over London. Over a cup of coffee, customers picked up the news of the day or made business deals. They also took part in lively discussions on politics and new ideas. In this picture of a London coffee house, the central figure is giving a speech to his fellow customers. **Critical Thinking** How would you describe the reactions of the speaker's audience?

Natural Rights in the American Colonies

People in Great Britain's colonies in North America were especially worried about government. A **colony** is a territory ruled by another nation, usually one far away. By the 1750s, these settlements were thriving communities that stretched from Georgia to New Hampshire. The British were finding that it was very expensive to protect their faraway colonies. To help pay for the defense of the colonies, the British wanted to collect taxes from the American colonists.

No Taxation Without Representation

Under British law, people could not be taxed unless their representatives had voted for the tax in Parliament. The colonists had no representatives in Parliament. How could it be fair, they asked, to make them pay taxes when they had no way of voting for or against a tax? Did this not mean that the British government was taking away their rights?

As American colonists protested, people in Britain grew worried. They felt that they were losing control of the colonies. They approved more taxes and stricter laws. Americans grew angrier. Leaders like Thomas Jefferson and Benjamin Franklin, who admired the ideas of John Locke, began to think about rebelling. The colonists began to gather weapons and ammunition.

On April 19, 1775, British soldiers marched into Lexington and Concord, towns outside Boston, Massachusetts. Their job was to take weapons and ammunition away from the Americans. The Americans, however, fought back.

The Colonies Declare Their Independence

The American Revolution began at Lexington and Concord. In 1776, during the course of the revolt, the Americans declared their independence from Britain.

Thomas Jefferson wrote a document called the Declaration of Independence to explain why the American colonists had rebelled. Jefferson based many of his ideas on those of John Locke. According to Jefferson, governments had power only because the people agreed that they did. He claimed that if a government starts taking away people's rights, the people have a right to change

Washington at Yorktown

Here, General George Washington lights a cannon to fire the first shot at the Battle of Yorktown. The American victory at Yorktown marked the end of the Revolutionary War. Washington led the colonial army from 1775 until the end of the war. He was elected the first President of the United States in 1789. **Critical Thinking** Why do you think people elect successful generals to important political offices?

the government or put an end to it. Thus, he said, the colonies had the right to rebel against Great Britain. Putting Jefferson's ideas into effect, however, took a long time.

The colonies had to fight Britain for their freedom. At first, it seemed that they would never win. Then, in 1778, the French came to the aid of the colonists. The colonial army, along with the French army and navy, forced the British to surrender at Yorktown, Virginia, in 1781. The United States of America had won its freedom.

SECTION 2 REVIEW

1. **Define** (a) Enlightenment, (b) scientific method, (c) natural law, (d) colony.

2. **Identify** (a) Galileo Galilei, (b) Isaac Newton, (c) John Locke, (d) Thomas Jefferson.

3. What did Galileo discover about falling objects and about the planets?

4. According to John Locke, when do people have the right to rebel against their government?

Critical Thinking

5. **Making Comparisons** How were the ideas of Isaac Newton and John Locke similar?

Activity

6. **Writing to Learn** Write a declaration in which you list what you think are the basic rights of all people.

Interpreting Line Graphs

Steve had worked hard on his report about Dallas, Texas. He had almost finished writing, and he had two days to hand it in. But the paragraph about the population growth of Dallas still worried him. Each time he tried to write about the number of people living in Dallas at different times in the city's history, it sounded too confusing. One number followed the other in a jumble. He thought about ways to show the population growth in a graph or a diagram.

"I could provide a population map of the city for each decade, but that's too many different maps," Steve thought. "I could make a table showing the population every 10 years, but that wouldn't show the changes at a glance. I need a good graph that will show growth over time."

Get Ready

Graphs are extremely helpful because they show a large amount of information in a simple, easy-to-read way. One of the most common types of graph is the line graph. Line graphs use lines to show amounts. Line graphs are the best graphs to use to show changes in amounts over time.

Try It Out

The graph below is a line graph. You can read, or interpret, it by following these simple steps.

A. Read the title. The title tells you what the line graph is about.

B. Read the labels on the axes. A line graph has two axes. The vertical axis runs up and down. What does this one show? How is it divided? The horizontal axis runs across. This one shows time in years.

C. Read the line. The line on the line graph shows how the amounts given on the vertical axis change over time. What trend, or general change, is shown by the line?

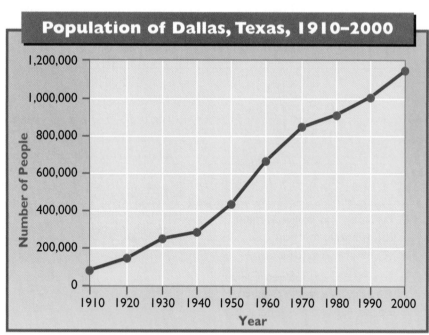

Population of Dallas, Texas, 1910–2000

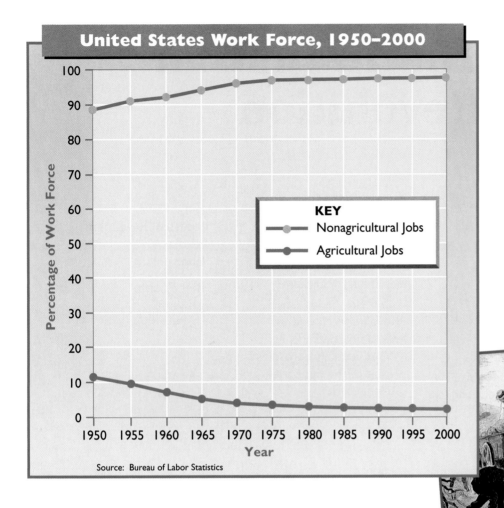

United States Work Force, 1950–2000

KEY
— Nonagricultural Jobs
— Agricultural Jobs

Percentage of Work Force

Year

Source: Bureau of Labor Statistics

Apply the Skill

The line graph above has two lines instead of one. But it works the same way, and you can apply the same steps to read it.

1 **Read the title.** What is this line graph about?

2 **Read the labels on the axes.** What does the vertical axis show? What does the horizontal axis show? How many years are covered by the graph?

3 **Read the lines.** What does the green line stand for? What does the purple line stand for? What percentage of the work force had agricultural jobs in 1950? What percentage of the work force had nonagricultural jobs in this same year? What percentage of workers had agricultural jobs in 2000? What percentage of workers had nonagricultural jobs in 2000?

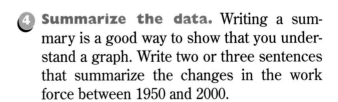

4 **Summarize the data.** Writing a summary is a good way to show that you understand a graph. Write two or three sentences that summarize the changes in the work force between 1950 and 2000.

The Industrial Revolution

Reach Into Your Background

You are surrounded by machines—cars, computers, telephones, television sets, and more. How do these machines influence your life? What would your life be like without them?

Questions to Explore

1. How did the Industrial Revolution change the way people earned a living?
2. What problems arose as a result of the Industrial Revolution?

Key Terms

Industrial Revolution
textile
labor union

Key People

Alexander Graham Bell
Thomas Edison

▼ Fountains of sparks stream from a modern steel furnace. The Industrial Revolution of the 1700s changed forever the way goods are produced.

“The thunder of the blast deafens you," wrote a visitor to an American factory around 1900. "The ever-brightening flame, flashing up finally as high as fifty feet, blinds you; sparks fall everywhere." Another described "the rumbling growl of rollers, the howls of horrible saws . . . the crashing thunder of falling iron plate, the hoarse coughing of great engines, and the hissing of steam.”

What an awful place to work! But it was also an exciting place because a revolution was going on in factories all across Europe and North America. This revolution continues today.

A New Kind of Revolution

The thunder and flames of the factories were all part of the **Industrial Revolution.** This was a period of time during which the production of goods shifted from simple hand tools to complex machines. People's lives changed a great deal. This change started in the 1760s, when industry began to grow rapidly.

Several factors made this possible. Trade from Britain's growing empire helped the economy grow rapidly. The British government supported this economic growth by building a strong navy to protect the empire and overseas trade. Businesspeople became wealthy from trade. Therefore, they had money to spend on new ventures such as factories. To support trade, people thought of new ways to make goods quickly and cheaply using machines. They also invented new ways to provide power for all the added machines. The Industrial Revolution changed the ways in which people today work, shop, and spend their free time.

The Industrial Revolution Begins The Industrial Revolution began in Great Britain in the 1760s. The **textile,** or cloth, business was one of the first to move into factories. Before the 1760s, cloth was made mostly by people working in their homes. People sheared wool from sheep, spun yarn, and wove cloth on a part-time basis. In some ways, this was good. Workers could be with their families and care for their children. It did, however, take a long time to make each piece of cloth. Textiles were expensive. Only the very wealthy had more than one change of clothes. Curtains, tablecloths, and other household items made of cloth were luxuries.

The invention of several machines made it possible to make cloth more cheaply. For example, people had spun fibers into thread using a wheel on a frame. A new invention, the spinning jenny, let each worker spin several bunches of thread at the same time. One worker using a spinning jenny could do the work of eight people using spinning wheels.

ACROSS TIME

The Spindle How did people make thread before there were spinning wheels? People in ancient Egypt, India, and South America used spindles that were long smooth sticks weighted on one end. The spinner started with a mass of short fibers, such as wool. Next, the spinner pulled fibers out and twisted them together. The spinner attached one end of the twisted fibers to the spindle, and twirled the spindle like a top to twist the thread. Finally, the spinner attached the thread to a notch in the spindle and started over.

A Textile Factory in the 1800s

Many of the workers in textile factories were women, like the weavers shown here. Factory owners often preferred women, because they could pay women lower wages for doing the same work as men. **Critical Thinking** What kind of job do you think the man in the center of the picture holds? Explain your answer.

The new textile machines, which spun thread and wove cloth, were so big and so fast that they needed more power than a human could supply. People came up with ways to use flowing water to supply power. They dammed rivers and built mills using water wheels. Later, steam engines were used to supply power. The machines had to be housed in one large building, a factory. This meant that people who wanted to work had to leave their homes and families and go to the factories.

The Industrial Revolution Grows Spinning and weaving machines powered by water were among the first inventions of the Industrial Revolution. Steam engines also provided power for textile machines. Soon other industrial inventions took advantage of the new power supply. Mighty steam-driven hammers forged iron parts. Drills and cutters made screws, rods, and other metal parts for farm machines, guns, railroad cars, and engines.

The new inventions made other developments possible. Steel girders could support taller buildings. Trains traveling on steel rails moved people and goods more quickly and cheaply.

New inventions also made the daily life of the average person easier. Inventors like Alexander Graham Bell and Thomas Edison used the power of electricity to create machines that revolutionized everyday life. Bell invented the telephone. Edison invented the phonograph, an early type of sound system. Later, he patented the electric lightbulb and developed a system to provide whole communities with electricity.

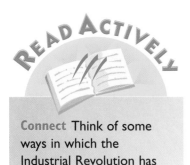

READ ACTIVELY

Connect Think of some ways in which the Industrial Revolution has made your life easier.

The Wizard of Menlo Park

In the 1870s, Thomas Edison set up a laboratory in Menlo Park, New Jersey. There, he and a team of scientists produced dozens of inventions, such as the electric lightbulb, the motion-picture camera, the microphone, and the phonographs shown above. People were so amazed with Edison's work that they called him "the wizard of Menlo Park."
Critical Thinking What impact do you think Edison's inventions had on everyday life?

The new department stores that opened in the late 1800s changed the way people shopped. Now, people could buy many different kinds of goods, from children's toys to furniture, under one roof. These stores also provided new job opportunities for store managers and shop clerks. This picture shows the busy food section of a London department store.

The Industrial Revolution also created new jobs. Managers were needed to run the factories. Merchants were needed to sell the goods made in the factories. The new jobs presented opportunities that allowed more people to move into the middle class of society—the group of people between the poor and the rich. More people than ever before were able to have comfortable lives.

The Problems of the Industrial Revolution

But not everyone had a better life. Many poor people's lives became harder during the Industrial Revolution. Farmworkers lost jobs to powerful machinery. Many farmers lost their land because they could not compete with wealthier farmers who were able to buy these expensive new machines. In Europe, many people left their homes hoping to make better lives for themselves across the ocean. Some went to the United States. They often found work in American factories. Others went to Canada, South America, Australia, or New Zealand.

Industrialization and Cities When Europe became industrialized, masses of people moved to the cities. From 1820 to 1900, London's population grew by more than 6 million. Paris's population grew by about 4.5 million between 1850 and 1930. Today, developing countries like Brazil are becoming industrialized. Again people are on the move. In 1991, the population of São Paulo, Brazil, was 9.6 million. By 2015, population experts say the population will be about 21 million.

A Factory Worker's Life   As more and more goods were made in factories, people had to move to cities to earn a living. They were no longer able to work at home at their own pace. Instead, many had to work 12 or more hours a day in the factory. They had few, if any, breaks.

Factories were noisy and dirty. Machines were often dangerous, and people were sometimes injured or killed. Factory workers were poorly paid. Often parents had to put their children to work so that the family could earn enough money to live. For many, life was nothing but endless work.

Workers lived in small, cramped quarters. Soot from smokestacks and trains covered everything, even indoors. The soot made it hard to keep anything clean. Often people in many different houses or apartments shared a single bathroom. Or they had no indoor plumbing at all. Many had to carry water in buckets from the nearest well or stream.

Garbage piled up in the streets. This attracted rats and packs of dogs. Dyes and dust from textile mills poisoned the air and water. Diseases swept easily through such cities. Many people died of cholera and typhus. Even minor diseases could be fatal under such conditions.

A London Street Scene

This drawing of a street in London's East End district was made in 1872. It shows the problems most working people faced in their everyday lives—poor housing, overcrowding, and pollution.

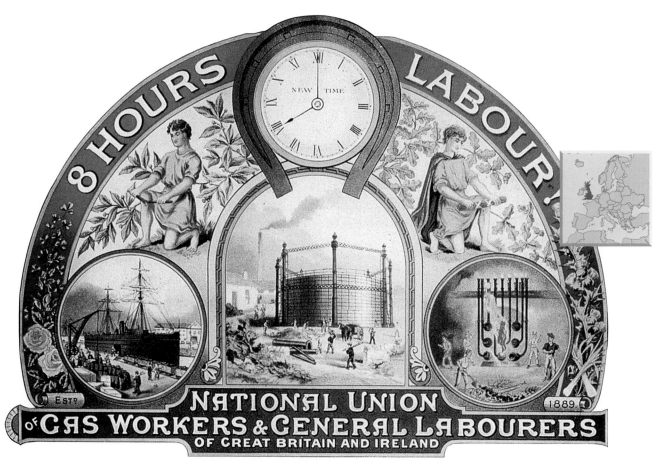

NATIONAL UNION
of GAS WORKERS & GENERAL LABOURERS
OF GREAT BRITAIN AND IRELAND

▲ In the late 1880s, one of the major campaigns of labor unions was for an eight-hour working day, as this British union membership card shows. Most workers did not achieve this goal until the early 1900s.

Workers Fight Back   As the Industrial Revolution went on, some workers formed labor unions. These were organizations that helped workers improve their pay and working conditions. At first, governments passed laws to keep the unions from becoming powerful. Over time, however, labor unions were accepted. Unions won shorter hours, better pay, and safer working conditions for their members and for other workers.

SECTION 3 REVIEW

1. **Define**   (a) Industrial Revolution, (b) textile, (c) labor union.

2. **Identify**   (a) Alexander Graham Bell, (b) Thomas Edison.

3. Why did so many people move from the country to cities during the Industrial Revolution?

4. Why did workers join together to form labor unions?

Critical Thinking

5. **Identifying Central Issues**   Do you agree or disagree with the following statement: "The Industrial Revolution has improved human life"? Explain your answer.

Activity

6. **Writing to Learn**   You are working in a textile mill during the late 1700s. Write a journal entry describing your work day.

Revolution and Imperialism

BEFORE YOU READ

Reach Into Your Background

Have you ever admired someone so much that you thought he or she could do no wrong? How did you feel when you realized that the person had faults, just like other people?

Questions to Explore

1. What changes did Napoleon bring to France?
2. Where and why did European powers seek to build empires in the late 1800s?

Key Terms

Reign of Terror
Napoleonic Code
nationalism
imperialism

Key People and Places

Maximilien Robespierre
Napoleon Bonaparte
Waterloo

▼ Women played an important role in the French Revolution. These poor women of Paris marched to the king's palace at Versailles to demand bread for their hungry children.

Famine gripped Paris in 1789. Thousands of people suffered because there was not enough food. Angry mobs gathered in the streets to protest. On October 5 of that year, thousands of women marched the 12 miles (19 km) from Paris to Versailles. Even though it was raining heavily, they were determined to see the king. They wanted him to come back to Paris so that he could no longer ignore the people's suffering.

The military was eventually able to control the large crowd. Still, the women would not leave without the king. Eventually, King Louis XVI agreed to return to Paris with the crowd. The royal family moved back to Paris. For the next three years, Louis and his family were practically prisoners in their palace in France's capital.

The French Revolution

What had brought the people of France to this situation? What factors led to the French Revolution?

King Louis XVI of France had helped the American colonists win their freedom from the British. Yet he was no great friend of liberty. He had helped because he wanted to reduce the power of the British. The Americans appreciated the help. The French people did not. They had to pay heavy taxes to support the army.

France's Problems France had always had tax problems. Under the French political system, only the working people paid taxes. The nobles and clergy, or church officials, paid nothing. The most successful merchants also found ways to avoid taxes. Thus it was the poorest people who carried the heaviest burden.

As France's money problems grew worse, taxes rose. Louis XVI was unable to solve these problems. The French began to demand that Louis share power. They used the arguments of Enlightenment thinkers to support their demands.

Then came the winter of 1788–1789. It was the worst winter in nearly 100 years. Crops were destroyed. Eighteen million people were starving. Riots broke out. Finally, in May 1789, the king called a meeting of representatives of the three estates, or divisions, of French society—the nobles, the clergy, and the middle class. These representatives formed a National Assembly that wrote a constitution, a plan for a government. France, like England, became a limited monarchy. This marked the beginning of the French Revolution.

When Terror Ruled The king of France had relatives in Austria and Prussia, a state in what is now Germany. They were absolute monarchs. They were afraid that if Louis' power was destroyed, theirs might be too. They sent armies to invade France to help the king. The French Assembly declared war on these foreign powers. When the war began to go badly for France, crowds of French citizens began to riot.

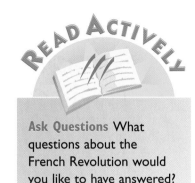

READ ACTIVELY

Ask Questions What questions about the French Revolution would you like to have answered?

The Tennis Court Oath

Louis XVI tried to prevent the National Assembly from writing a new constitution by locking them out of their meeting rooms. However, they gathered in an indoor tennis court. There, they took an oath not to disband until they had written the constitution. This painting of the Tennis Court Oath is by Jacques-Louis David, the most famous French artist of the revolutionary years.

To Be a Leader When news of the French Revolution reached the French island colony of Saint-Domingue (san duh MANG) in the Caribbean, enslaved Africans decided that they would fight for freedom, too. This revolt was led by a nearly 50-year-old former slave, Toussaint L'Ouverture (too SAN loo vur TOOR). He died in the struggle in 1803. His example, however, inspired the people of Saint-Domingue to keep fighting. Eventually they won out, founding the independent country of Haiti in 1804.

They stormed the palace and captured the king. A few months later, Louis XVI was executed.

A few men who called themselves the Committee of Public Safety seized power. They declared that the new constitution was no longer in effect. Maximilien Robespierre (rohbz PYAIR) led the committee in carrying out what became known as the **Reign of Terror.** For nearly a year, perhaps as many as 70 to 80 people were executed every day. No one was safe. Women and children were killed as well as men. Those who had helped to create the constitution were killed as well as those who had fought against it. Finally, Robespierre himself was executed, and the Reign of Terror ended.

The Age of Napoleon

France was still at war, however. The monarchs of Britain, Holland, and Spain had joined those of Austria and Prussia to defend the rights of kings. A young officer in the French army, Napoleon Bonaparte, won one remarkable victory after another against these foreign armies. In a little over a year, he rose from captain to general. Napoleon continued to astonish the world with his leadership. He took control of the French government in 1799.

Napoleon's Accomplishments Claiming that he was defending the ideals of the revolution, Napoleon brought many reforms

Napoleon Crossing the Alps

In 1797, Napoleon led French forces across the Alps into Austria. When he threatened the Austrian capital, Vienna, the Austrians decided to make peace. As a result, the French hailed Napoleon as a hero. This painting of Napoleon crossing the Alps, like that of the Tennis Court Oath, is by Jacques-Louis David. **Critical Thinking** What do you think David's purpose was in this painting?

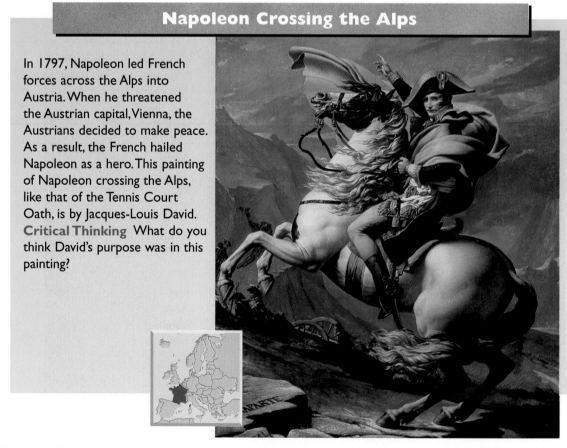

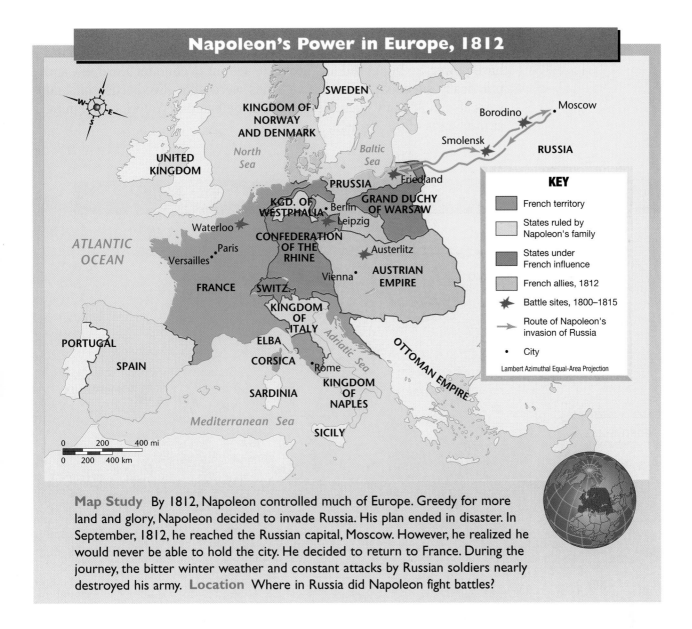

Napoleon's Power in Europe, 1812

KEY

- French territory
- States ruled by Napoleon's family
- States under French influence
- French allies, 1812
- ★ Battle sites, 1800–1815
- → Route of Napoleon's invasion of Russia
- • City

Lambert Azimuthal Equal-Area Projection

Map Study By 1812, Napoleon controlled much of Europe. Greedy for more land and glory, Napoleon decided to invade Russia. His plan ended in disaster. In September, 1812, he reached the Russian capital, Moscow. However, he realized he would never be able to hold the city. He decided to return to France. During the journey, the bitter winter weather and constant attacks by Russian soldiers nearly destroyed his army. **Location** Where in Russia did Napoleon fight battles?

to France. During the revolution, the government had taken control of the Catholic Church. Napoleon, however, knew that religion was important to many French people. He let the Catholic Church operate freely again. He also allowed other religions to have their freedom.

Perhaps Napoleon's most important accomplishment was to reform the laws. He had a team of lawyers study all the laws of France. Many of the laws were poorly written and confusing. The lawyers rewrote the laws so that they were clear and easy to understand. These new laws were called the **Napoleonic Code.**

Napoleon's Downfall In time, Napoleon convinced the French parliament to make him emperor. He received this honor at a grand ceremony in Paris.

As emperor, Napoleon kept many of the reforms of the revolution. For instance, he made sure that the laws applied to everyone, whether rich or poor.

However, Napoleon was no perfect hero. Like many people who have power, he hungered for more. He set out to conquer Europe—and practically succeeded. Yet his victories were short-lived. His constant wars also took many lives. He was finally defeated at Waterloo, Belgium, at the hands of the British.

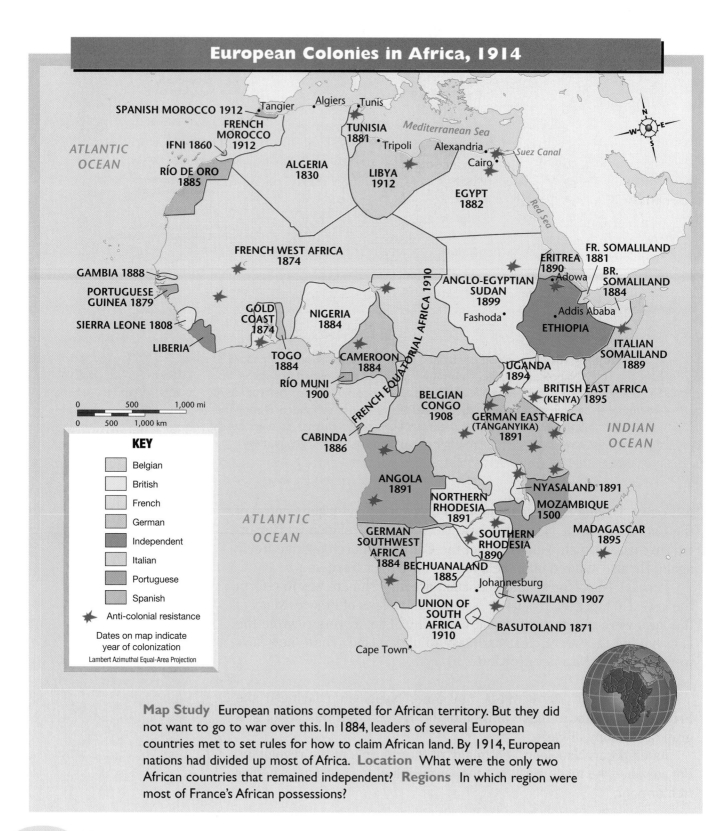

European Colonies in Africa, 1914

SPANISH MOROCCO 1912
FRENCH MOROCCO 1912
IFNI 1860
RÍO DE ORO 1885
ATLANTIC OCEAN
Tangier
Algiers
Tunis
TUNISIA 1881
Tripoli
Mediterranean Sea
Alexandria
Cairo
Suez Canal
Red Sea
ALGERIA 1830
LIBYA 1912
EGYPT 1882
GAMBIA 1888
PORTUGUESE GUINEA 1879
SIERRA LEONE 1808
LIBERIA
FRENCH WEST AFRICA 1874
GOLD COAST 1874
NIGERIA 1884
TOGO 1884
CAMEROON 1884
RÍO MUNI 1900
CABINDA 1886
FRENCH EQUATORIAL AFRICA 1910
ANGLO-EGYPTIAN SUDAN 1899
Fashoda
ERITREA 1890
Adowa
Addis Ababa
ETHIOPIA
FR. SOMALILAND 1881
BR. SOMALILAND 1884
ITALIAN SOMALILAND 1889
UGANDA 1894
BELGIAN CONGO 1908
BRITISH EAST AFRICA (KENYA) 1895
GERMAN EAST AFRICA (TANGANYIKA) 1891
INDIAN OCEAN
ANGOLA 1891
NORTHERN RHODESIA 1891
NYASALAND 1891
MOZAMBIQUE 1500
ATLANTIC OCEAN
GERMAN SOUTHWEST AFRICA 1884
BECHUANALAND 1885
SOUTHERN RHODESIA 1890
Johannesburg
MADAGASCAR 1895
SWAZILAND 1907
UNION OF SOUTH AFRICA 1910
BASUTOLAND 1871
Cape Town

0   500   1,000 mi
0   500   1,000 km

KEY

Belgian
British
French
German
Independent
Italian
Portuguese
Spanish
★ Anti-colonial resistance

Dates on map indicate year of colonization
Lambert Azimuthal Equal-Area Projection

Map Study European nations competed for African territory. But they did not want to go to war over this. In 1884, leaders of several European countries met to set rules for how to claim African land. By 1914, European nations had divided up most of Africa. **Location** What were the only two African countries that remained independent? **Regions** In which region were most of France's African possessions?

Nations and Empires

As Napoleon and his armies moved through Europe, they carried the ideas and the spirit of the French Revolution with them. The French Revolution told people that they had the right to rule themselves. It also taught them to appreciate their own nation. This desire for independence and pride in one's country is called **nationalism.**

Napoleon's wars gave some the chance to act on these ideals. While the European powers were busy fighting among themselves, some of their colonies took the chance to win their freedom.

Yet, as people in some parts of the world broke away from their foreign rulers, others came under foreign rule. By the 1800s, Europe was strong economically and politically. Confident of their power, European countries began to expand aggressively. There were several reasons for this. First, factories all over Europe needed more raw materials—more cotton, metal, coal, and rubber. Second, the goods the factories made had to be sold somewhere so factory owners could make money. The major countries of Europe set up colonies in Africa and Asia to get raw materials and sell goods. Nations also established colonies to protect trade routes. This effort to create an empire of colonies is called **imperialism.** The map on the previous page illustrates how imperalism affected Africa.

▲ In this cartoon from the late 1800s, the Chinese watch helplessly as the colonial powers of Britain, Germany, Russia, France, and Japan claim "slices" of China.

Closely linked to the economic reasons for imperialism were political and military interests. When one country established a colony, others did the same. No one country wanted to see its neighbors gain more power or greater wealth than it had.

France, Germany, Italy, the Netherlands, Portugal, and Belgium were all imperialists. The United States, too, claimed Puerto Rico and the Philippines. The greatest imperialist power of all, however, was Britain. By 1914, the British empire covered about one quarter of the Earth's land surface and included one quarter of the world's population.

SECTION 4 REVIEW

1. **Define** (a) Reign of Terror, (b) Napoleonic Code, (c) nationalism, (d) imperialism.

2. **Identify** (a) Maximilien Robespierre, (b) Napoleon Bonaparte, (c) Waterloo.

3. What did Napoleon do to improve life for the average person in France?

4. (a) Why did European nations create empires? (b) Where did they build their colonies?

Critical Thinking

5. **Making Comparisons** Compare the rule of King Louis XVI with that of Napoleon.

Activity

6. **Writing to Learn** Write a journal entry showing how one of the people discussed in this chapter was both a positive influence and a negative influence. List the ways in which this person was a positive influence. Then list the ways in which he or she was a negative influence.

Review and Activities

Reviewing Main Ideas

1. Name two things that made the Elizabethan Age a glorious time for England.
2. How did England become a constitutional monarchy?
3. How did Copernicus and Newton change the way people thought about the universe?
4. According to John Locke, what could people do if their government took away their right to freedom?
5. Why did so many people move away from farms during the Industrial Revolution?
6. Describe the working and living conditions of factory workers in the 1800s.
7. How did Napoleon reform the laws of France?
8. (a) In what parts of the world did European powers start colonies in the late 1800s? (b) Why did they do so?

Reviewing Key Terms

Use each key term below in a sentence that shows the meaning of the term.

1. civil war
2. bill of rights
3. revolution
4. constitutional monarchy
5. Enlightenment
6. scientific method
7. natural law
8. colony
9. textile
10. labor union
11. Napoleonic Code
12. nationalism
13. imperialism

Critical Thinking

1. **Recognizing Cause and Effect** In what ways did the American Revolution influence the French Revolution?
2. **Making Comparisons** Review the Glorious Revolution and the French Revolution. How were these two events similar? How were they different?

Graphic Organizer

Copy this chart on a separate sheet of paper. Then write the names of four events that grew out of the Enlightenment.

Enlightenment

Map Activity

Place Location

The Western World
For each place listed below, write the letter from the map that shows its location.

1. Versailles
2. Africa
3. France
4. Waterloo
5. Paris

Writing Activity

Writing a Tribute
Choose a person from this chapter about whom you would like others to know more. Write a short essay about this person, describing his or her accomplishments.

Take It to the NET

Activity Read about the working conditions of women in the textile and mining industries during the Industrial Revolution. For help in completing this activity, visit **www.phschool.com**.

Chapter 7 Self-Test To review what you have learned, take the Chapter 7 Self-Test and get instant feedback on your answers. Go to **www.phschool.com** to take the test.

Skills Review

Turn to the Skills Activity.
Review the three steps for reading a line graph. Then answer the following questions: (a) What is an axis? (b) How can line graphs be helpful in presenting information?

How Am I Doing?

Answer these questions to help you check your progress.

1. Can I discuss the ways in which the Enlightenment affected science and politics in Europe?

2. Do I understand how the Industrial Revolution changed the way people in Europe lived?

3. Can I explain how revolutions changed the governments of France and England?

4. What information from this chapter can I include in my journal?

CHAPTER 8

A Century of Turmoil

PICTURE ACTIVITIES

The picture above shows a momentous event in twentieth-century history—the fall of the Berlin Wall in 1989. For nearly 30 years, this mass of concrete and barbed wire separated parents from children and friend from friend. It also served as a symbol for the separation of two world views. Its fall, too, was also a symbol—of hope for a new, more peaceful world. To begin a study of twentieth-century history, do the following activities.

Study the picture
Look closely at the people in the picture. How would you describe their mood?

Write a caption
You are a newspaper editor. Write a 25-word caption describing what is happening in the picture.

World Wars and Revolution

BEFORE YOU READ

Reach Into Your Background

Have you ever promised to help a friend if he or she gets into trouble? What would you do if your friend asked you to fulfill that promise?

Questions to Explore

1. Why was Russia struck by revolution?
2. Why was the world torn by major wars twice in the 1900s?

Key Terms

czar   armistice
serf   genocide
communism   Holocaust
alliance   atomic bomb

Key People and Places

Vladimir Lenin
Adolf Hitler
Hiroshima
Nagasaki

Nicholas II and Alexandra, rulers of Russia, were very proud of their family. They had four daughters and a son, Alexis. A family friend described Alexis as "one of the handsomest babies one could imagine."

But Alexis was not as healthy as he looked. He had a disease that made it difficult for his blood to clot, or stop flowing. Even the tiniest cut or bruise could kill him. He could not play like other boys. He had to be careful not to get hurt. Everywhere he went, two guards followed him. They were there to try to catch him if he fell.

Alexis was next in line to become the **czar** (zar), or the Russian emperor. But Nicholas's advisors feared that Alexis might not survive long enough to come to the throne.

The Russian Revolution

Like Alexis, the monarchy of Russia was not as healthy as it seemed. Long before Alexis could grow up, the Russian people decided to end the rule of the czars. Nicholas and his family were forced to give up their power.

Why a Revolution? Russia had been ruled by czars for hundreds of years. The czars were absolute rulers. They controlled almost every part of their people's lives. Most people were **serfs,** poor peasant workers who were considered the

▼ This photograph of Czar Nicholas II and his family was taken in 1916. Alexis is seated at his mother's feet.

property of wealthy nobles. Serfs had to work the noble's land and also pay him part of the crops they grew for themselves. In exchange, they were allowed to live on the land.

The system of serfdom finally was ended in 1861. But the serfs remained poor. Freedom did not improve their day-to-day lives. The poor people in the cities, too, struggled to have a good life. Even those in the middle class felt that things could be better. Russians grew more and more unhappy with their government.

At the beginning of the 1900s, some Russians began to organize to remove the czar from power. They were willing to fight to create a better government. They were sure that ending the rule of the czars would mean a better life for everyone.

Revolution and War   A terrible war that started in Europe in 1914 helped to turn more Russians against the czar. This conflict was called World War I. When Russia entered the war, the people at home suffered greatly. Much of the country's food, fuel, and supplies were used for the war effort. This meant that the people at home had to do without basic needs. Support grew for the people who were calling for change. In 1917, Czar Nicholas was forced to give up the throne. Later, he and his family were executed.

Soon after Nicholas gave up power, rebels led by Vladimir Lenin took control of the government. These rebels wanted a communist government. **Communism** (KAHM yoo nizum) is a theory of government that says that all the people should own the farms and factories. Everyone should share the work equally. And everyone should receive an equal share of the rewards. The Communists withdrew Russia from the world

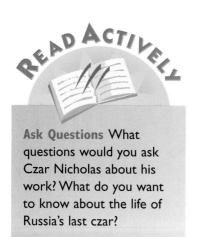

Ask Questions What questions would you ask Czar Nicholas about his work? What do you want to know about the life of Russia's last czar?

▼ The first half of the 1900s was a period of great upheaval.

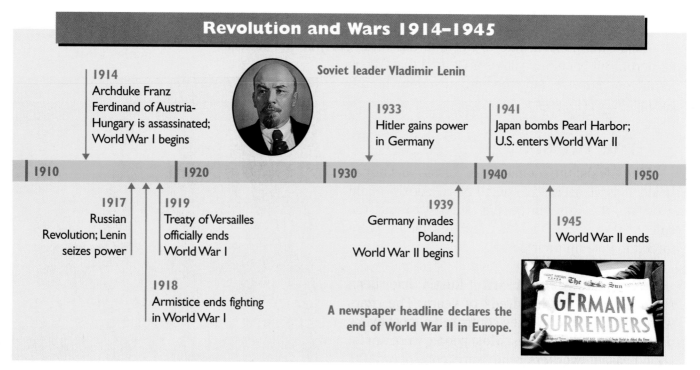

Revolution and Wars 1914–1945

1914
Archduke Franz Ferdinand of Austria-Hungary is assassinated; World War I begins

Soviet leader Vladimir Lenin

1933
Hitler gains power in Germany

1941
Japan bombs Pearl Harbor; U.S. enters World War II

1910   1920   1930   1940   1950

1917
Russian Revolution; Lenin seizes power

1919
Treaty of Versailles officially ends World War I

1939
Germany invades Poland; World War II begins

1945
World War II ends

1918
Armistice ends fighting in World War I

A newspaper headline declares the end of World War II in Europe.

GERMANY SURRENDERS

In March of 1917, angry Russian workers came face to face with the czar's troops in the city of Petrograd (St. Petersburg). The soldiers refused to follow orders to shoot the workers. Instead, they joined the rebellion. Here, soldiers patrol the streets carrying rifles with red flags—the symbol of the revolution. **Critical Thinking** Why do you think the soldiers turned against the czar and refused to obey orders?

war. But the fighting went on in Russia. The Communists fought forces loyal to the czar to hold on to power. They succeeded, creating a new communist nation called the Soviet Union.

Two World Wars

Even after Russia withdrew from World War I, the fighting in Europe continued for another year. World War I was one of the most terrible wars in human history. Never before had so many countries become involved in a single war. And never had the killing been so great.

The Spread of Nationalism For almost 100 years before World War I, Europe had seen only small wars. Two things made a large conflict like World War I possible. One was the growth of nationalism, feelings of loyalty to one's country. Among other things, nationalism encouraged countries to build big armies and to use force to reach their national goals. Feelings of nationalism also helped small conflicts blow up into big ones.

Countries Seek Allies The other main cause of World War I was the development of **alliances,** or agreements that nations make with one another. Usually these alliances include promises to protect each other in case of attack. Nations that have made an alliance are called allies. By teaming up before World War I, nations had hoped to discourage enemy attacks.

LINKS TO ART

Russian Ballet Both before and after the Russian Revolution, ballet was an important form of entertainment in Russia. The school of the Kirov Ballet in St. Petersburg was world famous. Dancers who trained at the school were known for the beauty of their movement. The school continued to train dancers even after the Revolution. Graduates of the Kirov Ballet include Rudolf Nureyev and Mikhail Baryshnikov, two of the greatest dancers of the 1900s.

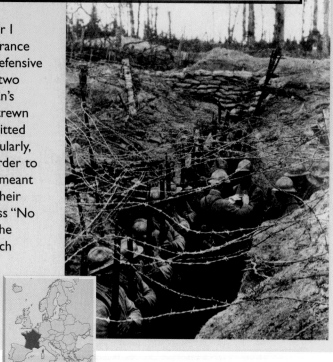

Shortly after World War I began, both armies in France dug a huge system of defensive trenches. Between the two trench lines lay "No Man's Land," an empty area strewn with barbed wire and pitted with bomb craters. Regularly, soldiers received the order to go "over the top." This meant that they had to leave their trenches and race across "No Man's Land" to attack the enemy lines. Here, French soldiers prepare for an inspection before going into battle.

LINKS ACROSS TIME

The Armenian Genocide A spirit of nationalism caused tensions in the empire of the Ottoman Turks during the 1890s. These tensions led to the genocide, or mass killing, of the Armenians, a minority group that lived in the eastern part of the empire. The Muslim Turks accused the Christian Armenians of plotting with the Russians against the Ottoman empire. Turkish leaders ordered a campaign of violence against the Armenians. Over the next 25 years, more than one million Armenian citizens of the Ottoman empire were killed.

But alliances also helped nations become unfriendly toward others. Each country knew that its allies would give their support. Because of alliances, many nations were soon drawn into wars against countries with whom they had no real argument.

World War I The spark that brought European alliances to war was the murder of Archduke Franz Ferdinand of Austria-Hungary. The leaders of Austria-Hungary declared war on Serbia. They suspected the Serbians of organizing the killing. Russia sided with its ally, Serbia. Immediately, Germany joined forces with Austria-Hungary. Then, Britain and France entered the war on the side of Russia. Most other European nations soon chose sides. Eventually, more than 20 nations joined the conflict, including the United States.

Tanks, fighter planes, submarines, machine guns, and poison gas were all used for the first time in World War I. These terrible new weapons led to more deaths than had occurred in any earlier war. Almost 10 million soldiers died. No one knows how many nonsoldiers were killed. The war left large areas of Europe in ruins.

In 1918, the warring nations agreed to an **armistice,** or cease-fire. The winning nations—Britain, France, and their allies—forced a harsh peace agreement on Germany and Austria-Hungary.

World War II The peace agreement that ended World War I left many nations unhappy. Germany, especially, felt it had been unfairly punished for its part in the war. A political leader named Adolf Hitler took advantage of the discontent among Germans. He formed an organization called the Nazi (NAHT see) party and seized power, promising to make Germany great again. He built up the armed forces. Then, using threats and military force, he began to take control of lands that bordered Germany.

Hitler's desire to build a German empire helped bring about World War II. This Second World War was even more terrible than the first. Germany, Italy, and Japan, or the Axis Powers, fought against Britain, France, the United States, and others, or the Allied Powers.

The immediate cause of World War II was Germany's invasion of Poland. The invasion was made possible by Hitler's agreement with the Soviet Union that the two countries would not fight one another. A secret part of this Nazi-Soviet agreement was that the two countries would divide up Poland and other Eastern European countries between them. Germany invaded Poland in September 1939, a month after the deal with the Soviets was signed. Two days after the invasion, Great Britain and France honored their treaties with Poland and declared war on Germany.

Japan quickly sided with Germany, attacking British and French colonies in Southeast Asia. The Japanese attack on Pearl Harbor, Hawaii, on December 7, 1941, drew the United States into the war. The German invasion of the Soviet Union, also in 1941, led Soviet forces to side with the Allied Powers.

World War II was fought all over the world. But most of the fighting took place in Europe, North Africa, Asia, and the Pacific. Almost all the nations of Europe

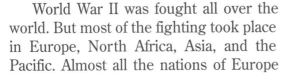

▼ ▲ German bombing in World War II left British cities such as London (below) in ruins. During World War II, many English children were sent to the countryside to escape the bombing (above).

and North Africa were involved. China, several Southeast Asian nations, and Australia took part in the fighting in Asia and the Pacific.

The Nazis committed some of the worst horrors of World War II. Hitler said that Germans were a "superior race." He began a campaign to destroy entire ethnic groups, particularly Jews. This planned killing of entire groups of people is called **genocide.**

The Nazis sent Jews and other "enemies of the people" to prison camps. In the camps, they were forced to work. Often they were worked to death. Others were tortured or simply killed. Millions of Jews and millions of other Europeans died in the camps. This genocide is now called the **Holocaust.**

The Holocaust

In Germany and in the countries that they conquered, the Nazis rounded up Jewish men, women, and children and sent them to prison camps. The roundup below took place in 1940 in the Polish city of Warsaw. These men at right managed to survive the horrors of Buchenwald (BOO kuhn wahld), a prison camp in central Germany.

A mushroom cloud rises above the Japanese city of Hiroshima on August 6, 1945 (below). The explosion destroyed practically every building in the city (left).

World War II also saw the use of a terrible new weapon, the **atomic bomb.** The United States developed this powerful bomb that could destroy whole cities. In 1945, United States President Harry S. Truman decided that an invasion of Japan would cost the lives of many Americans. He made the decision to use the atomic bomb to help end the war quickly. The United States dropped atomic bombs on the Japanese cities of Hiroshima (hir uh SHEE muh) and Nagasaki (nahg uh SAHK ee). The two bombs combined killed about 100,000 people instantly. Thousands of others died later from illnesses caused by radiation poisoning.

The war ended in Europe on May 8, 1945. It ended in Asia on September 2, 1945, shortly after the atomic bombs were dropped on Japan. The United States and its allies had won the war. Yet Europe was once again in ruins, as was much of Japan.

SECTION 1 REVIEW

1. **Define** (a) czar, (b) serf, (c) communism, (d) alliance, (e) armistice, (f) genocide, (g) Holocaust, (h), atomic bomb.

2. **Identify** (a) Vladimir Lenin, (b) Adolf Hitler, (c) Hiroshima, (d) Nagasaki.

3. What were the causes of the Russian Revolution?

4. What were some of the main causes of the two World Wars?

Critical Thinking

5. **Expressing Problems Clearly** How might alliances designed to protect nations draw those nations into war?

Activity

6. **Writing to Learn** Write down five words that describe one of the World Wars. Write a poem describing your feelings about the war. Be sure to include the words you wrote down.

Breaking Colonial Ties

Reach Into Your Background

Do you like to make your own decisions? How do you react when people make your decisions for you and tell you what to do?

Questions to Explore

1. How did colonies win independence in the time after World War II?

2. What challenges did the newly independent nations face?

Key Terms

civil disobedience
racism
developing nation
developed nation

Key People and Places

Mohandas K. Gandhi
Nelson Mandela
Ghana
Algeria
South Africa

▼ The newly independent nation of Ghana adopted a flag with a black star symbolizing African freedom.

It was a great day in world history. A new country was about to be born. More than 70 other countries sent representatives to witness the event.

For many years, the West African region known as the Gold Coast had been a British colony. On this day in 1957, it was breaking its colonial links. The Gold Coast had been ruled by the Portuguese, the Dutch, and then the British. Finally it would be governed by Africans. It would also leave its European name behind and take one that had belonged to an ancient African kingdom—Ghana (GAH nuh).

"We must set an example to all Africa," Ghana's new leader, Kwame Nkrumah (KWAH mee uhn KROO muh), said that day. He was right. After Ghana showed the way, the rest of Africa gradually won its independence from the colonial powers.

Fighting Colonialism

Africa was not the only region to free itself from the bonds of colonial powers. Newly independent nations sprang up in Asia and the Caribbean as well.

During the late 1800s and early 1900s, European countries claimed many areas of the world as their colonies. They sent officials to live in and govern these places. The colonies became a source of wealth for the European countries.

When Europeans colonized an area, they brought their cultures and religions with them. Sometimes, the colonial powers also brought useful new ideas to their colonies. But too often, Europeans expected the people already living in the colonies to start doing things their way.

The Europeans also took power away from the people who lived in the colonies. Often they destroyed the economies of the colonies. People who lived in the colonies were forced to grow crops that could be sold instead of crops they could use to feed themselves. People from colonized areas soon became tired of this treatment and wanted to end European rule.

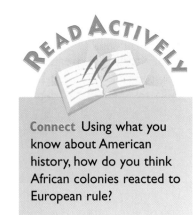

READ ACTIVELY

Connect Using what you know about American history, how do you think African colonies reacted to European rule?

The Colonies and the World Wars During the World Wars, the colonies were expected to side with their colonial rulers. The former French colony of Algeria is a good example. In World War II, Algeria at first sided with France. However, when France was invaded by Germany in 1940, Algeria came under German rule. Then, because Algeria was ruled by Germany, Britain, an ally of France, invaded it. Algerians believed that they had been unfairly caught in a war that was not theirs.

After the war, a number of colonies demanded their independence. Colonies that had helped Britain win the war wanted to be rewarded. And the United States and other nations had promised that all people of the world would be able to choose their own governments after the war.

African demands for self-government quickly gained ground. Africans were tired of being ruled by other countries. And Europeans, weakened by war, found it hard to deny these demands.

Independence in Algeria

Both those who wanted Algeria to remain part of France and those who wanted independence used terror to aid their cause. This picture (left) shows a street in Algiers on March 5, 1962, after more than 100 bomb explosions. The French government called for an end to the violence. This poster (above right) says, "For our children: Peace in Algeria."

Map Study Every nation shown in color on this map was controlled by another country in 1945. The map key indicates the different decades, or ten-year periods, during which each of these nations gained its freedom. Most of the countries in Africa and South and Southeast Asia were colonies of European countries. The countries shown in Eastern Europe came under the control of the Soviet Union after World War II. Most of the countries of central Asia were part of the Russian empire and came under Soviet rule after the 1917 Revolution.

Regions In 1945, which continent—not counting Australia—had the smallest number of independent nations? During which decade did the greatest number of countries on this continent gain independence?

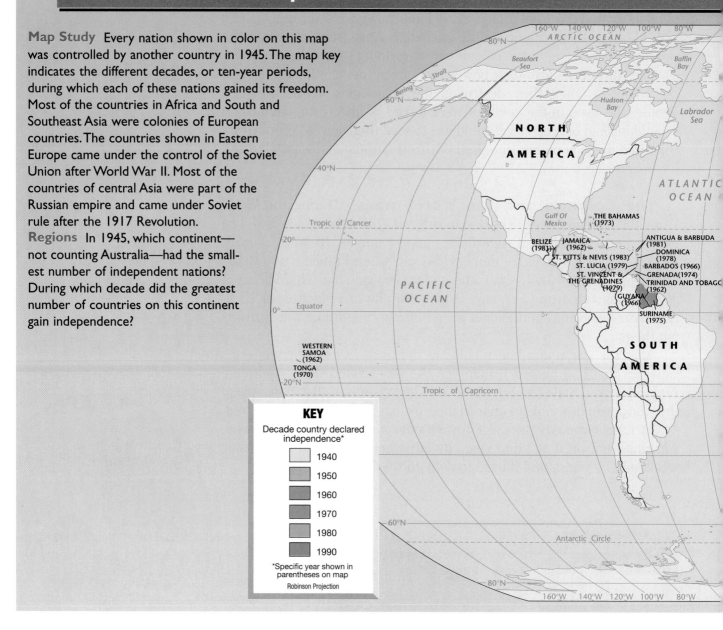

KEY

Decade country declared independence*

	1940
	1950
	1960
	1970
	1980
	1990

*Specific year shown in parentheses on map

Robinson Projection

From Self-Government to Independence Despite the growing world support for African independence, European nations were slow to give up their colonies. They tried to keep them by allowing Africans to have more power in colonial governments. But most Africans thought that this limited self-government was not enough. They wanted full independence.

In some countries, the change to independence was peaceful. Ghana is an example. In other places, like Algeria, it was violent. But whether peaceful or not, the changes were enormous. In 1950, only four African countries were independent of Europe. By 1990, all of Africa except Western Sahara was independent. More than 50 countries had gained their independence.

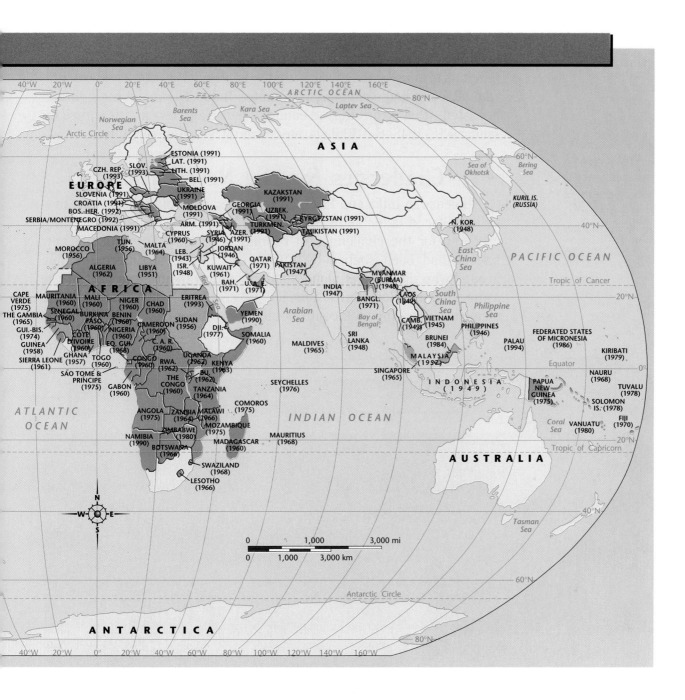

Map labels:

ARCTIC OCEAN

ASIA

Barents Sea

Kara Sea

Laptev Sea

Norwegian Sea

Arctic Circle

80°N

60°N

Sea of Okhotsk

Bering Sea

EUROPE

ESTONIA (1991)
LAT. (1991)
LITH. (1991)
BEL. (1991)
CZH. REP. (1993)
SLOV. (1993)
SLOVENIA (1991)
CROATIA (1991)
BOS.-HER. (1992)
SERBIA/MONTENEGRO (1992)
MACEDONIA (1991)
UKRAINE (1991)
MOLDOVA (1991)
GEORGIA (1991)
ARM. (1991)
AZER. (1991)

KAZAKSTAN (1991)
UZBEK. (1991)
TURKMEN. (1991)
KYRGYZSTAN (1991)
TAJIKISTAN (1991)

KURIL IS. (RUSSIA)

N. KOR. (1948)

40°N

PACIFIC OCEAN

CYPRUS (1960)
SYRIA (1946)
LEB. (1943)
JORDAN (1946)
ISR. (1948)
KUWAIT (1961)
BAH. (1971)
QATAR (1971)
U.A.E. (1971)

TUN. (1956)
MALTA (1964)

MOROCCO (1956)
ALGERIA (1962)
LIBYA (1951)

AFRICA

CAPE VERDE (1975)
MAURITANIA (1960)
MALI (1960)
NIGER (1960)
CHAD (1960)
ERITREA (1993)

THE GAMBIA (1965)
SENEGAL (1960)
BURKINA FASO (1960)
BENIN (1960)
NIGERIA (1960)
CAMEROON (1960)
SUDAN (1956)

GUI.-BIS. (1974)
GUINEA (1958)
SIERRA LEONE (1961)
CÔTE D'IVOIRE (1960)
GHANA (1957)
TOGO (1960)
EQ. GUI. (1968)
C. A. R. (1960)
DJI. (1977)
SOMALIA (1960)

SÃO TOMÉ & PRINCIPE (1975)
GABON (1960)
CONGO (1960)
RWA. (1962)
BU. (1962)
UGANDA (1962)
KENYA (1963)
THE CONGO (1960)
TANZANIA (1964)

ANGOLA (1975)
ZAMBIA (1964)
MALAWI (1966)
ZIMBABWE (1980)
MOZAMBIQUE (1975)
COMOROS (1975)
MADAGASCAR (1960)
MAURITIUS (1968)

NAMIBIA (1990)
BOTSWANA (1966)
SWAZILAND (1968)
LESOTHO (1966)

PAKISTAN (1947)
INDIA (1947)
BANGL. (1971)
MYANMAR (BURMA) (1948)
LAOS (1949)
VIETNAM (1945)
CAMB. (1949)

YEMEN (1990)

MALDIVES (1965)
SRI LANKA (1948)

SEYCHELLES (1976)

BRUNEI (1984)
MALAYSIA (1957)
SINGAPORE (1965)
INDONESIA (1949)

PHILIPPINES (1946)
PALAU (1994)
FEDERATED STATES OF MICRONESIA (1986)
KIRIBATI (1979)
NAURU (1968)
PAPUA NEW GUINEA (1975)
SOLOMON IS. (1978)
TUVALU (1978)
FIJI (1970)
VANUATU (1980)

East China Sea
South China Sea
Philippine Sea
Arabian Sea
Bay of Bengal
INDIAN OCEAN
Coral Sea
Tasman Sea

ATLANTIC OCEAN

Tropic of Cancer
20°N
Equator
0°
Tropic of Capricorn
20°S

AUSTRALIA

40°S

60°N

Antarctic Circle

ANTARCTICA

Scale: 0 1,000 3,000 mi / 0 1,000 3,000 km

A Global Movement

Independence movements also gained strength in other parts of the world. Great movements and great leaders appeared wherever people wanted self-rule. India's Mohandas K. Gandhi (GAHN dee) was one such leader. He led the movement for India's independence.

Gandhi used **civil disobedience**—breaking a law on purpose in order to protest it—in his movement. He urged people to protest without using force, or to be nonviolent. He organized strikes, fasts, and marches. And he helped Indians find ways to provide for their own needs so they did not have to depend on Great Britain.

After Britain granted India its independence in 1947, the country was split into two new nations. India became a country with a Hindu

Predict From what you know about Gandhi, what do you think he valued most?

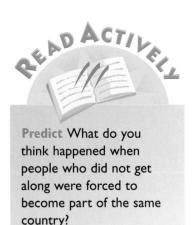
majority. Pakistan became a country with a Muslim majority. The two religious groups began a war with one another. This saddened Gandhi, who all along had struggled for a united India. To protest the fighting, he fasted—that is, he stopped eating. A peace agreement was signed on January 18, 1948. But 12 days later, Gandhi was shot and killed.

Challenges for the New Nations

Violence in India and Pakistan is one example of the problems new nations faced after independence. Often, their leaders were not prepared for the challenges of running a country. Some of the new nations had been shaped by Europeans. People of different ethnic groups who did not get along suddenly found themselves part of the same country. Sometimes this led to civil wars. In some of these countries, the army took control of the government.

Zoo

Nayeem Hassein
age 11
Bangladesh

Bangladesh (bahn gluh DESH), the home of this artist, was once the eastern part of Pakistan. In 1971, it broke away from Pakistan and became an independent nation. The painting shows a zoo in a Bangladeshi city.

Countries such as South Africa, Zimbabwe, and Namibia were free from colonialism. But they had another problem—**racism,** or the belief that one race is better than another. Like other countries around the world, some new African nations made laws that gave power to one group at the cost of another. In South Africa, for example, whites ruled the country for many years after independence. This was so despite the fact there were many more blacks than whites in the country.

Poverty was another problem faced by the new nations. Often their economies were troubled. Most of the world's poorer nations today are former colonies. Many are among the world's **developing nations,** countries with few industries. Most of the former rulers of colonies are **developed nations,** having strong economies and many industries.

The problems of the developing nations are slowly being solved. Government by soldiers is giving way to democracy in many countries. In 1994, South Africa's system of official racism ended for good when a black president, Nelson Mandela (man DEL uh), was elected. And nations have been working to improve their economies. The twenty-first century may be a time of success for the developing nations of the world.

▼ Nelson Mandela was a leader of the movement that resisted South Africa's harsh racist laws. For his activities, Mandela was sentenced to life in jail. He was finally released in 1990 to help South Africa move from white rule to majority rule.

SECTION 2 REVIEW

1. **Define** (a) civil disobedience, (b) racism, (c) developing nation, (d) developed nation.

2. **Identify** (a) Mohandas K. Gandhi, (b) Nelson Mandela, (c) Ghana, (d) Algeria, (e) South Africa.

3. Why did colonies want to become independent after World War II?

4. What challenges did colonies face when they became independent nations?

Critical Thinking

5. **Understanding Cause and Effect** How might fighting in World War II have led Africans to demand their independence?

Activity

6. **Writing to Learn** You are an Indian living in the time of British colonial rule. Write a letter to the editor of a newspaper stating your support for the independence movement. Before you begin, make a list of ideas you would include in such a letter.

SECTION 3

Our Shrinking Globe

BEFORE YOU READ

Reach Into Your Background

What personal challenges have you faced recently? What did you do to meet these challenges?

Questions to Explore

1. What was the Cold War and how did it end?
2. How are the countries of the world trying to protect their environments?

Key Terms

reunification
capitalist country
Cold War
arms race
interdependent

▼ The city of Dresden, in the former communist country of East Germany, now has many private businesses, such as this sidewalk café.

A young East German man was sitting in a West German restaurant in 1990. He turned to a friend and said, "I wonder what the waitress would say if I told her I was eating chocolate ice cream for the first time." He went on to explain that in East Germany "we have brown ice cream, but there is no chocolate in it."

After World War II, Germany had been divided. East Germany became a communist country. West Germany became a democratic country. Because life was so much better in West Germany, East Germans kept trying to escape to the West. In the early 1960s, the East German government tried to stop these attempts. In the divided city of Berlin, the East Germans built a big, ugly wall to stop people from escaping to the West.

In early November 1989, the East German government suddenly announced that its citizens were free to cross into West Germany. The next day, Germans in Berlin began to tear down the wall. Soon, the two Germanys were reunited.

Reunification, or the rejoining of the two parts of Germany, changed the lives of East Germans. Now they could do all sorts of things they had never done before. As one East German said, "I will live to be 101! The hope is so strong right now. Every day is wonderful!"

The First Computer

Built in 1946, the ENIAC, or Electronic Numerical Integrator and Calculator, was the first general-purpose computer ever made. It was so big that it filled a 1,500 square-foot (140 sq-m) room. It used 18,000 parts called vacuum tubes (inset, bottom left). Today, a laptop computer has more power and memory than the old room-filler. These modern computers use tiny silicon chips (inset, top right) instead of bulky vacuum tubes.

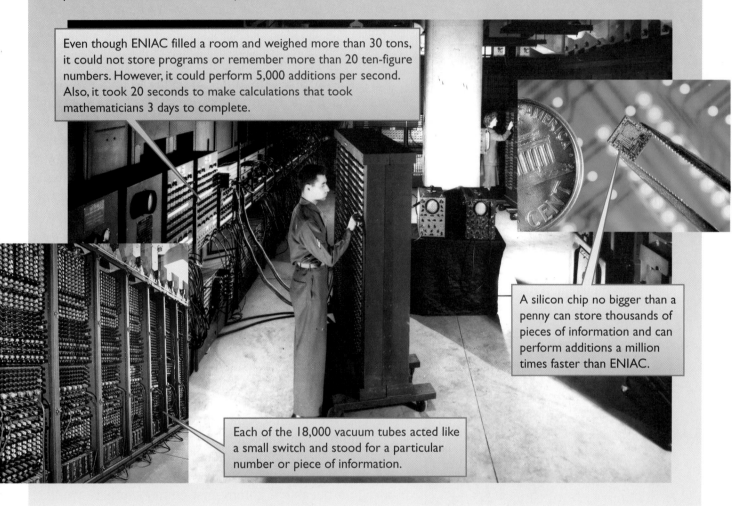

Even though ENIAC filled a room and weighed more than 30 tons, it could not store programs or remember more than 20 ten-figure numbers. However, it could perform 5,000 additions per second. Also, it took 20 seconds to make calculations that took mathematicians 3 days to complete.

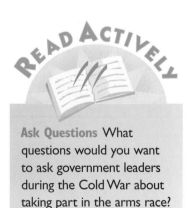

A silicon chip no bigger than a penny can store thousands of pieces of information and can perform additions a million times faster than ENIAC.

Each of the 18,000 vacuum tubes acted like a small switch and stood for a particular number or piece of information.

The Cold War

Today, it seems strange that Germany was ever divided. It happened because the Soviet Union and the United States fought on the same side in World War II. But they did not have a friendly relationship. The two countries had very different social and economic systems. The United States and its Western allies were capitalist countries. The Soviet Union was communist. One important difference between the two systems is that **capitalist countries** allow individuals to own property and businesses. In a communist system, the government usually owns and controls these things.

READ ACTIVELY

Ask Questions What questions would you want to ask government leaders during the Cold War about taking part in the arms race?

▲ In the 1950s, fear of nuclear war was real. People in the United States built bomb shelters and stocked them with food and water. The woman in this shelter is using a device to measure radiation.

▼ During the 1960s and 1970s, Americans organized protests against United States involvement in the Vietnam War.

How Tensions Grew   After World War II, the Soviet Union took control of several Eastern European nations and made them into communist countries. These countries—Poland, Czechoslovakia, Hungary, Romania, East Germany, and Bulgaria—were completely under the control of the Soviet Union.

In 1949, Communists also came to power in China. At about the same time, Korea split into communist and capitalist sections, like Germany. It seemed that the entire world was taking sides. One superpower, the United States, led the capitalist world. The other superpower, the Soviet Union, led the communist world. Each side accused the other of trying to take over the world. Each side believed its system was best. A period of distrust and a greatly increased risk of war followed. This period, from 1945 to 1991, is called the **Cold War.**

People call it the Cold War because the superpowers did not actually fight each other. Still, they created a great deal of tension. Each built more and more weapons. Each was afraid that the other was stronger. In this **arms race,** or attempt by both sides to assemble the biggest arsenal of weapons, the United States and the Soviet Union built many nuclear bombs. It was a frightening time because both countries had enough nuclear bombs to destroy the whole world.

Wars Break Out   The Cold War also resulted in some "hot" wars. In 1950, communist North Korea invaded South Korea. During the Korean War, the United States and other Western nations sent troops to support the South. China supported the North.

Another war happened after Vietnam split into two countries, a communist north and a noncommunist south. Some Americans believed that if one country in a region became a communist country, others would follow, one after another. To prevent this from happening, the United States sent hundreds of thousands of troops to fight the Communists in Vietnam. However, deaths soon started to increase in the Vietnam War. The United States withdrew its troops in the early 1970s. In 1975, North Vietnam defeated South Vietnam. The whole country became communist.

The Cold War Ends   The Cold War ended in the early 1990s, when communist rule collapsed in Eastern Europe and the Soviet Union. Communism had failed to provide its citizens with personal rights and freedoms. It had also failed to provide them with basic needs such as food, shelter, and clothing. In 1991, the Communists in the Soviet Union lost control of the government. The Soviet Union broke up into many smaller nations.

The leaders of the United States and Russia, the major power of the former Soviet Union, finally declared that they did not consider each other enemies. The 46-year-long Cold War came to an end.

Economic Development and the Environment

With the end of the Cold War, the world became more united. Now, more than ever, the nations of the world are **interdependent.** That means that they need one another. Developed nations need the resources of developing nations so that they can make goods.

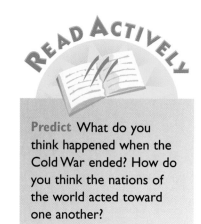

Predict What do you think happened when the Cold War ended? How do you think the nations of the world acted toward one another?

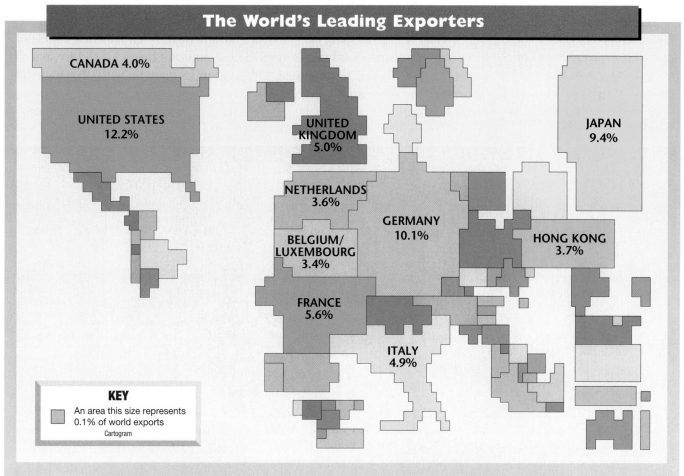

The World's Leading Exporters

CANADA 4.0%

UNITED STATES 12.2%

UNITED KINGDOM 5.0%

JAPAN 9.4%

NETHERLANDS 3.6%

GERMANY 10.1%

HONG KONG 3.7%

BELGIUM/ LUXEMBOURG 3.4%

FRANCE 5.6%

ITALY 4.9%

KEY
An area this size represents 0.1% of world exports
Cartogram

Map Study The map above is a cartogram. On other maps in this book, the size of each country is in proportion to its real area. On a cartogram, the size of a country reflects some other factor. This cartogram shows each country's share of the world's exports. Notice, for example, that the small country of Japan is fairly large on this map. That is because Japan produces a large share of the world's exports. **Movement** Which three countries account for almost one third of the world's exports?

Connect How have people reacted to the challenge of world pollution? Connect the global effort to what is happening in your community.

▼ In 1989, the *Exxon Valdez*, a huge oil tanker, ran aground along the southern coast of Alaska. The damaged ship spilled almost 11 million gallons (42 million liters) of oil into the sea. In this picture, workers clean up after the spill. Many were volunteers.

Developing nations need the tools and know-how of developed nations to become more developed.

Interdependence also means that if one nation has a problem, every nation has a problem. War in one country might make people move to another country, causing hunger or joblessness in the second country. If pollution occurs in one nation, it may spread to another.

Saving the Environment Controlling pollution has become one of the major challenges of today's world. The problem of pollution has been growing since the beginning of the Industrial Revolution in the 1800s. Factories pollute the water and the air. Pesticides—chemicals made to kill insects—pollute the soil. The taking of natural resources, including coal, oil, gold, and timber, has destroyed much of the environment where those resources lie. The wealthy nations have been eager to make use of their resources in spite of the dangers to the environment. And the developing nations have needed the money they can get by selling their resources.

Working Together Some nations have been working together to face environmental challenges. These nations have agreed to search for ways to balance the need for economic growth with the need to protect the environment.

Two girls put the finishing touches on a large globe for an Earth Day celebration. The purpose of Earth Day is to make people aware of environmental issues that affect everyone's health and well-being.

LINKS TO SCIENCE

The Recycling Effort
People around the world have come to understand that many of the Earth's resources cannot be replaced. Once these resources have been used, they are gone forever. People have learned that they must be more careful in their use of such resources. Today, many people are recycling goods. They realize that it is economical to reuse as many materials as possible. Paper, metals, and plastics are being reused in many different forms.

Some progress has been made. Ways have been found to clean certain kinds of pollution caused by smoke released from factories. Cars burn gasoline without giving off poisonous lead. Many materials can be recycled. Nations have joined in passing laws to protect endangered animals. People everywhere have become more aware of the importance of protecting the natural world for the health of all. The key to long-term success will be working together.

SECTION 3 REVIEW

1. **Define** (a) reunification, (b) capitalist country, (c) Cold War, (d) arms race, (e) interdependent.

2. How did the Cold War begin, and how did it end?

3. How have nations begun cleaning up the environment?

Critical Thinking

4. **Cause and Effect** Can you think of some ways in which the Cold War might have made environmental problems worse?

Activity

5. **Writing to Learn** Reread the paragraphs under the section "The Cold War." Make a list of words or phrases that could be used to describe a cold war. Make a similar list for a "hot" war. Use your lists to write a paragraph describing the two kinds of wars.

Expressing Problems Clearly

You belong to a very special generation. Your generation entered a new century as young adults.

As the human race begins a new chapter in history, you will begin a new chapter in your life. This is a good time for looking at the world around you and reflecting upon what you see. What do you like about the world today? What would you like to see changed?

There are a number of situations in the world that need changing, and there always have been. To make a change, you must first know what it is you would like to fix. You have to be able to identify problems and express them clearly.

Get Ready

Expressing problems clearly means stating problems in a direct, complete, and accurate way. The statements should contain facts, not opinions. The facts should be directly related to the problem. By stating problems clearly, you can search for solutions in a more appropriate way. In other words, you will have pinpointed the problem.

Try It Out

Read about the situation that follows and try to clearly express Ben's problem.

Ben had had a rough day. He had run into math class just as Ms. Brown was passing out the tests, and he was too flustered to answer the questions correctly. At soccer practice, he found everyone already playing when got there. He had to wait until the second half to play. When he got home for dinner, his family had practically finished eating, and his chicken was cold. He sat at the table with his meal while his brother and sister started on their homework. He felt so tired.

A. Identify the parts of the problem. What is Ben's problem at the moment? What has made his day so rough?

B. Think about the problem. Think about the events of his day. What do they have in common?

C. Express the problem. In one short sentence, describe the problem with Ben's whole day.

Apply the Skill

You can apply those three steps to larger problems. Read the selection in the box. Then complete the steps that follow.

1 Identify the parts of the problem. What problems are discussed in the selection?

2 Think about the problem. What do all of these problems have in common? What is the single major cause of the different problems?

3 Express the problem. Express the main problem discussed in the selection by writing a short, clear sentence. Then write a few sentences explaining how pinpointing the problem is necessary in order to find a solution to it.

The world's forests have been shrinking for hundreds of years. People have cut them down to make room for living and farming. Many of the woodlands in Europe, North America, and Asia have suffered great losses. Today, tropical rain forests face destruction as well.

The clearing of a rain forest often leaves behind eroded soil that is no good for farming. Trees disappear, and many other plant and animal species become extinct. About two thirds of the world's species live in tropical rain forests. Some people say that thousands of these species are dying out each year. Entire communities of people live in each of the major rain forest regions, and their homes are being destroyed with the rain forests.

▼ An aerial view of one part of the destruction of a rain forest in Brazil.

Review and Activities

Reviewing Main Ideas

1. What brought about the fall of the monarchy in Russia?

2. What were some of the causes and effects of the two World Wars?

3. Why did African nations fight to gain their independence after World War II?

4. What happened to the nations of Africa and Asia after they won their independence?

5. (a) What was the Cold War? (b) Why did the Cold War end?

6. What environmental challenges does the world face today?

Reviewing Key Terms

Use each key term below in a sentence that shows the meaning of the term.

1. czar
2. serf
3. alliance
4. genocide
5. Holocaust
6. atomic bomb
7. civil disobedience
8. racism
9. developing nation
10. developed nation
11. reunification
12. Cold War

Critical Thinking

1. **Making Comparisons** Compare and contrast the fight for independence by different colonized countries such as India, Ghana, and Algeria.

2. **Recognizing Cause and Effect** How did the Cold War lead to several "hot" wars?

Graphic Organizer

Copy this chart onto a separate sheet of paper. Then fill in the empty boxes with examples to complete the chart.

Challenges of the 1900s			
Wars			
Differences in Economic Systems			
Environmental Problems			
Colonialism			
Differences in Wealth			

Map Activity

Africa and India

For each place listed below, write the letter from the map that shows its location. Use information in this chapter and the Atlas in the back of your book to complete this activity.

1. India
2. Ghana
3. Algeria
4. South Africa
5. Zimbabwe

Writing Activity

Write an Outline

Outline the history of the 1900s. Use facts from this chapter to complete your outline.

Take It to the NET

Activity Use maps, personal accounts, and background information to learn about the Normandy invasion in World War II. For help in completing this activity, visit www.phschool.com.

Chapter 8 Self-Test To review what you have learned, take the Chapter 8 Self-Test and get instant feedback on your answers. Go to www.phschool.com to take the test.

Skills Review

Turn to the **Skills Activity**.

Review the three steps for expressing a problem clearly. Then answer the following questions: (a) What questions could you ask in step two? (b) How does expressing a problem clearly make finding the solution easier?

How Am I Doing?

Answer these questions to help you check your progress.

1. Can I explain why world conflicts developed in the 1900s?
2. Do I understand when and how colonies gained their independence?
3. Can I explain how the nations of the world are interdependent?
4. Can I give examples of ways in which nations are responding to environmental challenges?
5. What information from this chapter can I include in my journal?

History Quiz Wizards

Who figured out the law of gravity? How much has the United States grown since 1776? What was *The Tale of Genji?* If you know the right answers, you win three points!

A history quiz game can give you the chance to sharpen your memory and show what you know. And when you write some of the questions yourself, you will have to hunt through history for interesting facts.

Purpose

In this activity, you will create a game to help you and your classmates learn and remember many of the things you have read in this book.

Players will answer questions from all periods of history from medieval times to today. With a group of your classmates, you will write the questions for the quiz.

Take no more than one hour to look through this book and write questions about the history you find. Be sure to write answers as well. Look for information about the topics described on the next page.

Which ocean did Columbus cross on his journeys?

Maps and Globes

Find in this book descriptions of how geography has influenced history. For example, you will read that Christopher Columbus crossed the Atlantic Ocean. Thus you might write the question "Which ocean did Columbus cross on his journeys?" Geography questions will often be answered with the names of countries, cities, landforms, or bodies of water.

Wonderful Words

These questions have to do with language or literature. You can ask for definitions of special words in the text. You can also ask questions about the literature or language of a region. For example, ask, "Why do many Africans speak French?"

How the Earth Works

Questions in this category have to do with science. You might ask about inventors or important scientific discoveries, for example, "What scientist of the Muslim empire made important medical discoveries?"

History Counts

Challenge players to solve a math problem. Use numbers that have to do with historical facts. For example, "The Silk Road was about 3,400 miles long. If a caravan traveled at an average speed of 3 miles per hour, how long would it take to complete the journey?"

Wild Card

Write questions about health, art, music, or any other subject you come across as you read this book. Call this the "wild card" category.

Prepare Question Cards

Develop at least five questions for each of the categories. Write each question on a note card. Write the answer on the back of the card. Color-code your note cards for the five different question categories.

Play

Choose a scorekeeper. This person will ask the questions and keep track of players' right and wrong answers.

To begin, have the first player select one of the five question categories. The scorekeeper should then choose a card from that category and ask the question written on the card. If the player answers correctly, he or she gets a point for that category. Then the next player takes a turn. A player wins the game by correctly answering three questions in each category.

ANALYSIS AND CONCLUSION

1. Was it easier for you to come up with questions for some categories than for others? Why do you think this was so?

2. What did you learn about history by making this game?

3. What did you learn about history by playing this game?

MEDIEVAL TIMES TO TODAY
PROJECT POSSIBILITIES

As you study history from medieval times to today, you will be reading and thinking about these important questions.

☛ **GEOGRAPHY** How did physical geography affect the development of societies around the world?

☛ **HISTORY** How did each society's belief system affect its history?

☛ **CULTURE** What was the pattern of day-to-day life in these societies?

☛ **GOVERNMENT** What types of government were formed in these societies?

☛ **ECONOMICS** How did each society organize its economic activities?

It's time to show what you know about medieval times to today.

GEO LEO

Project Menu

The chapters in this book have some answers to these questions. Now you can find your own answers by doing projects alone or with a group. Here are some ways to make your own discoveries about history from medieval times to today.

One Job Through the Ages There were no airplane pilots 500 years ago, but there were doctors, carpenters, and teachers.

Learn about the history of a job that has been around at least since the Middle Ages. Find out how different cultures have practiced and changed this job over the course of history. For example, how has medicine been affected by doctors from the Muslim empire, medieval China, and Europe in the 1800s?

Put what you learn in a time line. Write brief descriptions of the important contributions of different cultures. Add them to your time line, along with illustrations and a title.

From Questions to Careers

JOBS IN HISTORY MUSEUMS

History museums preserve bits of the past for the enjoyment and education of the people of the present. Some specialize in local history. Others teach about the history of whole nations. Still others are dedicated to specific historical events, like wars or migrations.

Each is also a fascinating place to work. Since most history museums are open to the public, tour guides perform an important job. They show visitors through the museum, explaining exhibits and answering questions. Historians and designers create these exhibits.

Many museums have libraries for historical research. These are usually managed by professional librarians.

Most of these jobs require a college degree. Other jobs, however, do not. There are assistants in many history museums. Jobs in gift shops and information booths are also available for those without a degree. Today, many museums offer on-the-job training.

▶ A tour guide leads a group in the Air and Space Museum.

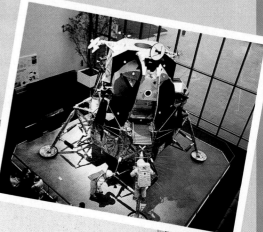

Two Tales of One City

Since medieval times, the great cities of the world have changed dramatically. Five hundred years ago, few cities existed in the Americas. African cities that are now home to millions were tiny villages.

As you read this book, pick a city that has existed for at least 300 years. Choose a year in that city's past, and compare life in that city then to life in that city today. How big was it? What did it look like? What jobs did the people have? Find the answers to these and other questions. Answer the same questions for today.

Make a poster that compares your city's past with its present. Draw pictures of the city then and now. Write captions describing city life in both times.

The Birth of a Nation

Today there are about 200 nations in the world. Each was formed sometime in the past and became a nation over the years. Choose one nation and learn how it came into being.

Conduct research to learn about the nation's history. What country or empire was it once a part of? How did it achieve its independence? Find the answers to these and other important questions. Identify the most important steps the nation took in arriving at the borders, government, and culture it has today.

Then write a short history of the nation. Discuss its birth and growth. Describe what it is like today. Present your work as part of a "Nation Celebration" in your classroom.

Major Migrations

One of the biggest stories in modern history is the vast movement, or migration, of people from some areas of the Earth to others.

As you read in this book about each major human migration, mark it on a world "Migrations Map" in your classroom. Label each migration with its name and date.

Answer these questions about each one: Who migrated? When? From where did they migrate? Where did they go? How did they travel? Why did they migrate? What were the effects of the migration?

Reference

TABLE OF CONTENTS

Handbook
MAP AND GLOBE

This Map and Globe Handbook is designed to help you develop some of the skills you need to be a world explorer. These can help you whether you explore from the top of an elephant in India or from a computer at school.

You can use the information in this handbook to improve your map and globe skills. But the best way to sharpen your skills is to practice. The more you practice the better you'll get.

GEO CLEO and GEO LEO

Table of Contents

Five Themes of Geography

Studying the geography of the entire world can be a huge task. You can make that task easier by using the five themes of geography: location, place, human-environment interaction, movement, and regions. The themes are tools you can use to organize information and to answer the where, why, and how of geography.

1 Location answers the question, "Where is it?" You can think of the location of a continent or a country as its address. You might give an absolute location such as "22 South Lake Street" or "40°N and 80°W." You might also use a relative address, telling where one place is by referring to another place. "Between school and the mall" and "eight miles east of Pleasant City" are examples of relative locations.

2 Place identifies the natural and human features that make one place different from every other place. You can identify a specific place by its landforms, climate, plants, animals, people, or cultures. You might even think of place as a geographic signature. Use the signature to help you understand the natural and human features that make one place different from every other place.

1. Location
Chicago, Illinois, occupies one location on the Earth. No other place has exactly the same absolute location.

2. Place
Ancient cultures in Egypt built distinctive pyramids. Use the theme of place to help you remember features that exist only in Egypt.

3 Human-Environment Interaction focuses on the relationship between people and the environment. As people live in an area, they often begin to make changes to it, usually to make their lives easier. For example, they might build a dam to control flooding during rainy seasons. Also, the environment can affect how people live, work, dress, travel, and communicate.

4 Movement answers the question "How do people, goods, and ideas move from place to place?" Remember that, often, what happens in one place can affect what happens in another. Use the theme of movement to help you trace the spread of goods, people, and ideas from one location to the next.

5 Regions is the last geographic theme. A region is a group of places that share common features. Geographers divide the world into many types of regions. For example, countries, states, and cities are political regions. The people in these places live under the same type of government. Other features can be used to define regions. Places that have the same climate belong to a particular climate region. Places that share the same culture belong to a cultural region. The same place can be found in more than one region. The state of Hawaii is in the political region of the United States. Because it has a tropical climate, Hawaii is also part of a tropical climate region.

3. Human-Environment Interaction
Peruvians have changed steep mountain slopes into terraces suitable for farming. Think how this environment looked before people made changes.

4. Movement
Arab traders brought not only goods to Kuala Lumpur, Malaysia, but also Arab building styles and the Islamic religion.

PRACTICE YOUR WORLD EXPLORER SKILLS

1. What is the absolute location of your school? What is one way to describe its relative location?

2. What might be a "geographic signature" of the town or city you live in?

3. Give an example of human-environment interaction where you live.

4. Name at least one thing that comes into your town or city and one that goes out. How is each moved? Where does it come from? Where does it go?

5. What are several regions you think your town or city belongs in?

5. Regions
Wheat farming is an important activity in Kansas. This means that Kansas is part of a farming region.

Understanding Movements of the Earth

Planet Earth is part of our solar system. The Earth revolves around the sun in a nearly circular path called an orbit. A revolution, or one complete orbit around the sun, takes 365 1/4 days, or a year. As the Earth revolves around the sun, it is also spinning around in space. This movement is called a rotation. The Earth rotates on its axis—an invisible line through the center of the Earth from the North Pole to the South Pole. The Earth makes one full rotation about every 24 hours. As the Earth rotates, it is daytime on the side facing the sun. It is night on the side away from the sun.

The Earth's axis is tilted at an angle. Because of this tilt, sunlight strikes different parts of the Earth at certain points in the year, creating different seasons.

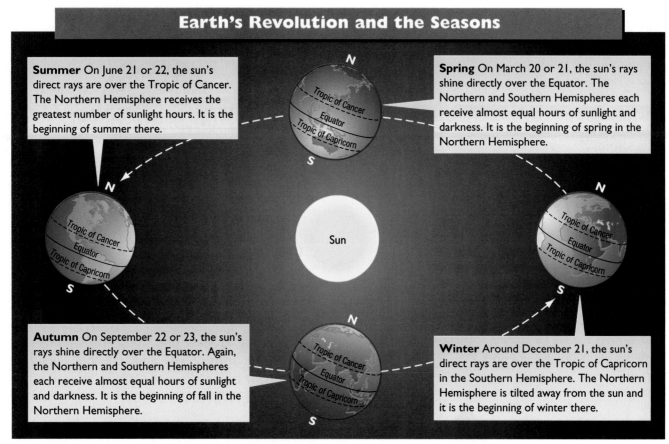

Earth's Revolution and the Seasons

Summer On June 21 or 22, the sun's direct rays are over the Tropic of Cancer. The Northern Hemisphere receives the greatest number of sunlight hours. It is the beginning of summer there.

Spring On March 20 or 21, the sun's rays shine directly over the Equator. The Northern and Southern Hemispheres each receive almost equal hours of sunlight and darkness. It is the beginning of spring in the Northern Hemisphere.

Autumn On September 22 or 23, the sun's rays shine directly over the Equator. Again, the Northern and Southern Hemispheres each receive almost equal hours of sunlight and darkness. It is the beginning of fall in the Northern Hemisphere.

Winter Around December 21, the sun's direct rays are over the Tropic of Capricorn in the Southern Hemisphere. The Northern Hemisphere is tilted away from the sun and it is the beginning of winter there.

▲ **Location** This diagram shows how the Earth's tilt and orbit around the sun combine to create the seasons. Remember, in the Southern Hemisphere the seasons are reversed.

PRACTICE YOUR WORLD EXPLORER SKILLS

1. What causes the seasons in the Northern Hemisphere to be the opposite of those in the Southern Hemisphere?

2. During which two months of the year do the Northern and Southern Hemispheres have about equal hours of daylight and darkness?

Maps and Globes Represent the Earth

Globes

A globe is a scale model of the Earth. It shows the actual shapes, sizes, and locations of all the Earth's landmasses and bodies of water. Features on the surface of the Earth are drawn to scale on a globe. This means a smaller unit of measure on the globe stands for a larger unit of measure on the Earth.

Because a globe is made in the true shape of the Earth, it offers these advantages for studying the Earth.

- The shape of all land and water bodies are accurate.
- Compass directions from one point to any other point are correct.
- The distance from one location to another is always accurately represented.

However, a globe presents some disadvantages for studying the Earth. Because a globe shows the entire Earth, it cannot show small areas in great detail. Also, a globe is not easily folded and carried from one place to another. For these reasons, geographers often use maps to learn about the Earth.

Maps

A map is a drawing or representation, on a flat surface, of a region. A map can show details too small to be seen on a globe. Floor plans, mall directories, and road maps are among the maps we use most often.

While maps solve some of the problems posed by globes, they have some disadvantages of their own. Maps flatten the real round world. Mapmakers cut, stretch, push, and pull some parts of the Earth to get it all flat on paper. As a result, some locations may be distorted. That is, their size, shape, and relative location may not be accurate. For example, on most maps of the entire world, the size and shape of the Antarctic and Arctic regions are not accurate.

PRACTICE YOUR WORLD EXPLORER SKILLS

1. What is the main difference between a globe and a map?

2. What is one advantage of using a globe instead of a map?

Global Gores

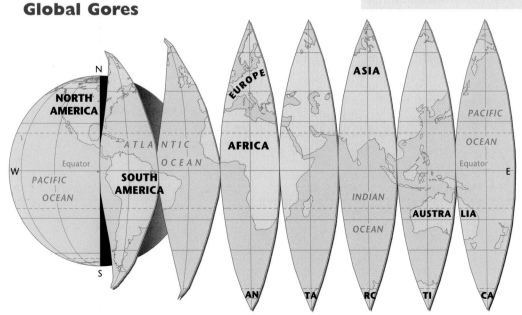

◀ **Location**
When mapmakers flatten the surface of the Earth, curves become straight lines. As a result, size, shape, and distance are distorted.

Locating Places on a Map or a Globe

The Hemispheres

Another name for a round ball like a globe is a sphere. The Equator, an imaginary line halfway between the North and South Poles, divides the globe into two hemispheres. (The prefix *hemi* means "half.") Land and water south of the Equator are in the Southern Hemisphere. Land and water north of the Equator are in the Northern Hemisphere.

Mapmakers sometimes divide the globe along an imaginary line that runs from North Pole to South Pole. This line, called the Prime Meridian, divides the globe into the Eastern and Western Hemispheres.

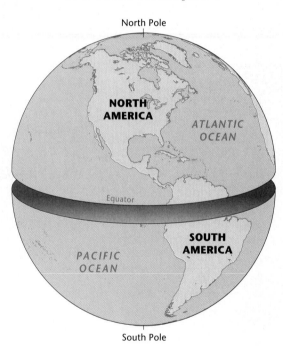

Southern Hemisphere

▲ The Equator divides the Northern Hemisphere from the Southern Hemisphere.

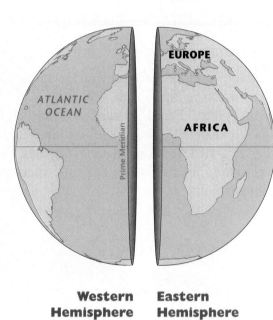

**Western   Eastern
Hemisphere   Hemisphere**

▲ The Prime Meridian divides the Eastern Hemisphere from the Western Hemisphere.

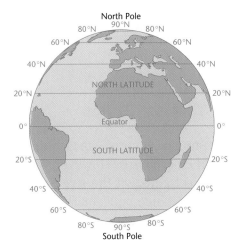

Parallels of Latitude

The Equator, at 0° latitude, is the starting place for measuring latitude or distances north and south. Most globes do not show every parallel of latitude. They may show every 10, 20, or even 30 degrees.

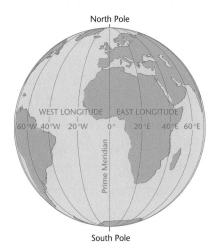

Meridians of Longitude

The Prime Meridian, at 0° longitude, runs from pole to pole through Greenwich, England. It is the starting place for measuring longitude or distances east and west. Each meridian of longitude meets its opposite longitude at the North and South Poles.

The Global Grid

Two sets of lines cover most globes. One set of lines runs parallel to the Equator. These lines, including the Equator, are called *parallels of latitude*. They are measured in degrees (°). One degree of latitude represents a distance of about 70 miles (112 km). The Equator has a location of 0°. The other parallels of latitude tell the direction and distance from the Equator to another location.

The second set of lines runs north and south. These lines are called *meridians of longitude*. Meridians show the degrees of longitude east or west of the Prime Meridian, which is located at 0°. A meridian of longitude tells the direction and distance from the Prime Meridian to another location. Unlike parallels, meridians are not the same distance apart everywhere on the globe.

Together the pattern of parallels of latitude and meridians of longitude is called the global grid. Using the lines of latitude and longitude, you can locate any place on Earth. For example, the location of 30° north latitude and 90° west longitude is usually written as 30°N, 90°W. Only one place on Earth has these coordinates—the city of New Orleans, in the state of Louisiana.

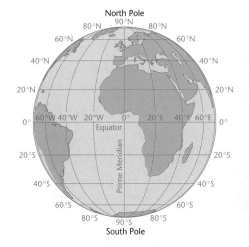

The Global Grid

By using lines of latitude and longitude, you can give the absolute location of any place on the Earth.

PRACTICE YOUR WORLD EXPLORER SKILLS

1. Which continents lie completely in the Northern Hemisphere? The Western Hemisphere?

2. Is there land or water at 20°S latitude and the Prime Meridian? At the Equator and 60°W longitude?

*I*magine trying to flatten out a complete orange peel. The peel would split. The shape would change. You would have to cut the peel to get it to lie flat. In much the same way, maps cannot show the correct size and shape of every landmass or body of water on the Earth's curved surface. Maps shrink some places and stretch others. This shrinking and stretching is called distortion—*a change made to a shape.*

To make up for this disadvantage, mapmakers use different map projections. Each map projection is a way of showing the round Earth on flat paper. Each type of projection has some distortion. No one projection can accurately show the correct area, shape, distance, and direction for the Earth's surface. Mapmakers use the projection that has the least distortion for the information they are studying.

Same-Shape Maps

Some map projections can accurately show the shapes of landmasses. However, these projections often greatly distort the size of landmasses as well as the distance between them.

One of the most common same-shape maps is a Mercator projection, named for the mapmaker who invented it. The Mercator projection accurately shows shape and direction, but it distorts distance and size. In this projection, the northern and southern areas of the globe appear stretched more than areas near the Equator. Because the projection shows true directions, ships' navigators use it to chart a straight line course between two ports.

Mercator Projection

Equal-Area Maps

Some map projections can show the correct size of landmasses. Maps that use these projections are called equal-area maps. In order to show the correct size of landmasses, these maps usually distort shapes. The distortion is usually greater at the edges of the map and less at the center.

Robinson Maps

Many of the maps in this book use the Robinson projection. This is a compromise between the Mercator and equal-area projections. It gives a useful overall picture of the world. The Robinson projection keeps the size and shape relationships of most continents and oceans but does distort size of the polar regions.

Azimuthal Maps

Another kind of projection shows true compass direction. Maps that use this projection are called azimuthal maps. Such maps are easy to recognize—they are usually circular. Azimuthal maps are often used to show the areas of the North and South Poles. However, azimuthal maps distort scale, area, and shape.

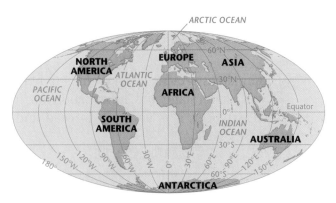

Equal-Area Projection

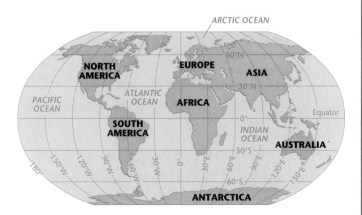

Robinson Projection

PRACTICE YOUR WORLD EXPLORER SKILLS

1. What feature is distorted on an equal-area map?

2. Would you use a Mercator projection to find the exact distance between two locations? Tell why or why not.

3. Which would be a better choice for studying the Antarctic—an azimuthal projection or a Robinson projection? Explain.

Azimuthal Projection

Parts of a Map

Mapmakers provide several clues to help you understand the information on a map. As an explorer, it is your job to read and interpret these clues.

Compass

Many maps show north at the top of the map. One way to show direction on a map is to use an arrow that points north. There may be an N shown with the arrow. Many maps give more information about direction by displaying a compass showing the directions, north, east, south, and west. The letters N, E, S, and W are placed to indicate these directions.

Title

The title of a map is the most basic clue. It signals what kinds of information you are likely to find on the map. A map titled *West Africa: Population Density* will be most useful for locating information about where people live in West Africa.

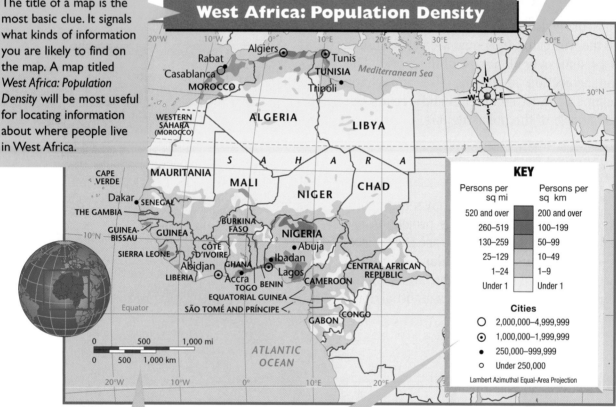

West Africa: Population Density

KEY

Persons per sq mi	Persons per sq km
520 and over	200 and over
260–519	100–199
130–259	50–99
25–129	10–49
1–24	1–9
Under 1	Under 1

Cities

○ 2,000,000–4,999,999
◉ 1,000,000–1,999,999
● 250,000–999,999
○ Under 250,000

Lambert Azimuthal Equal-Area Projection

Scale

A map scale helps you find the actual distances between points shown on the map. You can measure the distance between any two points on the map, compare them to the scale, and find out the actual distance between the points. Most map scales show distances in both miles and kilometers.

Key

Often a map has a key, or legend, that shows the symbols used on the map and what each one means. On some maps, color is used as a symbol. On those maps, the key also tells the meaning of each color.

PRACTICE YOUR WORLD EXPLORER SKILLS

❶ What part of a map tells you what the map is about?

❷ Where on the map should you look to find out the meaning of this symbol? ●

❸ What part of the map can you use to find the distance between two cities?

Comparing Maps of Different Scale

ere are three maps drawn to three different scales. The first map shows Moscow's location in the northeastern portion of Russia. This map shows the greatest area—a large section of northern Europe. It has the smallest scale (1 inch = about 900 miles) and shows the fewest details. This map can tell you what direction to travel to reach Moscow from Finland.

Find the red box on Map 1. It shows the whole area covered by Map 2. Study Map 2. It gives a closer look at the city of Moscow. It shows the features around the city, the city's boundary, and the general shape of the city. This map can help you find your way from the airport to the center of town.

Now find the red box on Map 2. This box shows the area shown on Map 3. This map moves you closer into the city. Like the zoom on a computer or camera, Map 3 shows the smallest area but has the greatest detail. This map has the largest scale (1 inch = about 0.8 miles). This is the map to use to explore downtown Moscow.

Map 1

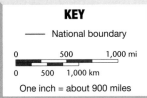

KEY

—— National boundary

0   500   1,000 mi

0   500   1,000 km

One inch = about 900 miles

Map 2

KEY

▨ Built-up area

—— Road or street

0   5   10 mi

0   5   10 km

One inch = about 12.5 miles

Map 3

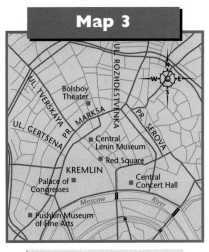

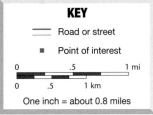

KEY

— Road or street

■ Point of interest

0   .5   1 mi

0   .5   1 km

One inch = about 0.8 miles

PRACTICE YOUR WORLD EXPLORER SKILLS

1. Which map would be best for finding the location of Red Square? Why?

2. Which map best shows Moscow's location relative to Poland? Explain.

3. Which map best shows the area immediately surrounding the city?

Political Maps

Mapmakers create maps to show all kinds of information. The kind of information presented affects the way a map looks. One type of map is called a political map. Its main purpose is to show continents, countries, and divisions within countries such as states or provinces. Usually different colors are used to show different countries or divisions within a country. The colors do not have any special meaning. They are used only to make the map easier to read.

Political maps also show where people have built towns and cities. Symbols can help you tell capital cities from other cities and towns. Even though political maps do not give information that shows what the land looks like, they often include some physical features such as oceans, lakes, and rivers.

Political maps usually have many labels. They give country names, and the names of capital and major cities. Bodies of water such as lakes, rivers, oceans, seas, gulfs, and bays are also labeled.

PRACTICE YOUR **WORLD EXPLORER** SKILLS

1. What symbol shows the continental boundary?

2. What symbol is used to indicate a capital city? A major city?

3. What kinds of landforms are shown on this map?

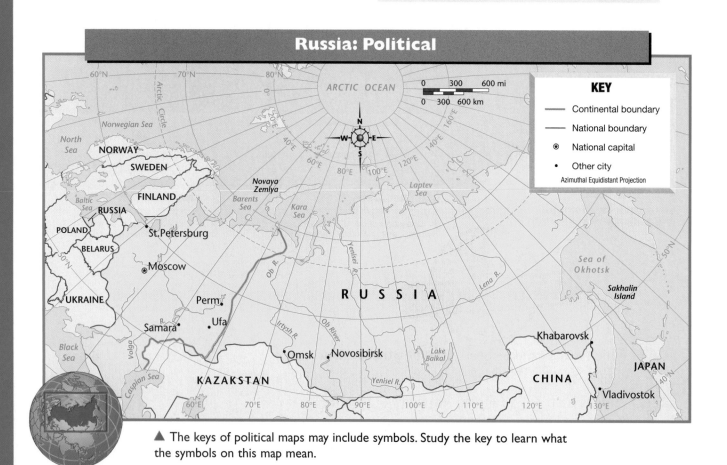

Russia: Political

KEY
— Continental boundary
— National boundary
⊛ National capital
• Other city
Azimuthal Equidistant Projection

▲ The keys of political maps may include symbols. Study the key to learn what the symbols on this map mean.

Physical Maps

Like political maps, physical maps show country labels and labels for capital cities. However, physical maps also show what the land of a region looks like by showing the major physical features such as plains, hills, plateaus, or mountains. Labels give the names of features such as mountain peaks, mountains, plateaus, and river basins.

In order to tell one landform from another, physical maps often show elevation and relief.

Elevation is the height of the land above sea level. Physical maps in this book use color to show elevation. Browns and oranges show higher lands while blues and greens show lands that are at or below sea level.

Relief shows how quickly the land rises or falls. Hills, mountains, and plateaus are shown on relief maps using shades of gray. Level or nearly level land is shown without shading. Darkly shaded areas indicate steeper lands.

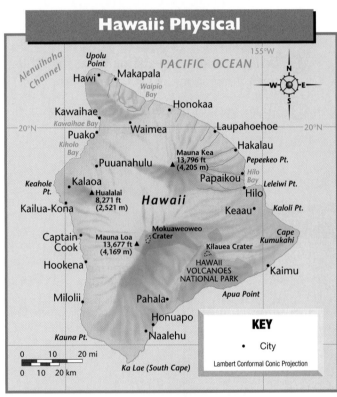

Hawaii: Physical

▲ On a physical map, shading is sometimes used to show relief. Use the shading to locate the mountains in Hawaii.

PRACTICE YOUR WORLD EXPLORER SKILLS

1. How is relief shown on the map to the left?

2. How can you use relief to decide which areas will be the most difficult to climb?

3. What information is given with the name of a mountain peak?

▼ Mauna Kea, an extinct volcano, is the highest peak in the state of Hawaii. Find Mauna Kea on the map.

Special Purpose Maps

As you explore the world, you will encounter many different kinds of special purpose maps. For example, a road map is a special purpose map. The title of each special purpose map tells the purpose and content of the map. Usually a special purpose map highlights only one kind of information. Examples of special purpose maps include land use, population distribution, recreation, transportation, natural resources, or weather.

The key on a special purpose map is very important. Even though a special purpose map shows only one kind of information, it may present many different pieces of data. This data can be shown in symbols, colors, or arrows. In this way, the key acts like a dictionary for the map.

Reading a special purpose map is a skill in itself. Look at the map below. First, try to get an overall sense of what it shows. Then, study the map to identify its main ideas. For example, one main idea of this map is that much of the petroleum production in the region takes place around the Persian Gulf.

1. What part of a special purpose map tells what information is contained on the map?

2. What part of a special purpose map acts like a dictionary for the map?

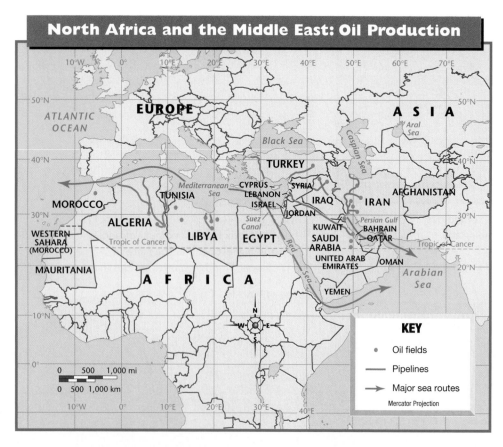

North Africa and the Middle East: Oil Production

◀ The title on a special purpose map indicates what information can be found on the map. The symbols used on the map are explained in the map's key.

KEY
- Oil fields
- Pipelines
- → Major sea routes

Mercator Projection

Landforms, Climate Regions, and Natural Vegetation Regions

Maps that show landforms, climate, and vegetation regions are special purpose maps. Unlike the boundary lines on a political map, the boundary lines on these maps do not separate the land into exact divisions. A tropical wet climate gradually changes to a tropical wet and dry climate. A tundra gradually changes to an ice cap. Even though the boundaries between regions may not be exact, the information on these maps can help you understand the region and the lives of people in it.

Landforms

Understanding how people use the land requires an understanding of the shape of the land itself. The four most important landforms are mountains, hills, plateaus, and plains. Human activity in every region in the world is influenced by these landforms.

- **Mountains** are high and steep. Most are wide at the bottom and rise to a narrow peak or ridge. Most geographers classify a mountain as land that rises at least 2,000 feet (610 m) above sea level. A series of mountains is called a mountain range.

- **Hills** rise above surrounding land and have rounded tops. Hills are lower and usually less steep than mountains. The elevation of surrounding land determines whether a landform is called a mountain or a hill.

- A **plateau** is a large, mostly flat area of land that rises above the surrounding land. At least one side of a plateau has a steep slope.

- **Plains** are large areas of flat or gently rolling land. Plains have few changes in elevation. Many plains areas are located along coasts. Others are located in the interior regions of some continents.

▶ A satellite view of the Earth showing North and South America. What landforms are visible in the photograph?

Climate Regions

Another important influence in the ways people live their lives is the climate of their region. Climate is the weather of a given location over a long period of time. Use the descriptions in the table below to help you visualize the climate regions shown on maps.

Climate	Temperatures	Precipitation
Tropical		
Tropical wet	Hot all year round	Heavy all year round
Tropical wet and dry	Hot all year round	Heavy when sun is overhead, dry other times
Dry		
Semiarid	Hot summers, mild to cold winters	Light
Arid	Hot days, cold nights	Very light
Mild		
Mediterranean	Hot summers, cool winters	Dry summers, wet winters
Humid subtropical	Hot summers, cool winters	Year round, heavier in summer than in winter
Marine west coast	Warm summers, cool winters	Year round, heavier in winter than in summer
Continental		
Humid continental	Hot summers, cold winters	Year round, heavier in summer than in winter
Subarctic	Cool summers, cold winters	Light
Polar		
Tundra	Cool summers, very cold winters	Light
Ice cap	Cold all year round	Light
Highlands	Varies, depending on altitude and direction of prevailing winds	Varies, depending on altitude and direction of prevailing winds

Natural Vegetation Regions

Natural vegetation is the plant life that grows wild without the help of humans. A world vegetation map tells what the vegetation in a place would be if people had not cut down forests or cleared grasslands. The table below provides descriptions of natural vegetation regions shown on maps. Comparing climate and vegetation regions can help you see the close relationship between climate and vegetation.

Vegetation	Description
Tropical rain forest	Tall, close-growing trees forming a canopy over smaller trees, dense growth in general
Deciduous forest	Trees and plants that regularly lose their leaves after each growing season
Mixed forest	Both leaf-losing and cone-bearing trees, no type of tree dominant
Coniferous forest	Cone-bearing trees, evergreen trees and plants
Mediterranean vegetation	Evergreen shrubs and small plants
Tropical savanna	Tall grasses with occasional trees and shrubs
Temperate grassland	Tall grasses with occasional stands of trees
Desert scrub	Low shrubs and bushes, hardy plants
Desert	Little or no vegetation
Tundra	Low shrubs, mosses, lichens; no trees
Ice cap	Little or no vegetation
Highlands	Varies, depending on altitude and direction of prevailing winds

PRACTICE YOUR WORLD EXPLORER SKILLS

1 How are mountains and hills similar? How are they different?

2 What is the difference between a plateau and a plain?

Atlas

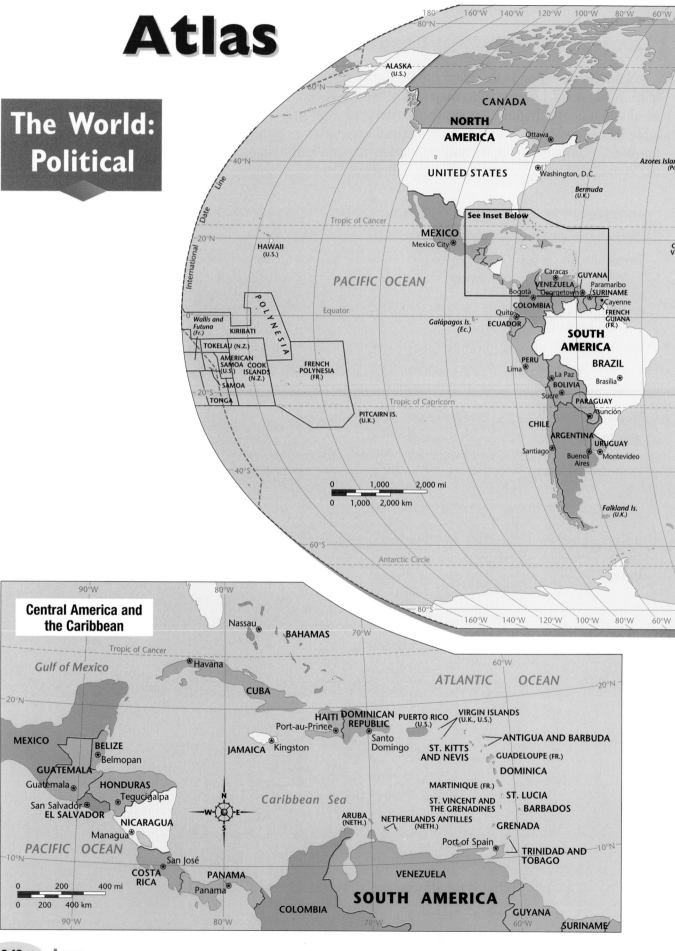

The World: Political

See Inset Below

180° · 160°W · 140°W · 120°W · 100°W · 80°W · 60°W
80°N

ALASKA (U.S.)

60°N

CANADA

NORTH AMERICA

Ottawa ⊛

40°N

UNITED STATES

Washington, D.C. ⊛

Azores Islands (Port.)

Bermuda (U.K.)

Tropic of Cancer

20°N

MEXICO

Mexico City ⊛

CAPE VERDE

HAWAII (U.S.)

PACIFIC OCEAN

Caracas ⊛ **GUYANA**

VENEZUELA Paramaribo ⊛

Bogotá ⊛ Georgetown ⊛ **SURINAME**

COLOMBIA • Cayenne

Equator

Quito ⊛ **FRENCH GUIANA (FR.)**

0° *Wallis and Futuna (Fr.)*

ECUADOR

Galápagos Is. (Ec.)

P O L Y N E S I A

KIRIBATI

TOKELAU (N.Z.)

SOUTH AMERICA

PERU

AMERICAN SAMOA (U.S.) COOK ISLANDS (N.Z.)

Lima ⊛

BRAZIL

FRENCH POLYNESIA (FR.)

La Paz ⊛ Brasília ⊛

BOLIVIA

SAMOA

20°S

TONGA

Sucre ⊛

Tropic of Capricorn

PARAGUAY

PITCAIRN IS. (U.K.)

Asunción ⊛

CHILE

ARGENTINA **URUGUAY**

0 1,000 2,000 mi

Santiago ⊛ Buenos Aires ⊛ Montevideo ⊛

0 1,000 2,000 km

40°S

Falkland Is. (U.K.)

International Date Line

60°S

Antarctic Circle

80°S

160°W · 140°W · 120°W · 100°W · 80°W · 60°W

Central America and the Caribbean

90°W · 80°W

Nassau ⊛

BAHAMAS

70°W

Tropic of Cancer

Gulf of Mexico

⊛ Havana

ATLANTIC OCEAN

60°W

20°N

20°N

CUBA

MEXICO

HAITI **DOMINICAN REPUBLIC** PUERTO RICO (U.S.) **VIRGIN ISLANDS (U.K., U.S.)**

BELIZE

Port-au-Prince ⊛

⊛ Belmopan

JAMAICA Kingston ⊛

Santo Domingo

ANTIGUA AND BARBUDA

ST. KITTS AND NEVIS **GUADELOUPE (FR.)**

GUATEMALA

Guatemala ⊛

HONDURAS

DOMINICA

Tegucigalpa ⊛

MARTINIQUE (FR.) **ST. LUCIA**

San Salvador ⊛

Caribbean Sea

ST. VINCENT AND THE GRENADINES **BARBADOS**

EL SALVADOR

NICARAGUA

ARUBA (NETH.) NETHERLANDS ANTILLES (NETH.) **GRENADA**

Managua ⊛

PACIFIC OCEAN

Port of Spain ⊛ **TRINIDAD AND TOBAGO**

10°N

San José ⊛

10°N

0 200 400 mi

COSTA RICA

PANAMA

VENEZUELA

0 200 400 km

Panama ⊛

SOUTH AMERICA

GUYANA

90°W

COLOMBIA

80°W

70°W

60°W

SURINAME

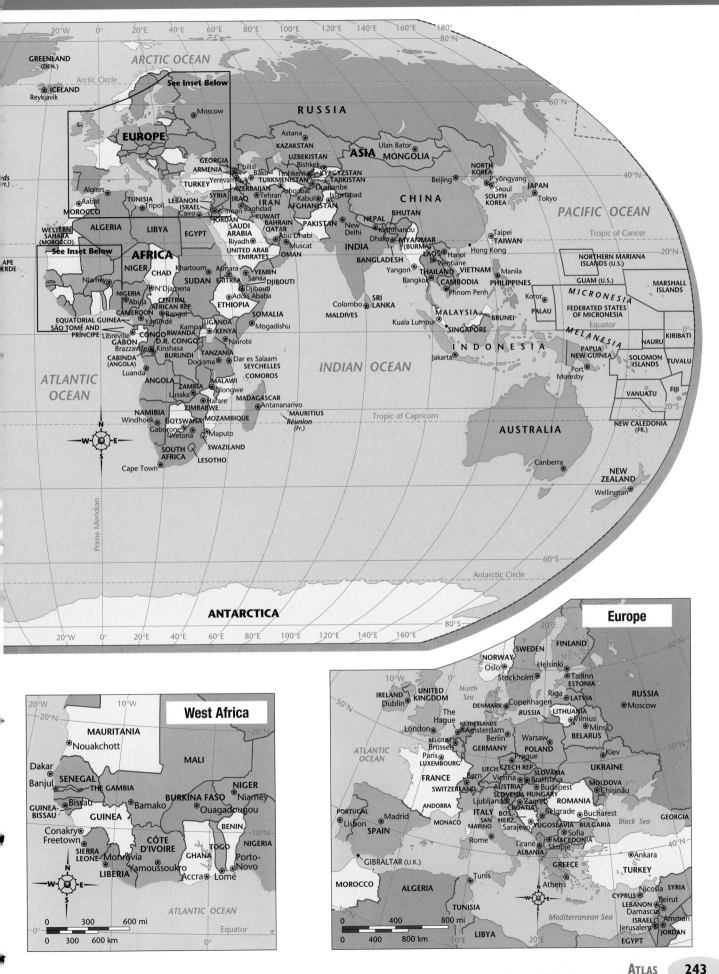

GREENLAND (DEN.)

ARCTIC OCEAN

Arctic Circle

⊛ ICELAND
Reykjavik

See Inset Below

EUROPE
⊛ Moscow

R U S S I A

Astana ⊛
KAZAKSTAN
Ulan Bator ⊛
ASIA **MONGOLIA**

⊛ Algiers
GEORGIA
⊛ Rabat
TUNISIA
⊛ Tripoli
MOROCCO

UZBEKISTAN
Bishkek
T'bilisi ⊛ **ARMENIA** Baku ⊛ Tashkent ⊛ **KYRGYZSTAN**
Yerevan ⊛ **TURKMENISTAN** **TAJIKISTAN**
TURKEY **AZERBAIJAN** Ashgabat ⊛ Dushanbe ⊛
SYRIA Tehran ⊛ Islamabad ⊛
LEBANON **IRAQ** **IRAN** Kabul ⊛
ISRAEL Baghdad ⊛ **AFGHANISTAN**
Cairo ⊛ Amman ⊛ **JORDAN** **KUWAIT**

Beijing ⊛

NORTH KOREA
P'yŏngyang ⊛
⊛ Seoul
SOUTH KOREA
JAPAN
Tokyo ⊛

CHINA

PACIFIC OCEAN

WESTERN SAHARA (MOROCCO)
ALGERIA **LIBYA** **EGYPT**
SAUDI ARABIA
Riyadh ⊛
BAHRAIN **QATAR**
Abu Dhabi ⊛
UNITED ARAB EMIRATES
OMAN
Muscat ⊛

NEPAL
New Delhi ⊛ Kathmandu ⊛ **BHUTAN**
Dhaka ⊛
INDIA **BANGLADESH**
MYANMAR (BURMA)
Yangon ⊛
LAOS Hanoi ⊛
Vientiane ⊛
THAILAND **VIETNAM**
Bangkok ⊛
CAMBODIA Manila ⊛
Phnom Penh ⊛
PHILIPPINES

Taipei ⊛
TAIWAN
Hong Kong

Tropic of Cancer

NORTHERN MARIANA ISLANDS (U.S.)
GUAM (U.S.)
MICRONESIA
FEDERATED STATES OF MICRONESIA
Koror ⊛ **PALAU**
MARSHALL ISLANDS

AFRICA
NIGER **CHAD** **SUDAN**
Khartoum ⊛
CENTRAL AFRICAN REP.
N'Djamena ⊛
Niamey ⊛
NIGERIA
Abuja ⊛
CAMEROON
Yaoundé ⊛
Bangui ⊛

Asmara ⊛ **YEMEN**
ERITREA Sanaa ⊛ **DJIBOUTI**
Addis Ababa ⊛ Djibouti ⊛
ETHIOPIA **SOMALIA**
Mogadishu ⊛

Colombo ⊛ **SRI LANKA**
MALDIVES

MALAYSIA **BRUNEI**
Kuala Lumpur
SINGAPORE

Equator

MELANESIA
PAPUA NEW GUINEA
NAURU
KIRIBATI
SOLOMON ISLANDS
TUVALU

EQUATORIAL GUINEA
SÃO TOMÉ AND PRINCIPE
Libreville ⊛ **CONGO**
GABON
Brazzaville ⊛ Kinshasa ⊛
CABINDA (ANGOLA)
Luanda ⊛

UGANDA
Kampala ⊛
RWANDA **KENYA**
Nairobi ⊛
BURUNDI
D.R. CONGO **TANZANIA**
Dodoma ⊛ Dar es Salaam ⊛
SEYCHELLES
COMOROS

INDIAN OCEAN

Jakarta ⊛
I N D O N E S I A

Port Moresby ⊛

ATLANTIC OCEAN

ANGOLA **ZAMBIA**
Lusaka ⊛
MALAWI
Lilongwe ⊛
ZIMBABWE
Harare ⊛
MADAGASCAR
Antananarivo ⊛
MAURITIUS
Réunion (Fr.)

Tropic of Capricorn

AUSTRALIA

VANUATU **FIJI**
NEW CALEDONIA (FR.)

NAMIBIA **BOTSWANA** **MOZAMBIQUE**
Windhoek ⊛ Gaborone ⊛ Pretoria ⊛ Maputo ⊛
SWAZILAND
SOUTH AFRICA **LESOTHO**
Cape Town ⊛

Canberra ⊛

NEW ZEALAND
Wellington ⊛

ANTARCTICA

Antarctic Circle

FINLAND
SWEDEN
NORWAY
Oslo ⊛ Helsinki ⊛
Stockholm ⊛ Tallinn ⊛
ESTONIA
Riga ⊛ **LATVIA**
RUSSIA
Moscow ⊛

North Sea

IRELAND **UNITED KINGDOM**
Dublin ⊛
DENMARK Copenhagen ⊛
RUSSIA
LITHUANIA
Vilnius ⊛ Minsk ⊛
BELARUS

The Hague ⊛
London ⊛
NETHERLANDS Amsterdam ⊛ Berlin ⊛
BELGIUM Brussels ⊛ **GERMANY**
Warsaw ⊛
POLAND
Kiev ⊛
UKRAINE

ATLANTIC OCEAN

Paris ⊛
LUXEMBOURG
FRANCE
LIECH. Prague ⊛ **CZECH REP.**
Bern ⊛ Vienna ⊛ **SLOVAKIA**
SWITZERLAND **AUSTRIA** Bratislava ⊛
SLOVENIA HUNGARY Budapest ⊛
MOLDOVA
Chişinău ⊛

PORTUGAL
ANDORRA
MONACO
Madrid ⊛
Lisbon ⊛
SPAIN
Ljubljana ⊛ Zagreb ⊛ **ROMANIA**
CROATIA Belgrade ⊛ Bucharest ⊛
ITALY **BOS. HERZ.** **YUGOSLAVIA** **BULGARIA**
SAN MARINO Sarajevo ⊛ Sofia ⊛
Rome ⊛ **MACEDONIA**
Tiranë ⊛ Skopje ⊛
ALBANIA
Black Sea
GEORGIA

GIBRALTAR (U.K.)

Ankara ⊛
GREECE **TURKEY**
Athens ⊛

MOROCCO **ALGERIA**
Tunis ⊛
CYPRUS Nicosia ⊛ **SYRIA**
LEBANON Beirut ⊛
Damascus ⊛
ISRAEL Amman ⊛
Jerusalem ⊛ **JORDAN**

TUNISIA
Mediterranean Sea
LIBYA **EGYPT**

0	400	800 mi
0	400	800 km

West Africa

MAURITANIA
Nouakchott ⊛

Dakar ⊛
Banjul ⊛ **SENEGAL**
THE GAMBIA
GUINEA-BISSAU Bissau ⊛
MALI
Bamako ⊛
BURKINA FASO
Ouagadougou ⊛
NIGER
Niamey ⊛

GUINEA
Conakry ⊛
Freetown ⊛
SIERRA LEONE Monrovia ⊛
LIBERIA
Yamoussoukro ⊛
CÔTE D'IVOIRE
GHANA
Accra ⊛
BENIN
TOGO
Porto-Novo ⊛
Lomé ⊛
NIGERIA

ATLANTIC OCEAN

Equator

0	300	600 mi
0	300	600 km

The World: Physical

NORTH AMERICA

ARCTIC OCEAN

Beaufort
Sea

Bering
Sea
60°N

Aleutian Islands

Greenland

Baffin
Island

Hudson
Bay

CANADIAN SHIELD

ROCKY MOUNTAINS

GREAT PLAINS

Great
Lakes

APPALACHIAN MTS.

Missouri R.

Mississippi R.

St. Lawrence R.

ATLANTIC
OCEAN

Hawaiian Islands

Tropic of Cancer

SIERRA MADRE
OCCIDENTAL

SIERRA MADRE
ORIENTAL

Gulf of
Mexico

West Indies

Caribbean Sea

PACIFIC OCEAN

P O L Y N E S I A

Equator

Orinoco R.

GUIANA
HIGHLANDS

AMAZON

Amazon R.

BASIN

**SOUTH
AMERICA**

BRAZILIAN
HIGHLANDS

ANDES MOUNTAINS

PAMPAS

Rio de
la Plata

PATAGONIA

Cape Horn

Drake Passage

Antarctic Circle

ANTARCTIC
PENINSULA

80°N
40°N
20°N
0°
20°S
40°S
60°S
80°S

180° 160°W 140°W 120°W 100°W 80°W 60°W

160°W 140°W 120°W 100°W 80°W 60°W

KEY

Elevation

Feet		Meters
14,000		4,270
7,000		2,135
1,500		457
700		213
(sea level) 0		0 (sea level)

Ice pack

Ice shelf

Orthographic Projection

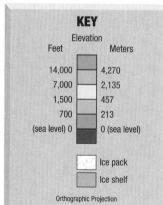

South Pole

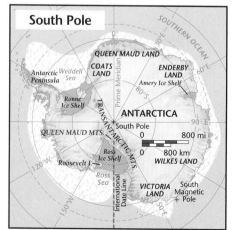

SOUTHERN OCEAN

QUEEN MAUD LAND

COATS
LAND

ENDERBY
LAND

Antarctic
Peninsula

Weddell
Sea

Amery Ice Shelf

Prime Meridian

Ronne
Ice Shelf

TRANSANTARCTIC MTS.

ANTARCTICA

South Pole

QUEEN MAUD MTS.

Ross
Ice Shelf

Roosevelt I.

WILKES LAND

Ross
Sea

VICTORIA
LAND

South
Magnetic
+ Pole

International
Date Line

0   800 mi

0   800 km

30°E

60°E

90°E

120°W

150°W

60°S

80°S

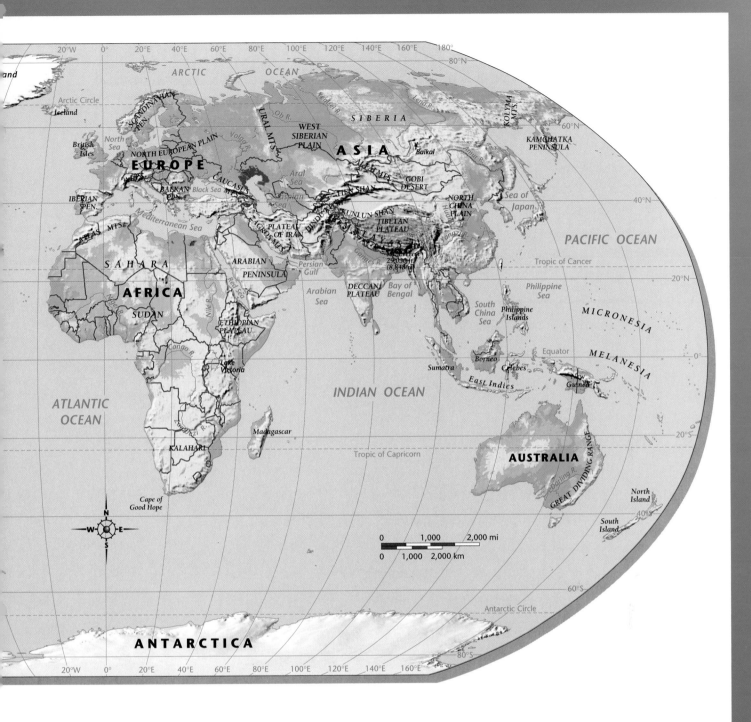

ARCTIC OCEAN

20°W · 0° · 20°E · 40°E · 60°E · 80°E · 100°E · 120°E · 140°E · 160°E · 180° · 80°N

Iceland

Arctic Circle

British Isles

North Sea

SCANDINAVIAN PEN.

NORTH EUROPEAN PLAIN

EUROPE

IBERIAN PEN.

BALKAN PEN.

Black Sea

CAUCASUS MTS.

Volga R.

URAL MTS.

Ob R.

Yenisey R.

S I B E R I A

Lena R.

A S I A

Baikal

KOLYMA MTS.

KAMCHATKA PENINSULA

60°N

ATLAS MTS.

Mediterranean Sea

ZAGROS MTS.

PLATEAU OF IRAN

Caspian Sea

Aral Sea

ALTAI MTS.

TIEN SHAN

HINDU KUSH

KUNLUN SHAN

GOBI DESERT

Huang He

NORTH CHINA PLAIN

Sea of Japan

40°N

S A H A R A

AFRICA

Red Sea

ARABIAN PENINSULA

Persian Gulf

HIMALAYAS

Mt. Everest 29,030 ft (8,848 m)

TIBETAN PLATEAU

Yangtze R.

PACIFIC OCEAN

Tropic of Cancer

20°N

SUDAN

Nile R.

ETHIOPIAN PLATEAU

Arabian Sea

DECCAN PLATEAU

Ganges R.

Bay of Bengal

South China Sea

Philippine Islands

Philippine Sea

M I C R O N E S I A

Congo R.

Lake Victoria

INDIAN OCEAN

Sumatra

East Indies

Borneo

Celebes

Equator

M E L A N E S I A

New Guinea

0°

ATLANTIC OCEAN

Zambezi R.

Madagascar

KALAHARI

Tropic of Capricorn

AUSTRALIA

GREAT DIVIDING RANGE

Darling R.

20°S

Cape of Good Hope

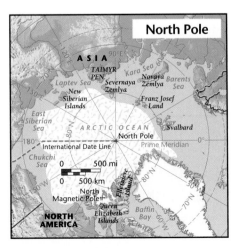

N · W · E · S

0 · 1,000 · 2,000 mi

0 · 1,000 · 2,000 km

North Island

South Island

40°S

60°S

Antarctic Circle

ANTARCTICA

20°W · 0° · 20°E · 40°E · 60°E · 80°E · 100°E · 120°E · 140°E · 160°E · 80°S

North Pole

A S I A

TAIMYR PEN.

Laptev Sea

Severnaya Zemlya

Kara Sea

Novaya Zemlya

Barents Sea

New Siberian Islands

Franz Josef Land

East Siberian Sea

ARCTIC OCEAN

North Pole

Svalbard

Prime Meridian

International Date Line

Chukchi Sea

0 · 500 mi

0 · 500 km

North Magnetic Pole

Ellesmere Island

Queen Elizabeth Islands

Baffin Bay

NORTH AMERICA

United States: Political

RUSSIA

ARCTIC OCEAN

Arctic Circle

70°N

70°N

ALASKA

CANADA

Yukon River

Bering Strait

60°N

60°N

Anchorage

Bering Sea

Gulf of Alaska

Juneau

0   250   500 mi
0   250   500 km

160°W   140°W

50°N   120°W   110°W

Seattle

Olympia

WASHINGTON   Spokane

River

Missouri   River

Minot

Columbia

Portland

Salem

Helena

MONTANA

Bismarck

OREGON

IDAHO

Billings

Boise

Sheridan

Klamath Falls

Snake River

Jackson

WYOMING

Pierre

40°N

Eureka

Twin Falls

Rapid City

Winnemucca

Great Salt Lake

NEBRASKA

Sacramento

Carson City

Salt Lake City

Cheyenne

San Francisco

NEVADA

UTAH

Denver

COLORADO

Grand Junction

Cedar City

Pueblo

CALIFORNIA

Las Vegas

Colorado River

Arkansas

Los Angeles

Santa Fe

PACIFIC

Albuquerque

OCEAN

ARIZONA

NEW MEXICO

Phoenix

San Diego

Roswell

Rio Grande

Tucson

El Paso

PACIFIC OCEAN

160°W   155°W

Honolulu

PACIFIC OCEAN

20°N   20°N

HAWAII

MEXICO

Hilo

0   50   100 mi
0   50   100 km

155°W

Tropic of Cancer

120°W   110°W

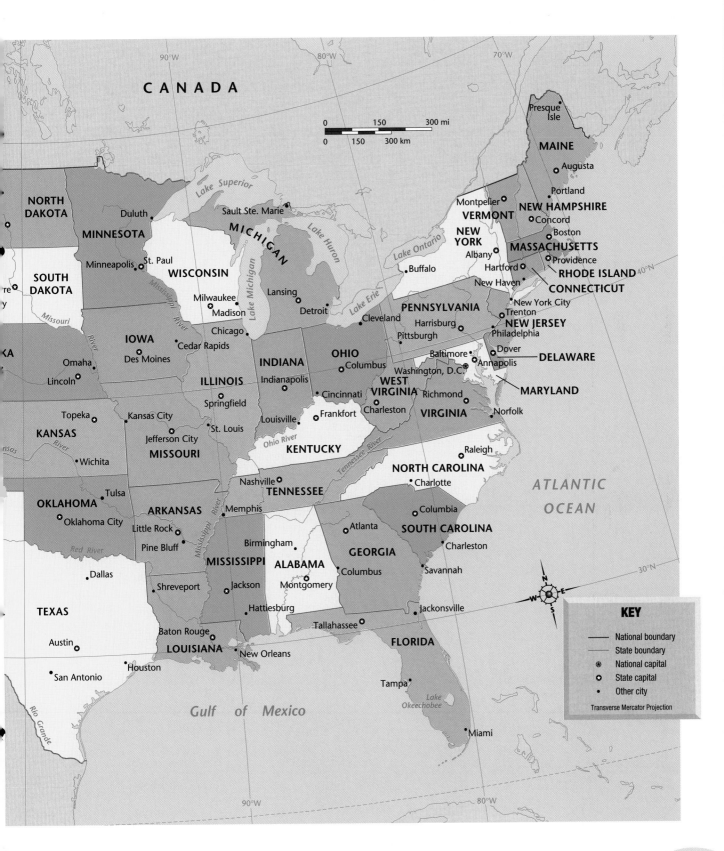

CANADA

0 150 300 mi
0 150 300 km

NORTH DAKOTA

MINNESOTA
Duluth

Lake Superior

Sault Ste. Marie

MICHIGAN

Lake Huron

Presque Isle

MAINE
Augusta

Portland

Montpelier
VERMONT
NEW HAMPSHIRE
Concord

SOUTH DAKOTA

WISCONSIN
Minneapolis • St. Paul

Lake Michigan

Milwaukee
Madison

Lansing

Detroit

Lake Erie

Lake Ontario

NEW YORK
Albany

Buffalo

Boston
MASSACHUSETTS
Providence
Hartford **RHODE ISLAND**
New Haven **CONNECTICUT**

Chicago

Cleveland

PENNSYLVANIA
Harrisburg
Pittsburgh

New York City
Trenton
NEW JERSEY
Philadelphia

IOWA
Cedar Rapids
Des Moines

ILLINOIS
Springfield

INDIANA
Indianapolis

OHIO
Columbus

Cincinnati

WEST VIRGINIA
Charleston

Baltimore
Washington, D.C.
Annapolis
Dover **DELAWARE**

MARYLAND

Omaha
Lincoln

Richmond
Norfolk

Missouri River

Topeka
Kansas City

KANSAS
Wichita

Jefferson City
MISSOURI

St. Louis

Louisville

Frankfort
KENTUCKY

Ohio River

VIRGINIA

Tennessee River

Raleigh

NORTH CAROLINA
Charlotte

OKLAHOMA
Tulsa
Oklahoma City

ARKANSAS
Little Rock
Pine Bluff

Nashville
TENNESSEE

Memphis

Columbia
SOUTH CAROLINA
Charleston

Red River

Birmingham

MISSISSIPPI
Jackson

ALABAMA
Montgomery

GEORGIA
Atlanta
Columbus

Savannah

Dallas

Hattiesburg

Tallahassee

Jacksonville

ATLANTIC OCEAN

Shreveport

Baton Rouge
LOUISIANA
New Orleans

TEXAS

Austin

San Antonio
Houston

FLORIDA

Tampa

Lake Okeechobee

Gulf of Mexico

Rio Grande

Miami

N
W   E
S

KEY

—— National boundary
—— State boundary
⊛ National capital
✪ State capital
• Other city

Transverse Mercator Projection

North and South America: Political

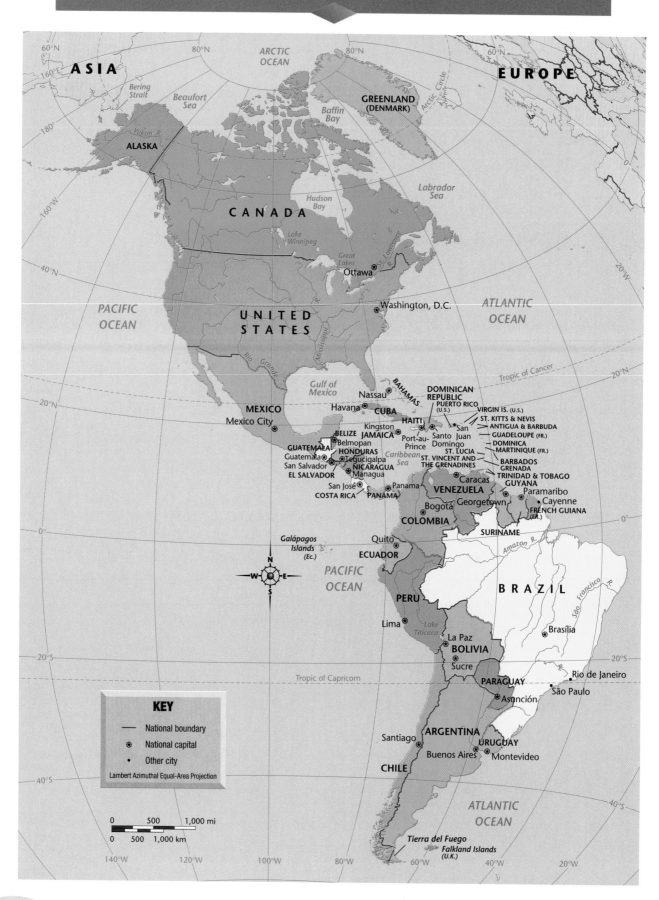

ASIA

ARCTIC OCEAN

EUROPE

Bering Strait

Beaufort Sea

GREENLAND (DENMARK)

Baffin Bay

ALASKA

Yukon R.

Hudson Bay

Labrador Sea

CANADA

Lake Winnipeg

Great Lakes

St. Lawrence R.

Ottawa

PACIFIC OCEAN

UNITED STATES

Washington, D.C.

ATLANTIC OCEAN

Rio Grande

Mississippi R.

Tropic of Cancer

Gulf of Mexico

MEXICO

Mexico City

Nassau

BAHAMAS

Havana

CUBA

DOMINICAN REPUBLIC

PUERTO RICO (U.S.)

VIRGIN IS. (U.S.)

ST. KITTS & NEVIS

ANTIGUA & BARBUDA

Kingston

JAMAICA

HAITI

Port-au-Prince

San Juan

Santo Domingo

GUADELOUPE (FR.)

DOMINICA

MARTINIQUE (FR.)

ST. LUCIA

BELIZE

Belmopan

GUATEMALA

HONDURAS

Guatemala

Tegucigalpa

San Salvador

NICARAGUA

Managua

EL SALVADOR

Caribbean Sea

ST. VINCENT AND THE GRENADINES

BARBADOS

GRENADA

TRINIDAD & TOBAGO

GUYANA

San José

COSTA RICA

Panama

PANAMA

Caracas

VENEZUELA

Georgetown

Paramaribo

Cayenne

FRENCH GUIANA (FR.)

Bogotá

COLOMBIA

SURINAME

Galápagos Islands (Ec.)

Quito

ECUADOR

PACIFIC OCEAN

Amazon R.

BRAZIL

São Francisco R.

PERU

Lima

Lake Titicaca

La Paz

BOLIVIA

Sucre

Brasília

Rio de Janeiro

Tropic of Capricorn

PARAGUAY

São Paulo

Asunción

KEY

—— National boundary

⊛ National capital

• Other city

Lambert Azimuthal Equal-Area Projection

Santiago

ARGENTINA

Buenos Aires

URUGUAY

Montevideo

CHILE

ATLANTIC OCEAN

0   500   1,000 mi

0   500   1,000 km

Tierra del Fuego

Falkland Islands (U.K.)

North and South America: Physical

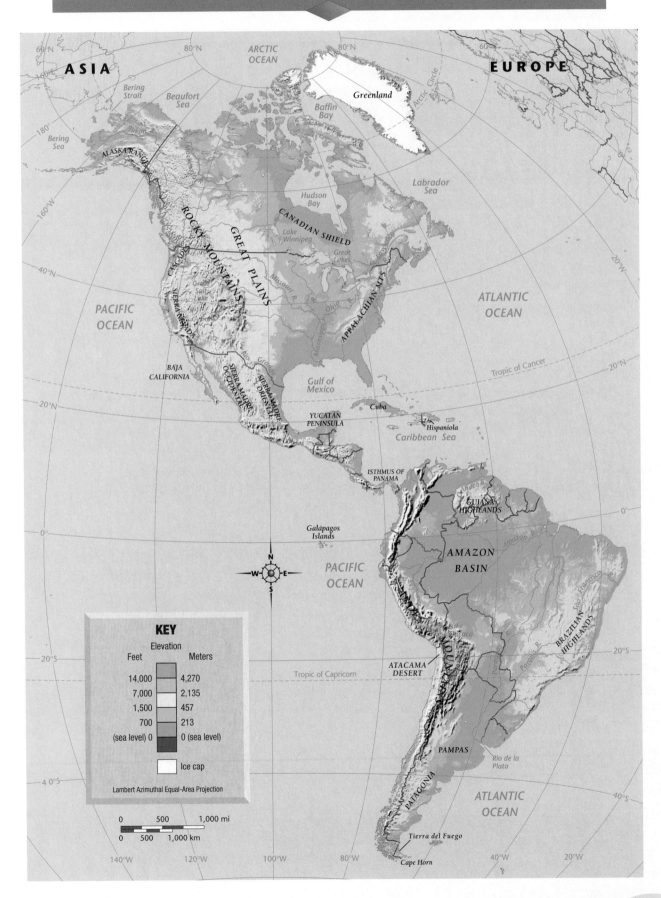

KEY

Elevation

Feet		Meters
14,000		4,270
7,000		2,135
1,500		457
700		213
(sea level) 0		0 (sea level)

Ice cap

Lambert Azimuthal Equal-Area Projection

0   500   1,000 mi

0   500   1,000 km

Europe: Political

KEY

— National boundary
⊛ National capital
• Other city

Lambert Azimuthal Equal-Area Projection

ARCTIC OCEAN

ATLANTIC OCEAN

ICELAND
Reykjavik ⊛

Faeroe Is. (Den.)

Shetland Is. (U.K.)

NORWAY
Lillehammer
Oslo ⊛

SWEDEN
Stockholm ⊛

FINLAND
Turku
Helsinki ⊛
Gulf of Bothnia

St. Petersburg

RUSSIA
Moscow ⊛

ESTONIA
Tallinn ⊛

Baltic Sea

LATVIA
Riga ⊛

Göteborg

LITHUANIA
Vilnius ⊛

BELARUS
Minsk ⊛

North Sea

DENMARK
Copenhagen ⊛

RUSSIA
Gdańsk

POLAND
Warsaw ⊛
Łódź

IRELAND
Dublin ⊛

UNITED KINGDOM
Manchester
London

Amsterdam
The Hague
NETHERLANDS

Berlin ⊛

Kiev ⊛

UKRAINE

English Channel

Brussels ⊛
BELGIUM

GERMANY
• Cologne
• Bonn
Frankfurt

Katowice
Kraków

CZECH REPUBLIC
Prague ⊛
Brno

SLOVAKIA
Bratislava ⊛

MOLDOVA
Chişinău ⊛

LUXEMBOURG
Luxembourg ⊛

Danube R.

Munich

Vienna ⊛

Budapest ⊛

Cluj-Napoca

Bay of Biscay

FRANCE
Paris ⊛

LIECHTENSTEIN
Bern ⊛
SWITZERLAND

AUSTRIA

HUNGARY

ROMANIA
Bucharest ⊛

Black Sea

Milan

Ljubljana ⊛
SLOVENIA
Zagreb ⊛
CROATIA

BOSNIA-HERZEGOVINA
Sarajevo ⊛

Belgrade ⊛
YUGOSLAVIA

BULGARIA
Sofia ⊛

PORTUGAL
Lisbon ⊛

SPAIN
Madrid ⊛

ANDORRA
Barcelona

Marseille

MONACO

SAN MARINO

ITALY
Rome ⊛
VATICAN CITY

Corsica

Adriatic Sea

Podgorica ⊛

ALBANIA
Tiranë ⊛

Skopje ⊛
MACEDONIA

GREECE

Sardinia

Balearic Is.

Tyrrhenian Sea

Naples

Ionian Sea

Aegean Sea

Strait of Gibraltar

GIBRALTAR (U.K.)

Mediterranean Sea

Sicily

MALTA

Crete

Athens ⊛

AFRICA

N
W E
S

0   250   500 mi
0   250   500 km

Arctic Circle

Prime Meridian

Europe: Physical

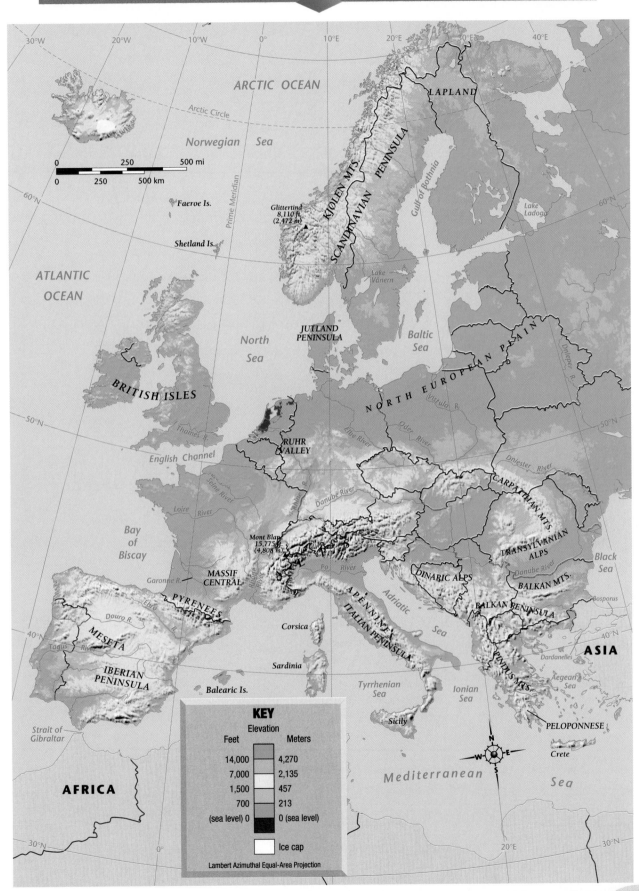

ARCTIC OCEAN

Arctic Circle

LAPLAND

Norwegian Sea

250   500 mi
250   500 km

Faeroe Is.

Glittertind
8,110 ft.
(2,472 m)

KJØLEN MTS.

SCANDINAVIAN PENINSULA

Gulf of Bothnia

Lake Ladoga

Shetland Is.

ATLANTIC OCEAN

Lake Vänern

North Sea

JUTLAND PENINSULA

Baltic Sea

BRITISH ISLES

Thames R.

NORTH EUROPEAN PLAIN

Dnieper R.

English Channel

Seine River

RUHR VALLEY

Elbe River

Oder River

Vistula R.

Dniester River

CARPATHIAN MTS.

Loire River

Danube River

Bay of Biscay

MASSIF CENTRAL

Mont Blanc
15,775 ft.
(4,808 m)

Rhône River

Po River

TRANSYLVANIAN ALPS

Danube River

Black Sea

Garonne R.

PYRENEES

DINARIC ALPS

BALKAN MTS.

Bosporus

Ebro R.

APENNINES

Adriatic Sea

BALKAN PENINSULA

Douro R.

MESETA

Corsica

ITALIAN PENINSULA

Dardanelles

ASIA

Tagus River

IBERIAN PENINSULA

Sardinia

Tyrrhenian Sea

Ionian Sea

PINDUS MTS.

Aegean Sea

Balearic Is.

Sicily

PELOPONNESE

Strait of Gibraltar

Crete

AFRICA

Mediterranean Sea

KEY

Elevation

Feet	Meters
14,000	4,270
7,000	2,135
1,500	457
700	213
(sea level) 0	0 (sea level)

Ice cap

Lambert Azimuthal Equal-Area Projection

Africa: Political

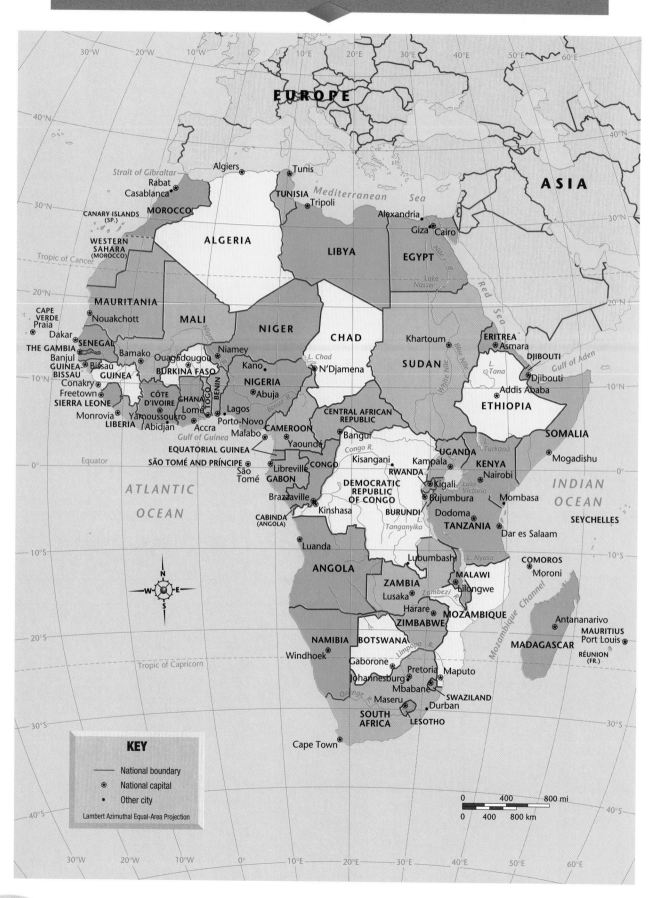

EUROPE

ASIA

Strait of Gibraltar
Algiers
Tunis
Rabat
Casablanca
Mediterranean Sea
TUNISIA
Tripoli
MOROCCO
Alexandria
CANARY ISLANDS (SP.)
Giza Cairo
WESTERN SAHARA (MOROCCO)
ALGERIA
LIBYA
EGYPT
Tropic of Cancer
Lake Nasser
Nile R.
Red Sea

MAURITANIA
Nouakchott
MALI
NIGER
CHAD
Khartoum
ERITREA
Asmara
DJIBOUTI
CAPE VERDE
Praia
Dakar
SENEGAL
Bamako
Niamey
L. Chad
N'Djamena
SUDAN
Blue Nile
L. Tana
Djibouti
Gulf of Aden
THE GAMBIA
Banjul
GUINEA-BISSAU
Bissau
GUINEA
Ouagadougou
BURKINA FASO
Kano
NIGERIA
Abuja
CENTRAL AFRICAN REPUBLIC
White Nile
Addis Ababa
ETHIOPIA
Conakry
Freetown
SIERRA LEONE
CÔTE D'IVOIRE
GHANA
TOGO
BENIN
Lagos
Benue R.
Monrovia
Yamoussoukro
LIBERIA
Abidjan
Accra
Lomé
Porto-Novo
CAMEROON
Malabo
SOMALIA
Gulf of Guinea
EQUATORIAL GUINEA
Yaoundé
Bangui
Mogadishu
SÃO TOMÉ AND PRÍNCIPE
Congo R.
Kisangani
Kampala
UGANDA
KENYA
L. Turkana
Equator
São Tomé
Libreville
CONGO
GABON
RWANDA
Kigali
Nairobi
DEMOCRATIC REPUBLIC OF CONGO
Bujumbura
Lake Victoria
Mombasa
ATLANTIC OCEAN
Brazzaville
Kinshasa
BURUNDI
Dodoma
INDIAN OCEAN
CABINDA (ANGOLA)
L. Tanganyika
TANZANIA
Dar es Salaam
SEYCHELLES
Luanda
Lubumbashi
L. Nyasa
COMOROS
Moroni
ANGOLA
ZAMBIA
MALAWI
Lilongwe
Lusaka
Zambezi R.
MOZAMBIQUE
Antananarivo
MAURITIUS
Port Louis
Harare
ZIMBABWE
Mozambique Channel
MADAGASCAR
RÉUNION (FR.)
NAMIBIA
BOTSWANA
Limpopo R.
Windhoek
Gaborone
Pretoria
Maputo
Johannesburg
Mbabane
SWAZILAND
Maseru
Durban
Orange R.
SOUTH AFRICA
LESOTHO
Cape Town

40°N 30°N 20°N 10°N 0° 10°S 20°S 30°S 40°S

30°W 20°W 10°W 0° 10°E 20°E 30°E 40°E 50°E 60°E

Tropic of Capricorn

KEY

—— National boundary

⊛ National capital

• Other city

Lambert Azimuthal Equal-Area Projection

0   400   800 mi

0   400   800 km

Africa: Physical

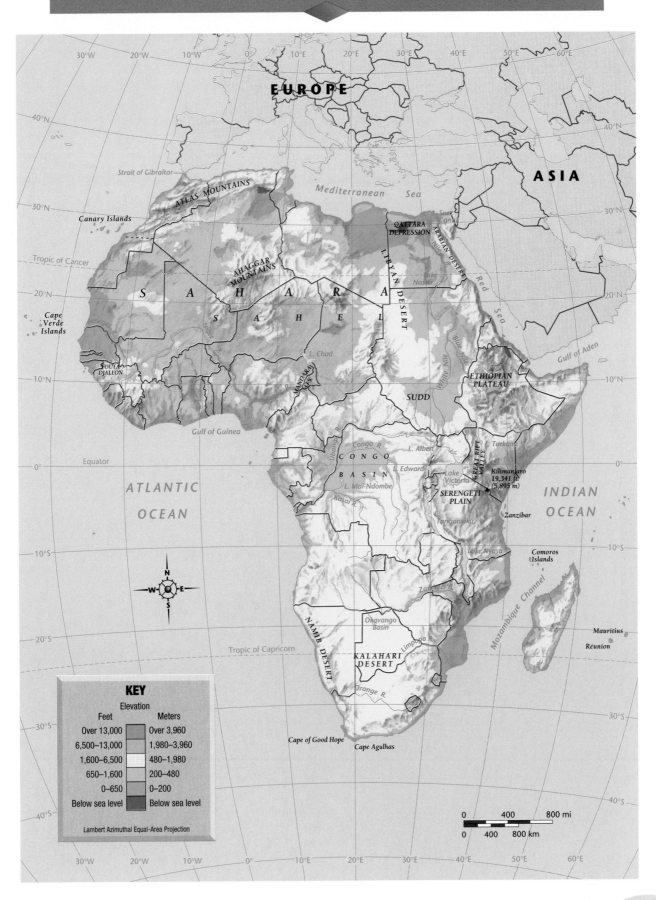

EUROPE

ASIA

Strait of Gibraltar

Mediterranean Sea

ATLAS MOUNTAINS

Canary Islands

Tropic of Cancer

QATTARA DEPRESSION

Suez Canal

ARABIAN DESERT

AHAGGAR MOUNTAINS

Lake Nasser

Cape Verde Islands

S   A   H   A   R   A

Senegal R.

Niger R.

LIBYAN DESERT

Red Sea

Gulf of Aden

FOUTA DJALLON

L. Chad

MANDARA MTS.

Blue Nile

White Nile

ETHIOPIAN PLATEAU

Gulf of Guinea

SUDD

Ubangi R.

Congo R.

CONGO BASIN

L. Albert

L. Edward

GREAT RIFT VALLEY

L. Turkana

Equator

Kasai R.

L. Mai-Ndombe

Lake Victoria

Kilimanjaro 19,341 ft (5,895 m)

SERENGETI PLAIN

Zanzibar

ATLANTIC OCEAN

Tanganyika

INDIAN OCEAN

Lake Nyasa

Comoros Islands

Mozambique Channel

Zambezi R.

Mauritius

Réunion

Okavango Basin

Limpopo R.

NAMIB DESERT

Tropic of Capricorn

KALAHARI DESERT

Orange R.

KEY

Elevation

Feet	Meters
Over 13,000	Over 3,960
6,500–13,000	1,980–3,960
1,600–6,500	480–1,980
650–1,600	200–480
0–650	0–200
Below sea level	Below sea level

Lambert Azimuthal Equal-Area Projection

Cape of Good Hope

Cape Agulhas

0   400   800 mi

0   400   800 km

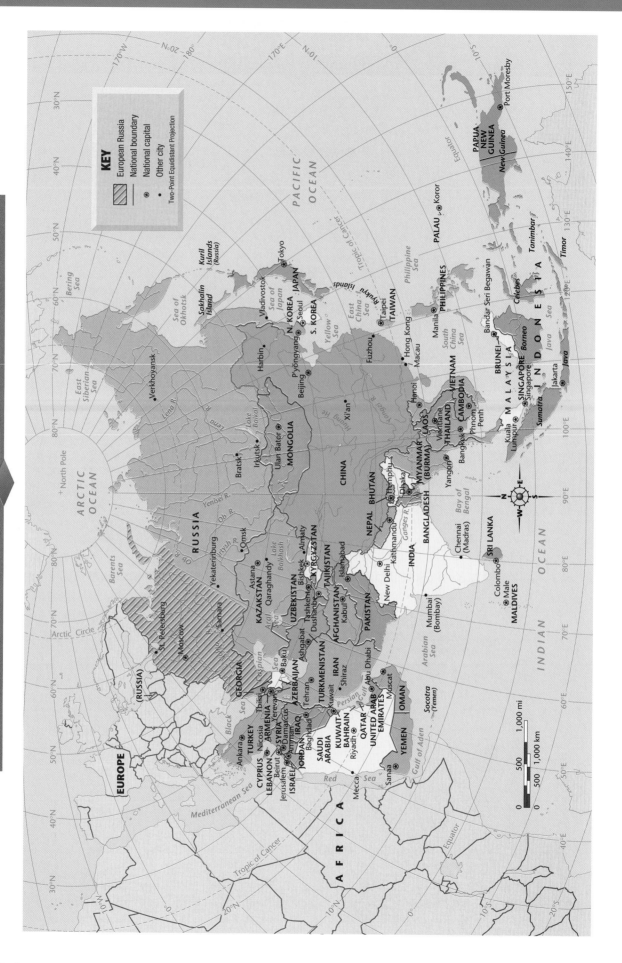

Asia: Political

KEY
- ///// European Russia
- — National boundary
- ⊛ National capital
- • Other city
- Two-Point Equidistant Projection

Asia: Physical

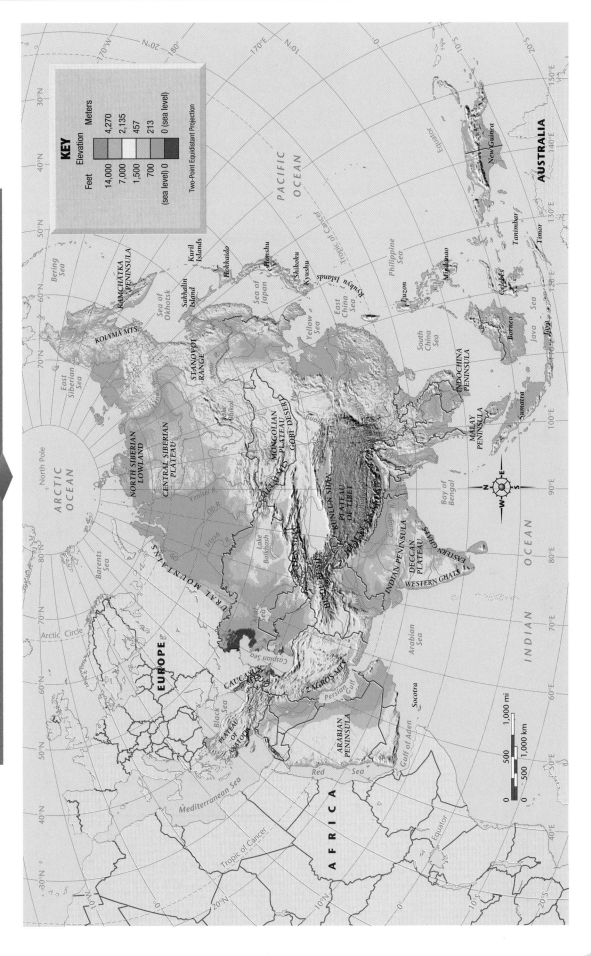

KEY

Elevation

Feet | Meters
14,000 | 4,270
7,000 | 2,135
1,500 | 457
700 | 213
0 (sea level) | 0 (sea level)

Two-Point Equidistant Projection

EUROPE

AFRICA

AUSTRALIA

ARCTIC OCEAN

North Pole

PACIFIC OCEAN

INDIAN OCEAN

Bering Sea

Sea of Okhotsk

KAMCHATKA PENINSULA

KOLYMA MTS.

STANOVOY RANGE

East Siberian Sea

NORTH SIBERIAN LOWLAND

CENTRAL SIBERIAN PLATEAU

Yenisei R.

Ob R.

Irtysh R.

Lake Baikal

Lake Balkhash

Aral Sea

URAL MOUNTAINS

Barents Sea

Arctic Circle

Black Sea

Caspian Sea

CAUCASUS MTS.

PLATEAU OF ANATOLIA

Mediterranean Sea

Red Sea

ARABIAN PENINSULA

ZAGROS MTS.

Persian Gulf

Gulf of Aden

Socotra

Arabian Sea

MONGOLIAN PLATEAU

GOBI DESERT

TIEN SHAN

KUNLUN SHEN

PLATEAU OF TIBET

HIMALAYAS

HINDU KUSH

Ganges R.

INDIAN PENINSULA

DECCAN PLATEAU

WESTERN GHATS

EASTERN GHATS

Bay of Bengal

Sakhalin Island

Kuril Islands

Hokkaido

Honshu

Shikoku

Kyushu

Sea of Japan

Yellow Sea

East China Sea

Ryukyu Islands

Tropic of Cancer

Philippine Sea

Luzon

Mindanao

South China Sea

INDOCHINA PENINSULA

MALAY PENINSULA

Celebes

Borneo

Sumatra

Java

Java Sea

Timor

Tanimbar

New Guinea

Equator

Tropic of Capricorn

1,000 mi
500
0

1,000 km
500
0

ATLAS 255

Australia, New Zealand, and the Pacific Islands: Physical–Political

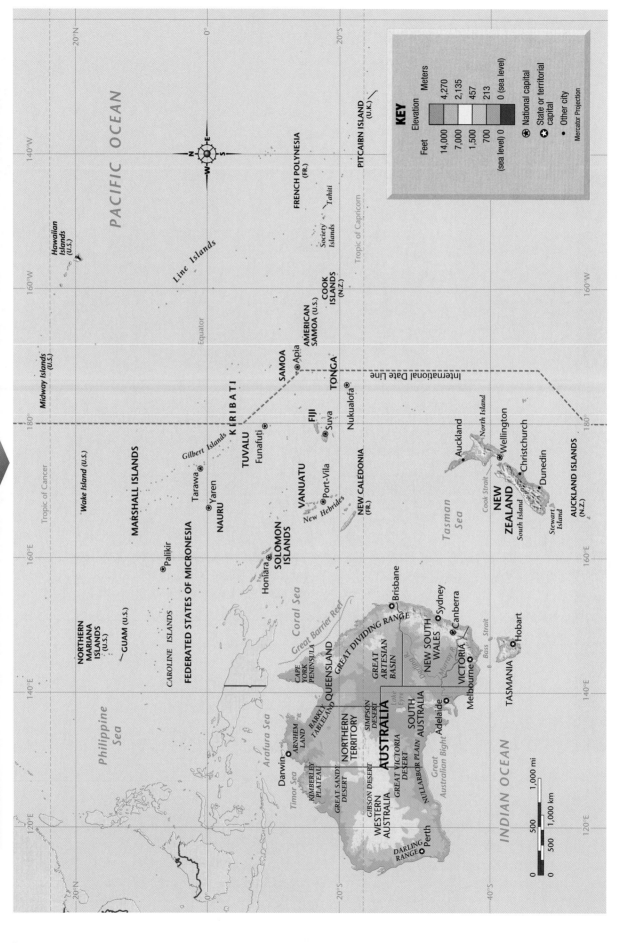

KEY

Elevation

Feet	Meters
14,000	4,270
7,000	2,135
1,500	457
700	213
(sea level) 0	0 (sea level)

⊛ National capital
✪ State or territorial capital
• Other city

Mercator Projection

PACIFIC OCEAN

PITCAIRN ISLAND (U.K.)

FRENCH POLYNESIA (FR.)

Tahiti

Society Islands

Tropic of Capricorn

Hawaiian Islands (U.S.)

Line Islands

COOK ISLANDS (N.Z.)

AMERICAN SAMOA (U.S.)

Equator

Midway Islands (U.S.)

SAMOA
⊛ Apia

TONGA
⊛ Nukualofa

International Date Line

Wake Island (U.S.)

Tropic of Cancer

MARSHALL ISLANDS

Tarawa

Gilbert Islands

KIRIBATI

TUVALU
Funafuti

FIJI
• Suva

NEW CALEDONIA (FR.)

North Island

Auckland •

⊛ Wellington
• Christchurch

NEW ZEALAND

• Dunedin

AUCKLAND ISLANDS (N.Z.)

South Island

Stewart Island

Cook Strait

Tasman Sea

Yaren
⊛ NAURU

VANUATU
Port-Vila

New Hebrides

NORTHERN MARIANA ISLANDS (U.S.)

GUAM (U.S.)

CAROLINE ISLANDS

FEDERATED STATES OF MICRONESIA
⊛ Palikir

SOLOMON ISLANDS
Honiara ⊛

Coral Sea

Great Barrier Reef

Brisbane •

QUEENSLAND

GREAT DIVIDING RANGE

GREAT ARTESIAN BASIN

NEW SOUTH WALES
✪ Sydney
⊛ Canberra

VICTORIA
Melbourne ✪

Murray

Darling

Bass Strait

TASMANIA
✪ Hobart

Philippine Sea

Arafura Sea

Timor Sea

Darwin •

ARNHEM LAND

KIMBERLEY PLATEAU

NORTHERN TERRITORY

BARKLY TABLELAND

CAPE YORK PENINSULA

GREAT SANDY DESERT

GIBSON DESERT

GREAT VICTORIA DESERT

SIMPSON DESERT

Lake Eyre

AUSTRALIA

SOUTH AUSTRALIA
Adelaide ✪

NULLARBOR PLAIN

Great Australian Bight

WESTERN AUSTRALIA

DARLING RANGE
Perth ✪

INDIAN OCEAN

1,000 mi

500

0

1,000 km

500

0

20°N

20°N

0°

20°S

20°S

40°S

120°E   140°E   160°E   180°   160°W   140°W

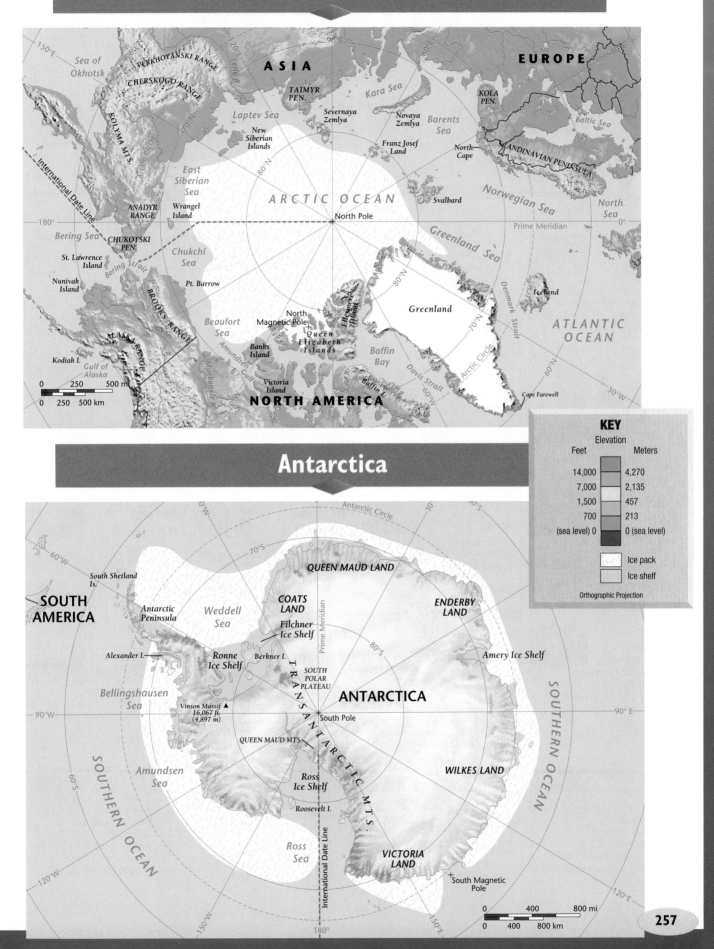

The Arctic

ASIA

EUROPE

Sea of Okhotsk

VERKHOYANSKI RANGE

CHERSKOGO RANGE

TAIMYR PEN.

Kara Sea

KOLA PEN.

Baltic Sea

Laptev Sea

Severnaya Zemlya

Novaya Zemlya

Barents Sea

KOLYMA MTS.

New Siberian Islands

Franz Josef Land

North Cape

SCANDINAVIAN PENINSULA

East Siberian Sea

80°N

ARCTIC OCEAN

Svalbard

Norwegian Sea

North Sea

ANADYR RANGE

Wrangel Island

North Pole

Prime Meridian

International Date Line

180°

CHUKOTSKI PEN.

Bering Sea

Chukchi Sea

Greenland Sea

Arctic Circle

Bering Strait

St. Lawrence Island

Nunivak Island

Pt. Barrow

80°N

Denmark Strait

Iceland

BROOKS RANGE

Beaufort Sea

North Magnetic Pole

Ellesmere Island

Greenland

70°N

ATLANTIC OCEAN

Kodiak I.

ALASKA RANGE

Gulf of Alaska

Queen Elizabeth Islands

Banks Island

Baffin Bay

Arctic Circle

0   250   500 mi

0   250   500 km

Victoria Island

Mackenzie R.

Baffin I.

Davis Strait

60°N

Cape Farewell

30°W

NORTH AMERICA

Antarctica

SOUTH AMERICA

Antarctic Circle

30°E

QUEEN MAUD LAND

South Shetland Is.

70°S

COATS LAND

ENDERBY LAND

Antarctic Peninsula

Weddell Sea

Filchner Ice Shelf

Prime Meridian

Amery Ice Shelf

Alexander I.

Ronne Ice Shelf

Berkner I.

80°S

SOUTH POLAR PLATEAU

Bellingshausen Sea

Vinson Massif ▲ 16,067 ft. (4,897 m)

ANTARCTICA

SOUTHERN OCEAN

90°E

90°W

South Pole

T R A N S A N T A R C T I C   M T S.

Amundsen Sea

QUEEN MAUD MTS.

60°S

WILKES LAND

Ross Ice Shelf

Roosevelt I.

Ross Sea

International Date Line

VICTORIA LAND

120°W

SOUTHERN OCEAN

South Magnetic Pole

120°E

180°

150°E

0   400   800 mi

0   400   800 km

KEY

Elevation

Feet		Meters
14,000		4,270
7,000		2,135
1,500		457
700		213
(sea level) 0		0 (sea level)

Ice pack

Ice shelf

Orthographic Projection

World View

Afghanistan

CAPITAL: Kabul
POPULATION: 21.9 million
OFFICIAL LANGUAGES: Persian and Pashtu
AREA: 251,770 sq mi/652,090 sq km
LEADING EXPORTS: fruits, nuts, hand-woven carpets, wool, and cotton
CONTINENT: Asia

Albania
CAPITAL: Tirana
POPULATION: 3.1 million
OFFICIAL LANGUAGE: Albanian
AREA: 10,579 sq mi/27,400 sq km
LEADING EXPORTS: textiles, footwear, asphalt, metals, and metallic ores
CONTINENT: Europe

Algeria
CAPITAL: Algiers
POPULATION: 30.8 million
OFFICIAL LANGUAGE: Arabic
AREA: 919,590 sq mi/2,381,740 sq km
LEADING EXPORTS: petroleum, natural gas, and petroleum products
CONTINENT: Africa

Andorra
CAPITAL: Andorra la Vella
POPULATION: 65,000
OFFICIAL LANGUAGE: Catalan
AREA: 181 sq mi/468 sq km
LEADING EXPORTS: tobacco products and furniture
CONTINENT: Europe

Angola
CAPITAL: Luanda
POPULATION: 12.5 million
OFFICIAL LANGUAGE: Portuguese
AREA: 434,235 sq mi/1,124,670 sq km
LEADING EXPORTS: crude oil, diamonds, refined petroleum products, gas, and coffee
CONTINENT: Africa

Antigua and Barbuda
CAPITAL: St. John's
POPULATION: 69,000
OFFICIAL LANGUAGE: English
AREA: 170 sq mi/440 sq km
LEADING EXPORTS: petroleum products, manufactures, food, and live animals
LOCATION: Caribbean Sea

Argentina
CAPITAL: Buenos Aires
POPULATION: 36.6 million
OFFICIAL LANGUAGE: Spanish
AREA: 1,056,636 sq mi/2,736,690 sq km
LEADING EXPORTS: edible oils, fuels and energy, cereals, feed, and motor vehicles
CONTINENT: South America

Armenia
CAPITAL: Yerevan
POPULATION: 3.5 million
OFFICIAL LANGUAGE: Armenian
AREA: 11,506 sq mi/29,800 sq km
LEADING EXPORTS: diamonds, scrap metal, machinery and equipment, and cognac
CONTINENT: Asia

Australia

CAPITAL: Canberra
POPULATION: 18.7 million
OFFICIAL LANGUAGE: English
AREA: 2,941,283 sq mi/7,617,930 sq km
LEADING EXPORTS: coal, gold, wool, aluminum, and iron ore
CONTINENT: Australia

Austria
CAPITAL: Vienna
POPULATION: 8.2 million
OFFICIAL LANGUAGE: German
AREA: 32,942 sq mi/82,730 sq km
LEADING EXPORTS: machinery and equipment, paper, and paperboard
CONTINENT: Europe

Azerbaijan
CAPITAL: Baku
POPULATION: 7.7 million
OFFICIAL LANGUAGE: Azerbaijani
AREA: 33,436 sq mi/86,600 sq km
LEADING EXPORTS: oil, gas, machinery, cotton, and foodstuffs
CONTINENT: Asia

Bahamas
CAPITAL: Nassau
POPULATION: 301,000
OFFICIAL LANGUAGE: English
AREA: 3,864 sq mi/10,010 sq km
LEADING EXPORTS: pharmaceuticals, cement, rum, and crawfish
LOCATION: Caribbean Sea

Bahrain
CAPITAL: Manama
POPULATION: 606,000
OFFICIAL LANGUAGE: Arabic
AREA: 263 sq mi/680 sq km
LEADING EXPORTS: petroleum, petroleum products, and aluminum
CONTINENT: Asia

Bangladesh
CAPITAL: Dhaka
POPULATION: 126.9 million
OFFICIAL LANGUAGE: Bengali
AREA: 51,703 sq mi/133,910 sq km
LEADING EXPORTS: garments, jute and jute goods, leather, frozen fish, and seafood
CONTINENT: Asia

Barbados
CAPITAL: Bridgetown
POPULATION: 269,000
OFFICIAL LANGUAGE: English
AREA: 166 sq mi/430 sq km
LEADING EXPORTS: sugar, molasses, rum, and other foods and beverages
LOCATION: Caribbean Sea

Belarus

CAPITAL: Minsk
POPULATION: 10.3 million
OFFICIAL LANGUAGES: Belorussian, Russian
AREA: 80,154 sq mi/207,600 sq km
LEADING EXPORTS: machinery and equipment, chemicals, metals, and textiles
CONTINENT: Europe

Belgium
CAPITAL: Brussels
POPULATION: 10.2 million
OFFICIAL LANGUAGES: Flemish, French, German
AREA: 12,672 sq mi/32,820 sq km
LEADING EXPORTS: machinery and equipment, chemicals, and diamonds
CONTINENT: Europe

Belize
CAPITAL: Belmopan
POPULATION: 200,000
OFFICIAL LANGUAGE: English
AREA: 8803 sq mi/22,800 sq km
LEADING EXPORTS: sugar, bananas, citrus fruits, clothing, and fish products
CONTINENT: North America

Benin

CAPITAL: Porto-Novo
POPULATION: 5.9 million
OFFICIAL LANGUAGE: French
AREA: 42,710 sq mi/110,620 sq km
LEADING EXPORTS: cotton, crude oil, palm products, and cocoa
CONTINENT: Africa

Bhutan
CAPITAL: Thimphu
POPULATION: 2.1 million
OFFICIAL LANGUAGE: Dzongkha
AREA: 18,147 sq mi/47,000 sq km
LEADING EXPORTS: cardamom, gypsum, timber, handicrafts, and cement
CONTINENT: Asia

Bolivia
CAPITAL: Sucre
POPULATION: 8.1 million
OFFICIAL LANGUAGES: Spanish, Quechua, and Aymará
AREA: 418,683 sq mi/1,084,390 sq km
LEADING EXPORTS: soybeans, natural gas, zinc, gold, and wood
CONTINENT: South America

Bosnia-Herzegovina
CAPITAL: Sarajevo
POPULATION: 3.8 million
OFFICIAL LANGUAGE: Serbo-Croat
AREA: 19,741 sq mi/51,130 sq km
LEADING EXPORTS: none of significance
CONTINENT: Europe

Botswana
CAPITAL: Gaborone
POPULATION: 1.6 million
OFFICIAL LANGUAGE: English
AREA: 218,814 sq mi/566,730 sq km
LEADING EXPORTS: diamonds, vehicles, copper, nickel, and meat
CONTINENT: Africa

Brazil
CAPITAL: Brasília
POPULATION: 168 million
OFFICIAL LANGUAGE: Portuguese
AREA: 3,265,059 sq mi/8,456,510 sq km
LEADING EXPORTS: manufactures, iron ore, soybeans, footwear, and coffee
CONTINENT: South America

Brunei

CAPITAL: Bandar Seri Begawam
POPULATION: 322,000
OFFICIAL LANGUAGE: Malay
AREA: 2,035 sq mi/5,270 sq km
LEADING EXPORTS: crude oil, liquefied natural gas, and petroleum products
LOCATION: South China Sea

Bulgaria

CAPITAL: Sofia
POPULATION: 8.3 million
OFFICIAL LANGUAGE: Bulgarian
AREA: 42,683 sq mi/110,550 sq km
LEADING EXPORTS: machinery and equipment, metals, minerals, and fuels
CONTINENT: Europe

Burkina Faso

CAPITAL: Ouagadougou
POPULATION: 11.6 million
OFFICIAL LANGUAGE: French
AREA: 105,714 sq mi/273,800 sq km
LEADING EXPORTS: cotton, animal products, and gold
CONTINENT: Africa

Burundi

CAPITAL: Bujumbura
POPULATION: 6.6 million
OFFICIAL LANGUAGES: French and Kirundi
AREA: 9,903 sq mi/25,650 sq km
LEADING EXPORTS: coffee, tea, sugar, cotton, and hides
CONTINENT: Africa

Cambodia

CAPITAL: Phnom Penh
POPULATION: 10.9 million
OFFICIAL LANGUAGE: Khmer
AREA: 68,154 sq mi/176,520 sq km
LEADING EXPORTS: timber, garments, rubber, rice, and fish
CONTINENT: Asia

Cameroon

CAPITAL: Yaoundé
POPULATION: 14.7 million
OFFICIAL LANGUAGES: English and French
AREA: 179,691 sq mi/465,400 sq km
LEADING EXPORTS: crude oil and petroleum products, lumber, and cocoa beans
CONTINENT: Africa

Canada

CAPITAL: Ottawa
POPULATION: 30,750,087
OFFICIAL LANGUAGES: English and French
AREA: 3,851,788 sq mi/9,976,140 sq km
LEADING EXPORTS: motor vehicles and parts, newsprint, wood pulp, and timber
CONTINENT: North America

Cape Verde

CAPITAL: Praia
POPULATION: 418,000
OFFICIAL LANGUAGE: Portuguese
AREA: 1,556 sq mi/4,030 sq km
LEADING EXPORTS: fuel, shoes, garments, fish, and bananas
CONTINENT: Africa

Central African Republic

CAPITAL: Bangui
POPULATION: 3.6 million
OFFICIAL LANGUAGE: French
AREA: 240,530 sq mi/622,980 sq km
LEADING EXPORTS: diamonds, timber, cotton, coffee, and tobacco
CONTINENT: Africa

Chad

CAPITAL: N'Djamena
POPULATION: 7.5 million
OFFICIAL LANGUAGES: Arabic and French
AREA: 486,177 sq mi/1,259,200 sq km
LEADING EXPORTS: cotton, cattle, and textiles
CONTINENT: Africa

Chile

CAPITAL: Santiago
POPULATION: 15 million
OFFICIAL LANGUAGE: Spanish
AREA: 289,112 sq mi/748,800 sq km
LEADING EXPORTS: copper, fish, fruits, paper and pulp, and chemicals
CONTINENT: South America

China

CAPITAL: Beijing
POPULATION: 1.3 billion
OFFICIAL LANGUAGE: Mandarin
AREA: 3,600,927 sq mi/9,326,410 sq km
LEADING EXPORTS: machinery, equipment, textiles, and clothing
CONTINENT: Asia

Colombia

CAPITAL: Bogotá
POPULATION: 41.6 million
OFFICIAL LANGUAGE: Spanish
AREA: 401,042 sq mi/1,038,700 sq km
LEADING EXPORTS: petroleum, coffee, coal, gold, and bananas
CONTINENT: South America

Comoros

CAPITAL: Moroni
POPULATION: 676,000
OFFICIAL LANGUAGES: Arabic and French
AREA: 861 sq mi/2,230 sq km
LEADING EXPORTS: vanilla, ylang-ylang, cloves, perfume oil, and copra
LOCATION: Indian Ocean

Congo (Democratic Republic of)

CAPITAL: Kinshasa
POPULATION: 50.3 million
OFFICIAL LANGUAGES: French and English
AREA: 875,520 sq mi/2,267,600 sq km
LEADING EXPORTS: diamonds, copper, coffee, cobalt, and crude oil
CONTINENT: Africa

Congo (Republic of the)

CAPITAL: Brazzaville
POPULATION: 2.9 million
OFFICIAL LANGUAGE: French
AREA: 131,853 sq mi/341,500 sq km
LEADING EXPORTS: petroleum, lumber, plywood, sugar, and cocoa
CONTINENT: Africa

Costa Rica

CAPITAL: San José
POPULATION: 3.9 million
OFFICIAL LANGUAGE: Spanish
AREA: 19,714 sq mi/51,060 sq km
LEADING EXPORTS: coffee, bananas, sugar, textiles, and electronic components
CONTINENT: North America

Côte d'Ivoire

CAPITAL: Yamoussoukro
POPULATION: 15.9 million
OFFICIAL LANGUAGE: French
AREA: 122,780 sq mi/318,000 sq km
LEADING EXPORTS: cocoa, coffee, tropical woods, petroleum, and cotton
CONTINENT: Africa

Croatia

CAPITAL: Zagreb
POPULATION: 4.5 million
OFFICIAL LANGUAGE: Croatian
AREA: 21,829 sq mi/56,538 sq km
LEADING EXPORTS: textiles, chemicals, foodstuffs, and fuels
CONTINENT: Europe

Cuba

CAPITAL: Havana
POPULATION: 11.2 million
OFFICIAL LANGUAGE: Spanish
AREA: 42,803 sq mi/110,860 sq km
LEADING EXPORTS: sugar, nickel, tobacco, shellfish, and medical products
LOCATION: Caribbean Sea

Cyprus

CAPITAL: Nicosia
POPULATION: 778,000
OFFICIAL LANGUAGES: Greek and Turkish
AREA: 3,572 sq mi/9,251 sq km
LEADING EXPORTS: citrus, potatoes, grapes, wine, and cement
LOCATION: Mediterranean Sea

Czech Republic

CAPITAL: Prague
POPULATION: 10.3 million
OFFICIAL LANGUAGE: Czech
AREA: 30,449 sq mi/78,864 sq km
LEADING EXPORTS: machinery and transport equipment, and other manufactured goods
CONTINENT: Europe

Denmark

CAPITAL: Copenhagen
POPULATION: 5.3 million
OFFICIAL LANGUAGE: Danish
AREA: 16,629 sq mi/43,070 sq km
LEADING EXPORTS: machinery and instruments, meat and meat products
CONTINENT: Europe

Djibouti

CAPITAL: Djibouti
POPULATION: 629,000
OFFICIAL LANGUAGES: Arabic and French
AREA: 8,950 sq mi/23,180 sq km
LEADING EXPORTS: reexports, hides and skins, and coffee
CONTINENT: Africa

Dominica

CAPITAL: Roseau
POPULATION: 74,000
OFFICIAL LANGUAGE: English
AREA: 290 sq mi/750 sq km
LEADING EXPORTS: bananas, soap, bay oil, vegetables, and grapefruit
LOCATION: Caribbean Sea

Dominican Republic

CAPITAL: Santo Domingo
POPULATION: 8.4 million
OFFICIAL LANGUAGE: Spanish
AREA: 18,815 sq mi/48,730 sq km
LEADING EXPORTS: ferronickel, sugar, gold, silver, and coffee
LOCATION: Caribbean Sea

Ecuador

CAPITAL: Quito
POPULATION: 12.4 million
OFFICIAL LANGUAGE: Spanish
AREA: 106,888 sq mi/276,840 sq km
LEADING EXPORTS: petroleum, bananas, shrimp, coffee, and cocoa
CONTINENT: South America

Egypt

CAPITAL: Cairo
POPULATION: 67.2 million
OFFICIAL LANGUAGE: Arabic
AREA: 384,343 sq mi/995,450 sq km
LEADING EXPORTS: crude oil, petroleum products, cotton, textiles, and metal products
CONTINENT: Africa

El Salvador

CAPITAL: San Salvador
POPULATION: 6.2 million
OFFICIAL LANGUAGE: Spanish
AREA: 8,000 sq mi/20,720 sq km
LEADING EXPORTS: offshore assembly exports, coffee, sugar, shrimp, and textiles
CONTINENT: North America

Equatorial Guinea

CAPITAL: Malabo
POPULATION: 442,000
OFFICIAL LANGUAGE: Spanish
AREA: 10,830 sq mi/28,050 sq km
LEADING EXPORTS: petroleum, timber, and cocoa
CONTINENT: Africa

Eritrea

CAPITAL: Asmara
POPULATION: 3.7 million
OFFICIAL LANGUAGE: Tigrinya
AREA: 36,170 sq mi/93,680 sq km
LEADING EXPORTS: livestock, sorghum, textiles, food, and small manufactures
CONTINENT: Africa

Estonia

CAPITAL: Tallinn
POPULATION: 1.4 million
OFFICIAL LANGUAGE: Estonian
AREA: 17,423 sq mi/45,125 sq km
LEADING EXPORTS: machinery and appliances, wood products, and textiles
CONTINENT: Europe

Ethiopia

CAPITAL: Addis Ababa
POPULATION: 61.1 million
OFFICIAL LANGUAGE: Amharic
AREA: 425,096 sq mi/1,101,000 sq km
LEADING EXPORTS: coffee, gold, leather products, and oilseeds
CONTINENT: Africa

Fiji

CAPITAL: Suva
POPULATION: 806,000
OFFICIAL LANGUAGE: English
AREA: 7,054 sq mi/18,270 sq km
LEADING EXPORTS: sugar, clothing, gold, processed fish, and lumber
LOCATION: Pacific Ocean

Finland

CAPITAL: Helsinki
POPULATION: 5.2 million
OFFICIAL LANGUAGES: Finnish and Swedish
AREA: 117,610 sq mi/304,610 sq km
LEADING EXPORTS: machinery and equipment, chemicals, metals, and timber
CONTINENT: Europe

France

CAPITAL: Paris
POPULATION: 58.9 million
OFFICIAL LANGUAGE: French
AREA: 212,394 sq mi/550,100 sq km
LEADING EXPORTS: machinery, transportation equipment, and chemicals
CONTINENT: Europe

French Guiana

CAPITAL: Cayenne
POPULATION: 152,300
OFFICIAL LANGUAGE: French
AREA: 35,100 sq mi/91,000 sq km
LEADING EXPORTS: shrimp, timber, gold, rum, and rosewood essence
CONTINENT: South America

Gabon

CAPITAL: Libreville
POPULATION: 1.2 million
OFFICIAL LANGUAGE: French
AREA: 99,486 sq mi/257,670 sq km
LEADING EXPORTS: crude oil, timber, manganese, and uranium
CONTINENT: Africa

The Gambia

CAPITAL: Banjul
POPULATION: 1.3 million
OFFICIAL LANGUAGE: English
AREA: 3,861 sq mi/10,000 sq km
LEADING EXPORTS: peanuts and peanut products, fish, cotton lint, and palm kernels
CONTINENT: Africa

Georgia

CAPITAL: Tbilisi
POPULATION: 5 million
OFFICIAL LANGUAGE: Georgian
AREA: 26,911 sq mi/69,700 sq km
LEADING EXPORTS: citrus fruits, tea, wine, and other agricultural products
CONTINENT: Asia

Germany

CAPITAL: Berlin
POPULATION: 82.2 million
OFFICIAL LANGUAGE: German
AREA: 134,910 sq mi/349,520 sq km
LEADING EXPORTS: machinery, vehicles, chemicals, and metals and manufactures
CONTINENT: Europe

Ghana

CAPITAL: Accra
POPULATION: 19.7 million
OFFICIAL LANGUAGE: English
AREA: 92,100 sq mi/238,540 sq km
LEADING EXPORTS: gold, cocoa, timber, tuna, and bauxite
CONTINENT: Africa

Greece

CAPITAL: Athens
POPULATION: 10.6 million
OFFICIAL LANGUAGE: Greek
AREA: 50,521 sq mi/130,850 sq km
LEADING EXPORTS: manufactured goods, food and beverages, and fuels
CONTINENT: Europe

Grenada

CAPITAL: St. George's
POPULATION: 98,600
OFFICIAL LANGUAGE: English
AREA: 131 sq mi/340 sq km
LEADING EXPORTS: bananas, cocoa, nutmeg, mace, and citrus
LOCATION: Caribbean Sea

Guatemala

CAPITAL: Guatemala City
POPULATION: 11.1 million
OFFICIAL LANGUAGE: Spanish
AREA: 41,865 sq mi/108,430 sq km
LEADING EXPORTS: fuels, machinery, and transport equipment
CONTINENT: North America

Guinea

CAPITAL: Conakry
POPULATION: 7.4 million
OFFICIAL LANGUAGE: French
AREA: 94,926 sq mi/245,860 sq km
LEADING EXPORTS: bauxite, alumina, gold, diamonds, and coffee
CONTINENT: Africa

Guinea-Bissau

CAPITAL: Bissau
POPULATION: 1.2 million
OFFICIAL LANGUAGE: Portuguese
AREA: 10,857 sq mi/28,120 sq km
LEADING EXPORTS: cashew nuts, shrimp, peanuts, palm kernels, and sawn lumber
CONTINENT: Africa

Guyana

CAPITAL: Georgetown
POPULATION: 855,000
OFFICIAL LANGUAGE: English
AREA: 76,004 sq mi/196,850 sq km
LEADING EXPORTS: sugar, gold, bauxite/alumina, rice, and shrimp
CONTINENT: South America

Haiti
CAPITAL: Port-au-Prince
POPULATION: 8.1 million
OFFICIAL LANGUAGES: French and French Creole
AREA: 10,641 sq mi/27,560 sq km
LEADING EXPORTS: manufactures, coffee, oils, and mangoes
LOCATION: Caribbean Sea

Holy See (Vatican City)
CAPITAL: Vatican City
POPULATION: 1,000
OFFICIAL LANGUAGES: Italian and Latin
AREA: 0.17 sq mi/0.44 sq km
LEADING EXPORTS: none
CONTINENT: Europe

Honduras
CAPITAL: Tegucigalpa
POPULATION: 6.3 million
OFFICIAL LANGUAGE: Spanish
AREA: 43,201 sq mi/111,890 sq km
LEADING EXPORTS: coffee, bananas, shrimp, lobster, and meat
CONTINENT: North America

Hungary
CAPITAL: Budapest
POPULATION: 10.1 million
OFFICIAL LANGUAGE: Hungarian
AREA: 35,652 sq mi/92,340 sq km
LEADING EXPORTS: machinery, equipment, and other manufactures
CONTINENT: Europe

Iceland
CAPITAL: Reykjavik
POPULATION: 279,000
OFFICIAL LANGUAGE: Icelandic
AREA: 38,707 sq mi/100,250 sq km
LEADING EXPORTS: fish and fish products, animal products, aluminum, and diatomite
LOCATION: Atlantic Ocean

India
CAPITAL: New Delhi
POPULATION: 998 million
OFFICIAL LANGUAGES: Hindi and English
AREA: 1,147,949 sq mi/2,973,190 sq km
LEADING EXPORTS: textile goods, gems and jewelry, engineering goods, and chemicals
CONTINENT: Asia

Indonesia
CAPITAL: Jakarta
POPULATION: 209.3 million
OFFICIAL LANGUAGE: Bahasa Indonesia
AREA: 699,447 sq mi/1,811,570 sq km
LEADING EXPORTS: oil and gas, plywood, textiles, and rubber
CONTINENT: Asia

Iran
CAPITAL: Tehran
POPULATION: 66.8 million
OFFICIAL LANGUAGE: Farsi
AREA: 636,406 sq mi/1,648,293 sq km
LEADING EXPORTS: petroleum, carpets, fruits, nuts, and hides
CONTINENT: Asia

Iraq
CAPITAL: Baghdad
POPULATION: 22.5 million
OFFICIAL LANGUAGE: Arabic
AREA: 168,869 sq mi/437,370 sq km
LEADING EXPORT: crude oil
CONTINENT: Asia

Ireland
CAPITAL: Dublin
POPULATION: 3.7 million
OFFICIAL LANGUAGES: Irish and English
AREA: 26,598 sq mi/68,890 sq km
LEADING EXPORTS: machinery and equipment, computers, and chemicals
CONTINENT: Europe

Israel
CAPITAL: Jerusalem
POPULATION: 6.1 million
OFFICIAL LANGUAGES: Hebrew and Arabic
AREA: 7,849 sq mi/20,330 sq km
LEADING EXPORTS: machinery, equipment, software, cut diamonds, and chemicals
CONTINENT: Asia

Italy
CAPITAL: Rome
POPULATION: 57.3 million
OFFICIAL LANGUAGE: Italian
AREA: 301,270 sq mi/294,060 sq km
LEADING EXPORTS: engineering products, textiles, clothing, and production machinery
CONTINENT: Europe

Jamaica
CAPITAL: Kingston
POPULATION: 2.6 million
OFFICIAL LANGUAGE: English
AREA: 4,181 sq mi/10,830 sq km
LEADING EXPORTS: alumina, bauxite, sugar, bananas, and rum
LOCATION: Caribbean Sea

Japan
CAPITAL: Tokyo
POPULATION: 126.5 million
OFFICIAL LANGUAGE: Japanese
AREA: 145,374 sq mi/376,520 sq km
LEADING EXPORTS: motor vehicles, semiconductors, and office machinery
CONTINENT: Asia

Jordan
CAPITAL: Amman
POPULATION: 6.5 million
OFFICIAL LANGUAGE: Arabic
AREA: 34,336 sq mi/88,930 sq km
LEADING EXPORTS: phosphates, fertilizers, potash, and agricultural products
CONTINENT: Asia

Kazakstan
CAPITAL: Astana
POPULATION: 16.3 million
OFFICIAL LANGUAGE: Kazakh
AREA: 1,049,150 sq mi/2,717,300 sq km
LEADING EXPORTS: oil, ferrous and nonferrous metals, and machinery
CONTINENT: Asia

Kenya
CAPITAL: Nairobi
POPULATION: 29.5 million
OFFICIAL LANGUAGES: Swahili and English
AREA: 218,907 sq mi/566,970 sq km
LEADING EXPORTS: tea, coffee, horticultural products, and petroleum products
CONTINENT: Africa

Kiribati
CAPITAL: Bairiki
POPULATION: 78,000
OFFICIAL LANGUAGE: English
AREA: 274 sq mi/710 sq km
LEADING EXPORTS: copra, seaweed, and fish
LOCATION: Pacific Ocean

Korea, North
CAPITAL: P'yongyang
POPULATION: 23.7 million
OFFICIAL LANGUAGE: Korean
AREA: 46,490 sq mi/120,410 sq km
LEADING EXPORTS: minerals and metallurgical products
CONTINENT: Asia

Korea, South
CAPITAL: Seoul
POPULATION: 46.5 million
OFFICIAL LANGUAGE: Korean
AREA: 38,120 sq mi/98,730 sq km
LEADING EXPORTS: electronic products, machinery and equipment
CONTINENT: Asia

Kuwait
CAPITAL: Kuwait City
POPULATION: 1.9 million
OFFICIAL LANGUAGE: Arabic
AREA: 6,880 sq mi/17,820 sq km
LEADING EXPORTS: oil and refined products, and fertilizers
CONTINENT: Asia

Kyrgyzstan
CAPITAL: Bishkek
POPULATION: 4.7 million
OFFICIAL LANGUAGES: Kyrgyz and Russian
AREA: 76,640 sq mi/198,500 sq km
LEADING EXPORTS: cotton, wool, meat, tobacco, and gold
CONTINENT: Asia

Laos
CAPITAL: Vientiane
POPULATION: 5.3 million
OFFICIAL LANGUAGE: Laotian
AREA: 89,112 sq mi/230,800 sq km
LEADING EXPORTS: wood products, garments, electricity, coffee, and tin
CONTINENT: Asia

Latvia
CAPITAL: Riga
POPULATION: 2.4 million
OFFICIAL LANGUAGE: Latvian
AREA: 24,938 sq mi/ 64,589 sq km
LEADING EXPORTS: wood, wood products, machinery, and equipment
CONTINENT: Europe

Lebanon

CAPITAL: Beirut
POPULATION: 3.2 million
OFFICIAL LANGUAGE: Arabic
AREA: 3,950 sq mi/10,230 sq km
LEADING EXPORTS: foodstuffs, tobacco, textiles, and chemicals
CONTINENT: Asia

Lesotho

CAPITAL: Maseru
POPULATION: 2.1 million
OFFICIAL LANGUAGES: English and Sesotho
AREA: 11,718 sq mi/30,350 sq km
LEADING EXPORTS: clothing, footwear, road vehicles, wool, and mohair
CONTINENT: Africa

Liberia

CAPITAL: Monrovia
POPULATION: 2.9 million
OFFICIAL LANGUAGE: English
AREA: 37,189 sq mi/96,320 sq km
LEADING EXPORTS: diamonds, iron ore, rubber, timber, and coffee
CONTINENT: Africa

Libya

CAPITAL: Tripoli/Benghazi
POPULATION: 5.5 million
OFFICIAL LANGUAGE: Arabic
AREA: 679,358 sq mi/1,759,540 sq km
LEADING EXPORTS: crude oil, refined petroleum products, and natural gas
CONTINENT: Africa

Liechtenstein

CAPITAL: Vaduz
POPULATION: 31,000
OFFICIAL LANGUAGE: German
AREA: 62 sq mi/160 sq km
LEADING EXPORTS: small specialty machinery, dental products, and stamps
CONTINENT: Europe

Lithuania

CAPITAL: Vilnius
POPULATION: 3.7 million
OFFICIAL LANGUAGE: Lithuanian
AREA: 25,174 sq mi/65,200 sq km
LEADING EXPORTS: machinery, equipment, and mineral products
CONTINENT: Europe

Luxembourg

CAPITAL: Luxembourg
POPULATION: 426,000
OFFICIAL LANGUAGES: French, Letzeburgish, German
AREA: 998 sq mi/2,585 sq km
LEADING EXPORTS: finished steel products, chemicals, rubber products, and glass
CONTINENT: Europe

Macedonia

CAPITAL: Skopje
POPULATION: 2 million
OFFICIAL LANGUAGE: Macedonian
AREA: 9,929 sq mi/25,715 sq km
LEADING EXPORTS: food, beverages, tobacco, and miscellaneous manufactures
CONTINENT: Europe

Madagascar

CAPITAL: Antananarivo
POPULATION: 15.5 million
OFFICIAL LANGUAGES: French and Malagasy
AREA: 224,533 sq mi/581,540 sq km
LEADING EXPORTS: coffee, vanilla, cloves, shellfish, and sugar
CONTINENT: Africa

Malawi

CAPITAL: Lilongwe
POPULATION: 10.6 million
OFFICIAL LANGUAGE: English
AREA: 45,745 sq mi/118,480 sq km
LEADING EXPORTS: tobacco, tea, sugar, cotton, and coffee
CONTINENT: Africa

Malaysia

CAPITAL: Kuala Lumpur
POPULATION: 21.8 million
OFFICIAL LANGUAGES: English and Bahasa Malay
AREA: 126,853 sq mi/328,550 sq km
LEADING EXPORTS: electronic equipment, petroleum, and liquefied natural gas
CONTINENT: Asia

Maldives

CAPITAL: Male
POPULATION: 278,000
OFFICIAL LANGUAGE: Dhivehi
AREA: 116 sq mi/300 sq km
LEADING EXPORTS: fish and clothing
CONTINENT: Asia

Mali

CAPITAL: Bamako
POPULATION: 11 million
OFFICIAL LANGUAGE: French
AREA: 471,115 sq mi/1,220,190 sq km
LEADING EXPORTS: cotton, gold, and livestock
CONTINENT: Africa

Malta

CAPITAL: Valletta
POPULATION: 386,000
OFFICIAL LANGUAGES: English and Maltese
AREA: 124 sq mi/320 sq km
LEADING EXPORTS: machinery, transport equipment, and manufactures
LOCATION: Mediterranean Sea

Marshall Islands

CAPITAL: Delap district
POPULATION: 59,000
OFFICIAL LANGUAGES: Marshallese and English
AREA: 70 sq mi/181 sq km
LEADING EXPORTS: fish, coconut oil, and trochus shells
LOCATION: Pacific Ocean

Mauritania

CAPITAL: Nouakchott
POPULATION: 2.6 million
OFFICIAL LANGUAGES: Arabic and French
AREA: 395,953 sq mi/1,025,520 sq km
LEADING EXPORTS: fish and fish products, iron ore, and gold
CONTINENT: Africa

Mauritius

CAPITAL: Port Louis
POPULATION: 1.2 million
OFFICIAL LANGUAGE: English
AREA: 718 sq mi/1,860 sq km
LEADING EXPORTS: clothing, textiles, sugar, cut flowers, and molasses
LOCATION: Indian Ocean

Mexico

CAPITAL: Mexico City
POPULATION: 97.4 million
OFFICIAL LANGUAGE: Spanish
AREA: 736,945 sq mi/1,908,690 sq km
LEADING EXPORTS: manufactured goods, oil and oil products, silver, coffee, and cotton
CONTINENT: North America

Micronesia

CAPITAL: Palikir
POPULATION: 109,000
OFFICIAL LANGUAGE: English
AREA: 271 sq mi/702 sq km
LEADING EXPORTS: fish, garments, bananas, and black pepper
LOCATION: Pacific Ocean

Moldova

CAPITAL: Chisinau
POPULATION: 4.4 million
OFFICIAL LANGUAGE: Romanian
AREA: 13,000 sq mi/33,700 sq km
LEADING EXPORTS: foodstuffs, wine, tobacco, textiles, and footwear
CONTINENT: Europe

Monaco

CAPITAL: Monaco
POPULATION: 32,000
OFFICIAL LANGUAGE: French
AREA: 0.75 sq mi/1.95 sq km
LEADING EXPORTS: not available
CONTINENT: Europe

Mongolia

CAPITAL: Ulan Bator
POPULATION: 2.6 million
OFFICIAL LANGUAGE: Khalka Mongol
AREA: 604,247 sq mi/1,565,000 sq km
LEADING EXPORTS: copper, livestock, animal products, cashmere, and wool
CONTINENT: Asia

Morocco

CAPITAL: Rabat
POPULATION: 27.9 million
OFFICIAL LANGUAGE: Arabic
AREA: 172,316 sq mi/446,300 sq km
LEADING EXPORTS: phosphates and fertilizers, food and beverages, and minerals
CONTINENT: Africa

Mozambique

CAPITAL: Maputo
POPULATION: 19.3 million
OFFICIAL LANGUAGE: Portuguese
AREA: 302,737 sq mi/784,090 sq km
LEADING EXPORTS: prawns, cashews, cotton, sugar, and copra
CONTINENT: Africa

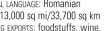

Myanmar (Burma)

CAPITAL: Yangon
POPULATION: 45.1 million
OFFICIAL LANGUAGE: Burmese
AREA: 253,876 sq mi/657,540 sq km
LEADING EXPORTS: pulses and beans, prawns, fish, rice, and teak
CONTINENT: Asia

Namibia

CAPITAL: Windhoek
POPULATION: 1.7 million
OFFICIAL LANGUAGE: English
AREA: 318,260 sq mi/824,290 sq km
LEADING EXPORTS: diamonds, copper, gold, zinc, and lead
CONTINENT: Africa

Nauru

CAPITAL: none
POPULATION: 11,000
OFFICIAL LANGUAGE: Nauruan
AREA: 8.2 sq mi/21.2 sq km
LEADING EXPORT: phosphates
LOCATION: Pacific Ocean

Nepal

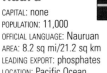

CAPITAL: Kathmandu
POPULATION: 23.4 million
OFFICIAL LANGUAGE: Nepali
AREA: 52,818 sq mi/136,800 sq km
LEADING EXPORTS: carpets, clothing, leather goods, jute goods, and grain
CONTINENT: Asia

Netherlands

CAPITAL: Amsterdam
POPULATION: 15.7 million
OFFICIAL LANGUAGE: Dutch
AREA: 13,097 sq mi/33,920 sq km
LEADING EXPORTS: machinery and equipment, chemicals, fuels, and foodstuffs
CONTINENT: Europe

New Zealand

CAPITAL: Wellington
POPULATION: 3.8 million
OFFICIAL LANGUAGES: English and Maori
AREA: 103,733 sq mi/268,670 sq km
LEADING EXPORTS: dairy products, meat, fish, wool, and forestry products
LOCATION: Pacific Ocean

Nicaragua

CAPITAL: Managua
POPULATION: 4.9 million
OFFICIAL LANGUAGE: Spanish
AREA: 45,849 sq mi/118,750 sq km
LEADING EXPORTS: coffee, shrimp and lobster, cotton, tobacco, and beef
CONTINENT: North America

Niger

CAPITAL: Niamey
POPULATION: 10.4 million
OFFICIAL LANGUAGE: French
AREA: 489,073 sq mi/1,266,700 sq km
LEADING EXPORTS: uranium ore, livestock products, cowpeas, and onions
CONTINENT: Africa

Nigeria

CAPITAL: Abuja
POPULATION: 108 million
OFFICIAL LANGUAGE: English
AREA: 351,648 sq mi/910,770 sq km
LEADING EXPORTS: petroleum and petroleum products, cocoa, and rubber
CONTINENT: Africa

Norway

CAPITAL: Oslo
POPULATION: 4.4 million
OFFICIAL LANGUAGE: Norwegian
AREA: 118,467 sq mi/306,830 sq km
LEADING EXPORTS: petroleum and petroleum products
CONTINENT: Europe

Oman

CAPITAL: Muscat
POPULATION: 2.5 million
OFFICIAL LANGUAGE: Arabic
AREA: 82,030 sq mi/212,460 sq km
LEADING EXPORTS: petroleum, fish, metals, and textiles
CONTINENT: Asia

Pakistan

CAPITAL: Islamabad
POPULATION: 152.3 million
OFFICIAL LANGUAGE: Urdu
AREA: 297,637 sq mi/770,880 sq km
LEADING EXPORTS: cotton, fabrics and yarn, rice, and other agricultural products
CONTINENT: Asia

Palau

CAPITAL: Koror
POPULATION: 18,000
OFFICIAL LANGUAGES: Belauan and English
AREA: 196 sq mi/508 sq km
LEADING EXPORTS: trochus (type of shellfish), tuna, copra, and handicrafts
LOCATION: Pacific Ocean

Panama

CAPITAL: Panama City
POPULATION: 2.8 million
OFFICIAL LANGUAGE: Spanish
AREA: 29,340 sq mi/75,990 sq km
LEADING EXPORTS: bananas, sugar, shrimp, and coffee
CONTINENT: North America

Papua New Guinea

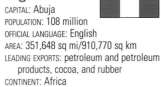

CAPITAL: Port Moresby
POPULATION: 4.7 million
OFFICIAL LANGUAGE: English
AREA: 174,849 sq mi/452,860 sq km
LEADING EXPORTS: oil, gold, copper ore, logs, and palm oil
LOCATION: Pacific Ocean

Paraguay

CAPITAL: Asunción
POPULATION: 5.4 million
OFFICIAL LANGUAGE: Spanish
AREA: 153,398 sq mi/397,300 sq km
LEADING EXPORTS: soybeans, feed, cotton, meat, and edible oils
CONTINENT: South America

Peru

CAPITAL: Lima
POPULATION: 25.2 million
OFFICIAL LANGUAGES: Spanish and Quechua
AREA: 494,208 sq mi/1,280,000 sq km
LEADING EXPORTS: fish and fish products, copper, zinc, and gold
CONTINENT: South America

Philippines

CAPITAL: Manila
POPULATION: 74.5 million
OFFICIAL LANGUAGES: English and Filipino
AREA: 115,830 sq mi/300,000 sq km
LEADING EXPORTS: electronic equipment, machinery, and transport equipment
CONTINENT: Asia

Poland

CAPITAL: Warsaw
POPULATION: 38.7 million
OFFICIAL LANGUAGE: Polish
AREA: 117,552 sq mi/304,460 sq km
LEADING EXPORTS: manufactured goods, chemicals, and machinery and equipment
CONTINENT: Europe

Portugal

CAPITAL: Lisbon
POPULATION: 9.9 million
OFFICIAL LANGUAGE: Portuguese
AREA: 35,502 sq mi/91,950 sq km
LEADING EXPORTS: machinery, clothing, footwear, and chemicals
CONTINENT: Europe

Qatar

CAPITAL: Doha
POPULATION: 589,000
OFFICIAL LANGUAGE: Arabic
AREA: 4,247 sq mi/11,000 sq km
LEADING EXPORTS: petroleum products, fertilizers, and steel
CONTINENT: Asia

Romania

CAPITAL: Bucharest
POPULATION: 22.4 million
OFFICIAL LANGUAGE: Romanian
AREA: 88,934 sq mi/230,340 sq km
LEADING EXPORTS: textiles, footwear, metals, and metal products
CONTINENT: Europe

Russia

CAPITAL: Moscow
POPULATION: 147.2 million
OFFICIAL LANGUAGE: Russian
AREA: 6,592,812 sq mi/17,075,400 sq km
LEADING EXPORTS: petroleum, petroleum products, and natural gas
CONTINENT: Europe and Asia

Rwanda

CAPITAL: Kigali
POPULATION: 7.2 million
OFFICIAL LANGUAGES: French and Rwandan
AREA: 9,633 sq mi/24,950 sq km
LEADING EXPORTS: coffee, tea, hides, and tin ore
CONTINENT: Africa

Saint Kitts and Nevis

CAPITAL: Basseterre
POPULATION: 41,000
OFFICIAL LANGUAGE: English
AREA: 139 sq mi/360 sq km
LEADING EXPORTS: machinery, food, electronics, beverages, and tobacco
LOCATION: Caribbean Sea

Saint Lucia

CAPITAL: Castries
POPULATION: 152,000
OFFICIAL LANGUAGE: English
AREA: 239 sq mi/620 sq km
LEADING EXPORTS: bananas, clothing, cocoa, vegetables, and fruits
LOCATION: Caribbean Sea

Saint Vincent and the Grenadines

CAPITAL: Kingstown
POPULATION: 111,000
OFFICIAL LANGUAGE: English
AREA: 131 sq mi/340 sq km
LEADING EXPORTS: bananas, eddoes, dasheen, and arrowroot starch
LOCATION: Caribbean Sea

Samoa

CAPITAL: Apia
POPULATION: 177,000
OFFICIAL LANGUAGES: English, Samoan
AREA: 1,093 sq mi/2,830 sq km
LEADING EXPORTS: coconut oil, cream, copra, and fish
LOCATION: Pacific Ocean

San Marino

CAPITAL: San Marino
POPULATION: 26,000
OFFICIAL LANGUAGE: Italian
AREA: 24 sq mi/61 sq km
LEADING EXPORTS: building stone, lime, wood, chestnuts, and wheat
CONTINENT: Europe

São Tomé and Príncipe

CAPITAL: São Tomé
POPULATION: 135,000
OFFICIAL LANGUAGE: Portuguese
AREA: 371 sq mi/960 sq km
LEADING EXPORTS: cocoa, copra, coffee, and palm oil
CONTINENT: Africa

Saudi Arabia

CAPITAL: Riyadh
POPULATION: 20.9 million
OFFICIAL LANGUAGE: Arabic
AREA: 829,995 sq mi/2,149,690 sq km
LEADING EXPORTS: petroleum and petroleum products
CONTINENT: Asia

Senegal

CAPITAL: Dakar
POPULATION: 9.2 million
OFFICIAL LANGUAGE: French
AREA: 74,336 sq mi/192,530 sq km
LEADING EXPORTS: fish, groundnuts (peanuts), and petroleum products
CONTINENT: Africa

Seychelles

CAPITAL: Victoria
POPULATION: 75,000
OFFICIAL LANGUAGE: Seselwa (French Creole)
AREA: 104 sq mi/270 sq km
LEADING EXPORTS: fish, cinnamon bark, copra, and petroleum products (reexports)
CONTINENT: Africa

Sierra Leone

CAPITAL: Freetown
POPULATION: 4.7 million
OFFICIAL LANGUAGE: English
AREA: 27,652 sq mi/71,620 sq km
LEADING EXPORTS: diamonds, rutile, cocoa, coffee, and fish
CONTINENT: Africa

Singapore

CAPITAL: Singapore
POPULATION: 3.5 million
OFFICIAL LANGUAGES: Malay, English, Mandarin Chinese, Tamil
AREA: 236 sq mi/610 sq km
LEADING EXPORTS: machinery and equipment, chemicals, and mineral fuels
CONTINENT: Asia

Slovakia

CAPITAL: Bratislava
POPULATION: 5.4 million
OFFICIAL LANGUAGE: Slovak
AREA: 18,933 sq mi/49,036 sq km
LEADING EXPORTS: machinery, transport equipment, and manufactured goods
CONTINENT: Europe

Slovenia

CAPITAL: Ljubljana
POPULATION: 2 million
OFFICIAL LANGUAGE: Slovene
AREA: 7,820 sq mi/20,250 sq km
LEADING EXPORTS: manufactured goods, machinery, and transport equipment
CONTINENT: Europe

Solomon Islands

CAPITAL: Honiara
POPULATION: 430,000
OFFICIAL LANGUAGE: English
AREA: 10,639 sq mi/27,556 sq km
LEADING EXPORTS: timber, fish, palm oil, cocoa, and copra
LOCATION: Pacific Ocean

Somalia

CAPITAL: Mogadishu
POPULATION: 9.7 million
OFFICIAL LANGUAGES: Arabic and Somali
AREA: 242,216 sq mi/627,340 sq km
LEADING EXPORTS: livestock, bananas, hides, and fish
CONTINENT: Africa

South Africa

CAPITAL: Pretoria
POPULATION: 39.9 million
OFFICIAL LANGUAGES: Afrikaans and English
AREA: 471,443 sq mi/1,221,040 sq km
LEADING EXPORTS: gold, diamonds, other metals, and minerals
CONTINENT: Africa

Spain

CAPITAL: Madrid
POPULATION: 39.6 million
OFFICIAL LANGUAGES: Spanish, Galician, Basque, Catalan
AREA: 192,834 sq mi/499,440 sq km
LEADING EXPORTS: machinery, motor vehicles, and foodstuffs
CONTINENT: Europe

Sri Lanka

CAPITAL: Colombo
POPULATION: 18.6 million
OFFICIAL LANGUAGES: Sinhala, Tamil, English
AREA: 24,996 sq mi/64,740 sq km
LEADING EXPORTS: textiles and apparel, tea, diamonds, and coconut products
CONTINENT: Asia

Sudan

CAPITAL: Khartoum
POPULATION: 28.9 million
OFFICIAL LANGUAGE: Arabic
AREA: 917,374 sq mi/2,376,000 sq km
LEADING EXPORTS: cotton, sesame, livestock, groundnuts, and oil
CONTINENT: Africa

Suriname

CAPITAL: Paramaribo
POPULATION: 415,000
OFFICIAL LANGUAGE: Dutch
AREA: 62,344 sq mi/161,470 sq km
LEADING EXPORTS: alumina, aluminum, crude oil, lumber, shrimp, and fish
CONTINENT: South America

Swaziland

CAPITAL: Mbabane
POPULATION: 980,000
OFFICIAL LANGUAGES: English and Swazi
AREA: 6,641 sq mi/17,200 sq km
LEADING EXPORTS: soft drink concentrates, sugar, wood pulp, and cotton yarn
CONTINENT: Africa

Sweden

CAPITAL: Stockholm
POPULATION: 8.9 million
OFFICIAL LANGUAGE: Swedish
AREA: 158,926 sq mi/411,620 sq km
LEADING EXPORTS: machinery, motor vehicles, paper products, pulp, and wood
CONTINENT: Europe

Switzerland

CAPITAL: Bern
POPULATION: 7.3 million
OFFICIAL LANGUAGES: French, German, Italian
AREA: 15,355 sq mi/39,770 sq km
LEADING EXPORTS: machinery, chemicals, vehicles, metals, and watches
CONTINENT: Europe

Syria

CAPITAL: Damascus
POPULATION: 15.7 million
OFFICIAL LANGUAGE: Arabic
AREA: 71,060 sq mi/184,060 sq km
LEADING EXPORTS: petroleum, textiles, and manufactured goods
CONTINENT: Asia

Taiwan

CAPITAL: Taipei
POPULATION: 21.7 million
OFFICIAL LANGUAGE: Mandarin Chinese
AREA: 12,456 sq mi/32,260 sq km
LEADING EXPORTS: electronics, electric and machinery equipment, metals, and textiles
CONTINENT: Asia

Tajikistan

CAPITAL: Dushanbe
POPULATION: 6.1 million
OFFICIAL LANGUAGE: Tajik
AREA: 55,251 sq mi/143,100 sq km
LEADING EXPORTS: aluminum, electricity, cotton, fruits, and vegetable oil
CONTINENT: Asia

Tanzania

CAPITAL: Dodoma
POPULATION: 32.8 million
OFFICIAL LANGUAGES: English and Swahili
AREA: 342,100 sq mi/886,040 sq km
LEADING EXPORTS: coffee, manufactured goods, cotton, cashew nuts, and minerals
CONTINENT: Africa

Thailand

CAPITAL: Bangkok
POPULATION: 60.9 million
OFFICIAL LANGUAGE: Thai
AREA: 197,255 sq mi/510,890 sq km
LEADING EXPORTS: computers and parts, textiles, and rice
CONTINENT: Asia

Togo

CAPITAL: Lomé
POPULATION: 4.5 million
OFFICIAL LANGUAGE: French
AREA: 21,000 sq mi/54,390 sq km
LEADING EXPORTS: cotton, phosphates, coffee, and cocoa
CONTINENT: Africa

Tonga

CAPITAL: Nuku'alofa
POPULATION: 97,000
OFFICIAL LANGUAGES: English and Tongan
AREA: 278 sq mi/720 sq km
LEADING EXPORTS: squash, fish, and vanilla beans
LOCATION: Pacific Ocean

Trinidad and Tobago

CAPITAL: Port-of-Spain
POPULATION: 1.3 million
OFFICIAL LANGUAGE: English
AREA: 1,981 sq mi/5,130 sq km
LEADING EXPORTS: petroleum, petroleum products, and chemicals
LOCATION: Caribbean Sea

Tunisia

CAPITAL: Tunis
POPULATION: 9.5 million
OFFICIAL LANGUAGE: Arabic
AREA: 59,984 sq mi/155,360 sq km
LEADING EXPORTS: textiles, mechanical goods, phosphates, and chemicals
CONTINENT: Africa

Turkey

CAPITAL: Ankara
POPULATION: 65.5 million
OFFICIAL LANGUAGE: Turkish
AREA: 297,154 sq mi/769,630 sq km
LEADING EXPORTS: apparel, foodstuffs, textiles, and metal manufactures
CONTINENT: Asia

Turkmenistan

CAPITAL: Ashgabat
POPULATION: 4.4 million
OFFICIAL LANGUAGE: Turkmen
AREA: 188,445 sq mi/488,100 sq km
LEADING EXPORTS: oil, gas, and cotton
CONTINENT: Asia

Tuvalu

CAPITAL: Fongafale
POPULATION: 10,000
OFFICIAL LANGUAGE: English
AREA: 10 sq mi/26 sq km
LEADING EXPORT: copra
LOCATION: Pacific Ocean

Uganda

CAPITAL: Kampala
POPULATION: 21.1 million
OFFICIAL LANGUAGES: English and Swahili
AREA: 77,046 sq mi/199,550 sq km
LEADING EXPORTS: coffee, fish and fish products, tea, and electrical products
CONTINENT: Africa

Ukraine

CAPITAL: Kiev
POPULATION: 50.7 million
OFFICIAL LANGUAGE: Ukrainian
AREA: 223,090 sq mi/603,700 sq km
LEADING EXPORTS: metals, fuel, and petroleum products
CONTINENT: Europe

United Arab Emirates

CAPITAL: Abu Dhabi
POPULATION: 2.4 million
OFFICIAL LANGUAGE: Arabic
AREA: 32,278 sq mi/83,600 sq km
LEADING EXPORTS: crude oil, natural gas, dried fish, and dates
CONTINENT: Asia

United Kingdom

CAPITAL: London
POPULATION: 58.7 million
OFFICIAL LANGUAGES: English and Welsh
AREA: 93,282 sq mi/241,600 sq km
LEADING EXPORTS: manufactured goods, fuels, chemicals, and food beverages
CONTINENT: Europe

United States

CAPITAL: Washington, D.C.
POPULATION: 281 million
OFFICIAL LANGUAGE: none
AREA: 3,717,792 sq mi/9,629,091 sq km
LEADING EXPORTS: capital goods and automobiles
CONTINENT: North America

Uruguay

CAPITAL: Montevideo
POPULATION: 3.3 million
OFFICIAL LANGUAGE: Spanish
AREA: 67,494 sq mi/174,810 sq km
LEADING EXPORTS: meat, rice, leather products, vehicles, and dairy products
CONTINENT: South America

Uzbekistan

CAPITAL: Tashkent
POPULATION: 23.9 million
OFFICIAL LANGUAGE: Uzbek
AREA: 172,741 sq mi/447,400 sq km
LEADING EXPORTS: cotton, gold, natural gas, mineral fertilizers, and ferrous metals
CONTINENT: Asia

Vanuatu

CAPITAL: Port-Vila
POPULATION: 200,000
OFFICIAL LANGUAGES: Bislama, English, French
AREA: 4,707 sq mi/12,190 sq km
LEADING EXPORTS: copra, beef, cocoa, timber, and coffee
LOCATION: Pacific Ocean

Venezuela

CAPITAL: Caracas
POPULATION: 23.7 million
OFFICIAL LANGUAGES: Spanish and Amerindian languages
AREA: 340,560 sq mi/882,050 sq km
LEADING EXPORTS: petroleum, bauxite and aluminum, steel, and chemicals
CONTINENT: South America

Vietnam

CAPITAL: Hanoi
POPULATION: 78.7 million
OFFICIAL LANGUAGE: Vietnamese
AREA: 125,621 sq mi/325,360 sq km
LEADING EXPORTS: crude oil, marine products, rice, coffee, and rubber
CONTINENT: Asia

Yemen

CAPITAL: Sana'a
POPULATION: 17.5 million
OFFICIAL LANGUAGE: Arabic
AREA: 203,849 sq mi/527,970 sq km
LEADING EXPORTS: crude oil, cotton, coffee, and dried and salted fish
CONTINENT: Asia

Yugoslavia

CAPITAL: Belgrade
POPULATION: 10.6 million
OFFICIAL LANGUAGE: Serbo-Croat
AREA: 39,449 sq mi/102,173 sq km
LEADING EXPORTS: manufactured goods, food, live animals, and raw materials
CONTINENT: Europe

Zambia

CAPITAL: Lusaka
POPULATION: 9 million
OFFICIAL LANGUAGE: English
AREA: 285,992 sq mi/740,720 sq km
LEADING EXPORTS: copper, cobalt, electricity, and tobacco
CONTINENT: Africa

Zimbabwe

CAPITAL: Harare
POPULATION: 11.5 million
OFFICIAL LANGUAGE: English
AREA: 149,293 sq mi/ 390,580 sq km
LEADING EXPORTS: tobacco, gold, ferroalloys, and cotton
CONTINENT: Africa

Glossary of Geographic Terms

basin
a depression in the surface of the land; some basins are filled with water

bay
a part of a sea or lake that extends into the land

butte
a small raised area of land with steep sides

▲ butte

canyon
a deep, narrow valley with steep sides; often has a stream flowing through it

cataract
a large waterfall; any strong flood or rush of water

◄ cataract

delta
a triangular-shaped plain at the mouth of a river, formed when sediment is deposited by flowing water

flood plain
a broad plain on either side of a river, formed when sediment settles on the riverbanks

glacier
a huge, slow-moving mass of snow and ice

hill
an area that rises above surrounding land and has a rounded top; lower and usually less steep than a mountain

island
an area of land completely surrounded by water

isthmus
a narrow strip of land that connects two larger areas of land

mesa
a high, flat-topped landform with cliff-like sides; larger than a butte

mountain
an area that rises steeply at least 2,000 feet (610 m) above surrounding land; usually wide at the bottom and rising to a narrow peak or ridge

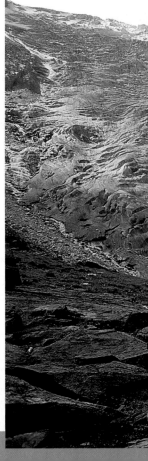

► glacier

◀ delta

mountain pass
a gap between mountains

peninsula
an area of land almost completely surrounded by water and connected to the mainland by an isthmus

plain
a large area of flat or gently rolling land

plateau
a large, flat area that rises above the surrounding land; at least one side has a steep slope

river mouth
the point where a river enters a lake or sea

strait
a narrow stretch of water that connects two larger bodies of water

tributary
a river or stream that flows into a larger river

volcano
an opening in the Earth's surface through which molten rock, ashes, and gasses from the Earth's interior escape

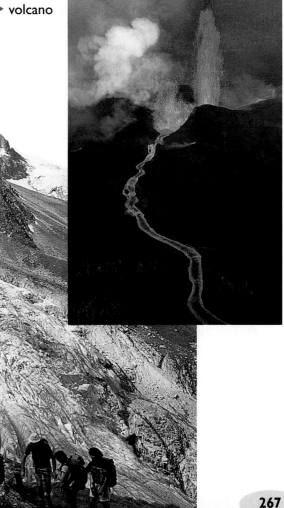

▶ volcano

Gazetteer

A

Aksum an ancient town in northern Ethiopia; a powerful kingdom and trade center about A.D. 200–600, p. 49

Algeria (28°N, 1°E) a country in North Africa; officially known as the Democratic and Popular Republic of Algeria, pp. 205, 258

Andes Mountains a mountain system extending along the western coast of South America, p. 65

Angkor (14°N, 104°E) capital of an ancient Asian empire; located in present-day Cambodia, p. 114

Arabian Peninsula (16°N, 65°E) a peninsula of Southwest Asia, on which are located the present-day nations of Saudi Arabia, Yemen, Oman, the United Arab Emirates, Qatar, Bahrain, and Kuwait, p. 15

Argentina (35°S, 67°W) a country in South America, pp. 66, 258

Arno River (43°N, 11°E) a river of central Italy, p. 138

Austria (47°N, 12°E) a country of central Europe, pp. 189, 258

B

Baghdad (33°N, 44°E) capital city of present-day Iraq; capital of the Muslim empire during Islam's golden age, p. 29

Bangladesh (24°N, 90°E) a coastal country in South Asia, officially the People's Republic of Bangladesh, pp. 95, 258

Belgium (51°N, 3°E) a country in western Europe, pp. 193, 258

Berlin (51°N, 13°E) the capital city of Germany, p. 210

Bolivia (17°S, 64°W) a country in South America, pp. 66, 258

Bosporus (41°N, 29°E) a narrow strait that separates Europe and Asia, and connects the Black Sea with the Sea of Marmara, p. 10

Brazil (9°S, 53°W) the largest country in South America, pp. 186, 259

Britain (56°N, 1°W) historically, the island of Great Britain; currently, a term used informally to describe Great Britain, the United Kingdom, or England, pp. 182, 265

Bulgaria (42°N, 24°E) a country in eastern Europe, pp. 212, 259

C

Cahokia (38°N, 90°W) a village in what is now the state of Illinois; formerly a large, prehistoric city known for its Native American mounds, p. 73

Cairo (30°N, 31°E) the capital and largest city of Egypt, located on the Nile River, p. 43

Cape Bojador (26°N, 16°W) an extension of the western Sahara coast into the Atlantic Ocean, p. 145

Chile (35°S, 72°W) a country on the west coast of South America, pp. 66, 259

China a country occupying most of the mainland of East Asia, pp. 10, 259

Constantinople (41°N, 29°E) a city located on both the European and Asian sides of the Bosporus; known as Istanbul in present-day Turkey; also known as Byzantium in the medieval Byzantine empire, p. 9

Cuzco (13°S, 72°W) a city in Peru; the capital city of the ancient Incan empire, p. 65

Czechoslovakia (49°N, 16°E) a country of eastern Europe, now known as the Czech Republic, p. 212

D

Delhi (29°N, 77°E) the third-largest city in India, popularly known as Old Delhi, p. 94

Denmark (56°N, 8°E) a country of northern Europe; considered part of Scandinavia, pp. 107, 260

Djenné city in Mali, Africa; was an important center of Muslim learning in the Kingdom of Mali in the 1300s, p. 46

E

Ecuador (0°N, 78°W) a country of northwest South America, pp. 65, 260

Ethiopia (8°N, 38°E) a country in East Africa, officially the People's Republic of Ethiopia, pp. 49, 51, 260

F

Florence (43°N, 11°E) a city in the Tuscany region of central Italy, p. 139

France (46°N, 0.47°E) a country in western Europe, pp. 107, 260

G

Gaul a region of France, Belgium, and parts of Germany and northern Italy occupied by the ancient Gauls, p. 107

Germany (51°N, 10°E) a country in central Europe, pp. 189, 260

Ghana (8°N, 2°W) a country in West Africa; officially known as the Republic of Ghana, pp. 45, 260

Grand Canal the 1,085-mile (1,747 km) channel connecting the Huang He and Yangzi rivers in China; the longest artificially made waterway in the world, p. 87

Great Zimbabwe former kingdom in the highlands of Southern Africa, located between the Zambezi and Limpopo rivers; founded in A.D. 1100 by the Shona people, p. 53

Greenland (74°N, 40°W) a large, self-governing island in the northern Atlantic Ocean, part of Denmark, p. 108

Gulf of Mexico (25°N, 93°W) an arm of the Atlantic Ocean in southeastern North America, bordering on eastern Mexico, the southeast United States, and Cuba, p. 62

H

Hiroshima (34°N, 132°E) a city in the southwestern part of the island of Honshu, Japan; the first city to be hit by an atomic bomb, dropped by the United States during World War II, p. 203

Holy Land (31°N, 35°E) a small region at the eastern edge of the Mediterranean Sea, also known as Palestine, which includes parts of modern Israel and Jordan; considered holy by Jews, Christians, and Muslims, p. 117

Huang He (35°N, 113°E) the second-longest river in China, p. 87

I

Incan Empire an empire ruled by the Incas that stretched along the Andes Mountains through present-day Ecuador, Peru, Bolivia, Chile, and Argentina; lasted from around the 1300s to the 1500s, p. 65

India (23°N, 77°E) a large country occupying most of the Indian subcontinent in South Asia, p. 94, 261

Iraq (32°N, 42°E) a country in Southwest Asia, pp. 16, 261

Israel (32°N, 34°E) a country in Southwest Asia, pp. 49, 261

Italy (44°N, 11°E) a boot-shaped country in southern Europe, including the islands of Sicily and Sardinia, pp. 138, 261

J

Japan (36°N, 133°E) an island country in the Pacific Ocean off the east coast of Asia, pp. 90, 261

Jerusalem (31°N, 35°E) the capital city of modern Israel; a holy city for Jews, Christians, and Muslims, p. 118

K

Kilwa a medieval Islamic city-state on an island near present-day Tanzania, p. 51

Koreas (40°N, 127°E) the nations of North and South Korea, which occupy the Korean peninsula in east Asia, surrounded by the Yellow Sea and the Sea of Japan, pp. 90, 261

Kyoto (35°N, 135°E) a city in west central Japan; was Japan's capital until the late 1800s, p. 90

L

Lake Texcoco a lake, now drained, in central Mexico, where Mexico City now stands; formerly the site of the ancient Aztec capital of Tenochtitlán, p. 59

M

Machu Picchu (13°S, 72°W) an ancient city in the Andes Mountains built during the Incan Empire; located near the present-day city of Cuzco in Peru, p. 69

Mali (15°N, 0.15°W) a country in West Africa, officially the Republic of Mali; powerful West African trading kingdom from about 1240 to 1500, pp. 43, 262

Mecca (21°N, 39°E) a city in western Saudi Arabia; birthplace of the prophet Muhammad; the holiest Muslim city, p. 15

Medina (24°N, 39°E) a city in western Saudi Arabia; one of the two holiest cities of Islam (the other being Mecca), p. 19

Mexico (23°N, 104°W) a country in North America, pp. 59, 262

Moscow (55°N, 37°E) the capital city of modern Russia and the third-largest city in the world; home of the czars, p. 9

Mozambique (20°S, 34°E) a country of southeast Africa, pp. 51, 262

N

Nagasaki (32°N, 130°E) a city on the island of Kyushu, Japan; the site of the second atomic bomb dropped by the United States during World War II, p. 203

Netherlands (53°N, 4°E) a country in northwestern Europe; also known as Holland, pp. 193, 263

Norway (63°N, 11°E) country in northwestern Europe, occupying the western part of the Scandinavian peninsula, pp. 107, 263

O

Orléans (48°N, 2°E) a city in north-central France; the site of the Hundred Years' War and the defeat of the English by the French under the leadership of Joan of Arc, p. 128

P

Pacific Ocean the largest of the world's oceans; extends from the western Americas to eastern Asia and Australia, p. 90

Pakistan (28°N, 67°E) country in South Asia, between India and Afghanistan, officially the Islamic Republic of Pakistan, pp. 95, 263

Paris (49°N, 2°E) capital of France, p. 116

Pearl Harbor (21°N, 158°W) an inlet of the Pacific Ocean on the southern coast of Hawaii, p. 201

Peru (10°S, 75°W) a country in northwestern South America, pp. 66, 263

Portugal (38°N, 8°W) a country in western Europe; with Spain, occupies the Iberian Peninsula, pp. 193, 263

Prussia (50°N, 8°E) a historical region and former kingdom in central Europe; includes present-day northern Germany and Poland, p. 190

R

Red Sea a narrow sea located between northeast Africa and the Arabian Peninsula; it is connected to the Mediterranean Sea in the north and the Arabian Sea in the south, p. 50

Romania (46°N, 23°E) a country in eastern Europe, pp. 212, 263

Rome (42°N, 12°E) the capital city of modern Italy; capital of the ancient Roman empire (753 B.C.–A.D. 476), p. 11

Runnymede (51°N, 0.34°W) a meadow along the Thames River in England, p. 126

Russia (61°N, 60°E) a country in northern Eurasia, pp. 9, 263

S

Sahara the world's largest desert, covering almost all of North Africa, p. 37

Silk Road a 4,000-mile-long (6,400-km) series of ancient trade routes linking China to the Mediterranean Sea, p. 86

Somalia (3°N, 44°E) a coastal country in eastern Africa, pp. 51, 264

Songhai an ancient empire and trading state in West Africa that reached its peak in the 1400s, p. 48

South Africa (28°S, 25°E) the southernmost country in Africa, officially known as the Republic of South Africa, pp. 209, 264

St. Petersburg (60°N, 30°E) one of the largest cities in Russia; formerly known as Leningrad, p. 155

Strait of Magellan (52°S, 64°W) the channel linking the Atlantic and Pacific oceans between the mainland tip of South America and the island of Tierra del Fuego; discovered by Ferdinand Magellan, p. 148

Sweden (60°N, 14°E) a country of northern Europe; occupying the eastern half of the Scandinavian Peninsula, pp. 107, 264

Syria (35°N, 37°E) a country in Southwest Asia, pp. 16, 264

T

Taj Mahal a spectacular tomb near Agra, India, built by the Mughal emperor Shah Jahan in memory of his wife, Mumtaz Mahal, p. 98

Tanzania (6°S, 34°E) a coastal country in southeastern Africa, pp. 51, 265

Tenochtitlán (approximately 19°N, 99°W) the capital city of the Aztec empire, located on islands in Lake Texcoco, now the site of Mexico City, p. 59

Thames River (51°N, 1°W) a river of southern England that flows to the North Sea, p. 126

Tierra del Fuego (54°S, 68°W) a group of islands off the southern coast of South America; part of Chile and Argentina, p. 149

Tombouctou (16°N, 3°W) a city in Mali near the Niger River; in the past an important center of Islamic education and a trans-Saharan caravan stop (also spelled Timbuktu), p. 47

V

Venice (45°N, 12°E) a city and major seaport in northern Italy, known for its canals, p. 13

Versailles (48°N, 2°E) a city in France; site of the Palace of Versailles built by Louis XIV, p. 152

Vietnam (18°N, 107°E) a country located in Southeast Asia, pp. 212, 265

W

Waterloo (50°N, 4°E) village south of Brussels, Belgium, where Napoleon was defeated, p. 192

West Africa countries in the western region of Africa, p. 39

Y

Yangzi (30°N, 117°E) the longest river in China and Asia and the third-longest river in the world, p. 87

Z

Zimbabwe (18°S, 29°E) a country in Southern Africa, pp. 53, 265

Biographical Dictionary

A

Akbar (AK bar) (1542–1605) greatest of the Mughal emperors and reformers of India, p. 97

Archduke Franz Ferdinand (1863–1914) Archduke of Austria, whose assassination in Sarajevo by a Serbian nationalist sparked World War I, p. 200

Aurangzeb (OR ung zeb) (1618–1707) Mughal emperor of India (1658–1707), who succeeded his father Shah Jahan, p. 99

B

Babur (BAH boor) (1483–1530) descendant of Genghis Khan and Tamerlane; founder of the Mughal dynasty and emperor from 1526 to 1530, p. 96

Bell, Alexander Graham (1847–1922) American scientist, born in Scotland, who invented the telephone and whose laboratory developed the phonograph, p. 184

Bi Sheng (bee shehng) Chinese printer who invented movable type printing around A.D. 1045, p. 87

Bonaparte, Napoleon (1769–1821) general, consul, and emperor of France; fought to extend France's rule, but was defeated and exiled, p. 190

C

Catherine of Aragon (1485–1536) daughter of Queen Isabella and King Ferdinand of Spain and first queen of King Henry VIII of England; popular with English people even when the king ended his marriage to her, p. 169

Charlemagne (SHAR luh mayn) (A.D. 742–814) king of the Franks who conquered much of Western Europe, great patron of literature and learning, p. 107

Charles I (1600–1649) king of England, Scotland, and Ireland (1625–1649); under his rule a struggle between the king and Parliament began, resulting in the English Civil War, p. 155

Charles II (1630–1685) King of England, Scotland, and Ireland, whose reign saw an increase in the power of Parliament, the rise of political parties in England, and the emergence of England as a great sea power, p. 173

Columbus, Christopher (1451–1506) Italian navigator who discovered the Americas in the process of looking for a sea route from Europe to Asia, p. 145

Confucius (kuhn FYOO shuhs) (551–479 B.C.) Chinese philosopher and teacher; his beliefs, known as Confucianism, greatly influenced Chinese life, p. 83

Copernicus, Nicolaus (koh PUR nuh kuhs) (1473–1543) Polish astronomer who developed the theory that Earth moves around the sun, upon which all modern astronomy is based, p. 174

Cortés, Hernán (kor TEZ, hur NAN) (1485–1547) Spanish explorer who reached Mexico in 1519, conquered the Aztecs, and won Mexico for Spain, p. 157

Cromwell, Oliver (1599–1658) military leader and later lord protectorate of England, p. 173

D

da Gama, Vasco (c. 1469–1524) (duh GAH muh, VAS koh) Portuguese navigator who was the first European to sail to India; his voyage opened the way for the expansion of the Portuguese empire, p. 145

Drake, Sir Francis (c. 1540–1596) English navigator and admiral, was the first Englishman to circumnavigate the globe, p. 171

E

Edison, Thomas (1847–1931) American inventor widely considered to be one of the greatest of his time, invented the telegraph, the light bulb, one of the first batteries, and entire distribution systems for the conduction of electricity, among many other inventions, p. 184

Edward III (1312–77) king of England (1327–77) during the time of the Black Death; oversaw great social change, p. 128

Elizabeth I (1533–1603) queen of England from 1558 to 1603; restored England to Protestantism; admired for her courage and intelligence, p. 169

F

Ferdinand II (1479–1516) Spanish king (1474–1504) who with his wife Isabella ruled the first united Spanish kingdom, p. 146

Franklin, Benjamin (1706–1790) American statesman, writer, printer, and scientist, whose works and political positions influenced all aspects of American life, p. 178

G

Galileo Galilei (gal uh LAY oh gal uh LAY ee) (1564–1642) Italian mathematician, astronomer, and physicist; his claim that Earth revolves around the sun and is not the center of the universe caused the Catholic Church to arrest him, p. 174

Gandhi, Mohandas K. (GAHN dee) (1869–1948) known as Mahatma ("great soul") Gandhi, he led Indian nationalists to use nonviolent methods to win freedom from British rule; assassinated in 1948, p. 207

Gregory VII, (c. A.D. 1020–1085) pope who reigned from A.D. 1073 to 1085; considered one of the great papal reformers of the Middle Ages, p. 124

H

Harun ar-Rashid (hah ROO nar ash EED) (A.D. 766–806) fifth caliph of the Abbassid dynasty who ruled Baghdad at the height of its empire, p. 30

Henry IV (A.D. 1050–1106) king of Germany and the Holy Roman Empire; argued with Pope Gregory VII and was banned from the Church, p. 124

Henry VII (1457–1509) king of England (1485–1509); during his rule England and Scotland were united, p. 155

Henry VIII (1491–1547) king of England from 1509 to 1547; had 6 wives; separated the English Church from Catholicism to begin the English Reformation, p. 169

Hideyoshi, Toyotomi (hih day yoh shee, toh yoh toh mee) (1536–1598) Japanese warrior who united the nation and became its ruler, p. 91

Hitler, Adolf (1889–1945) dictator of Nazi Germany; led military invasions that began World War II; led a campaign of genocide against European Jews and others, p. 200

I

Ieyasu, Tokugawa (ee yay ah soo, toh koo gah wah) (1543–1616) founder of the last shogunate in Japan; closed his country off from the rest of the world, p. 93

Ignatius Loyola (1491–1556) Spanish clergyman who founded the Jesuit Catholic order, he was recognized as a saint in 1622, p. 142

Igor, Prince (EE gor) (died A.D. 945) duke of Kiev (A.D. 912–45); concluded a new commercial treaty with the Byzantines during the last year of his life, p. 9

Isabella I (1451–1504) Spanish queen (1474–1504) who with her husband Ferdinand ruled the first united Spanish kingdom, p. 146

J

Jahan, Shah (shah juh HAHN) (1592–1666) Mughal emperor of India and builder of the Taj Mahal, p. 98

Jalal ad-Din ar-Rumi (juh LAHL ud DEEN ur ROO mee) a poet and Sufi, who established a religious group called the Whirling Dervishes, p. 33

James II (1430–1460) king of Scotland (1437–60) who regulated the courts and monetary system, he died in England during the War of the Roses, p. 173

Jefferson, Thomas (1743–1826) statesman, scientist, and architect, who was the author of the Declaration of Independence and became third president of the United States (1801–1809), p. 178

Jesus (c. 4 B.C.–A.D. 30) believed by Christians to be the Messiah, founder of Christianity; executed by the Roman government, p. 20

Joan of Arc (c. 1412–1431) peasant girl who led the French army to victory over the English in the Hundred Years' War, p. 128

John I (1167–1216) king of England who was forced to sign the Magna Carta in 1215 under threat of civil war, p. 126

Julius II (1443–1513) an Italian who was pope from 1503 to 1513; restored the Papal States to the Church, p. 140

Justinian (A.D. 483–565) Byzantine emperor who sponsored a code of laws, p. 11

K

Khadijah (kha DEE jah) (died A.D. 619) first wife of the Prophet Muhammad, the founder of Islam, p. 18

Khayyám, Omar (ky YAHM, OH mahr) (1048–1131) Persian poet, mathematician, and astronomer, p. 28

Kublai Khan (KOO bluh kahn) (c. 1215–1294) Mongol emperor who founded the Yuan dynasty in China; encouraged the Chinese arts, stimulated foreign trade and showed religious tolerance, p. 92

L

Lenin, Vladimir (1870–1924) founder of the Russian Communist party; leader of the Russian Revolution of 1917 and of the Soviet state, p. 198

Leo Africanus (c. 1465–1550) man from northern Africa who traveled around Africa and to the Middle East and wrote about his travels in Arabic, p. 47

Leonardo da Vinci (lee uh NAR doh duh VIN chee) (1452–1519) the most famous artist of the Renaissance, painter of the *Mona Lisa* and *The Last Supper;* also a talented sculptor, scientist, architect, and engineer, p. 137

Locke, John (1632–1704) English philosopher whose writings helped start the Enlightenment, p. 177

Louis XIV (1638–1715) king of France from 1643 to 1715 and the symbol of absolute monarchy; expanded France's borders in a series of wars, p. 150

Louis XVI (1754–93) king of France (1774–92) under whose reign the French Revolution was carried out, p. 188

L'Ouverture, Toussaint (loo vur TOOR, too SAN) (1744–1803) Haitian slave who joined in the rebellion to overturn slavery and later led a movement to drive out the British and Spanish; was captured and became a martyr after dying in a French prison, p. 190

Luther, Martin (1483–1546) German teacher who founded the Protestant Reformation of the 1500s in revolt against the Roman Catholic Church, p. 140

M

Magellan, Ferdinand (muh JEL un, FUR din and) (c. 1480–1521) Portuguese explorer whose crew was the first to sail around the world, p. 147

Maimonides (my MAHN uh deez) (1134–1204) a Spanish-born medieval Jewish philosopher and teacher, p. 31

Malinche (mah LIHN chay) (c. 1501–1550) Native American princess who became the companion, guide, and interpreter for conquistador Hernan Cortés, p. 157

Mandela, Nelson (man DEL uh) (1918–) South African lawyer and nationalist; imprisoned for 28 years; in 1994 elected as South Africa's first black President, p. 209

Mansa Musa (MAHN sah moo SAH) (died c. 1332) Muslim emperor of Mali known for his pilgrimage to Mecca in 1324; encouraged the arts and learning, p. 43

Mary II (1662–1694) queen of England who ruled with her husband, William of Orange; William and Mary accepted the English Bill of Rights during the Glorious Revolution, p. 173

Mazarin (maz uh RAN) (1602–1661) French cardinal of the Roman Catholic Church who became a statesman and effectively ruled for Louis XIV until his death, p. 152

Michelangelo (my kul AN juh loh) (1475–1564) Renaissance painter, sculptor, and architect; known for his painting of the ceiling of Rome's Sistine Chapel, p. 139

Moctezuma (mahk the ZOOM uh) (1466–1520) last emperor of the Aztec empire; his empire was destroyed by Spanish conquerors in 1521, p. 156

Muhammad (c. A.D. 570–632) prophet of Islam who proclaimed the message of God; considered by Muslims to be the last of the prophets, p. 15

N

Newton, Sir Isaac (1642–1727) English mathematician and scientist whose works explained the principles of gravity, p. 176

Nicholas II (1868–1918) last czar of Russia (1894–1917), whose suppression of the serfs and Russian minorities led to the Russian Revolution, p. 197

Nkrumah, Kwame (uhn KROO muh, KWAH mee) (1909–1972) African political leader who became prime minister and then president (1960–1966) of Ghana, p. 204

P

Paul III (1468–1549) Roman who was pope from 1534–1549, under him a new era called the Catholic Reformation began, p. 142

Peter the Great (1672–1725) emperor of Russia from 1682 to 1725; one of Russia's greatest statesmen, organizers, and innovators, p. 154

Peter the Hermit (c. 1050–1115) French religious leader who led one of the bands of the First Crusade, p. 119

Pizarro, Francisco (c. 1475–1541) Spanish explorer who conquered the Incas in South America and founded the city of Lima, Peru, p. 159

Prester John a legendary Christian priest and ruler of a vast African kingdom, p. 51

R

Raleigh, Sir Walter (c. 1554–1618) English courtier, poet, and explorer, who set up the first English colony in North America at Roanoke, Virginia, p. 171

Richard I (1157–1199) king of England and leader of the Third Crusade; a hero and central figure of English romantic literature, p. 120

Richelieu (RISH loo) (1585–1642) cardinal and chief minister to King Louis XIII of France and supporter of royal absolute power, p. 152

Robespierre, Maximilien (rohbz PYAIR) (1758–1794) radical Jacobin leader; figure in the French Revolution; led the Committee of Public Safety in the Reign of Terror, p. 190

S

Saladin (SAL uh din) (c. 1137–1193) Muslim leader who became sultan of Egypt and ultimately defeated the Crusades; was also a man of learning and a patron of the arts, p. 120

Shakespeare, William (1564–1616) English poet, actor, and playwright who is generally considered to be the greatest playwright who ever lived, p. 171

Solomon (died c. 932 B.C.) king of the Israelites (c. 972–932 B.C.) after his father David; built cities, temples, and established foreign trade and alliances, p. 49

Sundiata (sun JAHT ah) (died 1255) West African king who founded the Kingdom of Mali, p. 46

T

Tamerlane (TAM ur layn) (1336–1405) Turkish conqueror active in India, Russia, and the Mediterranean, known for his brutality, p. 94

Tang Taizong (tung ty zung) (A.D. 600–649) second emperor of the Tang dynasty, p. 83

U

Urban II (c. A.D. 1035–1099) pope who developed reforms begun by Pope Gregory VII, began the Crusades, and built political power for the papacy, p. 117

Uthman (ooth MAHN) (c. A.D. 574–656) son in-law and third caliph (A.D. 644–656) of the Muslim empire; he was eventually assassinated, p. 25

W

Washington, George (1732–1799) commander-in-chief of the Revolutionary Army during the American War for Independence and first president of the United States, p. 179

William of Orange (1650–1702) king of England who ruled with his wife, Mary II; William and Mary accepted the English Bill of Rights during the Glorious Revolution, p. 173

Y

Yoritomo, Minamoto (mee nah moh toh, yor ee toh moh) (1147–1199) founder of the shogunate, a Japanese feudal system that lasted for 700 years, p. 92

Glossary

This glossary lists key terms and other useful terms from the book.

A

absolute monarch a king or leader who has complete power over every part of life in a kingdom, for example, Louis XIV of France, p. 151

alliance an agreement between nations to support each other in case of attack by another nation; nations who have such an alliance are called allies, p. 199

Allied Powers in World Wars I and II, the countries who formed an alliance to fight against Germany and its allies, p. 201

Anasazi a Native American group that occupied parts of Colorado, Utah, New Mexico, and Arizona from about A.D. 100 on, and whose descendants are the present-day Pueblo peoples living in these places, p. 74

apprentice an unpaid worker who is being trained in a craft; in medieval Europe, boys became apprentices between the ages of 8 and 14 and trained for seven years, p. 115

aqueduct a system of pipes or channels to carry water from distant sources; used by the Aztecs to bring fresh spring water to Tenochtitlán, p. 62

armistice a cease-fire or end to fighting in a war; World War I ended with an armistice in 1918, p. 200

arms race the attempt by the former Soviet Union and the United States to each build nuclear weapons so as to have the largest arsenal in the world, p. 212

artisan a skilled worker who practices a trade, such as jewelry making, ceramics, or sculpture; in Aztec society, artisans were the third most important class, under the royal or religious leaders and warriors, p. 64

astrolabe a device used by sailors to measure latitude, or distance north or south of the Equator, p. 144

astronomer a scientist who studies the stars and other objects in the sky, p. 61

atomic bomb a powerful nuclear weapon developed in the United States during World War II and used on the Japanese cities of Hiroshima and Nagasaki, p. 203

Axis Powers in World War II, the alliance of Germany, Italy, Japan, and other nations that opposed the Allied Powers, p. 201

Aztecs a people who founded a civilization in central Mexico around 1325, that lasted until the Spanish conquest in the early 16th century, p. 59

B

Bantu-speakers (BAN too) people who speak Bantu, a family of languages; historically, those who migrated from West Africa southward, p. 39

bazaar a market selling different kinds of goods, p. 30

Bedouins Arab peoples of the Middle East, primarily nomadic, who live in tribes and practice Islam, p. 16

bill of rights a summary of all the rights held by the people under their government; in England, a statement that William and Mary had to accept when offered the throne after the Glorious Revolution, p. 173

bishop a Christian leader of high rank in the church hierarchy, p. 124

bubonic plague a contagious and often deadly disease spread from animals to humans; in medieval times, a bubonic plague known as the Black Death killed millions of Europeans, p. 116

bushido a Japanese samurai warrior's set of rules that stressed honor, discipline, bravery, and simple living, p. 91

C

caliph an Islamic ruler between the 600s and 1200s, p. 29

canal a waterway dug into the earth or modified by people to transport water or people, or provide drainage, p. 70

capitalist country a country that allows people to own property and businesses and compete for profit in a free market, p. 211

caravel a sailing vessel designed by Prince Henry's shipbuilders that was larger, stronger, faster, and easier to steer than other ships of the day, p. 144

caste system a Hindu social class system that controlled every part of daily life; the four castes were made up of: (1) priests, teachers, and judges; (2) warriors; (3) farmers and merchants; (4) craftworkers and laborers; casteless poor people were "Untouchables," p. 95

cathedral a large, important church, p. 111

causeway a raised street made of hard earth, used for travel over wetland or lakes; causeways connected the Aztec city of Tenochtitlán to the mainland, p. 62

chivalry the noble qualities that knights were to have: bravery, loyalty, and doing heroic deeds to win the love of a worthy woman, p. 116

Christianity the Christian religion, based on the life and teachings of Jesus and on the Christian holy book, the Bible, p. 50

Church of England national church of England, established by King Henry VIII in the 1500s, p. 169

circumnavigate to travel completely around Earth, p. 149

city-state a city that has its own independent government and often controls much of the surrounding land; Aksum was one of East Africa's ancient city-states, p. 51

civil disobedience the deliberate breaking of a law to protest it; practiced by Mohandas K. Gandhi in India to free his country from British rule, p. 207

civil war a war for power among groups within a single country, p. 172

clan a group of families who trace their roots to the same ancestor, p. 40

clergy persons ordained to perform certain religious duties, p. 111

Cold War the period from 1945 until 1991, during which there was great international tension and risk of war between the capitalist countries led by the United States and the communist countries led by the former Soviet Union, p. 212

colony a territory ruled by another nation, often one that is far away, p. 178

communism a kind of government where all people together own the farms and factories, share work equally, and earn rewards equally; revolutionaries who took over Russia under Lenin wanted a communist government, p. 198

conquistador a conqueror; the Spanish soldiers who traveled in the Americas and claimed the land and people for Spain and the Roman Catholic Church, p. 159

constitutional monarchy a type of government in which a monarch has only the powers granted by a constitution and the laws of the nation, p. 173

Crusades several military expeditions between A.D. 1095 and 1272, supported by the Catholic Church, to win the Holy Land back from the Seljuk Turks; the Holy Land included Jerusalem and parts of present-day Israel and Jordan, p. 117

czar a Russian emperor; Nicholas, the last czar, was forced to give up the throne in 1917, p. 197

D

daimyo the powerful estate owners in Japan who hired their own samurai warriors to protect them, and peasants to farm their lands, p. 91

democracy a system in which the people are governed by elected representatives, p. 151

developed nation a nation that has many industries; many former colonies are developed nations, p. 209

developing nation a nation that has few industries; some former colonies are among the world's developing nations, p. 209

divine right a belief that the right to rule comes directly from God; a belief held by many European kings during the 1600s, p. 151

drought a long period of weather with no rain, p. 61

dynasty a series of rulers from one family; periods of Chinese history are referred to by dynasty, for example, Tang or Song, p. 84

E

encomienda an economic system introduced by the Spanish in Mexico, in which settlers received the land and the forced labor of Native Americans, p. 158

Enlightenment a time when people in Europe emphasized reason and rational thinking; sometimes called the Age of Reason, p. 174

excommunicate to expel or prevent someone from taking part in Church life; in the Middle Ages, Catholic Church leaders threatened to excommunicate a lord who rebelled against Church power, p. 112

F

famine a time when there is so little food that many people starve, p. 61

feudal system a system of government in which less powerful people promise loyalty to more powerful ones; in Japan, the powerful person was the shogun, p. 91

feudalism a system of power in Europe during the Middle Ages, in which kings and queens had the most power, followed by nobles, knights, and peasants, p. 108

French Revolution a revolution in France that resulted in the overthrow of the French monarchy; it lasted from 1789 to 1799, p. 188

G

genocide the systematic killing of an entire group of people; in Nazi Germany during World War II, members of different ethnic groups, especially Jews, were murdered, p. 202

guild an association of all the people in a town or village who practiced a certain trade; weavers, grocers, masons, and others in the Middle Ages formed guilds and set standards for quality and prices, p. 114

H

hajj for Muslims, a pilgrimage or sacred journey to Mecca; Muslims throughout the world who can afford to do so try to make the hajj once in their lives, p. 23

hieroglyphs a kind of picture writing in which some pictures stand for ideas or things and others stand for sounds; in this text, the written signs and symbols used by the Mayan people; Egyptians and other groups also developed hieroglyphic writing systems, p. 61

hijra the migration in A.D. 622 of Muslims from Mecca to Yathrib (now called Medina), p. 19

Hinduism a religion developed in India, introduced by the Aryans, and based on sacred books called the Vedas; Hindus accept many gods as different aspects of one supreme being, p. 94

Holocaust the slaughter of millions of Jews and other Europeans by Nazi Germany during World War II, p. 202

Hopi a Pueblo people, descended from the Anasazi, who occupy reservations in northeastern Arizona, p. 74

I

icon a painting or an image of a holy person or saint, often painted on wood; icons are seen as sacred by some Christians, p. 12

imperialism a country's policy of extending its rule over other countries, or colonizing; during the 1800s, Europeans obtained raw materials and created markets for their goods using such a policy, p. 193

indulgence an official pardon given by the pope in return for money in the Middle Ages; people could pay the Catholic Church to be forgiven for their sins, a practice opposed by Martin Luther, p. 141

Industrial Revolution a period beginning in the late 1700s, when goods that had been produced by hand began to be made by machines in factories, p. 182

interdependent depending upon one another, p. 213

Islam the religion practiced by Muslims; based on the teachings of the prophet Muhammad and on the holy book of Islam, the Quran, p. 18

K

kachina ancestral spirits in the Pueblo culture, p. 75

kiva an underground chamber in a Pueblo village used for ceremonial purposes, p. 75

knight in medieval times, a man who received land and titles in exchange for serving a lord or king as a soldier, p. 108

L

labor union an organization to help workers improve their pay and working conditions, p. 187

M

Maasai descendants of Bantu-speakers who live in present-day Tanzania and Kenya, p. 41

Magna Carta the "Great Charter"; an agreement between King John of England and his nobles and clergy in which the king's power over his nobles was limited, p. 127

maize corn; the most important crop of Mayan farmers and other ancient Native American groups, p. 60

manor a large estate, often including a village and farmlands, ruled by a lord in medieval Europe, p. 108

Mayas a people who established a civilization in southern Mexico and Central America; their civilization flourished c. 300 to c. 900, p. 60

medieval of the Middle Ages, p. 106

merit system a system introduced in China to hire government officials for their ability, which was proved by taking tests, rather than for their family connections, p. 84

Middle Ages the years between ancient and modern times; from about A.D. 500 until 1500, p. 106

migration the movement of people from one place to another, p. 39

monk a man who lives in a monastery with other men and follows the practices of a religious order, p. 112

Moors Muslims of mixed African and Arab descent, who presently live in Northern Africa; in the 8th century, Moors established a civilization in Spain that lasted until the 15th century, p. 154

mosque an Islamic house of worship, p. 21

movable type a kind of printing first used in China and fully developed in Korea; each character is a separate piece of type, which can be moved and reused, p. 87

muezzin a man who calls all Muslims to prayer by chanting; in Islamic cities today, the call is broadcast over loudspeakers, p. 21

Muslim person who practices the religion of Islam, p. 18

N

Napoleonic Code a reform of the laws of France; Napoleon Bonaparte had all the laws rewritten so that they were clear and easily understood, p. 191

nation a community that shares a government and sometimes a common language and culture; in medieval Europe, kingdoms became nations as the kings gained power and unified their lands, p. 126

nationalism great pride in one's country, p. 193

natural laws patterns in the behavior of the universe, including laws of motion and gravity; observed during the European Enlightenment by thinkers such as Isaac Newton, p. 176

navigator an expert sailor who guides a ship across the ocean, p. 144

Nazi Party a political party founded in Germany in 1919 and brought to power by Adolf Hitler in 1933, p. 201

noble in certain societies, a person of high rank, sometimes inherited through family connections, p. 108

nomad a person who moves from one area to another and does not have a permanent home, p. 16

nun a woman who takes the vows of a particular religious order and often lives in a convent with other nuns, p. 112

O

oasis an area of vegetation fed by underground springs and surrounded by desert, p. 38

P

Parliament a council that advised the English king or queen in government matters; today, a group of elected officials who make up the legislative branch of the British government, p. 127

patriarch the founder of a tribe or family; in this text, the leader of the Byzantine Christian Church in Constantinople during medieval times, p. 12

patron someone who supports others or the arts; Caliph Harun ar-Rashid of Baghdad was a great patron of artists, p. 30

peasant a member of a class that makes its living through small-scale farming and labor, p. 108

perspective a technique in drawing and painting that shows objects as they appear to the eye, for example, making distant objects appear smaller in relation to closer objects, p. 139

porcelain a strong, beautiful kind of ceramic first made in China; porcelain vases, plates, cups, bowls, and figurines are often called "china," p. 85

prophet a religious leader or other person who claims to carry the message of God, p. 19

Protestants Christians who are not members of the Catholic or Orthodox churches; in this text, the people who shared the religious views of Martin Luther and others who protested against the Roman Catholic Church, p. 142

province a smaller region within a country or an empire, p. 47

pueblo a village built into the sides of steep cliffs or on top of tall mesas; the Pueblo and Anasazi people both adopted this style of building, p. 74

Pueblos groups of Native Americans, such as the Hopi, who live in parts of Arizona and New Mexico and are descended from the Anasazi, p. 74

Q

Quechua language spoken by members of the Incan empire; still spoken today in the Andes highlands from southern Colombia to Chile, p. 66

quipu a sequence of knotted strings used by Incan government officials to count and record information about births, deaths, taxes, and harvests, p. 67

Quran the holy book of Islam containing what God revealed to Muhammad: the rules of Islam, stories, promises, warnings, and instructions, p. 23

R

racism the prejudiced belief that one race is better than another, still a serious problem in many parts of the world, p. 209

Ramadan a month in the Islamic calendar during which all Muslims fast from sunrise to sunset, p. 22

Reformation the change or reform of the Catholic Church begun by Martin Luther that led to the establishment of Protestant churches, p. 140

Reign of Terror a period after the French Revolution when Maximilien Robespierre had 70 to 80 people executed each day; the Reign of Terror ended when Robespierre himself was executed, p. 190

religion an organized system of belief in a spiritual being or set of spiritual beings; usually centered around the creation and laws of the universe, p. 111

Renaissance a rebirth of learning in Europe between about A.D. 1300 and 1600, p. 137

reunification the rejoining of two or more things that had been separated; in this text, the rejoining in 1989 of East and West Germany into one nation, p. 210

revolution a complete overthrow of an established government; a sudden change in the way people think, p. 172

Roman Catholicism a Christian religion that is headed by the Pope and has a hierarchical organization of cardinals, bishops, and priests, p. 111

Russian Revolution a revolution in Russia in 1917 that resulted in the overthrow of the czar, p. 199

S

samurai the warriors in Japan who swore to serve their leaders and obeyed a strict code of rules without question, p. 89

Sanskrit an ancient language of India; Sanskrit is the language of Hinduism and of the Vedas, p. 95

savanna an area of gently rolling land covered by grasses, occasional trees, and thorny bushes, p. 38

schism a split, often in a church or religion, over different points of view; during the 1000s, a schism in the Christian Church split it into Byzantine and Roman Catholic sections, p. 13

scientific method a method of performing experiments under controlled conditions, recording the findings, and drawing conclusions; begun during the Enlightenment, p. 176

self-sufficient able to supply one's own needs; the residents of a medieval manor were self-sufficient, p. 109

serf a person who lived on and farmed a lord's land in feudal times; he or she did not own land and depended on the lord for protection, p. 110

shogun the most powerful lord in feudal Japan; the first shogun took power in 1192, p. 91

Shona Bantu-speakers who founded the kingdom of Great Zimbabwe around 1100, p. 53

silent barter trading without speaking; used by gold miners and salt traders in West Africa, p. 44

silk a valuable cloth originally made only in China from threads spun by caterpillars called silkworms, p. 85

slash-and-burn agriculture a type of farming in which farmers cleared forests, burned tree stumps, and used the ash for fertilizer; when soil was depleted, they moved to a new area; the Mayan farmers used this type of agriculture, p. 60

squire in feudal times, a young nobleman who serves a knight and is just below the knight in the social hierarchy, p. 105

Sufi a member of a Muslim branch that teaches its mystical ideas by means of philosophy and poetry, p. 32

sultan a Muslim king; between 1206 and 1526, a sultan ruled the Muslim empire, including what is now India, Bangladesh, and Pakistan, p. 95

Swahili the culture and language of the people of Kilwa and other East African city-states; today, Tanzania and Kenya use Swahili as their official language, p. 52

T

terrace a steplike ledge cut into a steep mountainside, used to grow crops and stop erosion; terraces were used by the ancient Incas of South America, p. 70

textile cloth; the textile industry was one of the first to move into factories during the Industrial Revolution, p. 183

tolerance the acceptance of differences; Muslims were tolerant of Jews and Christians who accepted Muslim rule during the golden age (about A.D. 800 to 1100), p. 30

troubadour a traveling performer who wandered from place to place in France, Italy, and Spain, singing songs and reciting poems about the chivalrous deeds of knights, p. 116

V

vassal in medieval Europe, a man who promised to be loyal to a landowner, who in return gave him a share of the land, called a fief, p. 108

Index

The *italicized* page numbers refer to illustrations. The *m, c,* or *p* preceding the number refers to maps (*m*), charts, graphs, and tables (*c*), pictures (*p*).

A

Abraham, 20, 23
absolute monarch, 151–152, 189–190, 276
absolute rule, 152
Activity Atlas, 2–7
Activity Shop
    Interdisciplinary, 220–221
    Lab, 166–167
Africa, *m 245, m 250, m 251*
    Bantu migrations in, 39–42, *m 40*
    colonization of, 192–193, *m 192*
    farming in, 38, 39
    independent nations of, 204, 206
    physical geography of, 38–39
Africanus, Leo, 47
Age of Reason. *See* Enlightenment
Agra, India, 99
Akbar, 97–98, *p 98,* 272
Aksum, 49, 268
    trade and, 50
Aladdin, 31–32
Alcazar Castle, *p 154*
algebra, *p 32*
Algeria, 205, *p 205,* 258, 268
alliance, 199, 276
Allied Powers, 201, 276
al-Mansur, 29
American colonies, independence of, 178–179
American Revolution, 178–179, *p 179*
Anasazi, 74, 276

Andes Mountains, *p 60,* 65–67, 69, 268
Angkor, 114, 268
Antarctica, *m 244*
apprentice, 115, *p 115,* 276
aqueducts, 62, 276
Arabian Peninsula, 8, 15, 268
    geography of, 15–17, *m 16*
    trade in, 16
Archduke Franz Ferdinand, 200, 272
armistice, 200, 276
arms race, 212, 276
Arno River, 138, 268
art
    Aztec, *p 63, p 64*
    in Baghdad, 30
    in Benin, 48
    Chinese, 86
    in Elizabethan England, 171
    Mayan, *p 61*
    in Mughal empire, 98
    Renaissance, 138–140
artisan, 276
    in Aztec culture, 64
Asia, *m 245, m 252, m 253*
astrolabe, 144, *p 144,* 276
astronomer, 61, 276
atomic bomb, 203, *p 203,* 276
Aurangzeb, 99, 272
Australia, 185, *m 245, m 254,* 258
Austria, 189, 258, 268
Austria-Hungary, 200
Axis Powers, 201, 276
Azimuthal projection, 233
Aztecs, 59, *p 59,* 62–64, 276
    conquest of, by Spain, 157–159
    floating gardens of, *p 62*
    role of women in culture of, *p 64*
    warlike way of life of, 63–64, *p 63*

B

Babur, 96, 97, 272. *See also* Mughal empire
Bacon, Francis, 176
Baghdad, 29–30, *p 29, p 30,* 268
ballet, 199
Bangladesh, 95, *p 208,* 258, 268
banking, beginnings of, *p 121*
Bantu languages, 42
Bantu migrations, 39–42, *m 40*
    physical barriers to, *p 39*
Bantu-speakers, 39, 276
baptism, *p 112*
Baryshnikov, Mikhail, 199
basin, 266
Battle of Orleans, 129
Battle of Yorktown, *p 179*
Battuta, Ibn, *p 52*
bay, 266
bazaar, 30, 276
Bedouins, 16–17, 276
Belgium, 192–193, 258, 268
Bell, Alexander Graham, 184, 272
Berlin, 210, 268
Berlin Wall, 196
Bi Sheng, 87, 272
Bible, 112
bill of rights, 173, 276
bishop, 124, 276
Black Death, 116, *p 116*
Black Sea, 9–10
Black Stone, 17, *p 17*
block printing. *See* China, invention of printing in
Bolivia, 66, 258, 268
Bonaparte, Napoleon, 190, 272
    accomplishments of, 190–191, *p 190, m 191*
    downfall of, 191–192
Bosporus strait, 10, 268

Acknowledgments

Cover Design

Bruce Bond, Suzanne Schineller, and Olena Serbyn

Cover Photo

Jon Chomitz

Maps

MapQuest.com, Inc.
Map information sources: Columbia Encyclopedia, Encyclopaedia Britannica, Microsoft® Encarta®, National Geographic Atlas of the World, Rand McNally Commercial Atlas, The Times Atlas of the World.

Staff Credits

The people who made up the *World Explorer* team—representing editorial, editorial services, design services, on-line services/multimedia development, product marketing, production services, project office, and publishing processes—are listed below. Bold type denotes core team members.

Joyce Barisano, Margaret Broucek, **Paul Gagnon, Mary Hanisco, Dotti Marshall,** Kirsten Richert, Susan Swan, and Carol Signorino.

Additional Credits

Art and Design: Emily Soltanoff. Editorial: Debra Reardon, Nancy Rogier. Market Research: Marilyn Leitao. Publishing Processes: Wendy Bohannan.

Program Development and Production

Editorial and Project Management: Summer Street Press
Production: Pronk&Associates

Text

28, from *The Concise History of Islam and the Origin of Its Empires* by Gregory C. Kozlowski. Copyright © 1991 by The Copley Publishing Group. Reprinted with permission from the Copley Publishing Group. **33,** from *Love's Fire: Re-Creations of Rumi* by Andrew Harvey. Copyright © 1988 by Andrew Harvey, published by Mother Meera Publications. **80,** from *The World in 1492* by Jean Fritz et al. Excerpt copyright © 1992 by The Native Land Foundation. Reprinted by permission of Henry Holt & Co., Inc. **88,** from *China's Examination Hell* by Ichisada Miyazaki. Copyright © 1981 by Yale University Press. Reprinted by permission of Weatherhill Inc. **89,** from *Legends of the Samurai* by Hiroake Sato. Copyright © 1995 by Hiroake Sato. Published by The Overlook Press, Woodstock, NY 12498. Used by permission. **132,** Reprinted with the permission of Atheneum Books for Young Readers, an imprint of Simon & Schuster Children's Publishing Division, from *Of Swords and Sorcerers: The Adventures of King Arthur and His Knights* by Margaret Hodges and Margery Evernden. Text copyright © 1993 by Margaret Hodges and Margery Evernden.

Photo Research

Feldman & Associates, Inc.

Photos

1 TL, © Ed Simpson/Tony Stone Images, **1 TR,** © Bibliotheque Nationale, Jerusalem/SuperStock International, **1 C,** © Renee Lynn/Tony Stone Images, **1 BL,** © North Wind Picture Archives, **1 BR,** © SuperStock International, **1 background,** Artbase Inc., **3,** © Michael Kirtley/National Geographic Society Image Collection, **5,** © Mark Thayer, Boston, **6 BL,** Phil Schermeister/© Corbis, **6 BR, 7,** © Felicia Martinez/PhotoEdit, **9,** © The Granger Collection, **10,** © Robert Frerck/Woodfin Camp & Associates, **11,** © North Wind Picture Archives, **12,** © Kammerhofmuseum, Gmunden, Austria/A. K. G., Berlin/SuperStock, **13,** © Bibliotheque Nationale, Paris Ms Fr. 9087, fol 207 v./Laurie Platt Winfrey Inc. **14,** © Robert Frerck/Tony Stone Images, **15,** © Robert Azzi/Woodfin Camp & Associates, **17,** © Nabeel Turner/Tony Stone Images, **18 BL,** © Sarah Stone/Tony Stone Images, **18 BR,** © Sylvain Grandadam/Tony Stone Images, **19,** © Bridgeman/Art Resource, **21,** © SuperStock International, **22,** © Reuters/Corbis-Bettmann, **23 TL,** © R. & S. Michaud/Woodfin Camp & Associates, **23 TR,** © SEF/Art Resource, **24,** © Tchehel Stun, Ispahan/Giraudon, Paris/SuperStock International, **25,** © Paul Chesley/Tony Stone Images, **26,** © Michael Newman/PhotoEdit, **28,** © Scala/Art Resource, **29,** © Nik Wheeler/Nik Wheeler, **30,** © The Granger Collection, **31,** © Bibliotheque Nationale, Jerusalem/SuperStock International, **32 TL,** © Private Collection/Bridgeman Art Library, London/The Granger Collection, **32 TR,** © Topkapi Serail-Museum, Istanbul, Turkey/Giraudon, Paris/SuperStock International, **32 BL,** © The Granger Collection, **32 BR,** © Roland & Sabrina Michaud/Woodfin Camp & Associates, **33,** © Oxford, U.K./Bodleian Library, **37,** © Jason Laure'/Laure' Communications, **39 TL,** © Daryl Balfour/Tony Stone Images, **39 TR,** © Ian Murphy/Tony Stone Images, **41,** © Renee Lynn/Tony Stone Images, **42,** © Boyd Norton/Boyd Norton, **43,** © L. Platt Winfrey/Woodfin Camp & Associates, **44,** © Explorer, Paris/SuperStock International, **45 BL, BR,** © Lee Boltin/Boltin Picture Library, **46,** © James Alan Brown/Visuals Unlimited, **47,** © Betty Press/Woodfin Camp & Associates, **48,** © Lee Boltin/Boltin Picture Library, **49,** © Getachew G. Hiwot, **50 BL, BR,** © Kjell B. Sandved/Visuals Unlimited, **51,** © Lawrence Manning/Tony Stone Images, **52,** © Marc & Evelyne Bernheim/Woodfin Camp & Associates, **53,** © Jason Laure'/Woodfin Camp & Associates, **54, 55,** © David Young-Wolff/PhotoEdit, **59,** © Robert Frerck/Woodfin Camp & Associates, **60 TL,** © North Wind Picture Archive, **60 TR,** © Tony Morrison/South American Pictures, **61,** © Kal Muller/Woodfin Camp & Associates, **63,** © ET Archive, London/SuperStock International, **64 TL,** © The Granger Collection, **64 TR,** © Mireille Vautier/Woodfin Camp & Associates, **65,** © Gianni Dagli Orti/Corbis, **66 TL, TM, TR,** © Lee Boltin/Boltin Picture Library, **67,** © Loren McIntyre/Woodfin Camp & Associates, **68,** © Douglas Mason/Woodfin Camp & Associates, **69 T,** © Jeremy Horner/Tony Stone Images, **69 B,** © Ed Simpson/Tony Stone Images, **70,** © Mireille Vautier/Woodfin Camp & Associates, **71,** © Kevin O'Mooney/Odyssey Productions, **72,** © SuperStock International, **73,** © John D. Cunningham/Visuals Unlimited, **74,** © North Wind Picture Archives, **75 T,** © Lee Boltin/Boltin Picture Library **75 M,** © Greg Probst/Tony Stone Images, **76,** © Steven W. Jones/FPG International, **77,** © Robert Frerck/Odyssey Productions, **81,** © North Wind Picture Archives, **83,** © Giraudon/Art Resource, **85 BL,** © SuperStock International, **85 BM, BR, 86 BL,** © Lee Boltin/Boltin Picture Library, **86 BM, BR,** © Viktor Ivanovich Sarianidi/National Geographic Society Image Collection, **87,** © Werner Forman Archive/British Library, London/Art Resource, **88,** © Tony Wiles/Tony Stone Images, **89, 91,** © Lee Boltin/Boltin Picture Library, **92,** © North Wind Picture Archives, **93,** © The Lowe Art Museum, The University of Miami/SuperStock International, **94,** © Giraudon/Art Resource, **96,** My Village, by Paramita Hazra, age 11, India. Courtesy of the International Children's Art Museum, **98,** © The Granger Collection, **99,** © David Sutherland/Tony Stone Images, **100,** © Michael Newman/PhotoEdit, **105,** © The Granger Collection, **107 T,** © Scala/Art Resource, **108,** © SuperStock International, **109,** © Biblioteca Civica, Padua, Italy/SuperStock International, **110,** © The Granger Collection, **111,** © Charles Harris Phelps/National Geographic Society Image Collection, **112,** © The Granger Collection, **114,** © SuperStock International, **115,** © Castle at Issogne, Valle d'Aosta, Italy/ET Archive, London, SuperStock International, **116,** © The Granger Collection, **117,** © North Wind Picture Archives, **118 T,** © North Wind Picture Archives, **118 B,** © Castle of Castelnaus, Prudhommat. (Dorka)/Laurie Platt Winfrey Inc., **120,** © The Granger Collection, **121,** © British Library, London/Bridgeman Art Library, London, SuperStock International, **122,** © The Granger Collection, **124,** © SuperStock International, **125,** © North Wind Picture Archives, **126,** © Hulton Getty/Tony Stone Images, **127 TL,** © Bridgeman/Art Resource, **127 TR,** © Brown Brothers, **128,** © The Granger Collection, **129,** © The Granger Collection, **133,** © North Wind Picture Archives, **134,** © Bob Krist/Corbis, **136,** CORBIS/MAGMA, **137**